GCP
in
Action

A practical guide to building and deploying secure,
scalable applications using Google Cloud Platform

Raymond Blum

bpb

www.bpbonline.com

First Edition 2025

Copyright © BPB Publications, India

ISBN: 978-93-65890-563

To View Complete
BPB Publications Catalogue
Scan the QR Code:

Dedicated to

Stephen McHenry, who always treated me as an equal and expected nothing less of me.
Eva, who encouraged me throughout many long days and nights of research and writing.
Joëlle Skaf, the best and truest teammate ever.

About the Authors

Raymond Blum is currently a senior staff engineer at Google DeepMind, where he works on Gemini policy compliance. Previously, he has been an engineering manager and tech lead at Google on a variety of technical infrastructure and site reliability teams. He led and advanced the data recovery and integrity teams at Google for several years and has published articles on the topic of digital data permanence and reliability for the Association of Computing Machinery and with Google.

Prior to this, he created and ran an internet services company for several years, after a career as a software developer in media and financial firms. During this time, he taught undergraduate computer science and professional skills workshops for the City University of New York.

Raymond holds a degree in computer science from the City University of New York. He contributes his time and guidance to organizations that promote and provide equal access to careers in the professional world to all.

About the Reviewers

❖ **Artiom Kuciuk** is a seasoned backend systems architect and technical leader with extensive professional experience in scalable payment infrastructures, backend development, system integration, and microservice-based architectures. His areas of expertise include high-performance system design, secure transaction processing, cloud-native technologies, and backend optimization.

Artiom is well-versed in technologies across AWS, Azure, and GCP, and he has worked extensively with multi-cloud platforms to deliver reliable, fault-tolerant applications. He has a proven track record in building payment ecosystems that support dozens of global providers, adhering to industry standards such as PCI DSS and leveraging encryption protocols like TLS.

He specializes in backend scalability and cloud-native architecture and is passionate about building resilient infrastructure that supports business growth and security. He is a frequent contributor to hackathons and engineering communities, where he shares his knowledge on system design and performance tuning.

He is currently working as a technical lead at Greentube GmbH, a leading online gaming solutions provider, and is part of the core team driving backend innovation and architecture.

❖ **František Krajňák** is a passionate DevSecOps specialist with over 10 years of professional experience in cloud security, infrastructure automation, and Google Cloud Platform solutions. He holds multiple industry certifications, including Google Cloud Professional Security Engineer, Professional Architect, and Data Engineer.

He specializes in system design and DevSecOps practices, with particular expertise in GKE optimization, Terraform infrastructure management, and vulnerability management. He enjoys working on complex cloud migrations and developing innovative solutions that bridge development and operations teams.

He is currently working as a senior cloud engineer - GCP specialist at Deutsche Börse in Prague, where he focuses on AI-powered solutions, including RAG and LLM-based chatbots, alongside enterprise-scale cloud deployments and compliance frameworks.

Acknowledgement

I would like to express my sincere gratitude to all those who contributed to the completion of this book.

First and foremost, I extend my heartfelt appreciation to my family and friends for their unwavering support and encouragement throughout this journey. Their love and encouragement have motivated me to always keep moving forward.

I would like to extend my special thanks to Alberto Rojas for their valuable input on this project. Your insights and feedback have been instrumental in shaping the content and improving the quality of this book. Thank you for your attention and your invaluable support.

I am immensely grateful to BPB Publications for their guidance and expertise in bringing this book to fruition. Their support and assistance were invaluable in navigating the complexities of the publishing process.

I would also like to acknowledge the technical reviewers and editors who provided valuable feedback and contributed to the refinement of this manuscript. Their insights and suggestions have significantly enhanced the quality of the book.

Finally, I want to express my gratitude to the readers who have shown interest in our book. Your support and encouragement have been deeply appreciated.

Thank you to everyone who has played a part in making this book a reality.

Preface

Understanding the role and the value of cloud infrastructure is crucial in the delivery of performant, secure, and sustainable distributed application systems. This book covers the emergent needs of today's highly scalable and available systems and the specific products that are provided by **Google Cloud Platform** (**GCP**) to fulfill those requirements. Products and technologies used in roles complementary to cloud services are also explored. The book provides experienced software engineers with an omnibus of cloud development practices and architecture patterns using GCP products.

Comprising fourteen focused chapters in four sections, this book covers a wide range of topics essential for understanding the structure of a distributed system and the design of a successful application.

The first section presents the reader with a classification of cloud products by their responsibility – the aspect of a computing system that they are provided to represent. Processing power, data persistence, and user authentication are delineated, and the various strengths and caveats of several GCP options are discussed. The second section then reviews the architecture of an entire application system: cloud services, frontend clients, and backend pipelines. Design patterns and engineering principles that have proven themselves through their use in the development of successful products are presented for each portion of the overall application system.

The third section of the book presents a case study, the design and development of a distributed global voting system. The reader is shown methods for the forecasting of demand and then presented with design practices to provide a reliable and highly available service. Monitoring and deployment practices are as important to the user experience as a well-developed codebase, and so site reliability considerations and practices that make use of GCP products are explored in detail.

The fourth and final section of the book applies both the lessons learned and the products of the case study to a wide range of business applications. A generalized view of the voting system can be used to design systems in other domains. The components of the voting application serve either as models or can be used directly in unrelated systems that have similar functional requirements. The design processes that lead to such reusability are recapped, and their value is reinforced through several examples.

Section 1: Cloud Services by Responsibility

Chapter 1: Responsibilities and Utility of a Cloud Platform- This introductory chapter will review the evolution of application development that has precipitated the need for

Cloud Service Platforms. The basic requirements of a distributed application will be described, and we will then explore how a cloud service adds value to an application. It will describe the architectural considerations of a distributed application and the types of services provided by a cloud platform to address those. Then, the chapter focuses on the GCP products for each of these types of service. We conclude with a review of those features that do not fit well on GCP services and what their optimal platforms are.

Chapter 2: Dividing Up Features of a Cloud Backed Application- In this chapter, the reader is shown a methodology for decomposing an application's features with a specific intent. The resulting feature set is then evaluated to identify the aspects of an application that are relevant to the selection of a cloud infrastructure platform.

The chapter discusses and exemplifies a process for designing a system architecture that focuses on the optimal fulfillment of requirements and has those requirements drive the selection of supporting services. The reader is given clear explanations of terms that are often sold in overly vague or hyperbolic terms, demystifying desirable features of a distributed systems framework such as GCP.

Chapter 3: Determining the Infrastructure to Build Features Upon- This chapter explores some common and often misunderstood technical requirements of application features, such as latency and transaction boundaries. Through the dissection of these requirements into their primary elements, the reader will be guided to identify the effects that are truly required by an application. Having requirements with a finer level of granularity increases the flexibility offered to the architect to meet those requirements. This chapter then reviews the cloud services that offer solutions to these fundamental requirements, and ways of arranging them to cooperatively meet the overall goals.

Chapter 4: Choosing Between GCP Options- This chapter disambiguates popular and commonly confused GCP products in four core domains: compute power, data storage, identity and authentication, and asynchronous processing. The reader learns how to determine which of the seemingly equivalent products in each of these domains is the most suitable choice for their application, considering both the product's strengths and any caveats.

Section 2: Cloud Backed Application Architecture

Chapter 5: Client-side Technology Choices- In this chapter, we will summarize both popular and up-and-coming client-side technologies that provide an end user's view of a system. The reader will be shown the costs of different approaches to initial development and maintaining an application on multiple platforms. The chapter will then guide the reader through consideration of developing a user interface as a platform-native client app, a cross-platform client app, a browser-based web application, or some combination of these.

Chapter 6: Cloud Services at the Backend Border- This chapter will present best practices that resolve ambiguity and confusion that result from feature overlap among sibling products in the GCP product suite. The reader will learn how to design components that encapsulate the details of their implementation and dependencies. The chapter will show how to design systems that can adapt to changes in the infrastructure landscape.

Chapter 7: Frontends at the Client Border- In this chapter, the reader will be acquainted with the high-level platform breakdown of a distributed application. The reader will learn criteria for isolating functionality and designating it to a particular architectural tier. Risks to application performance and integrity within each tier and at their borders will be exposed, and techniques for preventing or mitigating those risks will be explored and explained.

Section 3: End-to-End: A Global Voting System

Chapter 8: Making a Voting System Available and Reliable- This chapter will explore the real-world forces that challenge the reliability and availability of a distributed system, specifically in the context of our voting application. We will identify common aspects of these challenges, such as geographic and temporal distribution of demand. The chapter will examine detailed analyses of demand and then identify ways to mitigate risk to the integrity of the system exposed by these analyses.

Chapter 9: Identifying the Stress Points of our Voting System- In this chapter, the reader will be guided through the ways in which a system can fail and ways to mitigate these. This chapter will identify the dimensions of a service outage, describing the techniques and indicators used to categorize a specific incident. The reader will finish this chapter prepared with a methodology for categorizing failure modes and measures for mitigation, which can be applied to any highly available distributed system.

Chapter 10: Securing All User Votes- This chapter will review the features of Google Cloud Platform that address changes in user traffic. Both specific product features, such as auto-scaling and design patterns, will be discussed as means to dynamically shape system capacity to match demand.

Chapter 11: Guaranteeing Data Permanence- In this chapter, the reader will explore the different types of data stored in a business application and the different types of access. The chapter will categorize application behavior into typical access patterns.

The chapter will then lead the reader through evaluation of the need for data permanence over the lifetime of the application and the user. Practices and implementation mechanisms to guarantee the necessary permanence and availability of data will be identified and explained.

Chapter 12: Developing Voting Frontends- This chapter will examine the composition of a user visible feature, exploring specific implementation details of a feature's functionality The reader will be guided through the evaluation of an optimal tier for each of these features to reside within. The result will be a detailed design of user-visible features that clearly identifies the scope of a client application's responsibilities and dependencies. The design and codebase will be refactored to facilitate the independent development of multiple related software products.

Section 4: Recap: Applying the Case Study

Chapter 13: Replacing Components in Isolation- In this chapter, the engineering principles to maximize software reuse will be described. The chapter will show how to interface with GCP services in ways that maximize the independence of different components.

The reader will examine a case study of the replacement of an infrastructure component in a running system. This migration exercise will highlight the value of the best practices that have been described and followed. To avoid potential harm to the business, we will also construct plans for reducing and mitigating the remaining risks of the migration.

Chapter 14: Voting System as a Reference Implementation- The final chapter will examine two extensions of our voting system: the adaptation of the system to another business domain and the application of isolated components to an unrelated product with similar infrastructure requirements. The reader will be presented with insight of how general smaller problems are connected to solve a specific business problem. By the end of this chapter and the conclusion of the book, the reader will be shown the opportunity for reuse of the voting application as well as the usefulness of the principles and methodologies that were employed in future projects.

Code Bundle and Coloured Images

Please follow the link to download the
Code Bundle and the *Coloured Images* of the book:

https://rebrand.ly/xr0t3uq

The code bundle for the book is also hosted on GitHub at
https://github.com/bpbpublications/GCP-in-Action.
In case there's an update to the code, it will be updated on the existing GitHub repository.

We have code bundles from our rich catalogue of books and videos available at https://github.com/bpbpublications. Check them out!

Errata

We take immense pride in our work at BPB Publications and follow best practices to ensure the accuracy of our content to provide with an indulging reading experience to our subscribers. Our readers are our mirrors, and we use their inputs to reflect and improve upon human errors, if any, that may have occurred during the publishing processes involved. To let us maintain the quality and help us reach out to any readers who might be having difficulties due to any unforeseen errors, please write to us at :

errata@bpbonline.com

Your support, suggestions and feedbacks are highly appreciated by the BPB Publications' Family.

Did you know that BPB offers eBook versions of every book published, with PDF and ePub files available? You can upgrade to the eBook version at www.bpbonline. com and as a print book customer, you are entitled to a discount on the eBook copy. Get in touch with us at :

business@bpbonline.com for more details.

At www.bpbonline.com, you can also read a collection of free technical articles, sign up for a range of free newsletters, and receive exclusive discounts and offers on BPB books and eBooks.

Piracy

If you come across any illegal copies of our works in any form on the internet, we would be grateful if you would provide us with the location address or website name. Please contact us at **business@bpbonline.com** with a link to the material.

If you are interested in becoming an author

If there is a topic that you have expertise in, and you are interested in either writing or contributing to a book, please visit **www.bpbonline.com**. We have worked with thousands of developers and tech professionals, just like you, to help them share their insights with the global tech community. You can make a general application, apply for a specific hot topic that we are recruiting an author for, or submit your own idea.

Reviews

Please leave a review. Once you have read and used this book, why not leave a review on the site that you purchased it from? Potential readers can then see and use your unbiased opinion to make purchase decisions. We at BPB can understand what you think about our products, and our authors can see your feedback on their book. Thank you!

For more information about BPB, please visit **www.bpbonline.com**.

Join our Discord space

Join our Discord workspace for latest updates, offers, tech happenings around the world, new releases, and sessions with the authors:

https://discord.bpbonline.com

Table of Contents

Section 1:
Cloud Services by Responsibility

CHAPTER 1

Responsibilities and Utility of a Cloud Platform

Introduction

This book provides an end-to-end explanation and usage guide of Google Cloud Platform as a foundational layer for distributed computer applications. Both an abstract model of an application and a cloud service, and a specific concrete instance of each will be discussed and evaluated. By the end of the book, the reader will have both a conceptual understanding and a real reference implementation to use in designing their own distributed architectures.

In part one of this book, we will examine the architectural considerations of any distributed, scalable software system, remaining vendor agnostic. We then divide the functional requirements of an application into components, based on the features of our cloud platform.

After the planning is done, we then focus on the client in part two. Our users are not in the cloud; they are tethered to a phone, tablet, or computer. Client platforms will be described, including reasons to support each.

The border between client and cloud is next: we will consider the strengths and weaknesses of client and cloud environments and design well-defined interfaces for each of these.

We then put principles into practice. The third part of this book builds a distributed system where scalability and reliability are critical: a voting system for broadcast talent shows, the world's largest democracies.

With the voting system in place, part four of the book recaps a successful deployment. We will describe a common task, migrating our application to a new cloud service. A well-architected system allows migrating components of our system with minimal impact on the rest of the application.

We wrap up with a description of our voting system as a reference model for systems with similar technical requirements.

Structure

This chapter covers the following topics:

- Generic infrastructure considerations
- Identity and authentication
- Scalability
- Asynchronous processing
- Data permanence
- Response delivery
- Analysis of infrastructure responsibilities
- Google Cloud Platform product overview

Objectives

This chapter will review the evolution of application development that has precipitated the need for Cloud Service Platforms. We will then review the architectural considerations of a distributed application and the types of services provided by a cloud platform to address those. Then the chapter focuses on some of the **Google Cloud Platform** (**GCP**) products in each of these service categories. We wrap up the introductory chapter with a review of what features do not fit on GCP services and what each of their optimal platforms are.

The basic requirements of a typical distributed application will be described, and we will explore how a cloud service can add value to an application's solution to each of those requirements.

General infrastructure considerations

There are some common considerations that apply to all portions of a distributed system that should weigh heavily in your choice of an infrastructure provider and your overall design. First and foremost, what is the client interface? Client language libraries, a REST API, Socket-based remote procedure calls. How do you invoke an operation and get a response? Make sure that your infrastructure provider is a good fit with other considerations: the knowledge base of your engineers, the platforms you are targeting, and any domain-specific software products you have to interface with. Some other broad considerations include regional availability, billing model (provisioned capacity or demand-based), and technical and other support plans offered by the vendor or third parties.

Identity and authentication

This is who I am? and *May I do this?* are two of the most fundamental and stress-tested operations that an application system has to support. Fundamental in that all multi-user stateful systems have the notion of identifying a known user and the need for authenticating that user to prevent impersonation. These features are stress-tested by the many people, systems, and bot agents who are devoted to deceiving, bypassing, or breaking the authentication mechanism with the desired effect of spending someone else's money, authority, or reputation. Criminals are clever and persistent, so considerable effort is needed to stay one step ahead of them.

Scalability

The need to scale is the best problem to have. This is a surprising truth often encountered when one first delivers a large-scale popular system. For example, after spending months improving the quality and impact of a new internal system, users still complain about latency and capacity. Rather than be despondent, this is a cause for celebration. This means that the users cannot get enough of your service!

An unpopular system with no growth in the user base has no scaling challenges. In most business scenarios, it also has no future.

One of the most compelling reasons to host a system in the cloud is its elasticity. The number of workers is not limited by the amount of RAM in your servers, the size of your server room, the breadth of your IP block, or the number of watts your circuit breakers will allow. There are limits, of course, but they are someone else's limits, and that someone has made a profitable business of being able to provide more computing capacity on demand for a price. Your cloud provider's job is to fill data centers and buy network switches and to pay them when you need to use any amount of those.

Asynchronous processing

People do not need answers to their questions as immediately as they often think. What they really want is an acknowledgment that the question was heard and is being addressed. Take an example from an online banking system: you can use your checking account to pay your credit card balance. The request takes a few seconds to formulate; click a button, select a payment source, type in an amount, and click submit. In reality, banking systems are broad and deep: a transaction like this can take many seconds or minutes to fully execute and propagate through the banks' processes and data stores. Does the user see a spinning beach ball, or *please wait* for as long as it takes? They would probably close the window, or their browser would crash while they were waiting. Instead, the user is immediately told: *transaction pending*, with some details to confirm that the transfer request was, in fact, heard, and the bank's backend systems will process this transfer asynchronously, decoupled from the user's visible frontend. Eventually, the effect of the completed transaction is made visible to the user, and the pending payment is shown as complete, with balances and limits all updated in their respective accounts. The means to queue up pending requests like this for later processing without blocking the requester is an important capability offered by cloud platforms, usually in the form of a message queue service. A companion feature to this is an elastic work pool, where new tasks can be as needed to process a growing queue of pending requests.

Data permanence

Data permanence can be summed up by one simple invariant: *What you read is what you wrote. Period.* When you want to read some stored value, the only acceptable result is the value that you stored. There are no partial results, no garbled, incorrect values, and no timeouts. For example, after lunch with a coworker, you might write yourself a note *Joelle owes me $10.00*, and whenever you later wonder about Joelle's balance, you will calculate -10.0. After your friend repays you, you would write down, *Joelle now owes me $0.00*. When subsequently calculating Joelle's balance, you arrive at a balance of 0 and no awkward moments the next time you speak. This can only happen if you have confidence in the data permanence guaranteed by your storage service, in this case, your note-taking app or notebook. This is the most impactful and critical aspect of an application's reliability: a dropped user query can be retried, but lost data (and a slighted friend) is gone for good.

Response delivery

Response delivery is very similar to the decoupling of our credit card payment request from the processing it triggers. The delivery of a response to the client is also usually decoupled from the completion of a task. When our credit card payment system completes the complex transaction of applying for a payment, should it stop and wait for the updated status to be sent to the user? That would be a problem. Suppose they are offline, or network latency delays the message by several seconds. Another application of asynchronous processing, sometimes using the same message queue services, can be utilized to post responses for their intended recipients, with those recipients expected to retrieve them when they are available. A variation of this is support for push notifications, where a designated endpoint on the client is invoked by the messaging service rather than the client polling for any pending messages. Each model has its uses and will be explored in the course of this book.

Analysis of infrastructure considerations

The infrastructure platform that we use has distinct features to offer in implementing our final product. These features are not always clearly delineated, and capabilities can overlap or seem to be redundant between them. The following section discusses how and more importantly why an application can be decomposed into functional components.

Interdependence of platform responsibilities

Now that we can refer to the working definitions of these topics, we can look at the topography of an application and see how these considerations overlap. The following Venn diagram will be our guide through this exploration:

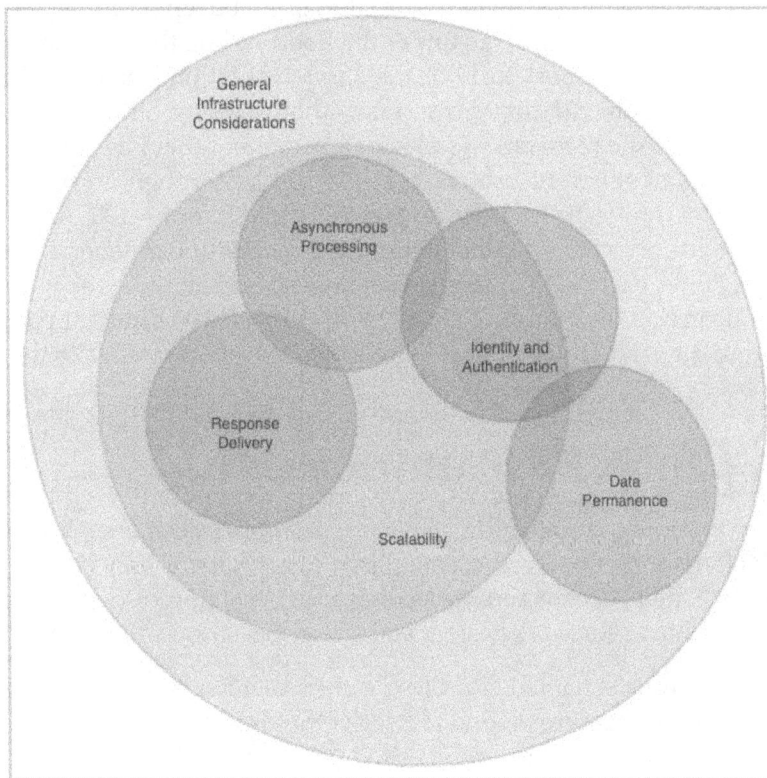

Figure 1.1: Critical responsibilities within a distributed application

It would be naive to consider any of these topics in isolation. For example, user requests are not the only source of demand that we expect to scale up. User logins, which provide the demand for *Identity and Authentication* processing, will introduce an increasing load on our system, and whatever mechanisms we use to keep up with an increasing rate of user requests could be brought to bear on the ever-increasing number of logins to our wildly popular product.

What makes an application system worthy or, better, suitable for incorporating a cloud service in its technical implementation? The answer is the same as for many other questions you face when you are under any pressure to deliver a product at some fixed cost or time. It should be the largest positive net-value option: the value provided the costs outweigh those of the non-cloud alternatives.

When you look at the codelabs or quickstarts (for some forgiving definition of quick) for GCP, it is daunting how much you have to learn before you can write a successful *Hello World from the cloud* application. This ramp-up is a high barrier to entry, and it is very tempting to believe that these services are unnecessarily complex or that the technical documentation is lacking. Many engineers have ended hours or days of frustrating attempts to get some simple solution working.

Any cloud service platform, GCP included, is a broad and deep machine. There are many internal gears, cogs, axles, and springs under the hood. While the designers of these very complex machines do their best to hide the implementation details, reduction of the publicly visible complexity can only go so far without sealing off access to much of the inherent capabilities of the platform. A software component that has the ability to service dozens or hundreds of different use cases cannot do so through an API with just one unparameterized method call. In practical terms, if there are N=100 different scenarios that a component can address, its public interface could be 100 independent methods, 50 independent methods, each with a Boolean argument, and 10 methods with 10 different meaningful sequences of invocation. or just 1 method with 100 different parameter value combinations, but there are going to be 100 invocable *somethings* visible to the users of that component.

Assigning roles by platform

A useful and entertaining engineering concept is that of *Antipatterns*. It is a category of design patterns frequently observed among large development projects that have failed. As a perfect complement to the accepted concept and catalog of design patterns, there were things to emulate in software design, and there were things to avoid.

One of these antipatterns is named *God Class*, a class that has *too much* responsibility and functionality. A common feature of God classes is the *doItAll()* method, which does it all. Everything the class does is in one long method body. This is the antithesis of the design practices of an application backed by a cloud service. In a cloud-backed application, responsibilities are made specific to both function and ideal form: function being the intended effect, and form being the particular runtime environment in which that function is most ideally executed. Some things *belong* near the user; some are more tightly coupled to a data store, global cache, or another software system with which your application interoperates.

Let us discuss some reasons why you should not write large and clumsy monoliths:

- **Different operations have different request rates**: Not every operation in a system has the same drivers of demand. A login operation occurs once per user session and maybe less if a client allows the user to remain logged in for extended periods. In contrast, a *view current high bid* in an auction happens constantly at short intervals throughout some stage of a user session. There are going to be some resources that are allocated to authenticate a user but are not needed once the user's identity is known, and isolating the login operations allows us to more conveniently free up resources that should be out of scope after they have served their purpose.

- **Long methods are hard to understand**: Readability and engineer comprehension are the factors that determine the accuracy of a computer program, not the understanding of a compiler or microprocessor. There have been notable bugs in language translators (aka compilers, interpreters, runtime bytecode interpreters) and processors, but they are notable because they are rare. On the other hand, there are bugs due to programmer errors, specifically misinterpreting the effect of some snippet of code in every software product, with more being introduced every day. One easy, obvious, and globally applicable factor in determining how well a software developer groks the method that they are reading and writing is how long the method body is. Once part of the method scrolls out of view in a typically sized source editor, around 24 lines or so, it is out of mind. Computer languages are dense, and maintaining awareness of 20, 30, or 100 lines of code is more than human consciousness is equipped to do.

- **Lack of isolation of values invites unintended side-effects and exploits**: Most programming languages provide a few options for the scope of a variable or function. Global, Class, or local to a method (or function). There are actually finer-grained scopes available, such as block level, but these are unfamiliar and seldom used intentionally because most for loops include them as the index, but the developers writing them do not think of them as an example of a block level variable, but rather as some *for loop specific thing*.

  Here is the problem: a large method that encapsulates many different operations will include local variables for those disparate operations but with nothing guarding operation A from accessing a variable declared and intended to be used by sibling operation B.

  This sort of undesirable side effect can be unintentional, such as in the following elided code snippet:

```
int x,y;
  ...
  x = height/2;
  y = width/2;
  ...
```

```
for (x=0; x<shape_count; x++) {
  reposition_shape(x);
}

…

  While (rect) {
    rect.resize_to_frame(x,y);
    rect = rect.nextShape;
    shape_count += 1;
  }
```

Look for the latent bug in the preceding code, syntactically correct but clearly a mistake.

The x in the for loop is the same method variable as the earlier assigned x and resets that value, which had been set to ½ of the height.

Of course, better variable names would help here as well; why is *x* such a common index name? However, that is a separate question.

Even worse than the unintended bug illustrated previously, this sort of side effect can be latent. This means that it does not arise in expected situations but is nonetheless there to be triggered in some edge cases. This is fertile ground for exploits such as stack-based buffer overflow attacks, commonly launched when a nefarious reader of the program source sees the potential for hijacking a piece of code and a way to change its behavior to some unintended and probably harmful effect.

One practice that minimizes this general class of defect is simple: keep methods' responsibilities well-defined and narrowly focused, with just the code they need to perform that very well-defined task. Reducing shared scope reduces the potential for and impact of destructive side-effects:

- **A specific degree of parallelism may be ideal for some operations but not for others**: This is a consideration more relevant to a distributed system than to a local, single runtime-platform application. Some tasks benefit from putting more workers on the job, and some tasks do not. There is an old adage that starts with *you cannot make a baby in one month*, but we can be more relevant than that. You can convert a large image to grayscale in ~1/100th the time by assigning each of 100 distinct segments of the bitmap to a different process. On the other hand, the precursor task of capturing the image itself from a camera is a one-worker operation.

All work requires the product of (time * space), and you want to decide how much to increase space to decrease time dynamically and appropriately to the specific task at hand. In the image grayscaling operation presented previously, processing a low-resolution bitmap of 340 x 240 pixels would not call for as many workers as an ultra-high definition 10 Megapixel image. The larger image has 130 times as many pixels to iterate over, and so if your goal is to keep processing time nearly constant, it would require 100+ workers to chew on the image in parallel. The *dynamically and appropriately* above is one of the strong points of a cloud service; they excel at providing workers on demand and equitably distributing work amongst the available workers in the pool.

By now, we hope that you realize how dangerous it can be to author a large system without following a good set of best practices. However, do not give up. It is not that dire: you have probably been producing software until now, and those applications have done their job. Building applications without a cloud service in your infrastructure does not make you incompetent any more than including one is a guarantee of success. What learning about and employing cloud services in your systems *will* do is increase development velocity and lower the effort required to produce systems of higher reliability, responsiveness, and in the end, user satisfaction!

Google Cloud Platform product overview

Let us start to explore the specific services offered by GCP and arrange them by their major theme. Let us first discuss another diagram, a partial taxonomy of GCP services, grouped by general theme:

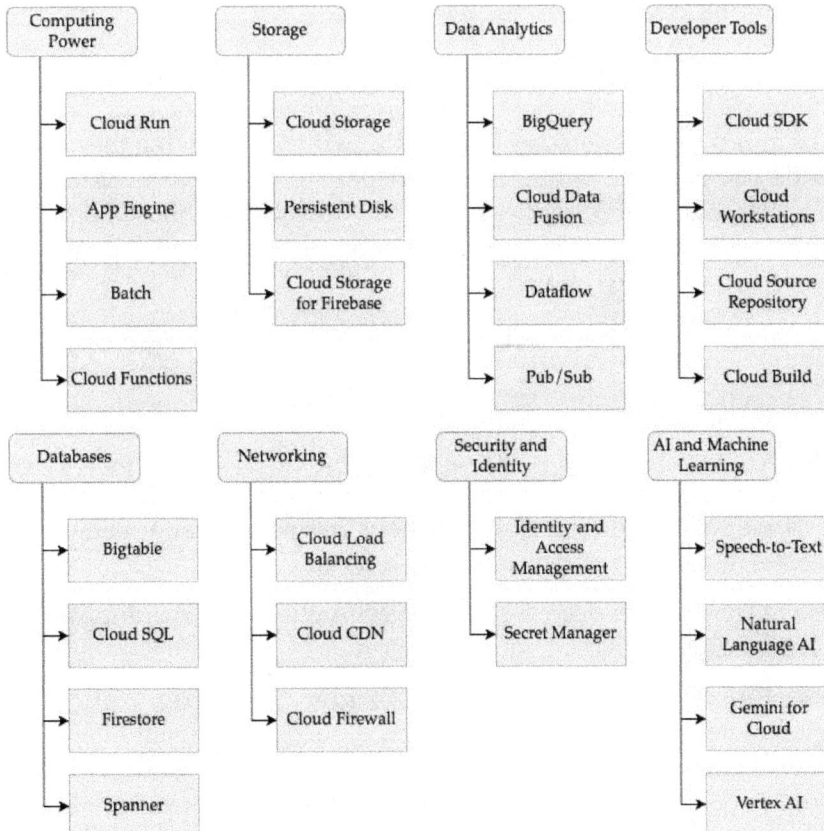

Figure 1.2: Taxonomy of major GCP services

Note: **As of summer 2024, GCP includes over 100 services, many of which exist to serve highly specialized use cases such as migration of existing VMWare workloads or managing fully dedicated hardware nodes that might be required to comply with specific requirements of a regulated industry. The preceding diagram and the overall content of this book focus on a large and most commonly applicable services. For a complete list of GCP services, always check Google's published product overview at https://cloud.google.com/products.**

Top level categories of Google Cloud services

GCP offers many services that address the same basic needs. Again, *Why can't they make it simple?* is a common response when someone first sees the long, long list of services offered up for consideration. There are two major reasons for having seeming duplication: **specialization** and **evolution**.

By specialization, we mean the wide breadth of some of these categories. Do you want to store many small files or fewer humongous files or maintain your own POSIX filesystems? Rather than reducing the many possible use cases to the greatest common denominator, which would leave many scenario-specific requirements unfulfilled, GCP offers different storage services to address different common sets of requirements.

Evolution is the changing characteristics of a solution over time due to either changes in the market or to feedback and lessons learned from previous solutions. There may be new paradigms or improved architectures to offer, but without removing the existing services that thousands of clients are built with and depend on. The balanced way to upgrade capabilities in this way is to introduce new, distinct services while keeping the old ones around, maintained, and supported until the user base has migrated to their newer, shinier, and hopefully more valuable counterparts.

Let us briefly review the mission of the categories and services represented in *Figure 1.2*.

Computing power

This class of services provides the ability to run a program. That is random access memory, a processor, and some largely ignored companion components. Relevant performance characteristics are speed, number of instructions per second, and memory, how many bytes (megabytes, gigabytes) of code and data can be held.

The services we are going to describe provide computing power optimized for different types of workloads. Let us learn about the services:

- **Cloud Run**: Cloud Run allows you to run a workload written in whatever language and frameworks that you choose, such as you would deploy and run on your own machines. Your deployable app is then packaged into a container image, either by you or by the Cloud Build tool, and is ready to run in production. Cloud Run automatically starts up new instances of your container to handle incoming requests and retires inactive, unneeded workers as demand lessens.

Cloud Run can run workers that process user requests, but can also manage non-interactive jobs that run for up to 24 hours.

- **App Engine**: App Engine is a managed service that is suited to run server-side rendered websites written in one of the supported languages: Node.js, Java. Ruby, C#, Go, Python, or PHP. Being a fully managed environment, App Engine hides all of the underlying infrastructure and OS; you simply build and deploy your application, which then runs in a sandbox environment with compute performance characteristics and storage limits for the instance type that you select from an available set. App engine scales the number of servers running your application to match traffic demands.

  App Engine has two types of environment: the **App Engine Standard Environment** and the **App Engine Flexible Environment**. The flexible environment supports a greater number of languages and frameworks but expects you to do some forecasting and planning of how traffic to your application will scale, whereas the standard environment handles rapid, dynamic changes in demand for you.

- **Batch**: Batch is the GCP equivalent of a classic Unix *Cron Job*. The batch service schedules, queues up, and executes non-interactive jobs and workloads that are not triggered by a user event. The batch service queues up instances of your batch jobs based on creation parameters that you specify. When the resource requirements that you specify are available, those queued jobs are run using scheduling parameters that you can override from calculated defaults.

  Batch is integrated with and is similar to Cloud Run and other compute services, but has options that make it a compelling choice for tasks that fit its constraints. Since the jobs run by batch are non-interactive and are presumed to have well-defined, existing inputs, fault tolerance, and the ability to be restarted, batch jobs can run on *Spot VMs* that have the same hardware profiles as other compute services but without guarantees of continuous availability. In other words, the VM that your batch worker is running on might be shut down or restarted, and your task will then be started on another VM when available. Running on these potentially short-lived instances and dealing with restart semantics buys you something: between 60% and 91% cheaper machines.

- **Cloud Run functions**: Cloud functions are an implementation of the ultimate infrastructure-abstract paradigm available: **function as a service (FaaS)**. To use cloud functions, you supply a single-purpose function in a supported language and couple it to a triggering event. When that event occurs, FaaS invokes your function, sending it the parameters of the triggering event.

  Cloud functions are written in a supported runtime: many versions of either Node.js, Python, Go, Java, Ruby, PHP, or .NET Core.

  This list may look familiar from the preceding App Engine description; The reader may ponder why this may be.

Databases

Database services are a collection of products that provide access to relational and non-relational databases, hosted and integrated with the other GCP services. GCP Database products can reside with the same regional specifications, identified and reached using Google Networking addresses, and protected with Google Security services.

Relational and non-relational databases are available and are of equal rank: The relational model has been the industry standard for decades, and the **Structured Query Language** (**SQL**) can describe and extract complex data models, but non-relational databases offer high scale and greater flexibility to support less-structured data. The following database products represent both of these paradigms:

- **Cloud SQL**: Cloud SQL is GCP's *generic* interface to many popular, existing relational database products: PostgreSQL, MySQL, and SQL Server. CloudSQL provides an abstraction layer common to all of these underlying products, allowing your application to be vendor-agnostic. In addition to this common API, Cloud SQL provides database management functionality; vendor-specific backups, database replication, capacity management (storage scaling), and software patches are all performed on your underlying database as you specify in a vendor-agnostic configuration specification.

- **Bigtable**: Bigtable is the original NoSQL database, written and used internally at Google for their own needs to support products like Search and Distributed Access through software such as MapReduce. The schema of these products was relatively simple. What was needed was speed and the ability to read and write extremely large rows. Bigtable data is not a relational database; the data model is a simple.

  `Key=[Value@Timestamp] map.`

  Bigtable databases can be distributed across many machines, hundreds of thousands, and hold Petabytes of data. Bigtable's access model can take some getting used to for developers used to a relational database but for the right fit of data, the schema can be simply expressed, and the performance unmatched.

- **Firestore**: Firestore is a managed, scalable, serverless document database. Its documents are JSON compatible and highly queryable with high-volume indexes. Firestore supports security and validation rules and **Atomicity, Consistency, Isolation, and Durability** (**ACID**) transaction support, guaranteeing data integrity.

  The Firestore service is part of the Firebase development platform, which provides direct access to the Firestore database from client apps on mobile devices and the web.

  A fully managed serverless product, Firestore database scaling, and maintenance are all performed internally, with no burden on the client.

- **Spanner:** Spanner is Google's newest database, incorporating features and lessons learned from earlier generation products such as Bigtable. Spanner is highly available and provides uniquely flexible control over scaling to separately match access demand and storage requirements. Database administration tasks such as sharding and scaling of compute resources are performed automatically. Dynamic schema changes are processed online and propagated while serving traffic, incurring no downtime.

  Spanner transactions provide strong ACID guarantees and region-independent (i.e., universal) time ordering.

  Spanner tables can be accessed using GoogleSQL, a Google supported dialect of the **Structured Query Language** (**SQL**), but Spanner also provides a PostgreSQL interface for easy porting to Spanner and to support migration of both applications and developer expertise.

Storage

Storage products offer what we traditionally think of as disk space. A storage service provides the ability to save, catalog, and retrieve independent blocks or objects with no overarching or imposed structure. Let us discuss them as follows:

- **Cloud Storage**: Cloud Storage is a managed service that stores unstructured data in *buckets* with one of several different access frequencies. The expected access frequency and storage type in Cloud Storage determine the cost and the service guarantees. All Cloud Storage options are either short-lived or highly durable and have maximum object lifetimes.

  Cloud Storage buckets, roughly analogous to volumes, can be replicated to optimize performance through localized/nearby access, support automatic, invisible failover among replicas, or guarantee data availability.

  For ease of application development and direct user manipulation, Cloud Storage FUSE can make your buckets available as a local file system.

- **Persistent disk**: The Persistent disk service provides a simple disk interface to redundant, automatically sized block storage.

  Persistent disks offer management options similar to, and often interchangeable with, the standard disk device paradigm. PDDs can be cloned, detached, and attached to different machines and can be encrypted with system or user-supplied keys.

  Persistent disks can be backed by either **hard disk drives** (**HDD**) or **solid-state drives** (**SSD**) to match a client's performance and cost requirements.

- **Cloud Storage for Firebase**: Cloud Storage for Firebase service facilitates storage and serving of user-generated content. Being geared towards client creation and delivery, Cloud Storage for Firebase provides fully featured client **software development kits** (**SDK**) to allow mobile and web clients to directly store and retrieve binary objects such as video, photos, and audio. To minimize the impact of client connectivity issues, storage and retrieval operations are resumable, retrying an interrupted operation where it left off.

For background or asynchronous processing of your Firebase objects, the Google Cloud Storage **application program interface** (**API**) can be used to access the objects from server-side GCP components. This is useful when a task may call for more compute power than you can expect a client platform to have, such as large-scale transcoding or image preparation and scaling.

Networking

Google Networking products are a combination of connectivity services and tools that support the network breadth and performance afforded by that connectivity. Informed dispatching, routing, and load balancing, request localization, and reducing bandwidth consumption are of high priority to make cost-effective use of a network by an application if it serves clients anywhere on the Internet, with no penalties for any user based on their locale. Google describes Google Cloud networking services as *One network, planet scale*. Let us look at them in detail:

- **Cloud load balancing**: Cloud load balancing allows you to choose a method by which Google's frontends will forward requests to your application. Several options are available to be selected from based on the type of traffic your application receives, the locality of your clients, and how broadly you wish to distribute the workers that receive these requests.

  Regardless of the type of load balancer, Google Cloud load balancing scales to process over 1 million **queries per second** (**QPS**). The frontends and the load balancers themselves are the same technologies that are used in Google's own production network that services Search, Ads, and YouTube.

- **Cloud and Media Content Delivery Networks (CDN)**: CDNs, also referred to as **Edge networks**, are a software layer above standard IP networking and are specialized to optimize the delivery of content such as video and audio files.

  Both of these GCP CDN services have the same basic operating principle: identify content that is being fetched from a distant source on the internet and establish a copy of that content as close as possible to as many requesting clients as possible. Then as subsequent requests for this same content are seen, intercept them and serve them from the close copy, avoiding repeated redundant fetches from that distant origin point. The result is lower latency for your users and lower network costs incurred by your application.

  Media CDN uses the same infrastructure as YouTube does to bring video streams and large file downloads closer to the user.

Cloud CDN uses Google's edge network to store and serve content from a Cloud CDN cache. The CDN cache itself uses your application's cloud load balancer to prime itself from the closest source of the content that your application offers. Cloud CDN can be used for any cacheable responses to GET requests, as determined by several criteria. Typically, static content types such as images, videos, audio, PDFs, and fonts are good candidates for CDN serving.

- **Cloud firewall**: GCP Cloud Firewall is a Next Generation Firewall that is an intrinsic part of Google's networking fabric and is always present. Cloud firewall is a stateful inspection model firewall that applies rules that you select and/or code to inspect all traffic and prevent suspect or malicious traffic from reaching your application.

  Google curates and publishes a set of global policies that you can call from your own firewall rules to keep up with emerging and evolving threats.

Data analytics

Google's data analytics suite includes products to both perform data analytics operations in a *GCP way* and several supporting products that themselves provide infrastructure for that infrastructure.

Let us step back and separate these two layers of product.

Data analytics, by the book, is the overall process of examining data sets to identify trends and then draw conclusions about the data they contain, with the goal of explaining and/ or forecasting movements and trends within the data.

Here is a very brief mental model of a data analytics task: multi-level derivatives in calculus. If your dataset of geolocation sync points is a series of timestamp + location values, you can derive velocity, and from a series of velocity values, you can compute your second-level derivative: acceleration.

Imagine a similar process but for consumer spending at a location or on a specific day of the week, and then finding the correlation between purchases of two seemingly independent items, each on some specific day of the week.

This kind of iterative calculation requires very large amounts of computation. Over the past decade or two, this kind of analysis has moved from one-off Excel workbooks, maybe with some macros, to highly specialized systems and programming languages.

These processing models are not of a scale that runs well on even the fastest workstation: both the computing power needed, and the size of the datasets and transient storage make that highly impractical.

One other thing to note before the big reveal that is coming up, these operations are iterative: a sequence of steps that each rely on the results of earlier steps.

To illustrate an expanded version of the preceding model to be used for road planning and urban safety studies, refer to the following figure:

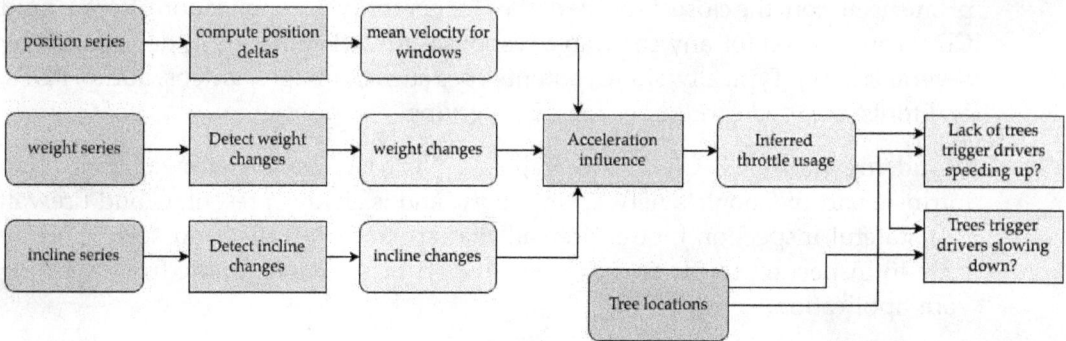

Figure 1.3: Pipeline to calculate the effect of roadside trees on gas pedal usage

Each of these calculations has dependencies and thus, the sequence is necessary. When we describe a set of dependent operations such as this, the term **Pipeline** is used, one in which the data flowing through the processes takes the place of water.

Back to GCP data analytics specifics. Some products in this suite, such as BigQuery and dataflow are used to specify and perform the actual calculations of the target values: acceleration, gas_pedal_usage and tree_locations in comparison to gas pedal usage. Other products, including Cloud data fusion, are used to build, run, and otherwise manage the pipelines themselves; they are the plumbers who install and maintain the pipeline:

- **BigQuery**: BigQuery is a data analytics platform that helps you build queries that unearth inherent but hidden information within your dataset. It offers query languages, connectors for your data to languages such as Python and frameworks including Apache Spark, and metadata operations such as data cataloging, lineage tracking, and data profiling.

  Gemini in BigQuery provides LLM-powered assistance for many of the tasks you will perform with the tools in BigQuery.

- **Cloud data fusion**: Cloud data fusion is a practical glue, or perhaps mediator, between data analytics tools such as BigQuery and the large datasets that they operate on. Your source data, those large collections of data points you have collected, are hopefully stored in some available and durable service such as Cloud Storage or Cloud SQL tables, and the data your pipeline computes at each intermediate step, as well as the final result, has to be stored somewhere.

  That is the job of an **extract, transform, and load** (**ETL**) product such as cloud data fusion. Fusion offers pre-built and helps create custom transformations and connections to be joined together into those pipelines we described earlier. As well as data centric components such as source and result data stores, Fusion also specifies and manages the *engines* that do the work: what compute capacity is used to perform the computations that transform your data in each step of the pipeline.

- **Dataflow**: The Dataflow service is specialized to support low latency, real-time analytics of streaming data so that you can spot and react to large-scale events as they occur: *People in Europe are asking about the prices of football jerseys 100 times more than they were hour ago* is a simple example of something that an online retailer should be aware of as it happens.

- **Pub/Sub**: Pub/Sub is Google's message queue service, and its grouping as a data analytics product is more a reflection of its popular usage rather than of its nature. Pub/Sub itself is not used to perform data analytics operations but it is a very convenient and commonly employed source of the large series of data that feed data analytics pipelines. Our discussion of Pub/Sub will focus more on its general capabilities and not its use with data analytics tools.

Pub/Sub is a simple abbreviation for *Publish and Subscribe*, the two core operations that a messaging service supports.

Think of an email list as a reference model for Pub/Sub. You sign up for an email list titled *space-battleship-Yamato-fandom* using a subscribe button on your favorite old-school anime website. A few hours later, someone else sends an email to the list telling everyone about an incredible new technical diagram of the Yamato that they have seen in a historical archive: they have just **published** a message.

As a **Subscriber** to the **Topic** of space-battleship-Yamato-fandom, you will eventually get this message in your inbox. It probably was not delivered immediately after it was sent, nor did you expect that; but it *will* be delivered to you, along with a few tens of thousands of other happy people with excellent taste in entertainment. The person who sent the message, the **Publisher**, did not stick around to check and see if everyone got the message, they trust that email infrastructure works.

That is the model of roles and responsibilities that Pub/Sub implements but for more structured data and programmatic access rather than correspondence among joyous anime fans.

Pub/Sub defines topics in a registry and allows client applications to subscribe to those Topics. Publisher clients then publish messages directed at a Topic. Subscribers have different ways by which their messages of interest can be delivered: Push, Pull, and Export:

o **Push subscriptions** are ones for which the Subscriber provides a callback, an endpoint for Pub/Sub to call when there is a message of interest.

o **Pull subscriptions** hold on to their messages until they are asked for. When ready, the Subscriber connects to their Pub/Sub Topic and retrieves each message that has been sent to that topic.

o **Export subscriptions** are for batch handling of large numbers of messages, messages are added to a BigQuery dataset or a Cloud Storage bucket, for whatever later processing the application performs. This is the overlap between Pub/Sub and data analytics cited earlier: Pub/Sub is a fast and reliable way to get data into an Analytics pipeline.

Security and identity

The security and identity suite is a large collection of products with the broad mission to *help you meet your policy, regulatory, and business objectives*. The offerings in this domain are constantly expanding and evolving due to the two irresistible, unplanned external forces driving this solution space: government regulators and criminal activity.

Used together, these two products provide both the means for secure access control, and for responsible management of the controls used to manage that access:

- **Identity and access management**: Identity and access management provides fine-grained access control to all the cloud resources that comprise your application.

  There are two major classes of features: Access control and role and group definition.

  Access control features to control who can access what and what forms that access can take. For example, many tasks in our application can write to logs, but they have got no good reason to read those logs, so that access should be controlled thus. Access to a resource can be logged, blocked or permitted; based on the access rules defined for the resource when applied to the attempting users defined roles and groups.

  Role and group support is based on the long-standing and proven best practice: do not count on an individual; count on a given role with appropriate responsibilities and privileges for which certain individuals have been designated. This allows for redundancy: stand-ins, substitutes and proxy individuals or teams can guard against single points of success and raise lottery factors of a system. This also provides security in the face of mobility: people can transfer, retire, or be terminated, but their critical responsibilities will be assigned to someone.

- **Secret Manager**: The Secret Manager service stores your most sensitive data: passwords, certificates, API keys, and other critical digital artifacts. Losing or inadvertently revealing these is arguably worse than accidentally losing or revealing the information that they protect.

  Encrypted data carries very little information without the means to decrypt it. It is very little as opposed to none, as there still may be visible metadata, such as the rough size of a file that has been encrypted. Strong encryption techniques are trusted enough so that a common and accepted method of data deletion is to simply destroy the keys needed to decrypt the data. This is a remarkably efficient way to destroy, say, all of the records written to all of our files in a given week if we rotate our encryption keys on a weekly basis. We can now execute a delete operation on millions of records within thousands of files by just deleting one small artifact: that week's decryption key. That is also a remarkably easy way to lose all of our business data for that week with that small deletion.

Hence, we should be particular about two things:

o   Not to lose the keys.

o   If you intentionally throw out those keys, be sure that they are really gone.

There is one additional statement to make:

o   Know who has the keys!

That is why you use Secret Manager.

Replication, access control, audit logging, and encryption of your secrets are among the features that keep your secrets safe.

Developer tools

GCP developer tools products remove a major obstacle to developing large, ambitious projects: our engineering workstations. Building, debugging, and deployment tasks for systems with a large number of technologies, components, and target environments of a cloud application tax the fastest workstations and saturate the fastest network connection.

Develop there, in the cloud, for the cloud. That is what cloud developer tools allow you to do. The development environment should be similar in both performance and scale to the deployment target, or you are trying to build a starship using stone knives and bearskins.

Developing in the cloud also democratizes the development experience: a modest and lightweight notebook is now as good as any top-end workstation and a lot easier to carry to a coworking space, café, or park. Let us discuss these tools:

- **Cloud SDK**: The Cloud SDK provides a set of command line tools that provide access to GCP resources similarly to how existing command line tools access local resources such as files, databases, and interactive shells that run on Compute Virtual Machines.

  Cloud SDK also includes client libraries for many GCP products that allow you to develop application that access such services as App Engine administration, Batch, Bigtable and Cloud Storage using familiar language idioms: classes and methods in language such as Python, Go and Java, rather than; for example, constructing and parsing calls to REST APIs over HTTP.

  The last category of Cloud SDK features follows a model that is in some ways an inverse of the other categories: local emulators for data services, including Bigtable, Spanner, Pub/Sub, Cloud Firestore, and Firestore. This allows rapid development and testing without the need to first setup and populate actual cloud data.

- **Cloud Workstations**: Google Cloud Workstations are virtual machines configured with current developer tools, including GCP and non-GCP products, that reside in your GCP environment. They are secure, fully managed, and local to your other GCP resources, reducing latency and vulnerabilities introduced by the network between a local workstation and the resources they access.

  Cloud Workstations are fully managed and configured from known options, and developers' environments are reproducible and consistent. This minimizes a common comical but frustrating syndrome: *But it works on my machine.*

- **GitLab integration with Google Cloud**: Google Cloud services are fully integrated with GitLab, which allows a GitLab project to deploy directly to Google Cloud. GitLab is an open-source collaborative software development platform which includes storage of source code. While they use much of the same underlying Git technology, GitLab is not GitHub, offering more comprehensive project management features.

  Developers who are familiar with GitHub will find the version control concepts and features GitLab to be familiar.

- **Cloud Build**: Google Cloud Build is a distributed continuous integration/continuous delivery system.

  Cloud Build brings dozens, hundreds, or thousands of compute workers to bear on a particular build, executing independent dependency chains in parallel, speeding up the time to build and deploy by several orders of magnitude. Cloud Build caches intermediate build artifacts so that redundant builds are often nothing more than retrieval of a reference to a cached object.

  Cloud Build provides lineage traceability and other guarantees for released packages, enabling SLSA Level 3 compliance and increasing recommended or required for high-impact industries and use cases. See **https://slsa.dev** for more info on supply-chain levels for software artifacts.

Artificial intelligence and machine learning

Artificial intelligence (**AI**) and **machine learning** (**ML**) products are a mix of those which provide AI/ML features such as Gemini, those which heavily depend on AI/ML functionality such as Natural Language AI and speech to text, and those that are used to manage AI/ML artifacts; aka, Models. Let us learn about these:

- **Speech to text**: The speech-to-text service provides a fast, high-quality, and broadly applicable solution to a problem that has been challenging since the 1980s: recognizing and transcribing human speech from encoded audio.

  Google Cloud Speech to Text sends an audio file or real-time stream, such as a live microphone, from a client to the cloud service, which can recognize and transcribe speech in over 100 human languages. Speech to text can identify the language being spoken with high confidence after listening to the first few seconds of audio-containing speech.

- **Natural Language AI**: Google natural language AI is a set of three related products: Natural Language API, AutoML, and Healthcare Natural Language AI.

  GCP's Natural Language API applies pre-trained ML models to transcriptions of human speech to achieve **natural language understanding** (**NLU**) of that text. NLU extracts syntactic information such as parts of speech, entity recognition, the identification of proper nouns, and sentiment analysis, classifying the emotional tone of the speech. Natural Language API is scaled automatically to keep pace with the text being analyzed and is capable of analyzing conversations in real-time.

  AutoML enables you to train your own ML models to classify Natural Language text and detect sentiment. While the Natural Language API exists for many cases of common speech, AutoML can be used to optimize NLU for specific jargon, conversation roles, or social situations.

- **Google Cloud Healthcare**: Natural Language AI provides ML solutions that apply ML models trained against various medical concepts such as diseases, medications, and procedures. The product can extract information about these concepts from unstructured medical records' text and map this information to standard medical industry vocabularies.

  The models and feature availability of Healthcare Natural Language AI are dependent on the location in which they are used, both for regulatory reasons and localized medical vocabularies and standards.

- **Gemini for Google Cloud**: Gemini is Google's public large language model product, trained on large amounts of data, against which inputs of many types can be applied to infer typical or expected responses based on patterns matched in the Model's training data.

  Gemini for Google Cloud provides a chat interface to models trained specifically on Google Cloud topics, for advice and best practice suggestions in using GCP services.

  Gemini is present in many places in GCP, like Code Assist in GCP developer tools which offers suggestions in the form of autocompletion, and even provides function definitions based on code comments and surrounding usage and context.

  Gemini in Google Workspace products, such as Gmail and Docs, provide writing assistance, generate likely responses to mail messages and suggest formulae in sheets.

- **Vertex AI**: GCP includes several Vertex AI products, with the common mission of providing support for building and using generative AI. Vertex AI includes hundreds of pre-trained models, including Gemini models and third-party and open models. Using Vertex products, you can customize the models with further training, tune them to certain use cases, and monitor their performance over time to detect skew and drift, which could lead to a model deviating from the behaviors it had been trained and tuned to achieve.

Vertex AI Agent Builder is a no-code interactive agent builder that creates AI agents based on existing models and with access to the client organization's data. For example, a customer service bot can check your company's product catalog and inventory.

Components outside of cloud services

With this exhausting list of products available in GCP, you might wonder what else you will need to build your application system.

Let us address the non-GCP components of a distributed application by platform:

- **Client-side code**: Not *everything* is in the cloud: your user for example. Most applications still interact with a human operator who is using some computing platform with one or more **human interface devices** (**HID**): touchscreens, displays, keyboards, mice, accelerometers, and compasses. These client platforms usually have less computing power and storage than their cloud/server-side counterparts, but what they lack in computing power, they make up for in portability and accessibility. There are several criteria for determining that a specific component or feature of an application is a good match for client-side residency:

  o **Presentation**: Showing the user some information, be it visual, audio, or haptic, requires some appropriate output device: screen, speaker, and vibration actuator, respectively, right there with the user. Fine-grained control over the device and real-time updating of the output are probable requirements, and so the code in charge of these outputs is best placed right there on the same device to which the output devices are attached.

  o **User input**: The counterpart to displays gets some information from the user: button presses, keyboard, microphone, or camera input, and the direction that the phone is pointing. These are all tightly bound to the user's presence. A controller and collector of these devices that do not reside on the client platform will be a challenge to the developer and a disappointment to the users.

  o **Telemetry**: Collecting telemetry such as location, light levels, and other features of the user's environment is a similar problem to that of getting user input and, by extension, of the arguments given there, is best run on the client.

Local, low cost but very latency-sensitive calculations.

There is an entire class of calculations that are not excessive in terms of computing demand but are highly latency sensitive. In these cases, the round trip of a request to the cloud may take longer than just doing it on the client. You are not obligated to move all of your application logic to the cloud. Do not incur two seconds to avoid doing one second of work.

- **Dependencies on industry or regulatory specific systems**: In many applications, there will be a required dependence on systems provided or mandated by a government or other industry-specific authority. These are likely to be outside of GCP and non-negotiable with regard to access and usage protocol. Such dependencies are usually in one of two forms:

  o **External services**: A **software as a service (SaaS)** product or other remote service can be abstracted away behind a thin layer in your GCP architecture that serves as a proxy for the actual external service. What GCP service you choose to implement these proxies is directed by particulars of the service: Several networking features, such as Google Cloud API Gateway, can implement this, or in more elaborate cases, a Cloud Functions or Cloud Run instance can be placed between your main application and the external service to perform any mechanical, repeated request pre-processing or response post-processing.

  o **Binaries**: Some external providers supply you with a binary, suitable to a specific runtime environment. These can be loaded into Cloud Storage or Persistent disk and run from one of the GCP VM or container compute service products.

Conclusion

You have reached the end of this chapter. It presented an overview of cloud service platform features and some of the Google Cloud Platform products that provide those. We have reviewed the entire landscape of a distributed application and discussed what considerations to bear in mind when deciding what features to host in the cloud and which to deploy on the client computer. We wrapped up with some of the use cases in which you have to include components that cannot be implemented in the best-fit GCP product and how to normalize those components as much as possible with the rest of your system architecture.

Next, in *Chapter 2, Dividing Up Features of a Cloud Backed Application,* we will go into some depth on how to divide up a cloud-based application's features into components with a level of granularity that affords our basing each of them on the most suitable GCP service or other platform.

Join our Discord space

Join our Discord workspace for latest updates, offers, tech happenings around the world, new releases, and sessions with the authors:

https://discord.bpbonline.com

CHAPTER 2

Dividing up Features of a Cloud Backed Application

Introduction

Now that we have some understanding of what services Google Cloud Platform offers us, which answers the question of supply, let us look at what requirements are presented by a distributed application, the question of understanding demand.

In this chapter, we will examine the technical aspects that an application's features may possess and how those translate or map to the technical requirements of the supporting infrastructure, such as GCP services. To do this, we will define a grammar for describing those features that can be applied directly or adapted to any potential user-driven software product.

Common implementation patterns, such as vertical and horizontal scaling of resources, will be described, and a method for determining both the applicability and actual need for these. Our grammar developed for application features will be extended to include the relevant aspects of infrastructure providers.

We will then apply this methodology that we have developed to select and designate GCP services suited to support features of a common application pattern, interactive shopping.

Structure

In this chapter, the following topics will be covered:

- Enumerating responsibilities and dependencies
- Grouping by topological locality
- Grouping by feature affinity
- Grouping by feature performance considerations
- Understanding feature requirements
- Defining application feature composition
- Describing infrastructure options

Objectives

The reader will learn how to methodically decompose an application's features and then identify the aspects of an application that are relevant to the evaluation of infrastructure platform features.

This chapter demystifies and clearly defines several desirable features of a distributed framework, such as GCP, giving the reader a clear explanation of terms that are often sold in overly vague or even hyperbolic terms.

We will discuss and exemplify a methodology for designing a system architecture that maximizes the product of **form** and **functional** considerations.

Enumerating responsibilities and dependencies

In theory, any modern computing platform could run any code. While it is an interesting thought experiment, our product has to satisfy our users, and it is certain that some tasks are better executed by our phone or web browser, some by our nightly log collector pipeline, and some work is most effectively accomplished by a swarm of workers; to get the job done this time, each time.

To decide where to perform each part of the overall work to be done, these design decisions must merge two independent sets of factors. First are the platform considerations of form, the shape or internal structure that the components of our system possess. The second design constraint is the scope of our product- what parts of our system should be. That is the set of functional considerations that we take into account. The best fit for both form and function is our ideal design product, and this chapter will illustrate a method for arriving at that optimal outcome.

To choose between alternative solutions for our competing problems of reliability, scale, and feature quality, the following historical, tried, and true techniques come to mind:

Figure 2.1: *Throwing darts*

Unrelated skills, such as a game of darts, or perhaps one of random chance, such as dice:

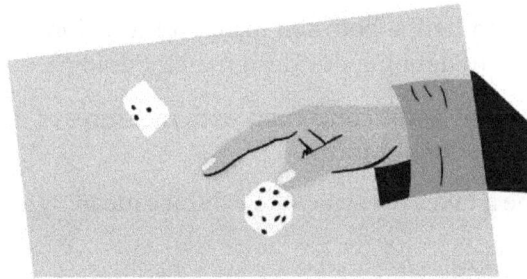

Figure 2.2: *A roll of the dice*

We could also try the following:

Figure 2.3: *Brainstorming sessions*

While the first two methods certainly have their strengths: ease of learning and a speedy execution, but they produce fairly low-fidelity results. We can apply some time, energy, and talent to get the job done right, so a fact-based, exploratory collaboration is how we will make our design decisions.

Different and valid points of view

An important concept, neglected in software engineering curricula and literature, is one posed by a thought experiment known as the Ship of Theseus. Details of the experiment can be found here: **https://open.library.okstate.edu/introphilosophy/chapter/ship-of-theseus/**

The philosophical problem this experiment addresses is that of material constitution, one aspect of which can be summarized by the statement *What something is and what it is made of are separate and different.*

Form and function: both are real, and each is crucial, but each can be considered and defined in isolation.

Understanding how we can define both the form and function of a distributed software application is the first step in defining our design methodology.

Let us start with a glossary of terms concerned with measures of a system's performance, typically bound to considerations of form:

- **Latency**: The time it takes the system to exhibit a meaningful response to a demand trigger

- **Latency sensitivity**: The tolerance of an application to perceptible latency in a response. We classify these largely as:

  o **Highly sensitive**: An increase in latency is noticed and is undesirable

  o **Low sensitivity**: A variance in latency is not consequential

  o **Latency insensitive**: There is no notice of latency. No one is timing the response, as long as the operation finishes

- **Computational expense**: The number of operations, in terms of executable instructions, an operation requires. This is analogous to the Big O notation of runtime cost. For our purposes, we will use relative values within our system:

  o Low (Trivial)

  o Medium

  o High

- **Parallelizable**: This measures how effectively a given task can trade space for time. If one worker takes ten hours, could ten workers, each of the same size as the original, get the job done in one hour? Some work is not divisible into independent sections, and those that are usually incur some cost in dividing the work and merging the results, so most cases do not achieve a straightforward tradeoff.

The degrees of parallelization we will assign are:

o   None.

o   **Low gain**: Sublinear reduction in time for increases in space.

o   **High gain with a ceiling**: Diminishing returns past some number of workers.

o   **High gain, unbounded**: A linear tradeoff of time for space. The more workers, the less time.

Now, let us define a similar set of terms centered around aspects of the *behavior* that a system demonstrates:

- **Demand**: The trigger or instigator of activity in our system.

- **Common classes of demand are**:

  o   **User request**: A user requests that some application take some action in response to that distinct request.

  o   **Accumulated activity reaching some threshold**: Some ongoing, repeated activities fill up a bucket to the point where we do some action on its contents.

  o   **A cumulative value reaching a threshold**: A value that increments over time reaches some significant value at which we take action.

  o   **Periodic (every hour)**: Regular scheduled activity, regardless of activity in the system.

  o   **Administrative action**: Some maintenance or governance action that is initiated by operators, not end-users, of the system

- **Feature affinity**: The features an application exhibits are all connected in some way, if they are truly part of the same application. The binding between any two features is stronger or weaker than that between any two others. Features that are tightly coupled should be implemented using services that are more accessible to each other; in other words, if the **vote** button incurs a **Add Tally to candidate** feature, the **Add Tally** should be invocable from the **Vote** code.

- **Topological proximity**: Similar to feature affinity, but with regards to platform, some features have the same runtime requirements as others and so belong on the same runtime platform. A convenient example is getting the user's vote and displaying a notification of the winning candidate. Both require interaction with the end user of our application and are best implemented in the same runtime platform.

- **Workflow duration**: Some tasks take milliseconds, and some may run for hours before making any observable progress that can be preserved as a milestone.

We will classify the duration of an operation with the following designations:

- **Immediate**: An operation is initiated, executed, and ended with no significant delay or external blocking factors. Stateless operations are most often immediate in their completion.

- **Transaction**: A group of sub-operations must be completed, typically in sequence, before an operation is completed. If any link in the chain fails, the entire operation fails, and so the lifespan of the primary operation is at least the sum of the component sub-tasks lifetimes.

- **User session**: A user engages an application to access some set of features, the exact set and sequence of which are determined to some degree by the individual user

- **Long-running**: Work that may be initiated by a trigger or request, which may take more time to complete than a typical user would wait before moving on to some other feature.

- **Multi-stage pipeline**: A *meta operation* that consists of many stages, each of which advances the state of the operation towards its completion.

The remaining terms defined are the ones that categorize the **functionality** of features of an application, with some examples for each:

- **System connection**: Login, logout, connection to another platform or service that an application is built upon.

- **User request**: The center of an interactive application. Making a purchase, sending a message, and casting a vote are all features that drive users to our product and which they directly invoke requests for.

- **User session**: Retrieving a user profile, retrieving the history of a user or system activity.

- **Client telemetry**: Client operations not explicitly requested by a user's request. Maintaining connectivity, updating location or other environment data.

- **Asynchronous delivery**: Receiving client updates, push notifications, and asynchronous responses to demand triggers.

- **User administration and control**: Changing user permissions or resources.

- **System administration and control**: Changing system-wide resources or availability.

- **On demand data analytics reporting**: Viewing system state in real-time. Current user count, request rates, latency, remaining inventory.

- **Offline, periodic data analytics reporting**: Aggregated system state, calculated at a point in time. Quarterly sales, month-over-month subscriber counts, and daily user activities are all examples of data that are both meaningless and prohibitively expensive to compute on demand in real-time.

With the glossary of terms defined, we need a way to apply them.

Note: **The following discussion refers to a subset of potential features of a voting system for the purpose of illustrating the methodology being explained. A full exploration of that application will be made in later chapters.**

Grouping by topological locality

The two aspects of application features described previously stand out from the others, those of *affinity* and *proximity*. Unlike the other feature attributes described, these are not characteristics of any one feature but rather of relationships between features. A convenient way to visualize such information for a potentially large set of features is commonly used in relational database design.

A *network graph* or *node-link diagram* primarily shows the relationships between entities rather than focusing on the entities and their composition. We can view our affinity features as a network graph where the nodes are the application features and the edges are the relationships between the features.

Here is a graph of the topological proximity of the features of our application:

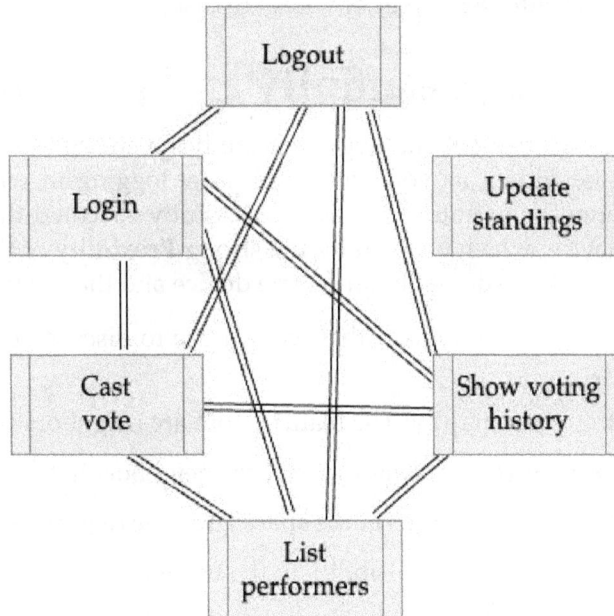

Figure 2.4: Graph of feature proximity

Grouping by feature affinity

The following graph reveals the feature affinity within our application:

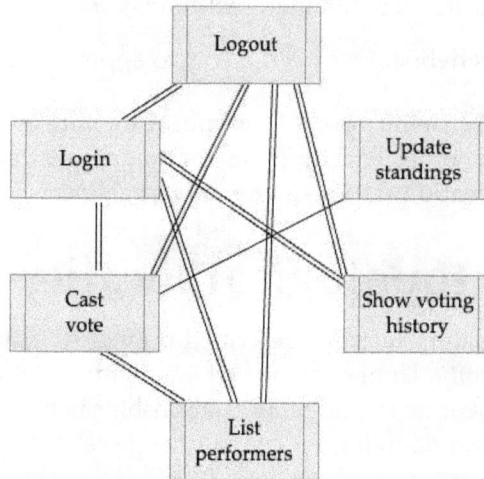

Figure 2.5: Graph of feature affinity

The strength of the relationship between the two nodes is depicted by the relative weight or thickness of the line used to draw the connection. In the preceding figure, the **Login** feature is tightly bound to the **Cast vote** operation, it is a frequent next action; whereas there is a tenuous relationship between casting a vote and updating standings, which is invoked asynchronously after a number of votes are cast.

Determining feature affinity and proximity

Looking at *Figure 2.5*, we see that the Login feature has a strong **Affinity** with the Cast vote feature, which is evident as you typically follow logging in with casting a vote. Additionally, you cannot vote until you have successfully executed the Login operation on the same client device, which is noted by the strong **Proximity** of the Login and Cast vote features in *Figure 2.4*. We do not login on one device and then vote on another.

We now have the following vocabulary that we can use to discuss our application from several points of view:

- **The application's geography**: The features that are neighbors in space.

- **The affinity of features**: The features that are neighbors in time.

- Questions of cost as the product of the space and time required to execute a feature.

- The immediacy of a feature's visibility to the trigger or activation requester.

- **The atomicity of a feature's operation**: The lifecycle and the persistent effect of a feature's execution.

We will use these tools to define the requirements of our system's architecture, mapped onto a set of platform capabilities. It is inevitable that you will make some compromise in any product you select, but there will always be an option that is the relatively best fit for the requirements. Reducing our application features into more discrete, atomic components aids the goal of being able to map those features as directly as possible to **Google Cloud Platform** (**GCP**) and non-GCP based infrastructure services.

Grouping by feature performance considerations

The next step in this process is to dive a bit deeper into the remaining feature categorizations or labels that we have identified.

A table of the feature-centric performance considerations allows us to see the overall composition of our application. Let us now define one with a subset of application features as an example:

Feature	Demand driver	Class of functionality	Latency sensitivity	Computational expense	Parallelizable	Duration
Login	User request	System connection	High	Medium	None	User session
Cast vote	User request	User request	High	Low	None	Transaction
List performers	User request	User request	High	Low	None	Immediate
Update standings	Accumulated activity	Asynchronous delivery	Low	Medium	High, ceiling	Multi-stage pipeline
Show voting history	Admin action	User admin	Low	Medium	High, ceiling	Long running
Logout	User request	Session Management	High	Low	None	Immediate

Figure 2.6: Feature performance characteristics

The preceding figure will help you view and compare the different values for each feature side-by-side. It makes it easy to make needed assertions such as *The most common driver of our application's features is User demand*. Additionally, more complex statements with broader domain like *Our application cannot make use of parallelization to reduce user request latency in the Cast Vote feature, but it can be employed to scale the Update Standings feature.*

Understanding feature requirements

Let us picture our system as a whole, in a rare moment when no one is logged in. There are no voters connected to the system from their mobile client app or our web page, and no features that are driven by user requests are currently being executed.

Although the system is definitely not quiet. Application logs are being anonymized, and aggregated, our data analytics pipeline is summing up all votes cast globally over the past day. In our European office, our Product Managers are compiling the voting history report for tomorrow's monthly business review. Thanks to our Cloud Service configuration, replication is copying our regional data stores to their global siblings to ensure both reliability and better performance for queries issued in any region.

These are all important features of our system but none of them are requested by any of our end-users. So, we will defer discussing those and first look at the features that are activated by user requests.

Let us start with the Login feature. An end-user can begin using the application by logging in, a process of identifying themselves as a known user and then authenticating that identity. This process does not get started without the user initiating it. We do not just start connecting users on random phones in the middle of the night.

A login operation begins when a User taps some icon or clicks on some link. The user explicitly requested that the system authenticate them now, so that some other features can be accessed.

There are a few things we can safely assume about all User Request features:

- The number of concurrent User Requests that the system should anticipate is O(N), where N=number of connected users, under normal circumstances.

- Any feature activated by a user request should be latency sensitive.

- Most User Request features will have feature affinity with some other User Request features; single-function end-user applications are rare, albeit not unheard of.

Examining another feature—cast vote, we have designated it to have a Class of functionality of User request unlike the Login feature, which is of the class System connection. The distinction is one of intent: the demand driver describes how the action is initiated, whereas the functionality class describes more of why the feature exists, and what purpose it serves. While Logging-in is something we all know we must do, casting a vote is the most central feature we provide: Casting votes is the *raison d'être* (reason for existence) of our voting system, and thus is truly a request by the user in the truest sense of the term.

The Cast vote feature is highly sensitive to latency. It would be unsettling and lower confidence in our system if users cast their votes and do not receive an acknowledgement of the vote being recorded. This acknowledgement has to be given fairly quickly, as the longer we delay, the more likely it is that a phone loses its signal, the browser crashes, or the user impatiently or accidentally closes the window.

The computational expense of casting a vote is not much for the actual recording of a vote. Recall the credit card payment example in the previous chapter: we do not have to tally all of the votes, update all copies of our records, and calculate the standing of all candidates now; what we have to do is guarantee that the user's vote has been recorded and that the effect of their vote will be felt. The response to casting a vote is acknowledgement that *Your choice is in the system and you need not worry* rather than *your vote has made its way through our system and been merged with every other vote that has been cast, and it is reflected in all data derived from votes.* The latter, handing off the user request to some durable mechanism in the system, can be inexpensive if we use the right Cloud product service. So, the **Computational expense** of casting a vote is **Low**.

Let us think about how parallelizable is the action of casting a vote, with the limited scope of the feature we have established. There is a function on the client that is invoked by an icon being tapped: this function's main responsibility is to get that vote into some other durable component of our application which is not tied to the relatively fragile and slow client platform. Let us envision something like this function in the client application:

```cpp
void handoff_selection(int vote_index) {
  if (vote_index <= 0 || vote_index > this->candidate_count) {
    throw std::invalid_argument("Received vote for invalid choice");
  }
  int errno = this->vote_recorder->accept_vote(vote_index);
  if (errno) {
    throw std::system_error("Error injecting. Vote not recorded.");
  }
}
```

There is one operation that is critical to this method's purpose: the invocation of **accept_vote()**. There are no *multiple independent processing steps* within this method to distribute among multiple workers to execute simultaneously. Looking at that one statement, we have identified as critical (**accept_vote(...):**), we pass only a single argument to that method, a scalar **int**, which does not present any method to *divide the data up* for consumption by more than one worker. So, we have labeled the parallelizable value of this feature with **None** as there is no reason or opportunity to use more than one worker to reduce the time needed to execute this feature.

Finally, the duration of casting a vote is the time taken for us to validate the choice we were given; the time that it then takes to invoke and get a response from the **accept_vote()** method of our **vote_recorder** service, and the time for us to confirm the response. Looking back at our description of **Workflow duration**, this matches the description of **Transaction**.

Defining application feature composition

The process of dividing the functionality of an application into clearly bounded components with optimal topography for performance consists of a sequence of three major steps, which we will now describe:

1. **Enumerate features**: First, you should spend some time identifying the features of your product, those operations that it will make available to satisfy your user cases or functional requirements.

   As an example, we will enumerate features of an application in a common domain, a shopping system for a retail business. Such an application might include the following functionality:

    a.   Login to the shopping account.

    b.   Create a new shopping account.

    c.   Add item from the inventory to the cart.

    d.   Commence inventory refresh for the item.

    e.   Review inventory refresh.

    f.   Order the inventory restock of item.

    g.   Remit the sales tax.

2.   **Determine the performance attributes of each feature**: This is non-trivial, but with a domain expert and system architect in the room, it can be a straightforward process. Lay out a table like the one in *Figure 2.7* with a row for each of the features that you have identified.

     Be prepared to go back and revise features as you discuss additional ones; after you describe the feature of refreshing inventory, you may realize that adding an item to the cart is more expensive or further reaching than you initially thought.

     The following figure describes the seven features we have identified for our retail shopping system:

Feature	Demand driver	Class of functionality	Latency sensitivity	Computational expense	Parallelizable	Duration
Shopping Login	User request	System connection	High	Medium	None	User session
Create new account	User request	User request	High	Medium	None	Transaction
Add item from inventory	User request	User request	High	Medium	Low	Transaction
Commence inventory item refresh	Accumulated activity	Asynchronous delivery	Insensitive	Low	None	Transaction
Generate inventory restock orders	Cumulative value	Offline batch	Insensitive	Medium	Low	Multi-stage pipeline
Order inventory item restock	Admin action	User request	Low	Medium	High, ceiling	Long running
Remit sales tax	Periodic	Offline batch	Insensitive	Low	Low	Long running

Figure 2.7: Shopping application features

3.   **Place the features**: With the features, their scope, and their cost described; we next illustrate their adjacency in space and in time.

     These seven features' *proximity* is shown in the following network diagram:

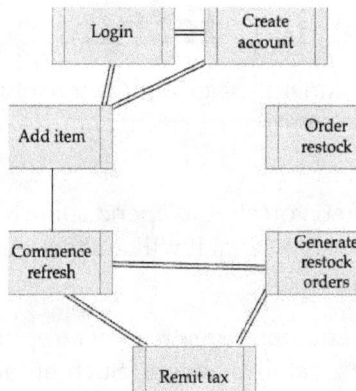

Figure 2.8: Proximity of shopping application features

The following network diagram illustrates the *affinity* of the same seven features:

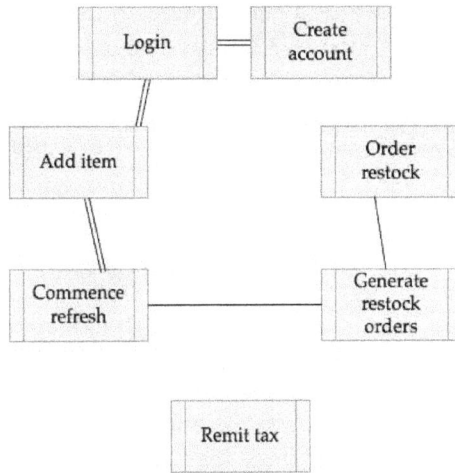

Figure 2.9: *Affinity of shopping application features*

At this point, we have a good understanding of the technical requirements of our described features. We can view that as demand for our infrastructure. Now that we can state the demand, the next step is to establish a counterpart vocabulary and grammar for the supply side of the equation: the infrastructure that we expect to satisfy those technical requirements.

Pertinent qualities of an infrastructure service or component

There is a myriad of infrastructure building blocks available for us to build our various features on, and rarely is there an absolute right or wrong choice: You could use a long-running virtual machine to run a request server, or you could implement a set of discrete cloud functions. The selection is not binary but rather one of degree, on several axes. Let us go over some of those dimensions now:

- **Performance**: The elapsed time that a given computing platform will require to complete execution of our workload. Not everything requires a supercomputer. A popular maxim when shopping for a new laptop is *I'm not folding proteins on this thing*. Serverless compute platforms share physical process space and power amongst (many) peers and you are usually not going to get the same speed out of 1/10th of a processor core as you would from 3 cores dedicated to your process. That may be fine, or you may have some compute-intensive tasks that make every millisecond of wall time count. Some services may have a quality-of-service guarantee, and some may be best-effort. Knowing the performance guarantee of each option lets us exercise flexibility for the features that we can and devote the more performant options to the workloads that we need them for.

- **Horizontal and vertical scalability**: The effort required to initiate an increase or decrease of the capacity of a service and the speed with such a change takes effect. Spinning up new Virtual Machines, registering them with load balancers and taking them out of service is not something that can be accomplished in a few seconds, whereas more concurrent requests to cloud functions or managed serverless applications can be handled quickly enough to transparently serve sudden spikes in traffic.

  On the other hand, each of those many cloud functions is only going to be so capable on its own, whereas a virtual machine with a more powerful processor and more RAM can take on larger tasks.

- **Cost**: The material cost of a platform per unit of effective compute power. The more of your cloud provider's actual resources a service consumes, the more they will charge you for that service. In the end, you cannot ignore practical concerns for long; the net cheapest product that satisfies your requirements should be considered the first best option. Remember to consider ancillary costs: a cheaper product that requires you to add-on another companion product may not be the cheapest option versus an expensive but completely self-contained alternative.

- **Long-Term Support**: The length of time that your investment in a product will be cost-effective when compared to alternative products. Obsolescence is the worst unexpected yet inevitable challenge that can disrupt a product's development lifecycle. After months of discovery and research, weeks of training, and quarters of development and deployment, a product team expects to focus on fulfilling feature requests from users and market analysts. No one welcomes a forced migration plan announced in even the cheeriest and most encouraging terms. Consider the following communique as a template of an announcement that might be sent by a product that your application has a strong dependency on. Some version of this generic notice has been an unwelcome surprise for many application developers, substituting any products and company for gadget, widget, and all-things. The announcement of deprecation of a service, whether cloud related or not, infrastructure or industry specific, usually follows the format of this fictional letter for the generic gadget service, and gives as little notice and as few options:

  To: gadget-users@

  From: support@all-things

  Subject: Announcing our newest component deployment product—Widget: built for the future!

  Dear customer

  We're excited to introduce you to Widget-service, our new, exciting and revolutionary replacement for Gadget-service.

  Over the next six months, we will be providing support for your migration to this feature filled and state of the art shiny thing. All clients of Gadget-service are encouraged to migrate to Widget-service by March 2025, at which time we will move Gadget support to best effort for one month.

…

Infrastructure churn can be viewed much like a companion cost of the product. A shorter lifespan implies a higher indirect cost: factors like training, re-engineering and redeployment that are inevitable with the most transparent and seamless infrastructure migrations, amortized over less time.

Note: This is why many Linux distributions offer releases labeled Long-Term Support (LTS). Many big clients of those distributions only run LTS versions because an operating system upgrade is expensive, complicated and has the potential to bring your entire operation down. So, you want to do it as infrequently as possible and only after a version has been in use and vetted for some significant window of time.

Describing infrastructure options

With these major considerations of an infrastructure product identified, let us outline a process for comparing the alternatives that our selected platform offers:

1. **Enumerate the options**: Much like the step of identifying our features earlier, this is simply listing the products we are evaluating.

    For brevity, let us restrict our options to a subset of the GCP products and non-cloud platforms we reviewed in the previous chapter.

    a. Google Cloud Run

    b. Cloud Functions

    c. Pub/Sub

    d. Batch

    e. Mobile client application framework

    f. Mobile client platform native development

    g. Identity and access management

2. **Describe the qualities of each product**: Let us use the same table format that we have for features: it is well suited to the task, provides consistency in our processes, and offers the convenience of familiarity:

Product	Performance	Horizontal scalability	Vertical Scalability	Cost	Long Term Support
Google Cloud Run	Medium	Highly scalable with demand	Configurable performance options	Relatively inexpensive	Long future roadmap
Cloud Functions	Medium	Highly scalable with demand	Fixed or limited performance options	Relatively inexpensive	Long future roadmap
Batch	Medium	Scalable, not transparent	Configurable performance options	Relatively inexpensive	Long future roadmap
Pub/Sub	Highly performant	Highly scalable with demand	Fixed or limited performance options	Medium cost	Long future roadmap
Mobile client platform native platform	Medium	Low scalability	Fixed or limited performance options	Relatively inexpensive	Newer options exist and promoted
Mobile client app framework	Low / Best effort	Low scalability	Fixed or limited performance options	Relatively inexpensive	Long future roadmap
Identity and Access Management	Highly performant	Highly scalable with demand	Fixed or limited performance options	Relatively inexpensive	Long future roadmap

Figure 2.10: Table of product qualities

It is important to recognize that the preceding figure is bucketing apples and oranges: IAM and batch are very different products, which will be considered in the next step of our process.

3. **Matching the features up with their suitable infrastructure**: With this analysis of the supply side, what each product has to offer, paired with that of the demand side and what each feature requires, we can make reasonably good choices of infrastructure to back each of our features. The value of a method such as this, based on microeconomics, is that it arrives at infrastructure choices based on the needs of the system, rather than a particular bias of the architect or platform provider.

    Since our features are defined with the boundaries of functional responsibility, not with the borders of any technical component in mind, it is likely (or a certainty) that there will not be a one-to-one mapping of infrastructure product to feature, but instead a combination of infrastructure products that will be useful in implementing a given feature.

Now, we will go through the process of matchmaking: pairing up a couple of features with infrastructure products and looking for the lowest-cost best match of requirements and capabilities.

What is a good platform for the user Login feature? Looking at *Figure 2.7*, it has low compute performance requirements, client platform proximity, and is latency sensitive. A Client app framework matches the proximity, latency, and compute requirements. We can confidently intuit that IAM is also needed to support a login function.

Let us select a product that is suitable to provide computing power for adding an item to a user's cart. The feature is latency sensitive, has no need for high computing power, and is driven by user requests. User requests are prone to spikes in concurrent demand, which in turn require horizontal scaling to keep up with those spikes and dips.

Cloud Run is highly horizontally scalable, provides medium performance relative among GCP compute products, and the worker's performance can be configured to meet expected processing demand. Adding items to a cart should have the same approximate performance requirements on any occasion, so the configurable vertical scalability of Cloud Run is a good match. It is not the only *potential* match, but it is an optimal choice from the set of products that we have considered in this example.

After going through this exercise for our seven features, the following figure shows the dependency graph that emerges:

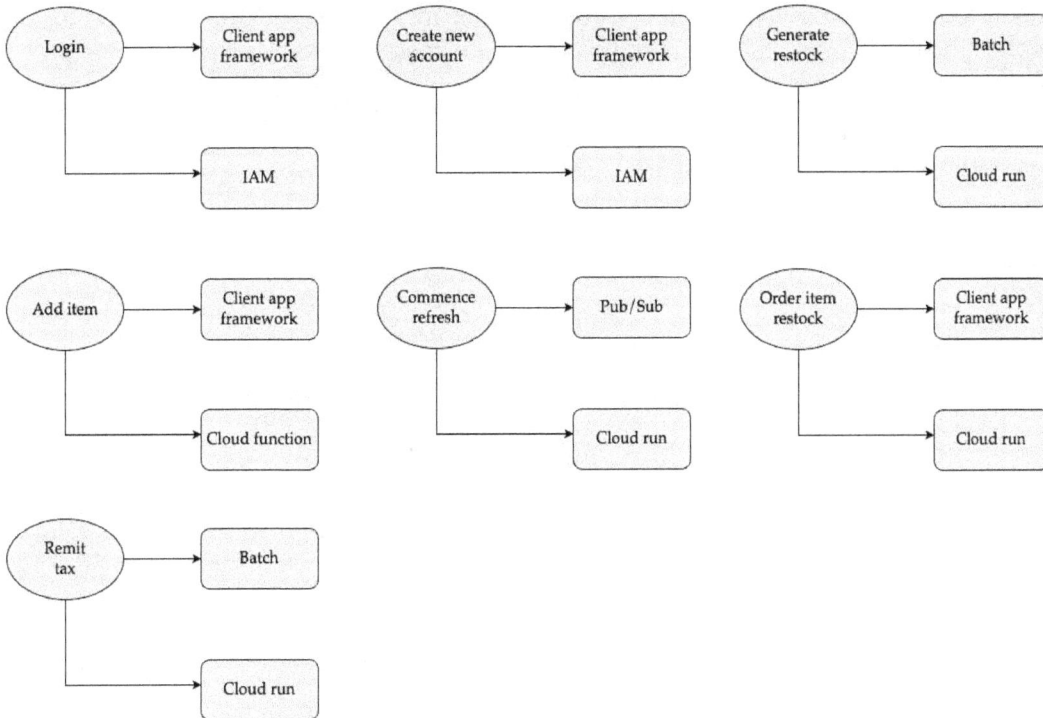

Figure 2.11: *Graph of feature infrastructure dependencies*

This graph makes an important point clear: it is rare that a single product delivers all that a feature may need. Two very different examples from the preceding figure drive this point home:

- A user-driven feature, such as Login, requires a client app to provide a user interface but uses cloud service to provide the backing functionality that would be difficult to implement well on a (for example) phone.

- The Remit tax feature uses the batch service, which must be coupled with a compute power product to perform the work that the batch service dispatches.

This lack of a monolithic product that handles everything is by design. Remember the description of, and arguments against, the *God class* back in the previous chapter. That anti-pattern is clearly respected and avoided by the GCP architects.

Conclusion

This chapter covered how to evaluate the features of your application in terms of functional requirements and to consider what technical demands those features will place on your implementation. We also looked at several infrastructure products with a critical eye to what dimensions they can be evaluated in and where they are each located on those axes.

This has culminated in a principled, informed selection of infrastructure products for our application based on suitability to the problem and cost.

Chapter 3, Determining the Infrastructure to Build Features Upon, will continue this process of feature decomposition and infrastructure assignment as we will look at optimizing features' infrastructure components: grouping and collapsing or merging them based on demand, affinity, and proximity.

Join our Discord space

Join our Discord workspace for latest updates, offers, tech happenings around the world, new releases, and sessions with the authors:

https://discord.bpbonline.com

CHAPTER 3

Determining the Infrastructure to Build Features Upon

Introduction

With a solid definition of the major components or subsystems of an application, it is important to know what platform each is best suited to reside on. The reader will gain knowledge of the strengths of cloud services and client platforms and how to optimally assign each subsystem to an appropriate infrastructure. Scalability determinants, latency considerations, and feature affinity are all arguments in the competition for the *most appropriate location* for each component. This chapter is a guide to the process of identifying these factors, evaluating the options and making principled selections from the candidates for each subsystem or feature.

Structure

In this chapter, the following topics will be covered:

- Request funneling to scale to O(N)!
- Guaranteeing user-visible responsiveness
- Security, privacy, and permanence
- Security in Google Cloud Platform

Objectives

This chapter will explore some commonly held and often misunderstood technical requirements of application features, such as latency and transaction boundaries. Dissecting the requirements to lay bare their actual needs will lead to an examination of what effects are truly required to reach those goals.

Having requirements with a finer level of granularity increases the flexibility offered to the architect to meet those requirements. We then look at the cloud services that offer solutions to these decomposed requirements, and ways of arranging them to cooperatively meet the overall goals.

Request funneling to scale to O(N)!

One of the major, perhaps the most significant, challenge in designing a reliable and performant application is that of scaling the system's capabilities to keep pace with demand. The mathematical notation known as Big O notation is used to classify the runtime complexity or cost of a resource. When faced with an increase in demand of $O(N)$ where N is the number of requests, we wish to serve this demand with a corresponding increase less than $O(N)$ and certainly not greater than $O(N)$. This section describes techniques to process requests through a funnel of staged resources, that is through an ever-narrowing series of resources.

Urgency versus importance

Our talent show voting system must **guarantee** that every vote in an election for the best act of the season is counted accurately and reliably.

The word **guarantee** is the most important point of that statement. A user must have reason to trust that the application will in fact do what it claims to. If a user is told *Your vote has been recorded*, it is **important** that their vote will be counted for their candidate of choice.

Tallying the votes for each candidate is of critical *importance*—but it is not **urgent**.

Recognizing the distinction between *urgency* and *importance* is key to understanding the value and appropriate reliance on *eventual consistency*, a transaction model that will be explained and examined in detail in this section. Before diving into that model, let us establish a common understanding of the underlying, often conflated principles of urgency and importance.

The decoupled definitions of urgency and importance are:

- **Important**: If we must complete something to achieve our goal, that thing is **important**.

- **Urgent**: If waiting to do something until beyond the near future makes it more costly or less valuable, then that task is **urgent**. In more direct terms: *Is it much* *better if you do it now instead of doing it tomorrow?* If the answer is *yes*, then it is urgent.

An *Eisenhower matrix aka priority matrix* popularized by *Dwight D Eisenhower*, who attributed it to an unnamed mentor figure, is the most popular illustration of these two distinct dimensions. The primary use of an Eisenhower matrix is to decide, in the most pragmatic of ways, how to prioritize scheduling individual tasks within a given set of tasks competing for your attention. After we examine a common situation to which this method can be applied, we will see how the method applies to feature design in a software product.

A relatable set of tasks a homeowner might face, having to prioritize is:

- Put out a kitchen fire.
- Buy a fire extinguisher.
- Put out the garbage bins on trash pickup night.
- Clean the attic window glass.

With these tasks on a to-do list, we then assign each position on each of the two dimensions on an Eisenhower matrix, urgency and importance, using the grading criteria for the preceding terms:

	Urgent	**Not Urgent**
Important	Put out fire	Buy fire extinguisher
Not Important	Put out garbage bins	Clean attic window

Figure 3.1: Eisenhower matrix for homeowners

The order in which the tasks in these quadrants should be carried out is clear for the highest and lowest priority work at any given time:

- Urgent, important tasks come first.
- Not urgent, not important tasks come last.

The other two are less clear but are in the middle of the top and the lowest priority work:

- Take care of important, not urgent tasks before they spawn urgent ones (like having to deal with future fires without an extinguisher in this example).

- If you do not get to urgent, not important tasks, it is not a significant problem. So, only do them when there is no work in any other quadrant competing for your attention.

The greatest value of arranging and prioritizing work using this method is the separation of immediacy and impact: urgency and importance. People often confuse important things as urgent things when the two aspects are, in fact, often mutually exclusive. Eisenhower summed this up in a famous statement later to be known as the **Eisenhower Principle**:

I have two kinds of problems: the urgent and the important. The urgent are not important, and the important are never urgent.

-Eisenhower

Eventual consistency in distributed systems

The recognition of immediacy and completion as separate requirements is embodied in the domain of distributed computing and popularized by Google's Bigtable.

We will take a commonly accepted definition of the concept of eventual consistency:

Eventual consistency, is the guarantee that all data read will be consistent with all data written, eventually; that is at some imprecise but foreseeable future time. That is not to imply non-deterministic chaos: you will be able to tell when the system has achieved consistency after sometime between data being written, all writes being merged, and the effects of those writes being resolved.

Being able to disentangle the portions of a large-scale or broad operation into those parts which are urgent and those which are actually non-urgent side-effects is a key step in streamlining our application design to optimize responsiveness. A question for application architects to keep in mind when designing a latency-sensitive feature is *Does the user really need to wait for this?*

A case study in eventual consistency

A brief examination of a use case in our voting system will illustrate the advantage of separating importance and urgency, introducing an eventually consistent model to implement this.

A voting app has one basic job: to allow a voter to cast a vote for a candidate. Any other functionality is icing on the cake. So, when it comes to reliable, responsive execution of the vote feature, do not mess it up.

Here is a simple requirement a user might have:

- **Requirement**: Tally the vote quickly, within 2 seconds. (latency sensitive)

This could be interpreted by an engineering team as *We have to add their vote (i.e +1) to the total number of votes for the chosen candidate, confirm that the candidate's total was incremented and then respond to the user Your vote has been counted within 2 seconds.*

That is easy to say, and the logic does not seem very complex, but in this case, the issues are largely consequences of scale.

Let us examine two issues we will face.

In a global talent competition, voters may be participating from anywhere and everywhere. A network round-trip to one centralized database within 2 seconds is not guaranteed from any potential end-point. You may employ a fast, reliable network on your backend, such as GCP's network fabric, but there is some portion of the route between the user's device and your application that is out of GCP's reach and out of your control.

Tens of thousands of voters will likely be casting a vote at any time, so relying on straightforward transaction semantics in real-time is going to lead to long delays, timeouts, race conditions and failures.

For 50,000 nearly concurrent votes to be processed by a single central task in 2 seconds (aka 2,000 milliseconds), we are expecting each vote to take no more than *2,000 ÷ 50000 = 0.04* or 40 microseconds. This is an overly simple means to calculate the load, but the theme it illustrates holds true. It is unlikely that a simple, serial stream of transactions with these performance constraints will succeed.

All is not lost; it is just that our expectations are in need of refinement.

The way we have defined it, the vote feature has strict requirements that we can plot on an Eisenhower matrix as follows:

	Urgent	**Not Urgent**
Important	Vote	
Not Important		

***Figure 3.2**: Eisenhower matrix for the vote feature*

This is bad news in light of our preceding quick feasibility study. The vote feature is *important*, as stated, it is the reason our application exists. The vote feature as we have defined it, is also *urgent*, the user wants to see that their vote was cast, and they would not wait for more than a typical response time of a couple of seconds.

However, remember the Eisenhower principle: few if any things are both urgent and important. Let us think about what our vote feature entails.

A user casts their vote for one of several candidates. Their selection must be recorded, and that recording must be durable and should be confirmed with the user quickly. We cannot confirm until the recording is actually durable, else we would be lying, so the end result of **confirmation of recorded vote** is both important and urgent.

However, the same is not true of the tallying or counting of votes, adding all votes cast to each candidate's totals. It is important to count all the recorded votes since that determines the outcome of the election. Although it is not urgent to count all the recorded votes for the candidates, as it does not affect the outcome, but only delays our announcement of the winner.

What about running totals during the election, that is, **results thus far...** it is *somewhat* arbitrary, whether you report on the results of an hour ago or five minutes ago, as long as you're transparent about which it is.

So let us break up the vote feature into two features: cast vote and update standings: the first being the recording and confirmation of a user's vote, and the second being the counting of all the votes cast to determine each candidate's total.

These features were described in the previous chapter, in *Figure 2.6*.

What we have done allows us to reposition these *two* features in different quadrants on the Eisenhower matrix:

	Urgent	Not Urgent
Important	Cast vote	Update standings
Not Important		

Figure 3.3: Eisenhower matrix of decomposed vote feature

The obvious benefit of this decomposition is that there is less work labeled as urgent, less work takes less time, and, thus, there is greater opportunity to meet our performance constraints.

However, there is more to consider: recall that the challenges in delivering the latency sensitive and reliable monolithic vote feature were largely raised by the coupling of the feature to a single choke point in the proposed implementation, the datastore to which all votes must be applied.

What we have described briefly previously decouples the user-visible cast vote feature from any such serial transaction processor. There can be as many places to record votes as we like, as long as each vote is recorded on one of them, the user's intention is safe.

There is no magic, all of those votes will have to be applied to some global datastore eventually; but that is a completely separate issue.

Let us look at a picture of a first pass at how this decomposed vote feature might be implemented:

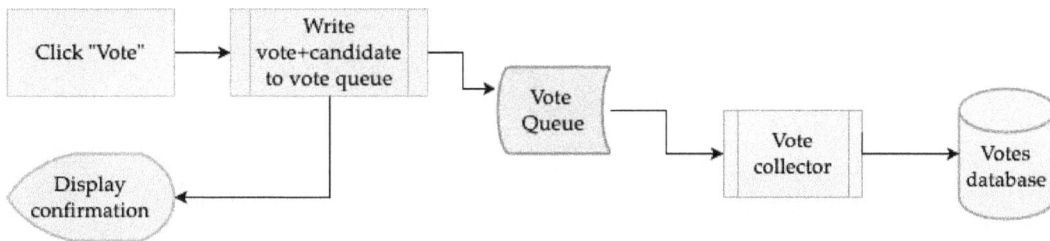

Figure 3.4: *Architecture of decomposed vote feature*

This is an improvement over the first vote feature in that there is less processing between clicking vote and getting confirmation, but as illustrated here, we have only put off the inevitable. The new Vote Queue is now a choke point, with its own performance limits, and it is inevitable that some stunning candidate will generate enough votes at once to overwhelm the Vote Queue's ingestion rate. Additionally, the performance concern of network round-trip time to the Vote Queue is just as real as the time to reach a database; the Vote Queue has to reside somewhere, and that will be far from some users of a globally available application.

However, we have given ourselves an out here by introducing the potential for horizontal scaling at that new bottleneck. There is no reason for everyone to use the same Vote Queue. We could have separate Vote Queues for each continent, country/province or even for each user.

Here is a horizontally scaled-up version of the preceding architecture with multiple Vote Queues for geographic locality:

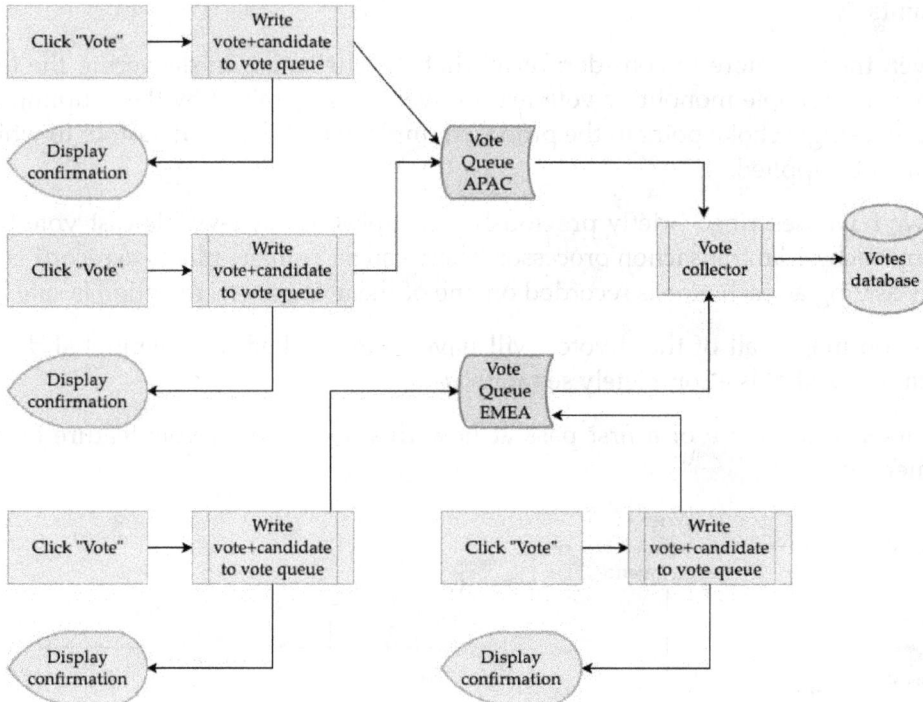

Figure 3.5: Architecture of scaled up decomposed vote feature

This has the effect of moving the choke point or bottleneck of this feature to the batch, non-latency sensitive Vote collector process; which we are free to place as near as possible to the Votes database to which it is tightly bound.

We have done it! At a very high level, we have designed an architecture for this feature that we can apply horizontal scaling to meet the requirements of latency. We can apply horizontal and vertical scaling as needed when we design the Vote collector in detail. The durability of cast votes depends on the implementation of Vote queue, but they are known GCP services that excel at providing such guarantees in this scenario.

Let us now recall the heading of this section: Request funneling. This is an apt description of the shape of the design: user requests are narrowed down from a very large set of endpoints to some reduced number of intermediate workers and then narrowed down further to the final, least horizontally scalable point in our design: a single logical database.

Guaranteeing user-visible responsiveness

With the concept of request funneling illustrated in the preceding example, this section will describe the use of GCP products to provide a concrete implementation of the example; and project the actual limitations on responsiveness that this technique overcomes.

Horizontal scaling via Pub/Sub

The end user of the voting application knows nothing of this complex, well-thought-out machine, and they should not. All they are really concerned about at the moment they cast their vote is the response: it should be fast, it should be certain, and it should be reassuring. While possibly better than nothing, if a frequent response to pressing the **vote** button is **Hmmm... something went wrong** or its common synonym **Server error**; people are not going to have much patience for the talent show or confidence in the fidelity of the results.

With that in mind, it should be a design goal to do *as little as possible* in the processing between the user request and response. The bare minimum required to guarantee the durability of the cast vote is the ideal: defer what you can.

The GCP service, well-suited to support the user end of the Vote Queue, Pub/Sub, is designed for this common and usually critical use case. From Google's Pub/Sub product description:

Pub/Sub is an asynchronous and scalable messaging service that decouples services producing messages from services processing those messages.

Pub/Sub allows services to communicate asynchronously, with latencies on the order of 100 milliseconds.

You can find the description here: **https://cloud.google.com/pubsub/docs/overview**

That is 100 milliseconds *on each client,* in parallel and completely decoupled from other concurrent clients. Unlike the earlier architecture, in which our clients' responses were competing for a slice of time, ending up with 40 microseconds each, this model carries a fixed cost of 100 milliseconds per client, virtually regardless of how many clients there are; they are not competing. With a target of 2,000 milliseconds for the cast vote, that leaves on the order of 1.9 seconds to execute whatever user interface and peripheral client-side processing our application ends up implementing. The durable recording of the user's vote has gone from a potential bottleneck in the execution of our feature to a minor fraction of the processing time.

Pub/Sub offers automatic capacity management to scale processing resources to keep up with demand. Pub/Sub's automatic replication of all data, to at least two network zones, provides a high guarantee of data durability and availability.

Two major concerns have been removed through the design of a feature set architected to meet our actual requirements, and the selection of infrastructure that is well suited to support those features' requirements.

Transaction guarantees

A transaction as we define it in computer science, is a set of operations for which all must complete for any to be considered to be complete. **All or nothing.** The classic example is the transfer of funds from one account to another, which is actually two operations: withdrawal from the source account and deposit to the target account. If you first record the withdrawal, reducing the amount of the source account and then the deposit to the target account, but the deposit target account were to fail due to a runtime exception in the process, then you would have a payer who is out for $100 and a payee who is still waiting for and expecting a payment. If you adjust the two accounts in the other order, first adding money to the payee account and then fail on the reduction of the source account. You have just *made money out of nothing*.

These two operations are to be wrapped in a *transaction*: withdraw the funds, add the funds, and only when both operations succeed, commit the changes and make them permanent. Without that commit, sealing the deal, the pending operations are eventually undone or *rolled back* - neither of them ever happened.

A reliable transaction system exhibits four basic properties, summarized by the acronym ACID:

- **Atomicity**: All changes within a transaction are atomic, they all happen or none happen, there is no sub-components.

- **Consistency**: At the end of a transaction, any invariants or integrity guarantees of the system are preserved, but the same may not be true during the internal state changes within a transaction.

- **Isolation**: Regardless of actual timing, each transaction appears to be executed before or after all other transactions without any awareness or dependence on concurrency between them.

- **Durability**: Once a transaction is complete and is committed, its effects are guaranteed to persist. There is no need to worry or check up later, a committed transaction happened and there is no subsequent failure or loophole in the protocol that will cause it to roll back.

Beyond the base transaction model

There are several transaction models that extend the basic ACID model, usually to accommodate the needs of highly distributed systems with extreme degrees of concurrency or those with updates to many sets of coupled datastores. The Two-phase commit protocol is one such algorithm; some others are implementations of the concept of eventual consistency described earlier in this chapter.

Much of the high value of GCP services is that they provide and adhere to transactional boundaries. By provide, it is meant that a product provides means to define a transaction and then enforces the integrity of that transaction, and in their API and usage patterns, gives the application developer clear points at which operations should be performed so as to participate in the well-defined transaction's boundaries. Adherence, in this case, means that the GCP products themselves respect and participate in transactions defined around their usage: if you insert a row to a GoogleSQL table and publish an event to a Pub/Sub topic within a transaction that fails, GoogleSQL and Pub/Sub do the right thing for the transaction.

In the example we developed previously, decomposing the vote feature into separate operations, we took an overly broad transaction which encompassed voting and updating the tallies for a candidate, and broke it into separate transactions: getting a vote recorded, and applying a vote to the election database. Recognizing and defining appropriate transaction scope is a large factor in optimizing the performance of a software system. Performance, in this statement, explicitly includes considering the integrity of a system's state, not just the responsiveness of user-visible behavior.

Security, privacy and permanence

Security and privacy are related but not the same. While privacy is drawing agreed-upon boundaries around the visibility of information, security is the guarantee that the behavior of a system; including those boundaries; cannot be subverted or altered outside of its design.

Cybersecurity

The definition of security is fairly straightforward and narrow: the state of being free of danger or threat. We use the term cybersecurity to refer to the security of computer systems, but in a computer system, what are the threats we wish to be free of?

Let us enumerate the challenges addressed or focus on the practice of cybersecurity:

- **Unauthorized operation**: Every system of consequence has rules governing who can access it and how they may do so. If we register to vote, we get to vote. If a registered voter gets to vote for their three favorite acts, we cannot vote for a fourth candidate, no matter how good a guitarist they are. A secure system guarantees that it can only be operated within the rules that have been declared and implemented for its use.

- **Corruption**: If we vote for the acrobatic canine act, that is the vote on record and my vote cannot be altered by some malicious party. If we authorize a 20 USD payment to a bubble tea shop, the amount of that charge has to remain 20, not be altered to 50 or 130 USD. A secure system is safe from alteration of its state by outside forces or by misuse of its features.

- **Theft**: Information is an asset, it has value. When people use a system, they typically leave some mark: their contact information, banking profile, voting history or shopping preferences. A secure system is one from which this information cannot be extracted or used for anything other than its understood and agreed upon purpose. Data breaches are the most popular frequent exhibition of insecure systems.

- **Denial of service**: This is a popular and forceful theft of a service, not theft of the *assets* of a system, but theft of the availability of the system itself. It is as if some criminal was forcefully keeping you from entering your car or your house. Of course, blocking every route to a destination takes a lot of energy, and there must be something in it for the perpetrators. Denial of service attacks are often used to extort a ransom to cease the attack, to starve a business by driving users to alternative services, or for some political or social agenda against the service. A secure system is highly resistant to, and/or can recover from a denial of service attack.

Security in Google Cloud Platform

GCP provides a high degree of security in two ways. First, as a suite of products, the GCP services themselves adhere to best practices and are resistant to the types of attacks and threats described previously, so GCP itself is secure.

Secondly, as an infrastructure provider. GCP includes many features that provide protection against cyberthreats. Cloud intrusion detection system detects and alerts when access patterns or artifacts are seen that are deemed to be malicious or dangerous. Several products offer sophisticated encryption for both data at rest and in transit. Cloud firewall can be enabled through the companion network security API and protects your cloud resources from both global, emerging threats and threats specific to your system or users.

Data privacy

Privacy in computer systems is more specifically termed data privacy. Data privacy is the ability of individual users of a computer system to determine who can access their personal data. Personal data is the information unique to an individual, not common to all users of a system. My username, login credentials, voting record are all personal, whereas the hours that the system was accepting votes are impersonal—it is not specific to any individual and cannot be used to determine anything substantial about an individual user.

A system that provides data privacy is one that protects personal and sensitive data from unauthorized access, manipulation, and misuse. This is only one aspect of providing privacy, the technical one. To provide privacy to its users, a service must also have a well-designed and transparent user data handling policy that makes it clear what control a user has over the use of their personal data and how to exercise that control.

Devising and publishing a suitable data handling policy is a series of business and product decisions. Once a policy is in place, several GCP products can be employed to ensure that the system remains in compliance with those policies, monitor policy compliance, detect any regressions of non-compliance, and help remediate the effects of those.

The GCP Sensitive Data Protection suite helps define, enforce, and monitor compliance with privacy policies, both external, such as regulatory requirements, and internal policies adopted and published to users. The sensitive data discovery product can detect the presence of sensitive data in a system. Anonymization and redaction requirements can be defined to remove **personally identifiable information (PII)** from data.

There's a set of vulnerabilities outside of GCP-backed systems: external sources and destinations of data are potential leaks of sensitive data. Options in Sensitive Data Protection allow the inspection of ingress and egress points to detect unexpected sources of PII and potential unplanned or manipulated releases of sensitive data to external systems and shut them down when detected.

Data permanence

Whatever information is read from the system should be the same as the information that was written. Data should not morph, transform, degrade, or mutate without design and intent. This concept of *what you read is what was written* is known as data permanence.

This was not a common problem throughout most of human history. Stone tablets, papyrus scrolls, newspapers, and checks inscribed with indelible ink are all fairly resistant to undetected alteration.

In the past few decades, the amount of data that civilization records has multiplied exponentially, increasing by many orders of magnitude. This has been accompanied by a companion shift towards more and more compact and volatile storage media, solid state drives and flash memory are all vulnerable to alteration, with no real evidence of such tampering.

Not all unintended alteration is the result of malice. Software and hardware defects (bugs), external events, such as power surges or electromagnetic pulses and the passage of time can render data unreadable or even worse readable as an altered value.

Google Cloud Platform's storage and database products provide several means of guaranteeing data permanence in your product. Data replicas protect against the loss of data due to some local, physical event such as a flooded datacenter. Audit Logging provides a means to prove the absence of unexpected alterations. The Bucket Lock feature can be used to provide immutable storage on Cloud Storage and guarantee a true archive, a faithful snapshot of your data at a specific point in time.

Conclusion

Defining application features should address user requirements, but must not do this in a vacuum. The real and digital worlds both impose constraints, and what is technically feasible must guide our definition of features that satisfy product requirements.

This chapter introduced compelling motivations for carefully defining application feature scope, considering technical feasibility alongside product intent. Examination of commonly conflated characteristics of urgency and importance was presented with some historical background.

The consideration of urgent versus important tasks was applied as a metaphor to technical counterparts: responsiveness versus data integrity. We applied the Eisenhower technique to a case study in our product and identified the different requirements that could be used to separate a monolithic feature into distinct components.

Transaction processing and variations on a theme were described in detail as those concepts are necessary background to make informed implementation choices to satisfy our feature's requirements. With scalability considerations explored, the chapter then separated and discussed another intertwined and often erroneously conflated issues: security and privacy. Requirements of a secure system were enumerated, and we identified some GCP services and features that can be used to satisfy those.

User privacy is as much a business decision as a technical one, and we identified the need for a data privacy policy and described the role of several GCP products used to monitor and enforce compliance with the policy. Chapter three wrapped up with a brief discussion of data permanence and GCP products that support data integrity and availability.

In the next chapter, we will focus on alternatives in a few main areas of application architecture, how to differentiate them, and determine the best fit for a particular use case.

Join our Discord space

Join our Discord workspace for latest updates, offers, tech happenings around the world, new releases, and sessions with the authors:

https://discord.bpbonline.com

CHAPTER 4
Choosing Between GCP Options

Introduction

Google Cloud Platform (GCP) contains multiple services which offer similar sounding utility and functionality. At the time of writing, the general domain of *compute power* includes 15 different GCP products; and there are 6 different database products in the GCP platform that could be used to store indexed rows of data.

While each of these products has specific strengths that distinguish them from the others, there is also sufficient overlap in their capabilities and descriptions to make the process of selecting a product for a particular use case difficult. Application architects often find themselves second-guessing or regretting their initial selection of an infrastructure product. Often, one product proves to be *good enough*, but some feature of another was missed, or aspects of the chosen product are suboptimal. This chapter will present several comparisons that will increase the suitability of long-term satisfaction with infrastructure selections.

Structure

In this chapter, the following topics will be covered:

- Choosing a server-side runtime platform
- Determining where best to store your data

- Identity and authentication
- Asynchronous message handling

Objectives

This chapter will focus on and disambiguate the strengths of some common and hard-to-distinguish GCP products in four core domains: Compute power, data storage, identity and authentication, and asynchronous processing. The reader will understand why one of the seemingly equivalent products in each of these areas would be the suitable choice for their requirements, both for the product's strengths and any caveats.

Choosing a server-side runtime platform

GCP offers many options for a platform on which to run application code, and in most cases, several of those options could be *made to work*; in other words, there is no *wrong* choice among them. In this section, we will discuss the benefits to look for when selecting a compute platform and the use cases for which several of these products are optimal fits.

The impact of compute platform selection

The choice of a runtime compute platform is the most significant factor and determinant of a software system's overall shape. There are going to be points where *save a record*, *read a record* or *display a value* will be called for in an application, but any of the relevant database or user interface frameworks will provide some function to plug into your application. In this case, the *how* of an operation may vary, but *what* and *where* to do will remain constant. In contrast, the mechanism used to run your code, serverless functions, an event-driven application framework, and an application abstraction library will dictate the points in time and the modular containment of the operations your application executes to fulfill its requirements.

The following figure shows the contrast, with some degree of abstraction.

In the following figure, the left diagram represents an event-driven client application storing application data using file-based storage, such as Google storage buckets. The diagram to the right shows the same application but using a relational Cloud **Structured Query Language** (**SQL**) database to store application data:

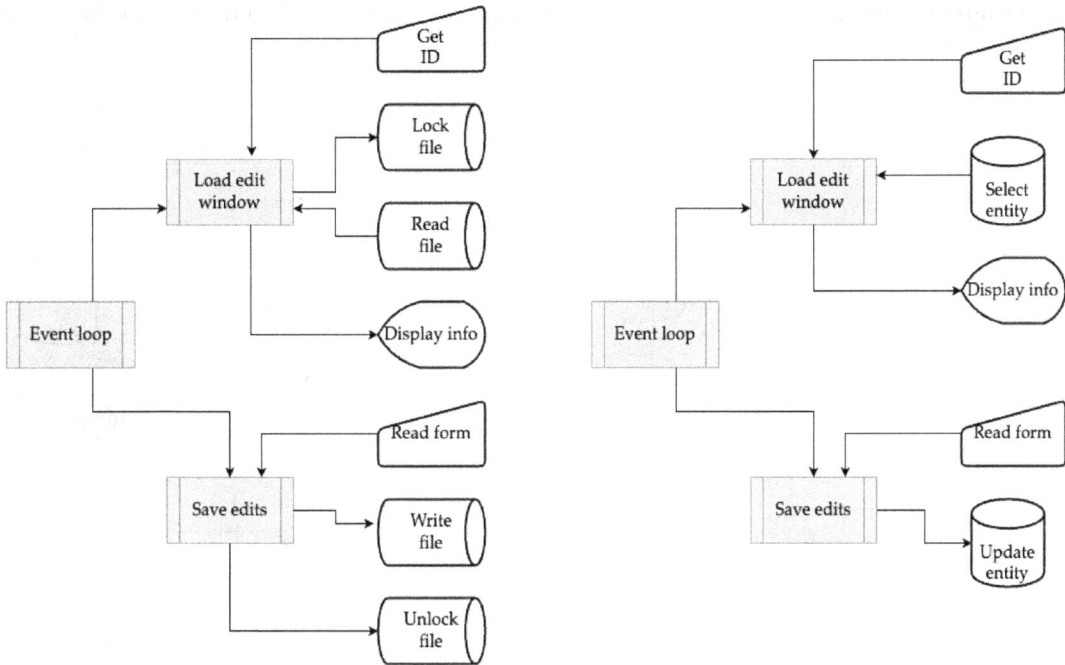

Figure 4.1: *Side-by-side comparison of storage platforms*

Note the strong similarity between the two application topologies. The overall flow of the application has not changed; the number of processing components and where they interface with storage and user interface functions is the same, just the specific features and their usage to fit each storage product's semantics varies.

Now, let us examine a similar side-by-side comparison of this application, but instead of varying the storage platform, we will design two different compute products with their distinct application paradigms.

The *left* diagram depicts our application using the same event-driven application framework and a relational database. The *right* diagram shows how the application might be designed using a **Representational State Transfer (REST)** API, while using the same database product for storage:

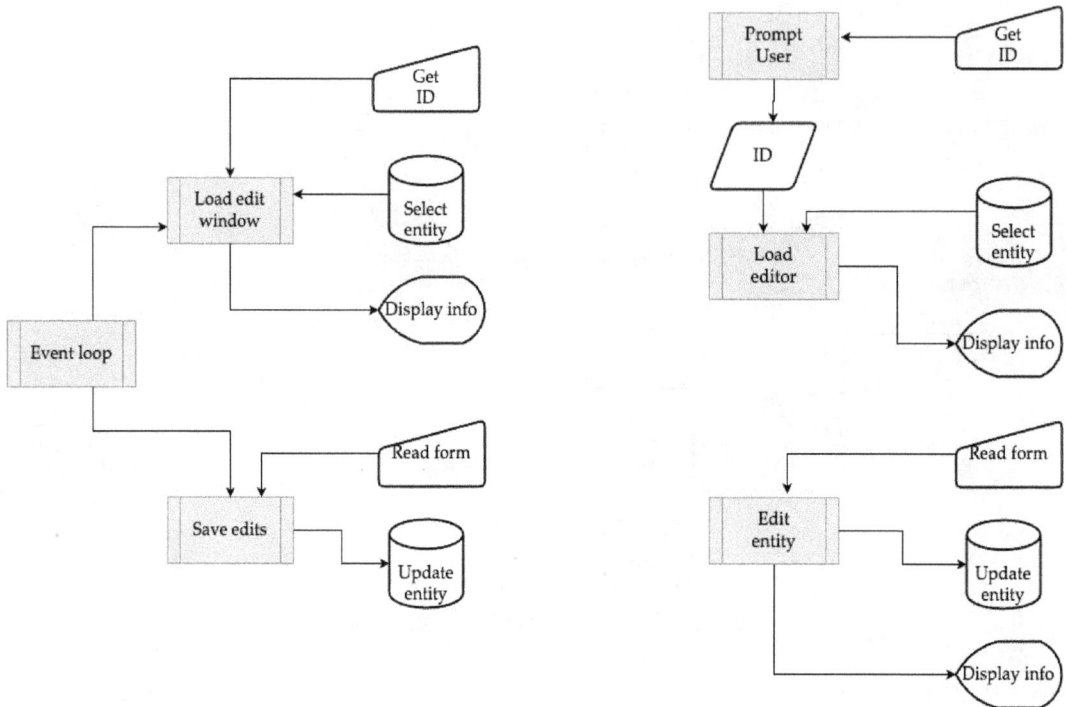

Figure 4.2: *Side-by-side comparison of event loop and REST architecture applications*

The differences between the left and right-side applications in *Figure 4.2* are more significant than the differences in *Figure 4.1*. There is no 1:1 correspondence of when different operations are dispatched in the latter diagram. In the REST design, the various functions have no central or unifying event loop from which they are coordinated and dispatched, any state must be established and published by the functions themselves, as with the ID value shown in *Figure 4.2*.

The effect of this distinction between compute platforms and other infrastructure categories is impactful enough for us to call out explicitly. If you find that some storage product X has some advantage over another storage product Y that you currently use in your system, the migration of your application may not be trivial, but it is going to be well-contained and localized within your application's codebase. On the other hand, deciding to use a microservice architecture, such as a REST API, rather than the event-driven client framework you are currently using, is going to call for a rewrite of your application; major changes are likely to result in a new codebase, perhaps you will reuse some modules or package scope but the changes will be significant from the top down.

Bearing this in mind, it is worth investing some time and energy to thoroughly understand and carefully choose from the available compute options in GCP. We will next describe each of the three GCP compute products independently before performing a comparative analysis.

Google Application Engine

Google Application Engine, commonly referred to as App Engine, is a service that runs monolithic server-side rendered websites. Monolithic, in this case, means that at the surface, the entire website is contained and defined by the code and resources managed within the App Engine instance. A server-side rendered website is one where the presentation of the website, aka the browser content, is rendered on the server, in the code executed within the App Engine, and then sent to the client browser.

App Engine is a serverless platform: the developer develops and deploys their application without any consideration of the underlying machine resources on which it executes at runtime. Configuration options, specified by the developer, are used to guide App Engine in how to start up and shut down instances of the managed application in response to changes in demand and traffic patterns.

App Engine offers two tiers of service, or environments: the App Engine standard environment and the App Engine flexible environment. The main distinction between the two environments are the degree of control offered over the scaling of the application at runtime in response to the number of requests and the amount of data that the application must handle.

First, let us look at some overall App Engine product features, which will provide context for an examination of the two environments.

App Engine supports web applications written using any of a number of programming languages. The applications you develop also typically make use of a web application framework or tools specific to your choice of programming language, such as Flask for Python; Apache Maven for Java; and Ruby on Rails for Ruby.

Administration of App Engine apps can be done through the *gcloud* **command line interface** (**CLI**) or the GCP console. For more experienced users or to efficiently manage large numbers of App Engine apps, GCP also offers App Engine **application program interfaces** (**APIs**) for programmatic, scripted execution of the administrative tasks you would manually perform with the CLI or console. This App Engine administrative API is available both as a REST interface and an **remote procedure call** (**RPC**) interface for language-specific client libraries.

The App Engine product provides compute resources, an *engine* to run your code, and does not venture into other classes of products such as storage, security, or messaging. App Engine apps can interface with other GCP services, such as Firestore, Pub/Sub and Cloud Storage.

Developing an App Engine application is well described with Google and the community providing numerous examples and prescribed solutions to many common problems. As such, App Engine is a good choice for a developer's first foray into GCP, if the application itself is suitable: a web-application without specific need for client-side rendering or other local processing. The serverless nature of App Engine platform gives the developer a chance to become familiar with the GCP tools, such as the gcloud command and developer console, without dividing their attention between those developer tools, their application itself, and the mechanics of managing runtime deployment.

The App Engine standard environment

The App Engine standard environment supports applications developed in Go, Java, Node. js, PHP, Python, and Ruby. A number of recent versions of each language are supported with a typical support schedule of a few years for each version offered. The support for a specific version of a language in App Engine is usually tied to the support offered by the language provider themselves and is offered in App Engine for some limited time after that version has been deprecated by the provider.

Applications deployed in the App Engine standard environment are run in a Sandbox environment, similar to a Python Virtual Environment or Linux chroot jail. The application is sealed off from unintentional interaction with other instances or applications and only has access to the App Engine and GCP services that are defined and explicitly offered; an app cannot make arbitrary calls to operating system services with the expectation that they will have any persistent effect outside of their own App Engine instance. In more direct terms, if your standard environment app were to use the Python OS package to remove arbitrary files in the root path, those file deletions would not be visible or have any effect in other concurrent or future instances of your application or in other developers' applications. Persistent changes to user and application data must be done through the appropriate services such as cloud storage or cloud database products.

The limited options and control over standard environment apps enables this environment to offer major consequential advantages over the flexible environment. Due to this isolation of instances, App Engine can treat all applications and instances as the same, that is, interchangeable. This agnostic view of instances, in turn, allows App Engine to start up new instances of your application very quickly, as minimal post-instance cleanup or pre-loading customization of a runtime environment is needed. Thus, the App Engine standard environment is optimal for applications that need to horizontally scale very quickly, keeping up with extreme spikes in request traffic. By virtue of this same *genericity* of instances, Standard Environment apps can run at very low cost, scaling your application down to zero instances during a lull in demand.

Many application developers first view the standard environment's constraints as being narrower than their current or preconceived portfolio of technologies and services and dismiss it as a non-viable option. This is worth deeper consideration. The standard environment should be evaluated from a fresh point of view, in terms of its own costs and benefits, rather than against a compatibility list with designs meant for other platforms. Many preconceived requirements of an application system for its infrastructure are, in fact, irrelevant in the presence of the serverless and low-maintenance features of App Engine standard environment; while the scaling and cost benefits are hard to match on other services.

The App Engine flexible environment

With both material and effort cost advantages of the standard environment; not every application can be developed within its predetermined menu options, nor can all systems take advantage of the scaling and cost savings it offers. The App Engine's flexible environment offers a greater range of development tools and increased freedom to pick and choose runtime options, hence the name flexible.

The first category in which the flexible environment offers more options is in the choice of development language and runtime support. The flexible environment allows development in the following languages, those which are exclusive to the flexible environment are in bold type: Go, Java, Node.js, PHP, Python, Ruby, .NET and custom runtimes.

As well as supporting a broader selection of languages, the runtime environment of your flexible environment application instances are under a far greater degree of your control. Flexible environment instances run in Google Compute Engine **Virtual Machines (VM)** for which you can configure custom software libraries and attach your own Docker containers. You can even access these virtual machines while they are running via a **Secure Shell (SSH)** to observe and debug a running application instance.

White the flexible environment does not manage your application to the degree where it can provide the same level of hands-off application deployment as the standard environment, it does provide a similar experience and advantage for the management of the VM instances on which your application runs, rather than of the application instances themselves.

The App Engine flexible environment VM instances can be configured with nearly the same freedom you have in setting up any machine of your own. *Nearly* because there are certain anti-patterns, such as software configurations that introduce known security risks, that are not supported.

The distinguishing features of a flexible environment VM over a machine of your own, or a VM that you lease directly from the underlying service, GCP Compute Engine, lie in the management of the flexible environment instances. These are managed in two ways: scaling for demand matching and system administration.

The number of concurrent instances of a flexible environment VM are auto-scaled, similar to how application instances are managed in the standard environment. As demand increases for your flexible environment application, the environment will start up more virtual machines to process the additional traffic. While the scaling may seem equivalent to that in the standard environment, the instantiation and shutdown of VMs is much more resource-intensive and time-consuming than that of the serverless resources in the standard environment. The flexible environment auto-scaling is not guaranteed to keep up if an application experiences sudden, steep and unpredictable spikes in demand. In such a case, other mechanisms should be employed to prevent shortfalls in capacity.

An important advantage of auto-scaling is that it is sensitive to the locale of user demand. Within the constraints that you configure, the flexible environment starts up instances in regions closest on the network to the origin of traffic, minimizing user latency and costs incurred by network services.

The second aspect of VM management that is handled by the flexible environment is that of System Administration: upkeep of your VM environment.

Let us describe the common administration tasks that are performed in a flexible environment.

Operating system and security updates to installed packages are automatically applied to your VM image; new instances will be running the updated software, and running instances will be automatically restarted up to once a week to ensure that old software is not left running in production for an extended period of time. If an operating system update is designated as critical and is known to be backward compatible with the previous version, it is automatically applied when it is available.

Running instances are health-checked, that is, they are queried with requests to confirm their liveness and readiness to serve user traffic. If an instance fails to respond to acknowledge its health, it is not considered available for routing of user requests and will be restarted if the unhealthy state persists.

As well as preserving system uptime, server health checks help to prevent both slow responses and dropped requests. For example, a common cause of server lockup, which leads to dropped requests, is a full, or nearly full, root file system. This is one condition that is detected and addressed by the flexible environment health checks, usually before the condition manifests.

At this point in the text, we have given an in-depth explanation of the Google App Engine product and its two variants: the App Engine standard and flexible environments. The App Engine product has been around since 2008, it was the first cloud computing service offered by Google. There is little reason to worry about obsolescence or deprecation, the App Engine service has evolved and advanced greatly since its introduction and has changed to integrate with the GCP ecosystem that has grown around it.

App Engine is a good choice for hosting a website for which the control and administration can be given over to the infrastructure's administrative features and tools. There are, of course, distributed components that do not fit within the App Engine model of a single indivisible website, and there are websites for which more precise control over the environment is needed. We will now examine some other GCP compute services to address those situations: Google Cloud Run, and Google Compute Engine.

Google Cloud Run

Google Cloud Platform offers a range of services, from the most abstract such as Cloud Functions and App Engine, to the most concrete known as bare metal. Google Cloud run lies somewhere near the midpoint of this spectrum, it provides a fully managed service but that service can run any type of workload you configure.

Containers, hermetic software packages

Central to many Google Cloud Platform services is the concept of containers. A container is conceptually a package of software artifacts: executables, configuration specifications and data, that is self-contained so that it can be run isolated from other containers that may be present and run on the same host computer system. This is similar to the sandbox environment that was described in the earlier section, *Google Application Engine,* for the App Engine standard environment, but at a lower level: that of operating system-level files and processes.

Cloud Run uses containers as the basic unit of user deployment. You, or GCP tools on your behalf, bundle together all the files that are needed to run your application within the boundaries of a known base operating system environment. The container is the world for the purpose of your application; directory paths, files, and processes are all present in the container with no unresolved external references. This allows the host system to load and run your containerized application as a hermetic task: sealed and air-tight, with no side-effects on the environment outside of the container and no worries about the side-effects from other similarly containerized siblings.

Let us look at some available languages and frameworks.

Since you fully configure the container environment in which your application will run, there is complete freedom to use any development language, framework and tools that you prefer as long as they are available for one of the base operating system images that are offered by Cloud Run. That is an advantage of containers: since you are isolated, you can explore and use options without worry, as the hermeticity of your runtime environment obviates any other parties' concerns about incompatibility or side-effects.

While any conceivable development suite can be used to develop and deploy under Cloud Run, there is a high degree of automation and tooling for common, well-defined development tools. Applications that are developed through following the published best practices in Go, Node.js, Python, Java, .NET Core, or Ruby, can be automatically built from the source and deployed to production with one command. The selection of supporting artifacts and other configurations of the runtime container are all done by the *gcloud* command, with the relevant command line flags.

Cloud Run application types: Cloud Run supports two models for running deployed containerized applications: services and jobs.

A Cloud Run *service* is meant to be a continuously running process, such as a web server or RPC server, that responds to incoming requests of a sporadic nature. These are the sort of jobs that respond to user queries or inputs and are typically scaled horizontally as the number of concurrent users grows and shrinks.

A Cloud Run *job* is a process model commonly referred to as batch. Not to be confused with the GCP Batch service, this refers generically to a workflow with a known input, predetermined processing stages, and a point where it is considered complete. This is not to say that the number, schedule, and inputs for every Cloud Run job instance are predetermined or even predicted, but rather that when a specific instance is started, its inputs are known and will be complete when all the job processing stages are completed.

Now, let us see the usage of Cloud Run service auto-scaling to match user demand.

Auto-scaling of a Google Run service is very similar to the parallel use case in App Engine. As new requests are routed to your job, they are either delivered to an available instance or a new instance is started up to process the request. After an instance has been idle for some time, it is removed from service and its resources are freed. Since starting up new instances takes time, you can configure your job to always preserve a minimum number of instances, even when there have been no recent requests; this avoids undue latency in processing the first requests after an idle period. While Cloud Run can auto-scale up to 1,000 service instances in response to traffic, you can configure a cap for the number of concurrent instances of your job to prevent any surprises on your usage bill. Let us explore how to use Cloud Run job scaling to match request profiles in the following exercise.

A typical batch job is much longer lived and presumed to experience more predictably shaped demand. There are three models by which a Cloud Run job can be run, which correspond to the common use cases for long-lived processes that are not attached to an individual user: tools, scheduled jobs, and array jobs. We will describe each of these and liken them to a non-GCP use case that they are a surrogate for:

- **Tool or script jobs**: A common requirement is to run some series of commands or a script that encapsulates them on demand as a one-off. This may be to accomplish some task with an asynchronous or unpredictable trigger, such as archiving all log files for this region, there is going to be a regulatory audit, or converting this database table to CSV files, that database is migrating to a new server. These would run when we say so and for some significant amount of time. Those are known as tool jobs or script jobs and are the sort of tasks that would be started in a terminal session in a non-cloud computing environment. In GCP, these would be run as a tool job with the output artifacts and execution logs directed to a persistent GCP product, such as a GCP storage bucket.

- **Scheduled jobs**: The need for some tasks is reliably predictable, proverbially like clockwork. Every day at midnight, a daily counter must be reset; every morning a message of the day should be updated; and every evening, temporary files from that day's processing are cleaned up. This is such a common requirement that every operating system has some mechanism to implement it: *cron, at jobs* and *scheduled tasks* to name a few.

Google Cloud provides this through the Cloud Scheduler service. You can configure the region and time specification, which includes frequency for a specific Cloud Run job to execute, and the scheduler will automatically start instances of your Cloud Run job to meet those scheduling criteria. The jobs can optionally be configured with a retry policy, specifying a maximum time that a scheduled job should be allowed to execute without successful completion, after which time the scheduler will stop the running job and start a new instance.

- **Array jobs**: Many tasks are easily divisible among many workers, so that the product of worker count and walltime needed to complete the task are a constant. To quote a popular proverb: *Many hands make light work*. The capability to execute a command for a number of inputs is offered by the Linux *xargs* command, and this command is the model on which Cloud Run array jobs is based.

We can state the tradeoff between walltime and worker count roughly in algebraic terms as follows:

$time\_to\_completion = total\_CPU\_seconds\_needed / number\_of\_workers)$

If it takes 100 CPU seconds to convert 20 color images to grayscale, it should take 100 seconds for **one** worker to complete or five seconds on the clock if you have **20** worker tasks, each concurrently converting one image:

$$walltime = 100 = 100/1$$

$$walltime = 5 = 100/20$$

The actual CPU time cost of the work (100 seconds) has not changed, but the *walltime* has been divided by the number of CPU seconds that were concurrently spent.

Many tasks are easily divisible into smaller, independent units of work. We call such splitting and distributing of work sharding. Another example is one of copying files; one task could be set to copy 1,000 files. Ten tasks could each copy 100 files or 100 tasks could each be assigned to ten files. Of course, not all files are the same size, but most sharding algorithms assume that the input data can be broken up into shards of equivalent size and have some means to do so.

This results in an easily understood linear trade-off between elapsed time and space occupied. When deciding how to configure the scaling of this function, we can research the cost of fewer longer-lived jobs versus a greater number of shorter-lived jobs to inform our decision.

Once we have decided on a suitable sharding method, such as number of files in a storage bucket or rows in a digital image, and a maximum number of tasks that we wish to scale to, we then setup a Cloud Run job that executes custom sharding code. This code selects a unique slice or shard of the input data based on the index or task number of a given task instance. In our file copying example, we will shard the input data by calculating the total number of files and then assign each shard an equal portion of those files, such as is done in the following code.

> **Note:** **The following task numbers and file indices are assumed to start at zero, as is the convention for arrays in most programming languages and libraries:**

```
total_file_count = len(input_file_list);
first_file_number_for_this_task = total_file_count /
        total_task_count * this_task_number;
last_file_number_for_this_task = total_file_count /
        total_task_count * (this_task_number + 1) - 1;
```

The computed boundaries for each shard are shown in the following figure:

total files	total task count	task number	first_file_number	last_file_number
1000	20	0	0	49
1000	20	1	50	99
1000	20	2	100	149
1000	20	3	150	199
1000	20	19	950	999

Figure 4.3: Array job shard boundaries

Then in our job's code, we would copy the range of files in the current task's shard as follows:

```
for (int file_index = first_file_number_for_this_task;
        file_index <= last_file_number_for_this_task;
        file_index++) {
    copy_file_to_output(input_file_list[file_index]);
}
```

To run this array job, you would configure the Cloud Run job to run the preceding code in a specified number of tasks, in this case, 20. Cloud Run would start the 20 tasks in parallel, and as each task is restricted to its own unique set of files by the preceding code, the tasks would run concurrently and independently of each other. When all 20 tasks have been successfully completed, the overall Array job is considered complete by Cloud Run.

Long-lived jobs in Cloud Run

One other advantage to note about Cloud Run jobs, they are able to run for a longer time than could be reliably expected from the non-GCP counterpart that was identified earlier, that is, a command in an interactive terminal session. Terminal sessions are considered either unreliable, a security risk, or both. The Linux operating system offers many ways to accommodate long-running commands: the *screen* and *tmux* commands, *at jobs*, and the *nohup* command are a few. Windows offers fewer options, but the *start* command is commonly used to achieve this.

Cloud Run jobs can run up to 24 hours and are not connected to an interactive terminal. Cloud Run monitors their completion, saves their exit status, and can be configured to automatically retry if a failure is detected. In addition, the output of your command is preserved for later examination. This replaces the features of the workarounds for long-running commands, with the added benefit of well-defined retry semantics.

To summarize, Google Cloud Run is a service that runs a custom executable of your own devising with a high degree of hermiticity through containerization. These jobs can be run with one of several models of execution: immediate execution, scheduled and periodic execution, and sharded, parallel execution. The completion status of jobs is monitored, and Cloud Run can be configured to retry failed jobs with several parameters governing the retry attempts.

Compute Engine

Now, we will look at a service that lies further away on the spectrum from serverless, managed application deployment and brings Google Cloud Platform's strength to machine management: Compute Engine.

Compute Engine offers similar management to the two services we have discussed thus far: App Engine and Cloud Run. Each can start instances, monitor them for failure, increase and decrease the number of active instances based on demand, and retry failed instances. This level of management is central to GCP compute products. The main distinction between the three compute products examined in this chapter is the nature of what they manage, and what sort of resource they control instances of.

Virtual machines

App Engine manages applications, Cloud Run manages sandbox environments, and Compute Engine manages virtual machines. For those unfamiliar with the concept, a virtual machine is the emulation of an entire computing system: CPU, memory, disk storage, network connections and sometimes even Human Interface Devices, such as keyboards and mice. The emulation of these hardware components is done entirely using software: it is not a disk you are writing data to, but rather a buffer in a program that behaves like a disk as far as the operating system can see. This offers many advantages over directly using a physical computer system, mainly hermeticity, cross system compatibility, and resource sharing. For detailed explanations, the reader is encouraged to Google the web for resources on the topic. For initial hands-on experience, the open-source Qemu project at **https://www.qemu.org/** is a great resource. For further exploration with production quality products, the reader is guided to the more advanced KVM project at **https://linux-kvm.org/** which is the hypervisor used within GCP.

Compute engine allows the user to configure a **virtual machine** (henceforth **VM**) image, specifying a processor type; amount of virtual memory; the number and size of attached disks; and network connections. The contents of the attached disks can be loaded with desired software, just as you would install software on any server or workstation.

Here is where the first advantage of VMs: the initial image of a VM is saved in a set of files somewhere on a real disk. Whenever you start or instantiate a running copy of your VM, it is loaded from the pristine image of your machine. If something goes awry, you accidentally delete needed directories, or the system is somehow corrupted through a bug, the initial, desired state of the system is still present in those image files. The damaged machine can be shut down, and a new instance can be started, ignorant or unaware of the events that afflicted the previous instance. The software that manages these underlying images and uses them to start VM instances is known as a **virtual machine monitor** (**VMM**) or *hypervisor*.

Many hypervisors, Compute Engine included, extend the management of images to provide support for *Snapshots*. A snapshot allows a picture of the current state of a running VM to be saved as an image, which can then be used to start later instances just as the initial pristine base image can. This, in effect, provides a time machine for VMs—a way to take a VM back in time to when a snapshot was previously taken.

Compute product comparison

The three GCP compute products that have been explored have very different scopes but share a common, unifying theme: they all manage specific aspects of *something*. What that something is that they manage differs, but the products all provide similar management capabilities and automation for the resources that they make available and deploy. We will first summarize the common aspects of these products and then review the discriminating factor: the unit of compute power that each product provides to its users.

GCP Compute resource management

To manage a resource means, in this context, to configure it; provision and deploy it into active service; monitor its execution; and finally respond to its termination in some way:

- **Configure**: A full description of the resource, both its contents and the parameters governing the later stages of its life cycle are collectively the resource's configuration.

- **Provision and deploy**: Setting aside or allocating the runtime dependencies needed to instantiate the resource is provisioning the resource. Some examples of runtime dependencies are real machines to run a VM on, an IP address for a service's endpoint, and sufficient quota in the user's budget.

- **Deploying a resource**: This is the ultimate act of making it so. Starting up a web server in App Engine to accept requests, booting a VM; deploying a resource makes an instance of it real, no longer just a description of the application we wish to run.

- **Monitoring**: Being aware of the state of a resource is the purpose of monitoring it. Knowing how much network traffic is being received, the amount of disk space is used, the CPU usage of an application's binary, and if a process is executing or has terminated.

- **Responding to termination**: When a resource has been terminated, either by external agents or from some internal mechanism, being able to take a prescribed action is needed for a highly available and reliable system. Restarting a web server that has exited, rebooting a VM that has frozen, and saving the logs from a long-running batch task are examples of some common termination actions.

Compute resources offered

The services we described provide resources along a spectrum of abstraction. We will summarize them from the most abstract to the most concrete.

On one end, the App Engine standard environment offers management of applications, typically web servers, with no transparency into the lower-level concrete compute resources used to provide those applications. The code exists independently, any dependencies or backing resources are hidden and opaque, handled behind the scenes.

The App Engine flexible environment provides VMs configured with an application and supporting software specified by the user. While the flexible environment does not hide the many layers of software and hardware that an application depends on, it does automate the creation and management of those lower-level dependencies.

Cloud Run manages containers; hermetic, self-contained runtime environments that run whatever code you configure, but isolated from affecting, or being affected by, neighboring container environments; including other instances of the same container.

Compute Engine manages complete VMs: idealized computer systems. These can run any of many available operating systems and contain arbitrary collections of devices, such as disks, network adapters and processors.

In an ideal world, the more abstract a specification is, the better it is to not require any specific dependency, as it confers the greatest freedom to adapt to the environment and situation. However, with abstraction comes a necessary loss of precision and control, which some systems cannot relinquish. So, as a very general rule of thumb, which should be viewed as a guiding principle rather than a prescription for success, the closer to the abstract end of the spectrum, the better.

Bear in mind that there are other GCP products which are even further abstractions, such as Cloud Functions; and products which are more concrete than Compute Engine VMs, including GCP Bare Metal Solution. The products that have been described here are the middle bands of the spectrum of abstraction and cover the requirements of the greater share of distributed applications.

The following figure positions the three compute products discussed on the spectrum of abstraction and roughly depicts the relative portion of application systems that they address:

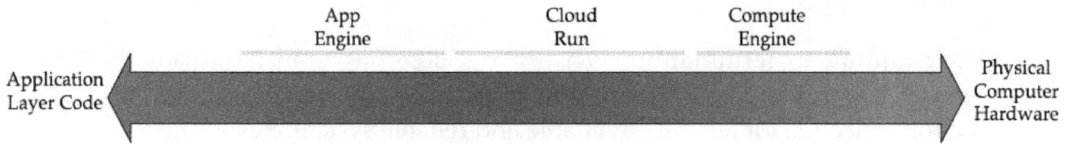

Figure 4.4: Products on the spectrum of resource abstraction

Determining where best to store your data

When selecting a new workstation or laptop, the first feature a consumer looks for after the computer itself is typically the specifications of the hard drive, or more accurately, solid-state drive. Likewise, after selecting the compute service for a given application feature, the means by which that feature persists in its state or stores its data is the usual next consideration.

Using a similar approach, as with compute products, we will examine several products that provide persistent, durable storage for application data. The services we will discuss cover a wide range of use cases and storage paradigms, and both the conceptual and pragmatic distinguishing characteristics of these products will be described.

Cloud Firestore

Cloud Firestore is not a relational database; it is a specialized NoSQL database used to store and retrieve data in the form of documents. As opposed to relational databases or row-centric non-relational databases, the unit of storage is itself fairly large: a document, such as a book, a form or a resume.

Firestore documents are structured. A document contains fields that Firestore represents in JSON format. A quick example of a book represented as a JSON document suitable for Firestore could look like the following:

```
{
  Book: {
    title: "The Hobbit",
    isbn: "9780345445605",
    author: "J.R.R. Tolkien",
    abstract: "Hobbits and dwarves look for gold with a wizard and
elves...",
    chapters: {
      "The beginning": "It was a rainy night in the hobbit hole...",
```

```
        "The middle": "The elven valley was fun...The mines are dark... ",
        "The end": "That was one scary big dragon... It's good to be home."
    }
  }
}
```

Collections of documents can be searched through, using filter values for a number of a document's fields. Cloud Firestore ensures optimal query performance by using indexes to quickly locate documents by their fields' values. Firestore automatically creates a set of basic indexes for your document collection; you can add indexes to support specific and complex queries that your application will issue. If a query is executed for which no suitable index exists, an error message will be returned that includes a link to create a suggested needed index in the Firebase developer console.

Cloud Firestore's query mechanism offers several operators and supports compound and nested queries, but it does not allow for as complex queries as a relational database using SQL. To address this, there are several dedicated third-party search services.

A Firestore query for books by other authors that contain references to hobbits in the description could be written in Python as follows:

```
from google.cloud import firestore

db = firestore.Client()
library_query = db.collection("books")
.where("author", "not-in", "Tolkien"))
.where("abstract, "in", "Hobbit")

books = query.stream()
for book in books:
    print(f"{book.isbn} => {book.title")
```

Documents can be created, updated and deleted as JSON using Firebase functions, with full support for **Atomicity, Consistency, Isolation, and Durability (ACID)** transactions as described in the previous chapter. Python's transaction semantics ensure data integrity both within individual documents and in the overall collection of documents.

Another distinguishing characteristic of Cloud Firestore is derived from the fact that it is an offshoot of another product, Firebase. Firebase is a development platform for mobile, primary Android and iOS, and web client applications. That being the aim of Firebase, it follows that Cloud Firestore has strong client library support. Firestore functions can be executed directly from code running on the client, not just from GCP infrastructure components.

Firestore's are as follows:

- Firestore is document based, rather than rows of data resembling a spreadsheet, Firebase stores structured data whose contents more closely resemble a text document with defined sections such as, heading, paragraph, and footnote.

- Firestore has exceptional accessibility from client code.

Its disadvantages are:

- FIrestore queries are not as capable as some other database products, such as relational databases.

Cloud Structured Query Language

GCP Cloud SQL is a product that acts as an abstraction for one of several relational database products, such as PostgreSQL, MySQL or SQL Server. The use of Cloud SQL as a proxy for any of these database systems offers two main advantages: Platform agnosticism in your application, and full management of your database resources.

- **Platform agnostic applications**: While all popular relational **database management systems (DBMS)** use the SQL to perform operations on data, that is where the similarity ends. Administration of the data objects, like tables, indices and supporting entities, vary greatly from one database system to the next. Even more problematic, the SQL language supported by database products possess variations in both syntax and capabilities. This can have undesired consequences: frustration for developers who are either familiar with or relying on the SQL supported by a different vendor and difficulty in porting or migrating from one database product to another.

  Cloud SQL positions itself between an application and any of the database systems it supports. Developers and administrators write application code, database specifications, and administration configuration without regard or knowledge of the backing DBMS; the capabilities offered by Cloud SQL are well-defined and consistent with an *ideal* relational database product. Through a combination of compile-time and runtime translation, Cloud SQL converts the database operations executed by an application into the corresponding operations that are native to whichever actual database product is in use at runtime.

- **Database management**: Cloud SQL is consistent with the management model that has been exhibited in the Compute products described earlier in the chapter. Regular and critical database administration tasks such as backups, replication, and managing storage capacity are all important to plan and urgent to execute when called for. Cloud SQL configures these tasks, as with its application interface, with tools and a grammar that are agnostic of the supported database product that the tasks will be executed on. Database administration is a complex field with little room for error and removing much of the product-specific arcana from the

Database Administrator's (DBA) role is both a reduction in stress for the DBA, and an increase in reliability and stability of the database and the products that rely on it. When you have configured replication of your database instances using Cloud SQL semantics, that replication will take place on PostGreSQ, MySQL or SQL Server using whatever the local expression of those semantics are.

The reliability of these tasks is as important as the proper configuration of them. Cloud SQL benefits from the high availability of all GCP products. In a local database server, scheduling of a backup or storage expansion typically depends on the availability of some local resource: a server process that launches administration tasks. If something goes wrong with that scheduling dependency, your task will not be executed and your system is placed at risk. GCP replicates the execution of management to different regions, so that even an outage of resources in one locale does not affect your system's integrity and availability.

Bigtable

Bigtable is the first popular NoSQL database that offers an alternative to the relational data model that is the basis for the majority of DBMSs that were in widespread use before it. While relational databases hold unstructured data elements and impose structure through defined relationships between these elements, Bigtable data columns can be unstructured or can possess their own inherent structure, without strong relational operators to apply to the columns. In contrast to relational databases' support of any columns being used to identify rows of data, Bigtable tables have a predetermined key, a rowID, and other columns' values are attributes of that row.

Bigtable performance

The non-relational model of data contributes to two main performance benefits of Bigtable: It is fast, and, as the name says, it is big. Data rows can be written and read from Bigtable at a greater speed than with a relational database, with the performance advantage becoming greater as the size of the rows and the number of operations increase. Bigtable is optimized to outperform with much larger data rows than most relational databases. This optimization makes sense in a non-relational model, as data in a relational database is typically split up amongst multiple *normalized* tables. So, a single large row is less often called for in a relational database design. The writing of correlated rows to many tables takes time, which is counter to Bigtable's design goals, that is, to access large amounts of data as quickly as possible. This is why the non-relational, denormalized, or flattened data model of Bigtable is needed to achieve its high rate of reads and writes. Bigtable data can be large in both breadth and depth: a single row can be up to 256 megabytes before any performance degradation is encountered, and a table can contain billions of rows and be several petabytes in size.

There are other implementation details of Bigtable that enable it to handle such large databases as well as it does. In brief, Bigtable accesses table data through *Tablet Servers*;

independent processing nodes that can be horizontally scaled to meet the requirements of individual tables and traffic patterns. So, if data grows or queries for certain portions of your data increase, Bigtable can scale the processes used to serve that demand.

Bigtable transactions are limited in scope. A corollary to the change from the relational database model is that of the transaction model supported by Bigtable. Since it is expected that a row of data in Bigtable does not relate or join to another row in any table, transactions are only supported within a single row.

This further encourages the flattening of data rows in Bigtable, to the point where all the data needed to represent a committed logical unit of work is contained within a single row.

When evaluating Bigtable versus relational databases, one should consider its performance and peculiar data semantics. If an application's data does not require large degrees of normalization or correlation between independent tables and the data will grow very large, Bigtable is a good candidate to provide persistence services for the application.

Bigtable's unique data model, structured and repeating column data, the preference for denormalized self-contained data rows and the narrower transaction scope require rethinking practices that are ingrained in developers when dealing with relational databases. The cost in developer time and effort to shift to Bigtable should be considered when evaluating a storage service. If an application does not require or use Bigtable's advantages of scale and speed, a more traditional database may be an efficacious and more practical choice.

Spanner

Spanner is the most ambitious database product with regard to scope in GCP and most likely in the world. Since this is a bold claim, let us justify it here by describing both the breadth and depth of Spanner's features:

- **Spanner's breadth of data models**: Spanner supports data stored in both relational and key-value models, like SQL based DBMSs and NoSQL systems. Spanner also allows developers to represent data in two additional paradigms: graph and vector data models.

  Spanner's support for relational data is offered both as a native GoogleSQL interface and though a PostgreSQL interface, which allows Spanner relational tables to be accessed using PostgreSQL commands, to allow fast migration of applications from PostgresSQL to Spanner, without a significant learning curve or application rewrite.

  Spanner's key-value table support is not equivalent to Bigtable's key-value store. Spanner introduces the concept of interleaved tables and child rows, and supports stronger consistency across rows, in place of Bigtable's wide-column support and single row philosophy.

Spanner also allows data to be represented and traversed as a graph through support of a recently published standard, the Graph Query Language; for which current info is always available at **https://www.gqlstandards.org/**.

Spanner additionally provides native support for a fourth data paradigm, that of a Vector Database. Also referred to as a Search Vector, vector data is stored as a mathematical representation and is intended to provide searches for similarities in data rather than exact value matches. The association by similarity makes vector search a natural fit for ML and generative AI applications which mostly deal with large sets of data which have fuzzy or statistical relationships.

- **Spanner's depth of runtime performance**: Spanner has been built with the experience of several generations of predecessor database, storage and distributed systems at Google. Some Spanner reliability and scaling features can be traced to the best of features in these earlier products, whereas some Spanner features have been designed to address lessons learned from years of running these proceeding services at scale.

    All Spanner databases are distributed: there are many copies of data stored in different locations and there are server processes associated with each of these copies. These replicas process reads and writes against their local data and cooperate in the background to apply local changes to their distributed counterparts. This is similar to the eventual consistency in Bigtable but offers much stronger transaction guarantees, as we will describe here shortly.

Spanner separates the compute power needed to serve database requests from the data stored, which allows for transparent horizontal scaling of compute resources so that different access patterns, many reads against a narrow subset of data; reads or writes of a large number of rows; complex queries cross referencing different slices of data, can all be provisioned for and served efficiently.

Replication, backups and even propagation of changes to a database schema are all performed automatically, with respect to configuration options specified by the user, in the background. Maintenance tasks such as schema conversion and migration that lock a user out of data while in flight are performed against replicas which are temporarily shielded from user access. In combination, these features allow a Spanner database to achieve zero downtime with regards to data availability.

Spanner offers Strong-ACID transaction guarantees, which are at least as strong as any relational database's, but due to Spanner's inherent distributed nature, Spanner must go one step further. Spanner implements TrueTime ordering of transactions that occur concurrently on a distributed database. As a result of this, a Spanner database provides *external consistency*, the strongest consistency defined for transaction processing systems. In plain terms, this means that Spanner offers well-defined semantics and rules for ordering and sequentially resolving transactions that occur across multiple replicas of a distributed, global database.

Evaluating Spanner as a product choice should consider its cost and the specialized strengths of competing alternatives. Since Spanner strives to include and exceed the capabilities of several other classes of database, why is there still competition in these classes? There are always other considerations, and specialized systems can be optimized for specific use cases. We will summarize a few of these counter-arguments to Spanner usage here:

- Reads of a large number of rows are faster in Bigtable. In its NoSQL model, tables of key-value pairs, Spanner offers more indexing options and matches or exceeds Bigtable performance in fetching specific rows. However, this is not the access pattern that Bigtable is optimized for. If reading a large series of rows, in some key range, the lower overhead of Bigtable's simple and smaller indexing mechanisms gives it a clear advantage in speed.

- The material cost of a Spanner is higher than that of a typical equivalent in competing products. While it can be argued that in the big picture or longer-term view, the additional reliability, and automation of Spanner make it a higher value for the investment, not every user needs or can afford the larger expense.

- The fixed cost of Spanner may outweigh the value of storing a small dataset. There is a non-trivial number of resources to create and maintain any Spanner database. If a given database is relatively small, the fixed overhead cost could be greater than the cost of the actual data. A small lookup table of product categories could be faster to access through a local NoSQL table than going through a Spanner node to get to these several dozen rows of unchanging data.

Cloud Storage

Google Cloud Storage is a different category of product than the databases that have been described to this point. Databases are used to store tables of repeating rows of data that each conform to the same description or layout of columns. At different points in time, the Invoices table may have no rows, one row or 10,000 rows, but each of those rows will have an invoice ID, amount due, date due, and billed party. You can process any subset of the rows with the same logic. The data is structured both horizontally into columns and vertically into rows.

Cloud Storage, on the other hand, is used to store, **Binary Large Objects (BLOBS)**. Apart from being an acronym, BLOB is also an apt description of a drop or lump of a liquid substance. A Blob in this sense has boundaries, but the contents, like that of a liquid, have no structure that is discernible from outside.

That is not to say that there can be no structure or definition of the data in a BLOB, but rather that that structure and definition is determined completely within the application that accesses it. The storage system itself, in our case Cloud Storage, keeps track of the boundaries of a BLOB: its size, location, and lifespan. Cloud Storage manages the BLOB as a whole, atomic unit. An application that processes a BLOB *knows* the meaning of various byte sequences contained therein.

Most software developers, in fact most computer users, are familiar with BLOBS by their common historic name: files. For all practical concerns, Google Cloud Storage is a File System, and BLOBS are files.

Cloud Storage stores data at the unit of a BLOB, which is, as we have described it, an implementation of a file. Cloud Storage's analogy to a typical OS based file system extends further to the use of a Bucket, which is the functional equivalent of a File System. Buckets are the containers in which Blobs are stored; the Bucket is configured with performance, retention, and reliability options which are then inherent in all Blobs stored in that Bucket.

A recently introduced option of Cloud Storage Buckets is that of a Hierarchical Namespace. A Bucket with a Hierarchical Namespace allows the Blobs to be stored in a folder hierarchy, just as directories in Linux or folders in a Windows system.

Cloud Storage distinguishes itself as a service in similar ways to all GCP services: availability, reliability, and scale. Additionally, Cloud Storage offers options for different service characteristics and costs. We will enumerate and briefly describe these facets of Cloud Storage shortly:

- **Performance and reliability**: Buckets can be configured to be present in any number of network regions. A replica of a Bucket can be written to and read from by processes in the same region, to reduce latency and the cost of network traffic. Cloud Storage automatically synchronizes data written to all regional copies of a bucket so that the data in any region is consistent with any other copy. This replication not only reduces latency but also provides reliability and data availability. If the data in a region is corrupt or lost, Cloud Storage will automatically route read and write requests in that region to a nearby sibling while repairing the damaged replica using data in the other copies.

- **Service options**: Cloud Storage supports a configured level of service for a bucket, referred to as the bucket Storage Class. Storage Class dictates the maximum retention time for the data stored in the bucket and the read and write latency for the bucket. Additionally, the Storage Class directs the durability of the data, that is, the guarantee of permanence for the data.

The cost of Cloud Storage is usage based. You pay for the bytes stored and accessed, without any flat fees for the service itself. The specific rates at which the user is charged for usage is based on the Storage Class used. The most common storage classes and some key facets of their intended use are enumerated in the following figure:

Storage Class	Retention limit	Relative durability	Access patterns	Relative cost
Standard	short lived	low	frequent access	most costly
Nearline	30 days	highly durable	infrequent access	low
Coldline	90 days	highly durable	infrequent access	very low
Archive	365 days	highly durable	rarely accessed	lowest

Figure 4.5: Storage classes offered by Cloud Storage

Evaluating Cloud Storage as a storage choice must consider the usage, needed durability, and size of the data being stored. Cloud Storage is a good choice for storing large amounts of data with an internal structure that has meaning specific to your application. An image file is an example, the amount of data in an image can be very large. Megapixels implies megabytes and the information within the image is encoded in a highly specialized format. It is not theoretically impossible to store the pixel values of an image in a relational database table, but there will be little to gain, and the additional time and storage required for such an implementation would be very high.

The selection of a suitable Cloud Storage storage class can be made by balancing the usage of stored objects against cost. Data that is produced inline and streamed, can be easily reproduced, and does not require high durability, whereas customer medical records should most likely be as durable and long-lived as possible.

Identity and authentication

We have now reviewed the major considerations of a computer-based system: compute power and data storage. These are fundamental to the application, which exists to store and manipulate information about the application-specific domain. We will now turn to classes of products that are more concerned with the requirements of the computing environment and the technical needs of the application, rather than inherent in the application domain.

Identity and authentication management (IAM) is the first class of product we discussed, that exists to satisfy the requirements of the *computing environment*, rather than the direct requirements of the *application user*. This is reflected in the fact that, while processing power and data storage have remained conceptually unchanged for the life of the commercial computing industry, IAM has emerged and evolved rapidly with major fundamental changes over the past few decades. Early computer users relied on simple, by today's standards naive, means of authentication. An early popular operating system, **Control Program/Monitor (CP/M)**, identified users by *User Number* with no authentication needed, you entered your user number and were trusted to go ahead and use the system.

We live in a world where many people are connected to computer systems and can access our applications and data, and so our barriers for access are higher. As more commercial, political and personal value is held on computers; there is unfortunately more incentive for malicious misuse of those systems as well as a greater impact of accidental cases of mistaken identity. As attempts to gain unauthorized access become more sophisticated, the mechanisms to prevent it improve in response, resulting in a state of mutual escalation.

Keeping up with the state of the affairs is something that a responsible application developer leaves to cybersecurity experts and products. We will describe and compare a few of those products that are offered as part of GCP.

Firebase Authentication

Firebase Authentication, like Cloud Firestore, is a product that is a discrete component of the Firebase client application development suite. Firebase Authentication is a complete end-to-end framework for managing user authentication from, and for, mobile or web-based client applications.

Firebase Authentication features

End-to-end in the case of Firebase is meant to convey the entire lifecycle of a user's identity. Signing up or creating a user account, session logins and logouts, maintenance of the user's profile and credentials are all handled by Firebase Authentication.

From providing complete coverage of an application's IAM requirements, Firebase Authentication offers several alternative implementations of user identity. A user of Firebase authentication can use an application-specific user identity or existing identities, such as Google and Apple accounts, that conform to industry standards for IAM; and can use phone or email-based authorization for accounts. Firebase Authentication also offers anonymous auth, the creation of a temporary anonymous account that can later be upgraded to a known user account while preserving the continuity of the user's activity. Firebase authentication is regularly upgraded and extended to keep pace with the latest developments in user identity protection, such as its support for **multi factor authentication** (**MFA**), which can be added to user accounts either as their opt-in or as required by an application's developers.

Evaluating the Firebase Authentication as a product choice should prefer it as a default choice, unless specific requirements rule it out. Firebase Authentication is available in several tiers of service which offer different features and varying cost structures. The cost of the Firebase Authentication service is usage based, consistent with the other GCP services that have been described. Firebase charges are calculated based on the number of **daily active users** (**DAUs**), which is the number of unique users, not user sessions, that signed in during a 24-hour period.

If an application will include a rich client platform presence, that is, a mobile or web-based client application, and wishes to offload or outsource domain-specific knowledge of identity and authentication, the Firebase Authentication should be strongly considered. Firebase Authentication can be configured and implemented in an application in minimal time. For developers who wish to control the look and feel of the authentication flow, Firebase allows developers to customize the **user interface** (**UI**) of the sign-in flow using FirebaseUI options. If a developer wants a truly unique sign-in UI, the code for Firebase UI can be forked on GitHub and customized.

Google Cloud IAM

Google Cloud IAM is an inherent and included service with every GCP product. Cloud IAM allows the definition of roles and users and the assignment of permissions for users to different GCP resources. In contrast to Firebase Authentication, Cloud IAM focuses on the cloud resources, such as your datastores and virtual machines, and on the abstractions, such as Roles to which operations on those cloud resources are permitted or denied. The **user experience** (**UX**) of identity management, such as the login or password change pages, are implemented outside of Cloud IAM; in Firebase auth or some other client-centric product.

Roles versus users

An important consideration when designing a secure system is the decoupling of access permissions from specific users. An example that illustrates this principle is one of a cloud function named **increase_credit_limit(username)** in a shopping system. This function, as the name implies, allows a user to purchase goods without paying. Permission to extend credit to shoppers is an ability that you want to limit to some inside, trusted members of your customer service staff.

One way of managing these permissions is to add every qualified user to a list of permitted invokers of the **increase_credit_limit()** method. This in itself is not an obvious problem, but then your developers realize that they needed to implement another method, **revoke_credit(user),** and another named **get_all_users_with_credit()**.

You are now keeping three separate but identical lists of permitted users, which will eventually lead to some inconsistency if they get out of sync. Rather than this double-triple or more entry method of keeping track of permissions, Cloud IAM in common with most access control systems, implements the concept of a *Role*; an abstraction of users. If a user is a *proper* noun such as *Larry Page*, a role is a related *common* noun such as *Chief Executive Officer*.

Applying this model to our shopper-credit example, we would define a role named **Credit_granter** and allow that role to invoke our three functions. When a new **customer service representative** (**CSR**) is allowed to manage shopper credit, we simply add the role **Credit_granter** to the roles that the specific CSR is assigned. When any signed-in CSR attempts to invoke **increase_credit_limit()** for some shopper, if the CSR's user has the **Credit_granter** role, the permission is transitively granted to the CSR and the operation is executed, else a permissions error is raised.

The concept of an entity who accesses resources, such as a **User** or a **Role**, is generally referred to as a **Principal**. It is convenient and usually holds true to think of a **Principal** as a specific user or some entity that stands in as a proxy or represents a user.

Let us now look at IAM policies.

IAM policies are rules, specifications governing how a requested operation by a Principal, on a given resource, can proceed. There are three types of policies, and any number of policies of any of these types can be defined for a resource. The determination of whether or not a requested access is allowed is the result of all of the policies attached to the resource being accessed.

The IAM policy types are:

- **Allow policies**: Specification of what principals are allowed to access the resource.

- **Deny policies**: Specification of what principals are denied access to the resource.

- **Principal access boundary (PAB) policies**: Specification of the boundaries of the resources that Principals can access.

Cloud IAM should be considered as a recommended basis for an application's overall identity management solution. Google Cloud IAM is not a product that an application developer opts-in to incorporate in a GCP-backed application. The access management features of GCP IAM are inherent in every other GCP service and are used to some degree in even the simplest of distributed applications. The choices facing developers designing a GCP application are what specific features of IAM they will utilize, and how sophisticated a policy hierarchy they will develop for their application's resources.

There are many predefined primitives in the IAM product to use when constructing the overall access policy of your application. Predefined Roles for each GCP service, an inherent Resource hierarchy and a suite of Policy Intelligence tools are available to all Google Cloud projects and developers, to help understand and control the access control requirements of GCP applications.

Identity Platform

Identity Platform is a set of **software development kits** (**SDKs**) used to provide a customizable authentication service for your GCP-backed application. Identity Platform can be thought of as a counterpart or equivalent to Firebase Authentication which has been described in the earlier section *Firebase Authentication*. Developers using Firebase Authentication can choose to use Identity Platform as a backend for the Firebase UI in place of Firebase's own components. Identity Platform provides the user experience for the access control policies defined and enforced by Cloud IAM.

The Identity Platform includes SDKs for client apps on iOS, Android and the web (browser-based). There are client SDKS for Identity Platform administration tasks in several languages.

The entire user identity lifecycle: signing up a new user, user session login and logout, and credential management, such as password change or upgrading to MFA, can be done with the SDKs that Identity Platform provides.

Identify Platform authentication features

Identity Platform provides the capability to support a number of identity types, at the discretion of the application developer. Some of the identity types supported are as follows:

- **Email/password**: An email address is used as the user identity and as a means of verifying the user. A strong password is associated with the user and managed through secure processes.

- **Social media**: Existing user accounts on federated identity providers, such as Google, Apple, and GitHub, are used to identify the user on this application, and authentication is done through those providers.

   Phone: A phone number identifies a user, and access to that phone is used to authorize a user's identity.

- **Security Assertion Markup Language (SAML)** and **OpenID Connect (OIDC)**: These are industry IAM standards that are used by many corporate systems. Identity Platform can interoperate with systems that use these to extend GCP applications to be included in the **Single Sign On (SSO)** experience within a corporate environment.

- **Custom authorization system**: If none of the existing identity management systems meet the particular needs of an application, Identity Platform provides a set of SDKs that allow a developer to design and implement their own user identity model.

Identity Platform provides the needed support to implement a complete solution for the user-facing side of identity management: self-service signup and profile management, login and logout, and even some levels of account recovery. The product also includes libraries to support the administration of users. Note the choice of words in the previous sentences: Identity Platform provides the needed support, but is not the ready out-of-the-box identity management user experience that Firebase Authentication provides. The developer must select from and incorporate the available functionality from the Identity Platform in their client application. A useful analogy is that of a restaurant menu; while Firebase Authentication offers a number of set, curated meals, Identity Platform offers a large number of à la carte items from which the developer must choose a compatible set of selections to make a satisfying meal.

Like most Google Cloud Platform products, a developer is charged for Identity Platform based on usage. Usage of the Identity Platform is measured in **monthly active users (MAUs)**, which is the number of users that have signed in during a given month, regardless of how many times they accessed the system. Some sign-in methods, such as phone authentication, might incur third-party charges, and so the use of those methods are also charged per message sent.

Asynchronous message handling

An important factor in designing a responsive, reliable application is the distinction between importance and urgency, which was discussed in the previous chapter. An underlying implementation choice is that between synchronous and asynchronous operations, which we will define for our purposes now.

The classic synchronous operation is one that every software developer has dealt with, a function or method call. This is an operation involving two parties: the invoker or caller of a function and the invoked function. The synchronous nature of a method call lies in the strict ordering and rigid sequence of operations, as shown in this sequence diagram of a call to the **add_item** method of a **cart** object:

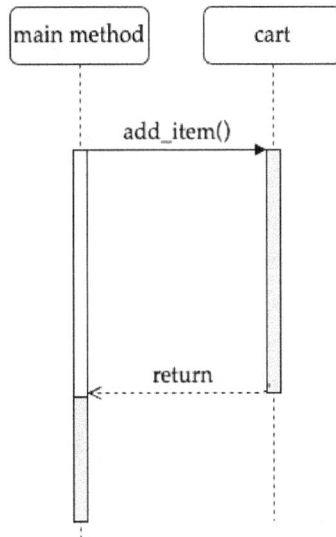

Figure 4.6: Method call sequence diagram

The blue bar represents the location of any instructions being executed. As we can see, when the main method invokes the **add_item** method, it surrenders control of the processor to the code in the cart's method, and the main method only resumes executing when the **add_item** method returns control. The **add_item** method is invoked *synchronously* and operations between the two parties are executed sequentially.

When the invoker of a function is in a different operating system process than the function that is invoked, the term RPC is used. Aside from the cross-process boundary of the invocation and return, nothing is changed from what was described earlier; the invoker waits, in its process, while the remote function executes.

In contrast, an asynchronous operation is one that is invoked by a caller, who does not wait for the invoked function to complete or return control; in fact, control is never relinquished.

Relating these two execution models back to the question of urgency and importance, a synchronous operation is needed to provide an *urgent response*, whereas if a response to a request for an operation is not urgent, an asynchronous method of execution can also be used.

The GCP products we will describe in the following section are two that support the asynchronous execution of operations, which are almost certainly important but not urgent in the manner just described.

Pub/Sub

Pub/Sub is a messaging service. Its sole purpose is to deliver a *message* from the sender to the receiver. The first thing we will discuss is the terminology used in messaging systems to name the entities involved:

- **Messages**: An envelope of data, defined by the application, that is to be delivered from one party to another. The message does not contain any knowledge or forward references to a specific destination.

- **Publishers or message producers**: A process that creates a Message and places it in transit to be received and further processed in the future by some other process.

- **Subscribers or message consumers**: A process that is open to receive Messages and submit them to further processing.

An important point to highlight is that there is no direct connection between a Publisher and a Subscriber. Publishers know nothing of Subscribers, and Subscribers only see the Messages that they receive, not the parties who created them.

Scalability of a messaging architecture

Since a Subscriber that processes a message is independent and in fact unaware of the process that published the message, a message-based approach allows a uniquely fine degree of control over the scale of processing power. Pub/Sub can be configured to horizontally scale the number of subscribers to match the rate at which messages are published to ensure that the queue is kept to a specified number of published messages pending consumption by a subscriber.

Consider the following diagrams in the discussion that follows.

As our application runs at a typical rate, two Processes have produced messages that will have to be processed.

In the first diagram, an existing message was created earlier and placed on the *queue* of messages, referred to as a Topic in Pub/Sub, to be delivered to Subscribers. Our one Subscriber process checks this Topic to see if there are any messages to be processed. At the same time, our two publishers are each enqueuing additional messages:

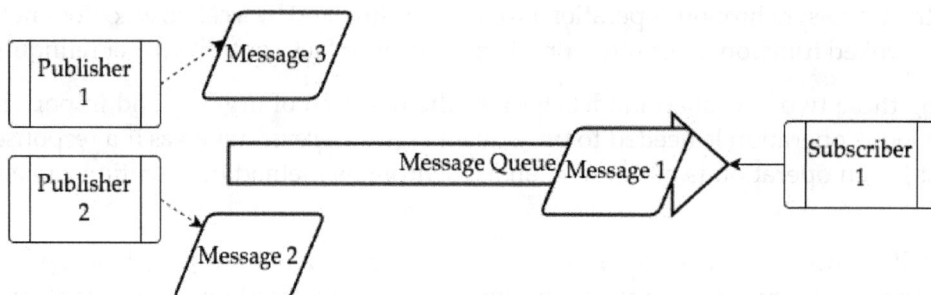

Figure 4.7: The first state of our message processing

At the next step, the subscriber has taken the message from the queue and begins to process it. While this happens, our publishers have placed their new messages on the queue:

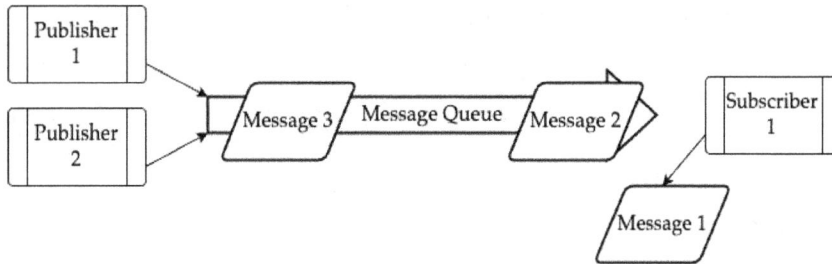

Figure 4.8: The second state of our message processing with a backlog building up

Now, we have more messages on the queue than subscribers, and our publishers are creating new messages. We can increase the number of subscribers to avoid a backlog of queued messages, as shown in the following figure:

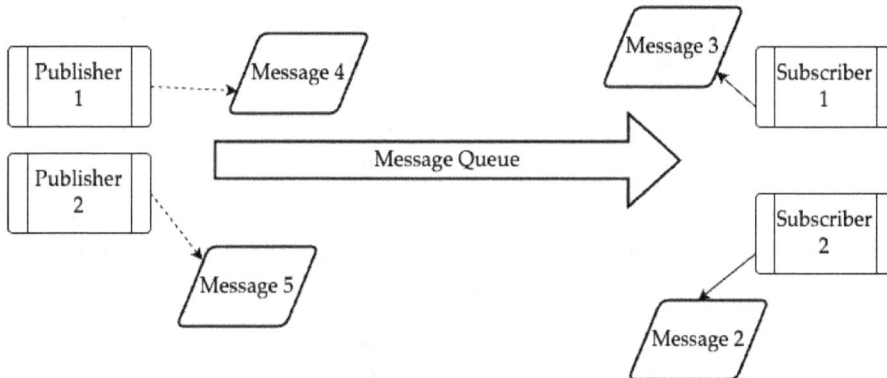

Figure 4.9: The third state of our message processing, a steady state of message consumption

An alternative scaling opportunity that could be performed instead of, or in tandem with, the horizontal scaling depicted previously is the vertical scaling of subscribers to increase their message processing rate. The flexibility to do this sort of adaptive scaling without any risk of disruption to the upstream processes on the publishers' side of the message queue, is possible because of the asynchronous, decoupled relationship between the message generators and their processors.

Evaluating Pub/Sub as a product choice should be based on a consideration of its features, constraints, and cost. The use of Pub/Sub only adds value when paired with a suitable service to implement the subscriber/processor tasks. In such an arrangement, and in a situation where an application can make use of this model, incorporating Pub/Sub can provide hand-in-hand gains in application throughput and reliability. Publishers and Subscribers one-way communication through Pub/Sub occurs on the order of 100 milliseconds, which is paid back in the steady processing rate under load that a Pub/Sub-based architecture achieves.

Pub/Sub is charged with a more complex cost model than many of the products examined thus far. In brief, Pub/Sub is charged based on the following three factors:

- Throughput costs for message transit from Publishers to Subscribers.

- Data transfer costs for messages that cross network regional boundaries.

- Storage costs for snapshots of the queues and messages that are retained after being delivered.

Cloud Tasks

Cloud Tasks is a managed service for the dispatching and delivery of work to a large number of worker tasks. Cloud Tasks is not a compute provider that runs your code; it is the dispatcher of processes that are run on one of the GCP compute products, such as App Engine, Cloud Functions, or a Cloud Run service. Cloud Tasks are similar to Pub/Sub as both are services that allow the asynchronous execution of work to be done, rather than immediate synchronous execution. The key difference between them is that Cloud Tasks publishers are not decoupled from the endpoint that will process the task; a publisher specifies the worker to which a task will be delivered, but without the expectation that it will be executed immediately. Cloud Tasks defers the execution of a specific RPC. Contrast this to Pub/Sub, where the publishers of messages have no knowledge of where the message will be delivered, only that it has been queued to be available until it is delivered somewhere.

The following figure illustrates the running state of a Cloud Tasks-based execution model:

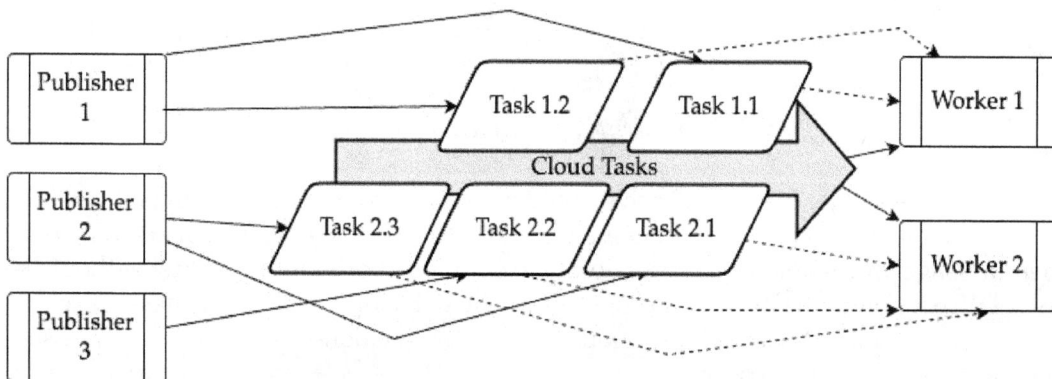

Figure 4.10: Three publishers sending tasks to two subscribers through Cloud Tasks

In this scenario, Publisher 1 has created two tasks and dispatched them to Worker 1 using Cloud Tasks. Concurrently with this, Publisher 2 and Publisher 3 have created three tasks that are dispatched for Worker 2. When Worker 1 is available for work, it will be sent Task 1, and when it finishes processing that task and signals to Cloud Tasks that it is available for work, it will be sent Task 1.2. Similarly, when Worker 2 indicates that it is available for work, Cloud Tasks will first send it Task 2.1 and subsequently Task 2.2 and Task 2.3. The distinction here from Pub/Sub is that Worker 2 will never be sent one of the tasks meant for Worker 1, and likewise, Worker 1 could be idle without being sent a Task dispatched to Worker 2.

Assigning asynchronous work to any available worker instance is not always an option. In a real-world example, consider a system which processes different types of orders: credit card, bank account, etc. You would have to enable every worker to process every order type, which could raise complexity and resource issues, *or* have specialized order processing workers for each type of order, and dispatch an order for eventual fulfillment processing by the correct worker.

Evaluating Cloud Tasks as a product choice must bear its hard limits in mind. Cloud Tasks is abstracted so that it can deliver Tasks to workers configured on virtually any GCP compute product that can provide an HTTP endpoint. Cloud Tasks guarantees that Tasks will be delivered and acknowledged by the designated worker, with configurable retries. Cloud Tasks has a ceiling of 500 **queries per second** (**QPS**) or 500 dispatched tasks per second, unlike Pub/Sub, which scales to any delivery rate needed. Cloud Tasks does not scale workers; it manages the delivery of the tasks, leaving the management of the workers to the service on which they are implemented.

Cloud tasks are charged by usage, as most GCP products. At the time of writing, Cloud Tasks are free for the first 1 million operations per month and charged $0.40 USD per million operations for up to 5 billion per month.

Conclusion

There are several technical requirements for a *distributed* application-specifically to consider, and for each of these, GCP offers multiple options to choose from. The selection of products can be made by reviewing the suitability of each option against the application feature under scrutiny and considered in relation to the other products chosen. Certain compute products may be a better or worse fit with specific storage services. Rather than scoring each product's use in isolation, the goal is to select the set of products that provide the greatest collective value.

Cost factors were reviewed as material cost, especially for services that can scale up by orders of magnitude, should be considered as strongly as the technical capabilities of a product.

With this, the reader has the information needed to evaluate the GCP products discussed and a framework for researching and describing the relevant aspects of any of the other products that were not explicitly covered herein.

The next chapter turns its attention to the portions of a system that are furthest from GCP, the client platform application. The three most popular client platforms: browser-based web applications, iOS, and Android mobile apps will be described along with development options for each.

Join our Discord space

Join our Discord workspace for latest updates, offers, tech happenings around the world, new releases, and sessions with the authors:

https://discord.bpbonline.com

Section 2:
Cloud Backed Application Architecture

CHAPTER 5
Client-side Technology Choices

Introduction

How a user accesses your product is what defines your app to them. In recent years, this point of interaction has been embodied by a few classes of devices: smartphones or tablets and desktop or notebook computers. This chapter will explore the different technologies used to represent a computer-based system to the human actors who are the primary users and reason for that system. The reader will be introduced to the development tools and techniques for optimizing developer effort while also producing the best user experience on each client platform.

Structure

The following topics will be covered in this chapter:

- Native mobile applications
- Cross-platform mobile frameworks
- Web applications
- Desktop client applications
- In-browser client applications
- Chatbots and voice agents

Objectives

Mobile application development, web apps, and local desktop or in-browser applications all have their own strengths and potential markets. This chapter summarizes common and up-and-coming client-side technologies that act as the public face of your product. The costs of both initial development and maintaining an application on multiple platforms will be explored. The reader will understand the considerations in choosing to develop their user interface as a platform-native client app, a cross-platform client app, a browser-based web application, or some combination of these.

The taxonomy of client development platforms and tools is illustrated in the following figure:

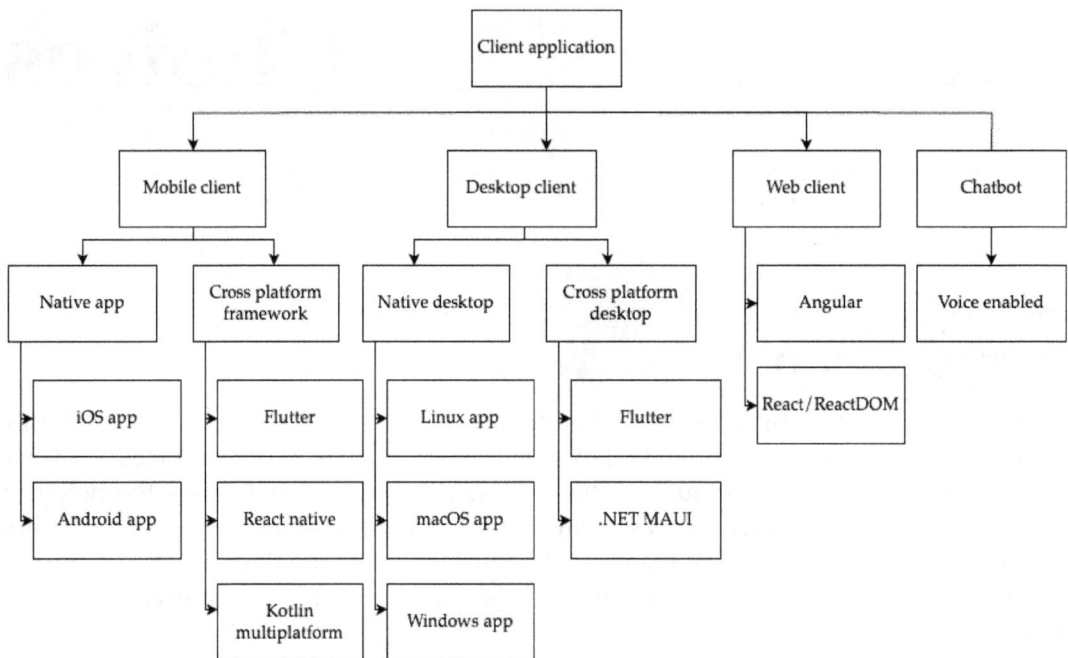

Figure 5.1: *Client application development taxonomy*

Native mobile applications

The applications you use on your smartphone or tablet, showcasing the best, unique and newest **user interface (UI)** features, are almost certainly written using the native, platform-specific development frameworks and libraries for that phone or tablet OS. A great scrolling experience, the smoothest window management, and the latest icon animations are accomplished using UI features that are specific to the hardware and operating system.

The incentive for the developer to use these vendor-specific libraries in an application is to have the best-looking and most idiomatic app possible. The vendors' incentive to you using their development tools is to have applications that are available only on their platform, or with the best user experience on their platform, driving more users to their hardware.

There is, of course, a downside for the developer: cross-platform incompatibility. An iOS application will not run on Android and vice-versa. The two platform application models are different enough to make porting the source code from one to the other difficult, to the point of impracticality.

We will now briefly describe the dominant tools for native platform development on Android, iOS, and iPadOS. We will also discuss the techniques for interfacing with GCP products from within those native applications.

Android development tools

Native Android client applications are developed primarily using Android Studio, Google's free **integrated development environment** (IDE). There are other development toolchains, some other IDEs similar to Android Studio, such as IntelliJ IDEA, and some collections of command-line tools run from a terminal window.

Android Studio is available for Windows, Mac, and Linux operating systems, and the installation includes a comprehensive suite of tools. An editor, Android runtime, compiler, build system, an interactive debugger, and device simulators for many Android phones and tablets are all integrated within Android Studio.

Android apps can be written in several programming languages. Java, Kotlin, C++, C#, Node.js, Ruby, and Go are all popular choices, but the languages with the greatest support by the primary tools are Kotlin and Java. Kotlin is a derivative, or perhaps evolution of the Java language and Java programmers find that they can recognize and understand most Kotlin constructs. While Google promotes Kotlin for new application development, Java is a first-class citizen in the Android ecosystem and is the most commonly used in community support and third-party examples.

When developing an Android app using Google's recommended tools, it seems predictable that a developer would find good support for interoperating with other Google products, such as GCP services. This assumption is true. Google Cloud provides client libraries that encapsulate much of the boilerplate code of accessing GCP products in language-specific idiomatic code. The amount of code required of the application developer to specify their GCP project metadata and credentials is often more than the code required to perform any specific GCP product operation.

As an example, the code to upload a local file from a client application to a Google Cloud Storage BLOB is as simple as this snippet of Java:

```
String bucketName = "my-unique-bucket";
String fileName = "readme.txt";
Storage storage = StorageOptions.newBuilder()
```

```
    .setProjectId(projectId).build().getService();
BlobId blobId = BlobId.of(bucketName, fileName);
BlobInfo blobInfo = BlobInfo.newBuilder(blobId)
    .setContentType("text/plain").build();
storage.createFrom(blobInfo, Paths.get(fileName));
```

Apart from these native language client-side libraries for most Google Cloud Platform products, a developer can also use a language agnostic **REpresentational State Transfer** (**REST**) API for any GCP product from within the client code. While more work and more code, this approach offers the advantage of being nearly identical in all client applications, regardless of language or version.

iOS development tools

For developing iOS and iPadOS applications (hereafter collectively referred to as iOS), Apple provides Xcode. Xcode is available for all users of macOS and is similar to Android Studio in scope. Source editors, an interactive debugger, simulators for specific Apple devices and OS versions, and a build system are all bundled into Xcode.

While people do write iOS applications in a variety of languages, Apple exerts much tighter control over the development ecosystem for iOS than Google does for Android. This results in a more consistent and predictable user experience for the users of Apple devices and a narrower set of toolchain choices for developers. Apps for iOS can be developed in Swift, and Objective-C. While other languages can be used through various third-party tools and wrappers, these are the primary languages supported in Xcode for iOS. Objective-C is a fairly old language, and Apple strongly encourages developers to use Swift for new application development.

Google does not provide the same full set of native libraries for iOS as they do for Android development. However, developers can access the full set of GCP products through their REST APIs, which are language and client-agnostic. Additionally, many GCP products are available through Firebase interfaces that provide most of the functionality of the service through a Firebase mediator. For example, here is a Swift code snippet that uses Cloud Storage for Firebase to upload a file to a Google Cloud Storage **Binary Large Object** (**BLOB**):

```swift
// File on local client
let localFile = URL(string: "resources/readme.txt")!

// Create a reference to the destination Storage BLOB
let storageRef = storageRef.child("files/readme.txt")

// Upload the file
let uploadTask = storageRef.putFile(from: localFile, metadata: nil) {
metadata, error in
```

```
guard let metadata = metadata else {
    // Error occurred
    return
}
```

While GCP products differ in the exact mechanisms used to support native iOS and Android client application development, the equivalent GCP functionality is available to both. If a developer chooses to build separate native applications for both mobile platforms, there are much larger differences in their codebases than the GCP interfaces, and this should be a minor consideration.

Cross-platform mobile frameworks

One step towards a common codebase and, correspondingly, one step away from a completely native application user experience is the use of a cross-platform application framework. This is a set of code classes and libraries that offer an abstracted or generic view of a mobile application and its components, such as panes, menus, icons, and scrolling lists. Instead of coding calls to Android or iOS classes such as *LinearLayout+ScrollView* and *UiTableView*, respectively, a developer would use a *ListView* (in Flutter), which would be rendered as a vertically scrolling list on either Android or iOS using the native widgets on each platform.

Cross-platform compatibility and a native application look and feel like a panacea. In fact, this is a good fit for the common user interface and experience elements on both platforms, but there is a gap between this and native application frameworks. The following Venn diagram depicts where a cross-platform framework is lacking:

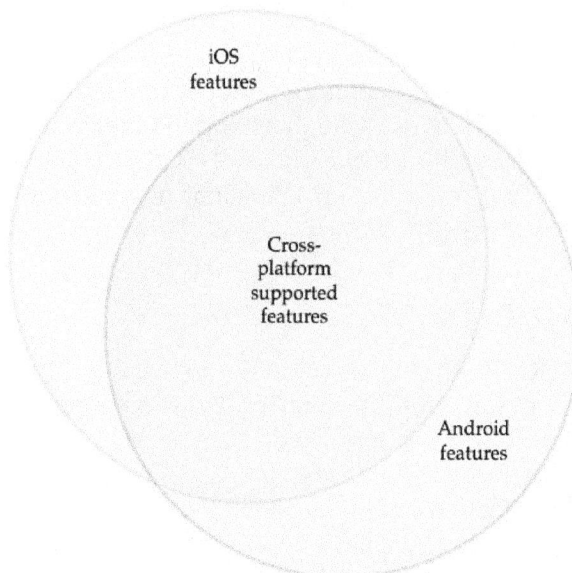

Figure 5.2: *Cross-platform features*

While most concepts and user interface elements are common for all mobile platforms, there are a number of features that are unique to Apple, Android, or specific devices under each of these umbrellas. Such iOS features as floating action buttons have no equivalent on Android, while Android's navigation drawer has no iOS counterpart. Fine-grained control of such platform-specific features often requires a developer to use a native mobile application framework. Additionally, direct use of the native implementation of a feature will be more performant than the indirect use or the generic equivalent provided through a cross-platform abstraction.

Flutter

Flutter is a framework for building client applications that run natively on iOS and Android. In addition, Flutter can build web applications for Windows, macOS, and Linux.

Flutter is an open-source project supported by Google. Flutter applications are written in Dart, an open-source programming language. Google provides client libraries for several GCP products and other Google products such as Google Translate and Docs. While a developer can use the REST APIs to access all GCP services, using native libraries where available will result in simpler and less error-prone code.

React Native

React Native is an open-source user interface framework developed by Meta. React Native can build applications that are rendered natively on iOS and Android. React Native applications are written in JavaScript, which guarantees a large body of technical resources. One strength of React Native is the extensive, committed developer community and their available technical knowledge.

Google does not offer React Native client libraries for GCP products. Several GCP products can be used from React Native apps through a supplied mediator Firebase client library, similar to the support described for iOS earlier. All GCP products can be accessed using their universal REST APIs through an HTTPS client or by using each product's gRPC interface through a JavaScript gRPC library.

Kotlin Multiplatform

Kotlin Multiplatform (KMP) is a feature of the Kotlin language that takes a very different approach from Flutter. Kotlin Multiplatform provides a framework for separating the business and control flow logic of an application from the UI code, with the understanding that the former is device-independent, and the latter is implemented using platform-specific code. So, while Flutter implements all the application's code, including UI rendering, a KMP application isolates the User Interface code into modules that are developed separately for iOS and Android using the native frameworks for each.

The UI code could be developed using Java or Kotlin on Android and Swift on iOS. JetBrains, the creator of KMP, also offers declarative UI toolkits such as Compose Multiplatform that allow developers to create shared UIs across Android, iOS, desktop, and web applications. Applications built with this cross-platform UI framework are closer in effect to the Flutter app; while the client code is rendered using native platform frameworks, the level of specification and control do not include features that are unique to one platform.

Support for Google Cloud Platform products in KMP applications is inherent in Google's support of the Kotlin language. The points where a client application will interface with GCP services would be within the business logic modules of a KMP application, which are coded in the Kotlin language. Google provides the Kotlin language libraries for several GCP products, including Cloud Storage, Bigtable, Firestore and Pub/Sub, along with others. If a particular GCP product does not yet provide a Kotlin library, the product's REST API can be used to access all its features.

Web applications

A web client application does not refer to a server-side rendered site, such as a web page using markup languages such as HTML and CSS. With the debut of JavaScript (circa 1996), web pages were able to download code to the browser that would execute rather than just be rendered by the browser. When an application is referred to as a web application, it consists of code that is run within the client's or end user's browser on their device, be that a desktop, tablet, or phone.

JavaScript is the programming language that all modern browsers can execute, and which web client apps are written in. However, the complexities of a typical web application lead practically all sizable web clients to be written using a framework or libraries of JavaScript modules.

We will describe the frameworks and architecture considerations in detail in a later section on in-browser client applications.

Desktop client applications

While many distributed applications offer platform-specific mobile frontends, for several years, the trend has been to rely on browser-based clients for desktop users.

Note: Desktop in this usage refers not only to desktop PCs but also to laptops, or in general, a computer with a keyboard and mouse.

The reason for this is the increasing capabilities of desktop browsers and the divergence of the desktop operating systems. Writing separate versions of an application for different versions of Windows, macOS, and Linux operating systems is significant work. The developers of browsers such as Chrome and Safari have put that effort into making their products render the same web pages and in-browser apps on these different client OSes. So, if a client developer writes their application using the features offered by these browsers, they can be isolated from the cross-platform differences and concerns.

However, there are some features that are not available or performance requirements that cannot be met by an in-browser web client application. In these cases, a binary native to the desktop operating system is the solution.

Native desktop development

Desktop applications are developed in a wide variety of programming languages and supporting frameworks and libraries. Python, Go, C++, Ruby, Java, and other languages are available and supported to some degree within desktop application development environments. For any of these, Google offers native language client-side libraries that can be used to access their GCP products from a client application.

The ultimate in-client responsiveness and familiar look-and-feel will be achieved by writing desktop applications in the preferred language and framework for each operating system. Choosing the ideal language and framework for each operating system is an involved process and involves balancing the vendor's (Apple and Microsoft) recommendations against community support and developer preference. As a rule of thumb, if a developer is making an investment in native desktop development, the vendor-recommended solutions will provide access to the most features and introduce the least friction in the development experience. Those vendors' recommended development tools for each client OS are identified as follows:

- **Windows**: Microsoft provides Visual Studio, an IDE that is useful for more than just Windows development. The strongest development framework and language support offered within Visual Studio is naturally for Windows development on Windows desktop PCs. This target is supported by Microsoft Foundation Classes and Windows Presentation Foundation frameworks which can be used with several languages, but C# is the premier language for Windows application development.

- **macOS**: Apple has always invested heavily in the developer community's tools and has provided strong development tools and support. Xcode is the suite of tools gathered under an IDE that Apple provides on macOS to develop applications for all Apple platforms, including macOS desktop applications. Swift is Apple's language of choice for app development, and while Objective-C is supported, it is meant to support older codebases, and new application development should favor using Swift. Apple offers a few application and UI frameworks: SwiftUI and AppKit are both interactive app builders in which a developer writes custom code to add application-specific behavior and business logic. The underlying macOS application framework, Cocoa, provides access to all macOS UI features and can be used by a developer without any app builder.

- **Linux GUI apps**: Linux desktop **graphical user interface (GUI)** applications are harder to define an environment for, than for Windows or macOS as there is no one official vendor whose standard is canonical. Instead, we will discuss the popular and community supported framework that has evolved and has broad support in many Linux distributions, GTK.

GTK is an open-source user interface toolkit maintained by the GTK Team, contributors that include several of the most prominent providers of Linux products, as well as many individuals whose combined expertise keeps GTK both technically pertinent and vendor agnostic. GTK can also produce apps for macOS and Windows with a native look and feel, although GTK support for new or specialized platform-specific features lags behind that support in Apple and Microsoft development tools.

GTK provides a collection of cooperative UI elements referred to as widgets. GTK is available for many programming languages and relies heavily on the principles of object-oriented programming to arrange and customize the user interface elements it encodes. As well as the construction of an application's UI through code, there are several app builders and frameworks that provide a layer above GTK's class hierarchy.

Cross-platform desktop development

There are many products that support the development of applications for deployment on multiple desktop client platforms. The most popular and widely supported ones that follow include products that are provided by major platform vendors and are explicitly supported by GCP:

- **Flutter**: Flutter was discussed earlier in the chapter as an option for multi-platform mobile application development. The same multi-platform support in Flutter includes the three desktop environments, and the same codebase used to develop mobile applications can support desktop client applications. As well as generating native client UI components for Windows, macOS, and Linux, the same GCP support offered for mobile apps is available for all Flutter apps. Therefore, native Dart libraries are provided for many GCP products, and any services' REST APIs can be used to access its complete feature set. As well as the Flutter components within the Dart language, Flutter for desktop includes plug-ins that are specific to each desktop environment and can be used to interact with custom native code written in the platform's language of choice.

- **.NET MAUI**: .NET is Microsoft's cross-platform framework for building apps and cloud services. .NET is free and open-source and is contributed to by a large developer community, but with a leaning towards developers experienced in Microsoft platforms.

  .NET Multi-platform App UI (MAUI) is a specific framework within .NET that supports the development of cross-platform desktop and mobile apps. There are several third-party development environments that can be used to develop MAUI applications, but Microsoft Visual Studio Code is the preferred and most popular choice. .NET applications can be written in C# or F#, the two can be mixed in the same project.

Google provides .NET client libraries for all GCP products. In addition, there are popular, value-added third-party client libraries that support connecting to GCP products from .NET client applications. Finally, the REST APIs of any GCP product can be used from a .NET MAUI application.

In-browser client applications

A client application that runs completely within, or more accurately, is executed by a web browser has many advantages. Such an application can delivered to the client when it is invoked so that there is central control over the version of an application that the user executes. Cross-platform compatibility is entrusted to the few developers of browsers rather than being the responsibility of thousands of individual application developers. Finally, the security of a *web application,* as they are commonly called, is somewhat guaranteed by the sandbox environment imposed by a browser; there is limited access to local resources such as root directories of disks or USB ports.

These strengths of the browser environment can also be viewed as limitations or caveats from a different point of view. The same sandbox environment, preventing a rogue or defective web application from overwriting or uploading sensitive files, also curtails your application's ability to copy data to a thumb drive. The advantage of downloading the application just in time also means that the application is unavailable or useless without an internet connection. Finally, as has been seen as a recurring pattern, the further an application is from the native operating system and user interface features, the fewer of that native platform's unique features will be available for use in the application.

With all of that considered, a web application is a good choice for an application where much of the functionality is in the cloud, and a consistent experience across client platforms is more desirable than the most native look and feel on any particular platform.

Web application programming languages

The language that is supported in all major browsers is *JavaScript*, which is also meant to include its derivative, *TypeScript*. There are many frameworks and libraries that are used in frontend web application development, such as *React* and *Angular*, but these are actually JavaScript frameworks that present a high-level grammar and component hierarchy but are effectively *macros* for JavaScript code that is executed by a browser. These frameworks add high-level support for user interface elements and user interaction, but the code that ties these together and implements business logic is written in JavaScript. To work effectively with these frameworks, a developer must first understand JavaScript.

Angular

Angular is an open-source web application framework that was created and actively maintained by Google based on an earlier project, AngularJS. Angular is contributed to by a wide community of corporate and individual contributors.

Angular developers write declarative statements using HTML templates, which are compiled into JavaScript instructions and optimized based on static analysis of the declared templates. Strictly speaking, Angular compiles into TypeScript, which is a statically typed language extended from JavaScript. TypeScript is supported by all major browsers as part of JavaScript support, so the distinction between the two has no effect on portability but does aid in Angular's optimization of compiled code.

Google does not provide specific Angular client libraries for GCP products. There are several techniques that can be used to access Google Cloud Platform services from an Angular app. In the most direct solution, the Node.js client library for any GCP product is accessed from within Angular declarative components and GCP documentation offers examples of doing so. A more involved solution includes creating a backend service to act as a server-side proxy for GCP product access and invoking that proxy service from an Angular application.

React and ReactDOM

React is a library for rendering UI components, written in JavaScript. React extended JavaScript with the Markdown syntax, known as JSX. React is open-source, created and released to the public by Facebook after it has been in use there internally.

React is not a framework for building an application, and so it is used with a companion library to make client applications. For web applications, React is used in combination with the ReactDOM package which provides the methods needed to manipulate objects within the browser **Document Object Model (DOM)**.

Google Cloud Platform supports React, but for components deployed to Google Cloud rather than as a local client of GCP services. There are a few ways to access most GCP products from a React/ReactDOM web client.

Firebase offers proxy services for several GCP products, such as Cloud Storage. This is the solution that was described for React Native applications earlier in the section *Cross-platform mobile frameworks*. For more direct control using more the same APIs that are used in other client platforms, the REST JSON APIs and gRPC APIs for GCP products can be used from JavaScript, and thus from React/ReactDOM. This solution is also supported by GCP for React Native mobile applications.

Web application development tools

The need for integrated environments, bringing together design tools, code editors, debuggers, and version control, is just as strong for web applications as for any other type of component. Due to their inherently distributed nature, web applications are best developed using tools that are themselves integrated with web services and have strong collaboration features. Some of the best and most popular tools are Visual Studio Code, IntelliJ IDEA, Android Studio, WebStorm, and Codeanywhere. Of this list, Codeanywhere stands out for being a web application itself, with the cross-platform support and internet access requirement that it confers.

GCP support for web application clients

There are many ways that web applications can access GCP products. Google provides a Node.js client library for all GCP products, which is the highest level of support and functionality for application structures that can utilize it. The Google API Client Library for JavaScript, aka *gapi*, provides access to the JSON API of many Google services, including GCP products such as Cloud Storage and Pub/Sub. There are also popular third-party libraries that can be used to access the JSON and gRPC APIs of GCP services.

Chatbots and voice agents

A new, novel and increasingly popular user interface is that of a chatbot. A chatbot is a pseudo-conversational interface to an application's features, relying on natural language to manipulate the state of a user session. Examples: the use of Google Assistant to control smart-home devices, play music or search the web. Another chatbot with a very different user experience is the WHO chatbot of the World Health Organization, available on Facebook Messenger.

Chatbots and GCP

There are many frameworks for developing a chatbot, some of which rely on LLMs such as OpenAI's ChatGPT or Gemini by Google. These frameworks typically include frontend and backend components written in suitable languages, such as a React frontend and Python for the backend portion.

The experience of tying a chatbot to GCP products varies greatly depending on the backend and level of customization desired. Gemini itself is integrated into Google Cloud as Gemini for Google Cloud and can help GCP developers with coding assistance, data analysis, and cloud application administration. For integrating Gemini into your applications functionality, as opposed to its management, the Vertex AI API is used to train ML models, and Google's Conversational Agents, aka DialogFlow CX, are used to build conversational interfaces. The Vertex AI Agent Builder is an application builder for conversational agents.

For access to GCP products in use cases other than those that are supported by these products, or for chatbots built with non-Google backends, such as OpenAI's products, a recommended path is to select languages for the frontend and backend tiers of the chatbot implementation that are well-supported by GCP APIs. For example, if user queries involve retrieving content from Google Cloud Storage buckets, a chatbot backend written in Python could use the GCP Python client libraries to fetch the relevant content called for by the user request.

Any use of a large language model introduces the risk of either unintended or intentional misuse and of harmful content being generated. The tools and processes included in the Google Responsible Generative AI Toolkit should be used to ensure the safety and privacy of users of a chatbot.

Chatbot voice frontends

The use of voice, rather than keyboard input, to talk to a chatbot requires the transcription of user speech to text and the complementary conversion of the computer's textual response to speech.

As much as the common factors of platform and programming language support, there are additional considerations in selecting voice services: language and dialect support. A speech transcriber must be trained in the natural languages that an application's users might speak and should be able to reliably auto-detect the language being spoken. Similarly, audio speech generated by a computer must be comprehensible by users of the application, and pronunciation and inflection must be appropriate to the language, dialect, and tone of the text being converted.

There are two types of service that are required of a voice frontend:

- **Transcription**: Transcription services rely on trained machine learning models and are very CPU-intensive. There are many open-source and commercial speech transcription packages, both local and cloud-based. The Whisper library is free from OpenAI and runs ML models locally to intesrpret speech. A companion product, the OpenAI API for Whisper, runs the models on OpenAI's cloud for use with clients that lack sufficient compute power to run the transcription locally. The Google Speech-to-text API provides a distributed transcription service that relies on both local and cloud components to provide streaming and bulk speech transcription

- **Text-to-speech**: The conversion of text to speech is computationally demanding but is a more straightforward problem than transcription, with many available solutions. These services are referred to as **text-to-speech** (**TTS**) engines. Some well-known and high-quality products are eSpeak, Mozilla TTS, and MaryTTS. While there are products with cloud-based backends, many produce good-quality speech running on typical client platform hardware.

Use of GCP with speech: The introduction of a speech transcriber and text-to-speech frontend is a layer above a text chatbot's existing functionality and should not affect the use of GCP services within the chatbot client application. Wherever a chatbot application has an invocation of a Google Cloud service, the application should present user input and output the response, whether directly as text or converted from and to audio.

Conclusion

This chapter reviewed the different client platforms that are available to provide a portal for users into a distributed system. The different development paradigms, like native, compatibility layers and browser-based, were discussed, along with a description of some of the languages and tools that are used for each of these.

To tie these application models to our Google Cloud focus, the chapter identified the techniques used to access GCP services from each of these types of applications, including the direct support provided by Google.

In the next chapter, we will focus on the other side of the fence between client and server, the design considerations, and methodology for decomposing the backend functionality to minimize hard dependencies between specific implementations of application and infrastructure features. We will learn how to design components with interfaces that are accessible from as many technologies and in as many contexts as possible.

Join our Discord space

Join our Discord workspace for latest updates, offers, tech happenings around the world, new releases, and sessions with the authors:

https://discord.bpbonline.com

CHAPTER 6
Cloud Services at the Backend Border

Introduction

Google Cloud Platform includes many rich services, among which there is some overlap in functionality. Additionally, some of these products have competing or conflicting requirements. These two factors can result in a complicated architecture that reflects particular aspects and idiosyncrasies of the selected cloud service components. A robust, long-lived application avoids such abstraction leaks and presents well-defined, capable public interfaces at the border between tiers. Public APIs should offer distinct operations, striving for component hermeticity that guarantees predictable, visible effects of defined requests and states.

This chapter presents key design considerations and recipes for addressing these concerns in the high-level system design of a distributed application. These practices yield applications that can adapt to the one constant, change, in computing technology.

Structure

The following topics will be covered in this chapter:

- Maintaining backend agnostic clients
- Visibility levels to the client
- Planning migration to substitute or equivalent cloud services

- Visibility between cloud services
- Identifying and packaging tightly coupled services

Maintaining backend agnostic clients

The line separating client-side code, running on the platforms described in *Chapter 5 Client-side Technology Choices,* and cloud or server-side code should be the hardest line in an application's design. By this it is meant that the code on either side of that line should have as little view or consideration of the implementation of components on the other side. Phrased differently, the interfaces that are visible between client and cloud platforms should be as narrow and as shallow as possible. Narrow in this context means defining as few methods, while shallow means having as simple parameters and return values as needed to get the job done.

Client and server components should access the other only through public methods that converge on parameters and return values that contain only logical, platform-independent data types. There is an overarching systems design maxim that all APIs should be as narrow as possible, composed of atomic operations, and the benefits of adhering to this principle are magnified by some specific aspects of a client/cloud interface. We will review both the general principle and the stronger considerations when using a cloud service.

General API design principles

There are many general patterns for successful API design in software engineering. What follows is not an exhaustive list, nor a deep dive, but a brief review of major relevant points that will be expanded on in the client/cloud-specific sections to follow.

To promote an easily understood API, use standard, easily digestible formats for data interchange.

Parameter lists, responses, and exported types should be readable and usable without incurring a tax. The tax, in this case, is an incurred, indirect cost that must be paid to unlock the directly purchased asset. To put this in context, if you adopt a new or uncommon data format in your parameter lists that would require most users of your API to spend time installing, learning, or debugging this new format, those additional tasks are a tax. No matter how novel or arguably better a new format is, your users do not want to spend their valuable time and resources on the tax. In addition, there are tools, documentation, and community support for existing, well-known standards that users of a novel format cannot take advantage of. If your data exchange requires more than a few instances of simple types, such as ints or strings, encode complex types using JSON. Your users are either already familiar with JSON or will find that the large amount of available documentation and tooling makes ramping up easy. In addition, learning such standards is an investment in broadly useful technical skills.

To keep a design simple, avoid lengthy, complicated parameter lists.

Encoding and decoding a long list of parameters is an exercise in complexity. All methods should be critically examined for an excessive number of parameters. Two tests can be applied to each parameter of a method to determine if it can be removed:

- **Flag the parameter as an unused parameter**: Does this parameter present information that is used by the invoked method?

- **Identify the parameter as a redundant parameter**: Is this parameter needed to provide the necessary information, and can the information be inferred from other parameters' values or visible state?

An additional refinement can be used to shorten a parameter list, overly precise parameters. The specification of individual parameters, which are actually individual details of one value, should be refactored into compound types. For example, two parameters **first_name: string, last_name:string** could be replaced by the one parameter **full_name: string[]**

Software modules or packages gain brevity, comprehension, and robustness from the definition and utilization of custom domain and implementation-specific data types. In a classic example, this snippet of C allows us to replace four fields with one throughout a codebase:

```
typedef struct Rectangle {
    int x, y;
    int width;
    int height;
} Rectangle;
```

Without this type definition, code that compares two rectangles requires undue effort to understand and verify:

```
int [] overlap_region;
...
overlap_region = overlap(shape1_left, shape1_top, shape1_width, shape1_height,
    shape2_left, shape2_top, shape2_width, shape2_height);
overlap_left = overlap_region[0];
overlap_top = overlap_region[1];
overlap_width = overlap_region[2];
overlap_height = overlap_region[3];
```

This code, which makes use of our custom Rectangle type, makes the intent more clear and is more compact:

```
Rectangle overlap_region;
...
overlap_region = find_overlap(shape1, shape2);
```

The second snippet provides several advantages, with greater brevity, contextual awareness, and reliability as the first snippet relies on unenforced array boundaries.

A more complex example would involve nested types or types with a larger number of constituent fields.

Responses should be easily understood by the clients of an API.

Responses have greater potential than parameters to introduce confusion and, thus, merit even greater attention regarding ease of comprehension. The reason for this is that while the parameters of a method are items that you expect a client of the API to possess, and have some knowledge of the response is an artifact of the invoked method. Since the response is a piece of the service that provides the API, it thus may be completely foreign to the caller. A response may contain a custom type defined and exported by the API or a value that is relevant within the environment of the API provider.

To avoid requiring detailed knowledge of the invoked service, the service API's responses should be well-defined and documented, and not incur heavy taxes as described earlier in this section. Use standard, idiomatic response codes, such as HTTP response codes for an HTTP API; return data in a format such as JSON with descriptive metadata; and provide necessary response headers. As an example, the following response contains descriptive metadata in the names that makes meanings clear and aid in documentation:

```
{
    "product_list": [
        {
            "product_id": "S001A",
            "quantity_in_stock": 25
        },
        {
            "product_id": "Z010A",
            "quantity_in_stock": 12
        },
        {
            "product_id": "Z095B",
            "quantity_in_stock": 0
        }
    ],
    "page»": 10,
    "max_items_per_page": 3
}
```

Keep APIs narrow to make the intent of methods clear and usage of the API flexible.

Another approach is to use a different remote invocation mechanism, such as gRPC, an open-source remote procedure call framework that is well supported by Google and has some level of support from Amazon and other cloud providers. gRPC libraries provide language and platform idiomatic request and response fields which abstract away the platform-specific data formats of parameters and return values of remote methods.

While a service must be fully featured, providing for all potential use cases, the desire to be all things to all users should not result in an API with many methods or with methods whose responsibilities vary based on the parameters' values or on the sequence of events. A given component should represent one thing and do it well. While there is no hard limit for how many operations are too many for a component or service or how atomic a method should be, there are some tests an API developer can apply to a proposed design to detect possibly overly precise or overly broad methods:

- **Too precise**: If two methods are tightly coupled so that a call to the first method is *only* made as a precursor to the second method, and the second method *must* always be prefaced by the first. The two are most likely one operation and should be combined into a single method.

- **Too broad**: A method that takes in a variety of data and operates on different parts of it, based on some discriminating parameter or flag, may actually be multiple distinct operations under one umbrella name. Refactoring these behaviors into independent methods will allow greater flexibility in their application to more use cases, lower overhead per invocation, and easier understanding of each method's purpose.

Special considerations for client or cloud interfaces

The previous section described several best practices of API design and techniques for implementing them, regardless of platform. These principles bring benefit to any situation but in a use case where an API is used to cross a major topographical boundary, such as that between a local client app and a cloud-based service, the gains are magnified, or more accurately, the **price** of **not** following them is magnified when compared to the average within-boundary case. We will now revisit the same set of design patterns and identify their benefits, which are amplified when applied to a cross-platform API.

The use of standard, easily digestible formats allows common understanding when involving multiple platforms.

A cloud platform, such as GCP, is made up of many related but independent services. It is a natural outcome of their development that these services will share highly specialized data types and formats due to their internal common ground and the need for them to interoperate. Such specialized data types are idiosyncratic, possessing attributes and design patterns that evolved to meet specific requirements within the platform. This presents a problem for clients of that platform; those specialized types and formats may not be familiar or translate efficiently into every client platform.

Consider a mobile app that makes heavy direct use of many GCP products; the amount of memory or open sockets that is the norm on a GCP component is likely to be prohibitive on a phone.

Another aspect of portability is one of grammar: a binary resource bundle format that is standard on iOS might have no direct equivalent in a cloud database product.

These challenges to interoperability are reduced if parameters are encoded by the client as JSON and responses are supplied by the service in JSON. A mutual format, used on each side of an API, protects both parties from having to accommodate foreign or incompatible formats and values.

Avoiding lengthy, complicated parameter lists reduces cross-platform translation and traffic.

The presence of many parameters can be a challenge to code readability and a signal that a function may have vague or multiple responsibilities, which hinders reuse. When a function is called locally, parameters may be passed by value or by reference, with the latter being relatively inexpensive: a pointer or handle is small and easily obtained. When a function is invoked remotely, the luxury of low-cost references is no longer a given.

A remote reference can be implemented in different ways, but in the end, there is always an address, albeit a logical one in a context rather than an offset in virtual memory, passed as the remote handle. To make use of this remote reference, there must be some means of translating that handle's value into the location of the actual object in the platform of origin's memory. This sort of resolution is highly optimized in modern **remote procedure call (RPC)** mechanisms, but it is not *zero* cost, whereas a local memory address is. In the case of a complex object, a remote reference is often implemented as a proxy object that itself has internal logic to retrieve the attributes of the remote object as they are needed.

As the number of parameters to a remote method increases, each parameter has one of two preparatory operations: either its value is serialized, or a remote reference is constructed and then serialized. Then each of these serialized parameters is sent over a network, which is an additional cost over local function calls, and finally, it is deserialized by the receiver. When one of the remote proxies described earlier is used, it may generate more network traffic as it fetches the values of attributes that are stored remotely on the platform of origin.

These considerations are masked by the RPC mechanism used, and those mechanisms are optimized to the point where the overhead of one or a few parameters is not a consideration in API design. However, excessively lengthy parameter lists will inflate this overhead, and at some point, the impact will be noticed. At some further point, the impact will be significant, and at a yet further point, the impact will be harmful. Keeping the parameter lists simple and brief is the best way to prevent those points from being reached.

Keeping responses easy to understand reduces cross-platform imposed paradigm shifts.

A remote method call is expensive, and it incurs architectural complexity and runtime cost over that of a local function. If a design has been vetted and a remote method passes review, there must be good reasons to justify its existence. The most common and obvious justification is to access states or capabilities that are not practically available on the invoking platform.

Let us dissect that statement into the following two parts:

- **First**: *state...not practically available* refers to some data that is simply located elsewhere. This could be a value in an in-memory key-value cache, the result of a complex query on a set of database tables, or the current global counter value from a transaction processing system. Whatever the information is, if it is available on some other remote platform, that platform should publish an API to make the information available where it is needed.

- Now for the other part of the justification, *capabilities ...not practically available.*, there are things that some compute platforms are good at and some that they are not. Delegating operations to a platform where they are more practical is another valid reason for a remote procedure call. Complex, parallelizable operations, such as edge detection on many digital images and machine learning model training, are prohibitively expensive to execute on any arbitrary client platform. A cloud service can bring terabytes of RAM and hundreds of processors to bear on a problem, providing capabilities that a phone or laptop would be unable to match.

With this established, there is an implied disconnect between concepts and structures that are idiomatic on the invoker and on the remote provider platforms. Having established that the two sides of an RPC are fundamentally different, their common practices and implementation patterns are also different.

With this built-in tendency towards counterintuitive implementation details across platforms, the need to simplify methods' responses is even stronger. There is significant work for the client of a remote API in understanding the concepts, design patterns, and implementation details of the foreign platform, so API developers should do what they can to reduce the overall cognitive load of their API. Fewer fields, good naming, and better documentation can all serve as counterweights to the comprehension challenges introduced by a remote platform.

Keeping APIs narrow increases the gains of other best practices. A good API is focused on the needs of the client. Providing methods that do what the users require to get their job done is as much functionality as any API should provide. There is no direct, special consideration for this in a remote API, but fewer methods have a fanout effect, resulting in fewer parameter lists to cull and fewer responses to optimize and construct JSON (or similar) representations of. This last principle is one whose payoff is realized by its role as a force multiplier, it increases the advantage of the other practices that have been discussed.

Visibility levels to the client

The safest, most reliable code that is most resilient in the face of change has no public methods and only private state. Consider an instance of the **Obelisk** class defined here in C++:

```cpp
#include <iostream>
using namespace std;

class Obelisk {
private:
  int counter;
  unsigned long int target;
protected:
  void increment() {
    if (counter >= this->target) {
      cout << "target " << this->target " has been met for " << counter;
    } else {
      counter+=1;
    }
  }
public:
  Obelisk(unsigned long int target=32000) {
    this->target = target;
    counter = 0;
  }
};

int main() {
  Obelisk *rock = new Obelisk();
  cout << "rock is steady";
}
```

It would be *difficult* for any direct client of the **Obelisk** class to cause an Obelisk to become corrupted or behave outside of its specifications. That is a side-effect of the fact that it is difficult to get an Obelisk to do *anything* at all. This is one example of a common trope in information technology, another example being the most secure system is one that's powered down.

While this class is too stable to be useful, it does serve as a starting point. All software components strive to achieve a balance between being feature-rich and being reliable. If an object (or method) that, in effect, offers nothing is the most reliable, an object on the other end of the spectrum, one which reveals every internal operation and piece of state, is capable of the most functionality but is also the least reliable. In short, potential functionality usually has a reciprocal relationship with reliability.

An often-stated principle in software design is *Start out with everything private. Expand access as little and as seldom as necessary to get the job done.* While this maxim is recommended for software design in general, it has special significance when designing interfaces between platforms. The API provided by cloud components should provide a few and minimal methods as possible to minimize both the design dependencies and runtime dependencies of the client on the cloud platform. There are several design practices that can be applied to accomplish this, but one to consider early on is a mediator: the use of server-side proxies for the client that collects a number of cloud dependencies and presents them as one minimal, unified face to the-client.

As an example, one might initially propose an architecture like this:

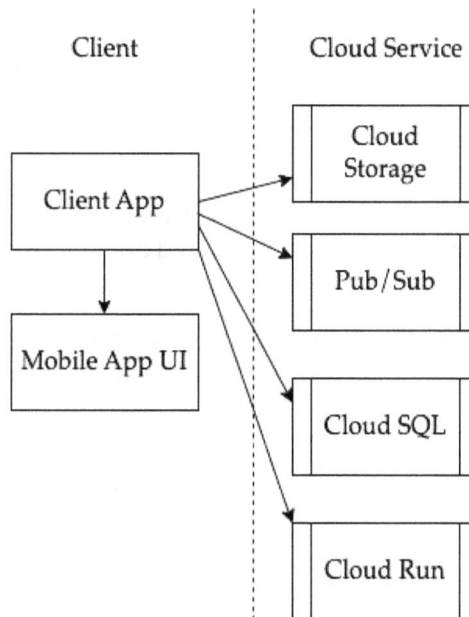

Figure 6.1: Client which directly accesses several cloud APIs

In this architectural design, the client application has direct *knowledge* of several cloud services. There are calls to various GCP services' methods scattered throughout the modules of the Client App. As a result, any changes to the Cloud Service APIs or their usage are likely to require refactoring, revision, and new testing of the client. If there are multiple clients, such as different mobile, desktop, and web applications, the impact of such a change will be multiplied. Additionally, there are other methods published by these cloud services that are not required for the Client's features, but their accessibility may lead to mistaken use due to confusion or intentional misuse by a bad actor in any of those clients.

Consider refactoring the preceding architecture, shown in *Figure 6.1*, into this functional equivalent:

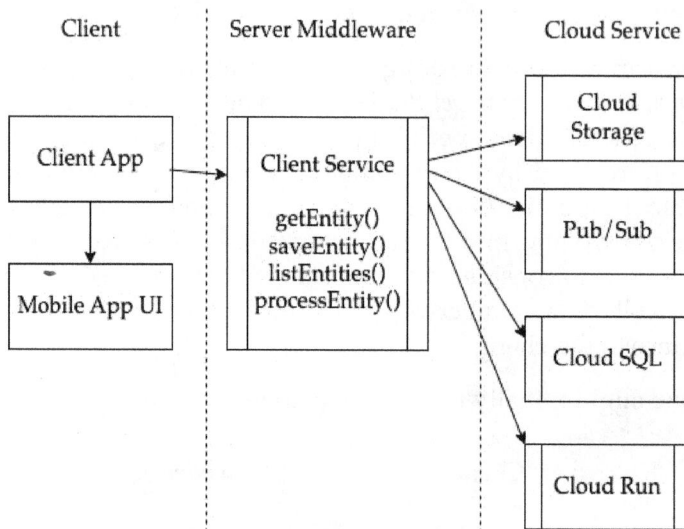

Figure 6.2: Client which goes through a cloud-side proxy

This design has gathered up all of the cloud operations, reducing what is visible to the client to only one component with only a few needed operations. There are several benefits to this technique, such as:

- The client app has no need to import or invoke the complete APIs of the four cloud services used, so there is a reduced learning curve for developers working on client applications.

- The unintended use of cloud services' features is prevented by hiding any irrelevant or unnecessary cloud methods from the client.

- Any changes to cloud service APIs or usage are contained on the cloud; the clients are isolated from any effect.

The proxy Client Service can be implemented using as lightweight a cloud service as possible, such as an App Engine or a Cloud Run service.

Planning migration to substitute or equivalent cloud services

Minimizing hard dependencies is a best practice in software architecture that is constantly and widely espoused, seldom challenged, but seldom actually explored. We will do that now, as a launching point for this section.

First, we should define hard dependency versus soft dependency. A hard dependency is commonly meant to refer to an existential requirement; that is, if X has a hard dependency on Y, it implies that without Y, X itself cannot function or perhaps exist. In contrast, a soft dependency is one on which you could still fulfill your primary function but to some reduced degree or with non-trivial workarounds. A good litmus test to determine if something is a hard dependency is, that if the presence of a resource is *critical*, that resource is a hard dependency.

Being beholden to another party is an undesirable position, we all wish to be masters of our own destiny. This section will explore a few factors that provide impetus to migrate from one cloud service to another and then practices that a developer can follow to make such migrations as easy and low-cost as possible.

Vendor lock-in

Let us turn this notion to the selection of a cloud platform. A cloud platform provider typically provides several important infrastructure services to an application, such as storage and user identity management, each of which is a hard dependency. While it is critical to have *some way* to store application state and sign up and authenticate users, due to the connections and shared context between the different services that comprise a cloud platform, it quickly becomes the case that a *specific* vendor, such as GCP, is a hard dependency. Rather than requiring *a SQL database* we find that GoogleSQL is explicitly required, carrying along with it dependencies on Google IAM and Google Cloud Storage. This situation is known as vendor lock-in. Vendor lock-in is a problematic state of affairs in which a customer is unable to transition from a specific product to a competitor's product.

When is this a problem? Maybe never for some users. If your cloud provider offers the proverbial best value for the dollar, always leading the industry in terms of features that are useful to you and never costs more than your budget, you've no reason to leave them; they truly have no competition.

That, of course, is a fictional situation. No matter how dedicated and resourceful a technology provider is, there are others out there with good ideas. For decades, the computer industry has been in a state of companies leapfrogging each other with new technologies, seizing the position of *best in class,* and then losing it to the next innovator. More constant than this series of revolutionary products is a slow but steady process of improvement, optimization, and specialization by established vendors. A vendor may decide to focus on supporting customers in certain industries or at specific scales of operation, leaving other customers better served by other vendors.

Of course, you cannot avoid locking into a chosen supplier at some point. What you *can* do to mitigate the cost of vendor lock-in is to adopt design principles and engineering practices that ease the process of migration and minimize the impact (including material cost) of substituting one vendor's product with that of another.

Product obsolescence

A dependency that is deprecated and unsupported too quickly is a large expense. Even without being discontinued, a product might simply be dated. Solutions based on new paradigms or that offer unique performance advantages may arise, and your existing product will no longer be the best choice. It is not broken, but there are more attractive options on the market.

Either of these cases is one of product obsolescence, but with different amounts of force compelling a customer to take action. In the case of a discontinued product, you are forced to identify and migrate to a substitute, whereas in the case of a dated product, you are missing out on a potential advantage offered by an alternative. We will call the first case one of forced migration and the second case one of **fear of missing out** (**FOMO**) or the cost of a missed opportunity. The concept of a **Long-Term Support** (**LTS**) model was introduced and briefly discussed in chapter two, but that is, at best, a buffer or an extended lease against a forced migration. You may still have very valid FOMO, and reliance on an LTS product will not address that.

Designing for migration

There is no way to completely remove the specific, hard references to your dependencies. You can introduce layers of abstraction and refactor class hierarchies and config files to relocate where product-specific grammar or imported resources are located, but there is no way to reduce them below the amount needed to configure and control the product in question. What you can do is use the aforementioned techniques to reduce the number of modules, be those classes, packages, or file, that are explicitly reliant on external resources. We will call this *reducing dependent components,* and while we cannot remove the functional dependencies on these resources in downstream components, we can make those non-specific to the external product in effect, we can concentrate all the dependencies with external scope to as few places as possible.

Introducing proxy components allows a developer to concentrate on external dependencies.

Refer to *Figure 6.2,* which presents a solution to a similar problem, how to minimize inter-platform coupling. The solution described introduces a mediator between the client and several cloud services, gathering knowledge of the cloud services in one place that is topographically closer to those cloud services and logically closer to the client. That design pattern has the side-effect of reducing the breadth of dependencies on external services, and there is no better validation of good practice than repeated benefits. When employing this pattern for reducing the breadth of a vendor product's influence on our architecture, we will make the proxy less specific to the four operations that were required by the client and, instead, provide non-product-specific abstractions for operations provided by each of the cloud platform products.

These components serve as stand-ins for the cloud products that are their counterparts. When used to its maximum effect, this practice can isolate large portions of an application from infrastructure considerations, separating an application into client presentation, business logic, and entities, infrastructure mediators, and infrastructure components. The following figure illustrates one possible arrangement of this architectural pattern in the context of an online shopping application:

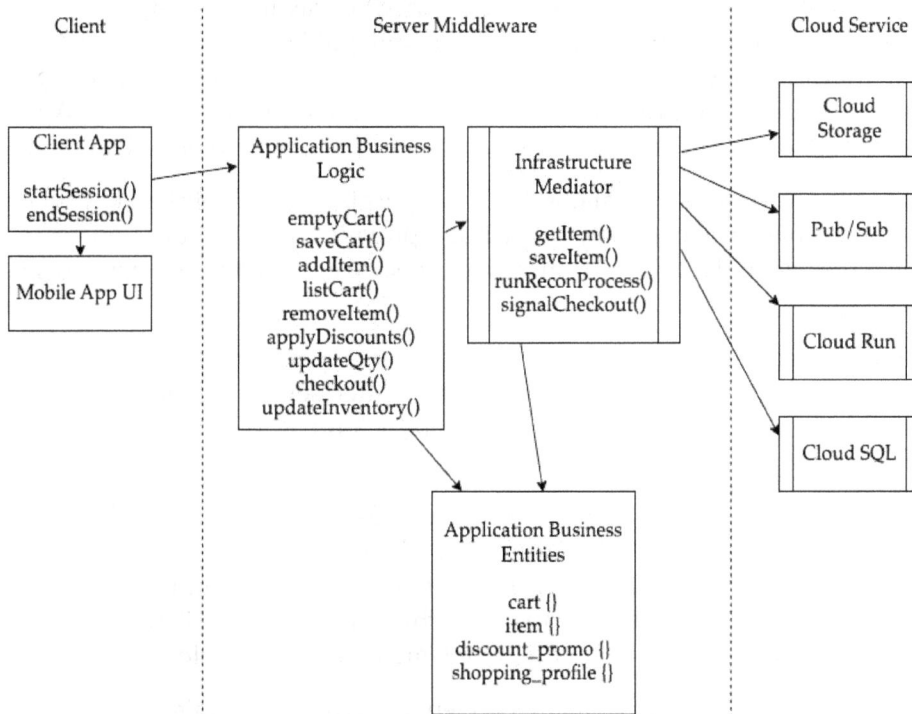

Figure 6.3: Shopping application using an infrastructure mediator

Some description of the four tiers in this diagram will point out explicit facets and advantages of the pattern.

The business logic of the application, which encodes the processes and state of a user's session, is contained in a module that we have labeled **Application Business Logic**. This code is presumably required in every client: mobile, web, or desktop. In keeping with good software design, we eliminate redundantly coding this in every client and extract it to one service, shared by and callable from all client applications.

The **Client App** module is reduced to the code that is tightly bound to the client, and the companion module, *Mobile App UI,* is only that code that is highly specific to the individual client platform's user interface. This tier is far removed from any notion of a cloud service provider and *ideally* communicates with the Application Business Logic tier as its sole provider of functionality, using the types defined in the Application Business Entities module.

The **infrastructure mediator** component is the focus of this design pattern. This is the code that abstracts infrastructure products into their functional roles and strives to free the rest of the application from hard dependencies on our cloud platform. There is likely to be a direct correspondence between methods defined within the mediator and methods offered by one of the cloud services, which is expected, as the goal here is not brevity but translation. The data structures that represent entities in our application are defined in a business-centric rather than infrastructure-specific way in the companion *Application Business Entities* module. This module defines and publishes the data needed by our application business logic, but with no infrastructure-specific references or types. The infrastructure mediator abstracts the *functions* of our cloud platform, and the Application Business Entities module abstracts the data provided by or sent to our cloud platform.

The use of an infrastructure mediator in this way isolates much of the dependency on a specific cloud provider to one component, but it provides further protection and does not fully shield the rest of the system from vendor-specific knowledge and dependencies. We will discuss both points here.

A well implemented meditator encapsulates a dependency in its entirety, not just its vendor or provider. Since a cloud provider may offer several products which overlap in functionality, such a Google App Engine and Cloud Run, the mediator allows the developer to experiment or switch between such potential counterparts with relative ease.

While a mediator serves as a proxy for many cloud-based functions within the system, there is a bootstrapping problem it does not address. A server-side platform is used to run the mediator itself, as well as the components that make use of its services. The best practice is to keep all server-side components that rely on the mediator to be as generic and platform-agnostic as possible in their implementation and deployment.

There may be cases where an explicit dependency between a cloud service and a specific component is difficult or impractical to break; in such a case, it is pragmatic to document and accept such a relationship. We will see a few such scenarios in the following sections. It is important to remember that the goal is to maximize the isolation of external dependencies rather than guaranteeing it to any specific degree or number of modules.

Finally, the Cloud Platform Services comprise a tier furthest from our control and expertise. These are the services, such as GCP storage and compute products, that have been enumerated and described in *Chapters 3, Determining the Infrastructure to Build Features Upon* and *Chapter 4, Choosing Between GCP Options*. These services provide enormous benefits to a distributed application, but also require a significant investment in infrastructure and vendor-specific expertise. Limiting their exposure to fewer modules of our application allows our development team to focus on specialties: a mobile app developer need not become an expert in GCP administration or GCP API practices.

Once we have implemented an architecture along these lines, we can truly separate development cycles driven by internal concerns, such as the cost or scalability of our cloud services, from release cycles driven by market forces such as new features. Suppose a developer designs a new structure for items in inventory that removes the storage of items' descriptions as **Binary Large Objects** (**BLOBS**) in Cloud Storage and completely stores items in a Spanner table. We can find and replace the code of the `getItem()` and `saveItem()` operations of the infrastructure mediator and restructure our dependencies to refactor this tier with zero effect on business logic or clients.

Similarly, and more drastically, we may someday migrate our application to another service provider completely such as Amazon Web Services or Microsoft Azure. The mediator may have to take on additional complexity to make up for feature disparity between the products or platforms, but the mediator is within our control and allows us to weigh such added complexity against the advantages provided by a new infrastructure platform.

Visibility between cloud services

One more type of external dependency remains to be addressed: the dependencies between sibling products within the cloud platform. The problem is less obvious and the solution complex than the cases addressed so far, but the potential for improvement is real and worth exploring.

Dependencies between cloud service products

Let us examine the solutions presented in the earlier sections. One advantage gained is the ability to migrate infrastructure features, such as the persistence of application data, to new representations. Changing the infrastructure products used for these features empowers a developer to change from a BLOB representation to one based on database rows or from a long-running process to a managed serverless one. Another scenario this pattern frees a developer to pursue is the move from one platform product to a different provider while limiting the changes to our application design and codebase.

The common technique used was refactoring code to limit direct references to specific products to designated modules. We can apply this same general strategy to some cases *within and between* cloud products, removing their direct dependencies upon each other.

We will use a specific case study as an illustrative example. Take the case of a service run on Google Cloud Run, a long-running inventory reconciliation process. Such a process could be signaled at the end of a user session when a shopper has completed checkout. The dependencies involved with this feature would look like the following figure:

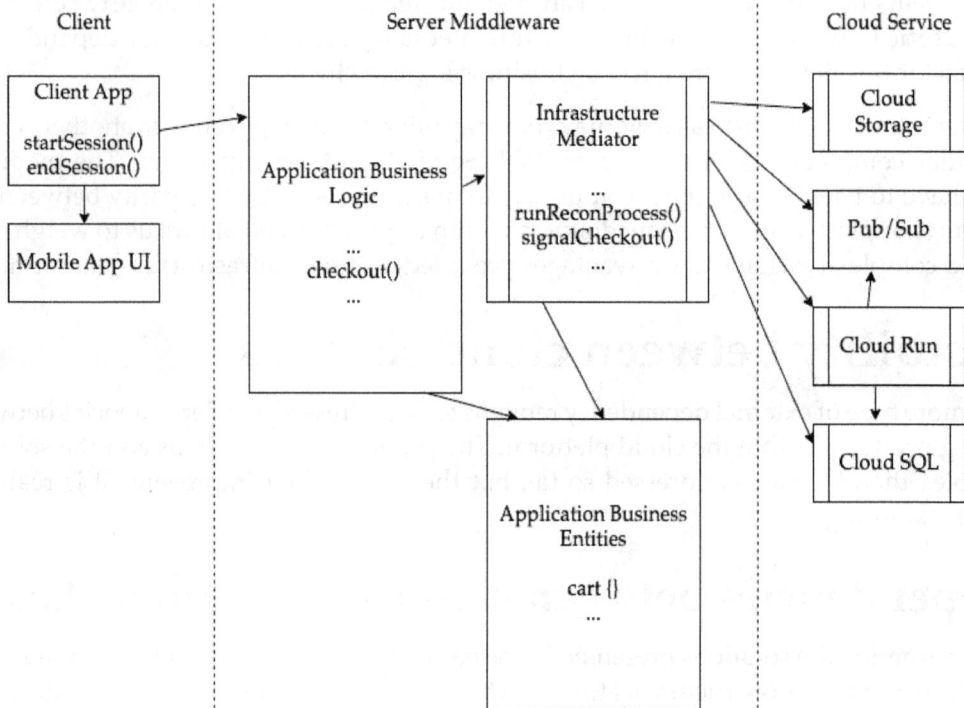

Figure 6.4: *Shopping application with infrastructure dependencies*

In this implementation, the infrastructure mediator initially starts a long running *Reconciliation* service on Cloud Run, which then waits for work. When a shopper checks out, the mediator publishes that checkout event using Pub/Sub. The mediator has successfully isolated the cloud platform tier from the business logic; there are no dependencies between the two.

However, what about the service running on Cloud Run? It subscribes to a Pub/Sub-topic and is notified of checkout events when it receives one. Its job is to update inventory and flag items below a quantity threshold for reordering. As part of this, it queries and updates the Inventory and possibly inserts rows into our Orders table. So, the server running on Cloud Run has specific hard dependencies on Pub/Sub and Cloud SQL services.

This is not as obvious a problem as having dependencies on infrastructure within our application client and logic was: the migration to another platform would have roughly the same impact and effect, regardless of these dependencies. However, the other reason for isolation, migrating from one product to a substitute within the same platform, is still a problem. The specialized platform expertise is not the issue that it was before introducing the infrastructure mediator, but moving from GoogleSQL to Google Cloud Storage buckets still requires us to search for references in code and make changes in multiple modules.

Isolating cloud service products

The dependencies between cloud services can be easily (in theory) addressed by extending the responsibilities of the mediator to serve as a proxy for services in our Cloud Service tier, as well as a proxy for our Business Logic modules.

Rather than our Reconciliation process on Cloud Run accessing our databases and subscribing to Pub/Sub directly, we can add methods to the mediator to provide these features for the Reconciliation process. These methods can be published using a separate API if needed to avoid a circular dependency. The dependencies of this feature would then resemble the following figure:

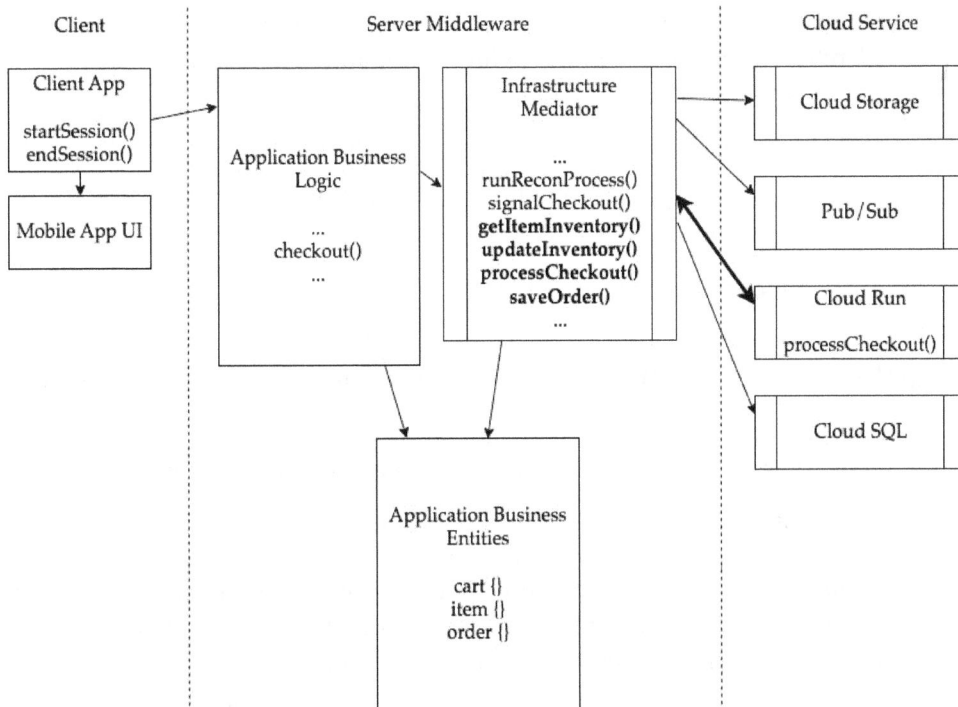

Figure 6.5: *Shopping application with bilateral infrastructure mediator*

The principal difference to note is the two-sided arrow between the mediator and the Cloud Run service. Our Reconciliation process now calls back to the same mediator that launched it and dispatches work to it. This allows the mediator to accept requests to fetch and store data from our cloud run service and then execute Cloud SQL operations to satisfy those requests. To remove dependencies between our Reconciliation service and Pub/Sub, the mediator now both sends events to Pub/Sub and asynchronously pulls events from the queue, invoking a method of the Reconciliation service to process those events.

With this step, we now have contained dependencies on Cloud Platform products to within the infrastructure mediator module.

Identifying and packaging tightly coupled services

We have identified the motivation for decoupling as much of our architecture as possible from external dependencies and described a strategy for doing so. We will now dive deeper into a case study, which includes the problematic case of modules with explicit dependencies that are difficult to break.

First, recall the mediator, which was created to be the sole dependent of all Cloud Platform infrastructure products. The basic design principle behind this mediator can be stated as:

If the application feature Z needs feature X from a cloud product Y, add a feature to the mediator that retrieves X from Y and provides a version of X that has no datatypes or references that are specific to Y.

Let us dissect that statement and assign some actual values for placeholders:

- Y is a cloud platform product, in this case, Pub/Sub.

- X is an operation of Pub/Sub, such as publish a **checkedout** message to the **pending_reconcilations** topic.

- The application feature Z is a business logic operation named **applyCheckoutToInventory** that is executed after a user has completed checking out.

  o   The contents of the completed cart are passed to this operation.

With our first mediator in place, the architecture of our shopping application is illustrated in *Figure 6.5*. The discussion and process were purposefully limited to the checkout feature, conveniently ignoring other features of our application for the moment. We will now discuss one of those ignored features that breaks the isolation mechanism of our infrastructure mediator, that of user login and authentication.

Users connect to our distributed system from the client platform. To limit the potential for unauthorized or malicious misuse of our system, we should provide as few windows into our larger system as possible to untrusted, unauthorized parties. This introduces a classic chicken-and-egg problem when employing a cloud-based user authentication service. If we rely on our infrastructure mediator that resides *in the cloud* to act as a proxy for user authentication, this implies that we connect to that mediator before our identity has been authenticated as an authorized user of the application.

This is where it is important to remember the goal of isolating and narrowing the dependent components in a design. Having no components with hard external dependencies is not feasible, assuming that the dependencies' features are actually needed. One such dependent component in a system is ideal. However, two dependent components are better than an unbounded number and may be the best possible fit for a multi-tiered distributed application. This number two is not arbitrary: one mediator for cloud-based components and one mediator for client-side components that are bound to their client platform.

The introduction of a client-side infrastructure mediator still affords us the advantages of containing product-specific dependencies in designated, focused modules and frees us from the chicken-and-egg conundrum encountered in the design of user authentication described earlier in this section. Adding a mediator for the required client services results in the following architecture:

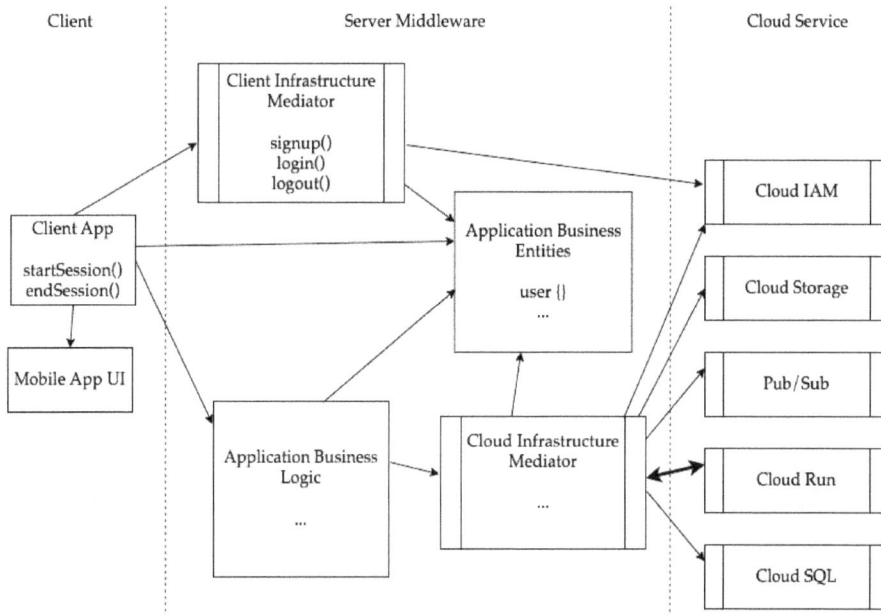

Figure 6.6: Shopping application with local infrastructure mediator

Note that the components involved in this refactoring, *Client App, Client Infrastructure Mediator, Application Business Entities*, and *Cloud IAM*, mirror their counterparts in the earlier refactoring that introduced the Cloud Infrastructure Mediator, respectively: *Application Business Logic, Cloud Infrastructure Mediator, Application Business Entities*, and several GCP products. This is evidence of a consistently employed design pattern; the roles are constant, and the specific components assigned to those roles vary as relevant to the situation in which the pattern is being applied.

In general, the result of the design patterns we have employed in this section is the separation of application-centric code from code centered around cloud infrastructure. This is a logical extension of the classic separation of business logic from user interface frameworks and controllers. The overarching benefit is that of shielding code that is driven by one external force, such as a specific mobile client platform's toolkit, from code that is shaped by a completely different external force, such as a specific cloud platform service. These two external dependencies are independent influences and isolating them allows us to accommodate changes dictated by either one with as little impact as possible on our application. Furthermore, the separation of business logic from *any* of these external dependencies ensures that we can encode and validate an application's market-critical feature set without worrying about polluting side-effects of our user interface or backend infrastructure.

Conclusion

When designing any significant software system, certain design patterns and practices have emerged to maximize robustness, maintainability, and performance. In a highly distributed, multi-tiered application such as one backed by a cloud service platform, the benefit of these patterns is magnified due to a greater scale of demand and the typically larger codebases.

This chapter reviewed principles of API design that are especially pertinent in the construction of Remote APIs. Distributed application-specific considerations were pointed out, which act as a force multiplier for the benefits of several of these practices when designing a cloud-backed application.

The reader was then guided through motivations and practices for isolating the presence of any specific cloud product within an application's architecture and codebase. Case studies were used to illustrate the practices discussed to reinforce the relevance of these design patterns.

The next chapter delves into the design of a backend agnostic client, one that defines and implements all behavior that is specific to the client platform rather than specified by the business logic of the encompassing application. Robustness in the face of unexpected server-side interactions will be considered and planned for, as well as isolating the application backend from unexpected states on the client.

CHAPTER 7
Frontends at the Client Border

Introduction

The frontend is the public, immediately visible and heavily judged portion of a distributed system. There can be many times more substance in the backend and infrastructure of an application, but those are invisible to the typical user, who only sees the controls and experiences the latency and flow of the client components that reside on their local phone, tablet or computer.

To control the user experience well, a client cannot simply dispatch requests to a subservient and user-ignorant backend. The client must have an internal plan and set of guarantees for what it handles internally, what it delegates to the backend, and what responses it will issue to user requests. In addition to responding to the client, the backend may present its own requests to the client and the frontend must define how it will serve as A representative of the system's own state, as well as responding to user actions

This chapter presents design principles and recipes for addressing these considerations in the high-level system design of a distributed application. Following these practices yields applications that deliver a consistent user experience that earns and maintains user trust, while working with the capabilities and limitations of the global, cloud-based tiers of the application.

Structure

The following topics will be covered in this chapter:

- Client-side logic
- Defining client requests to the backend
- Blocking and non-blocking request responses
- Pushback and handling unexpected responses
- Defining and handling non-user-initiated actions

Objectives

Through this chapter, the reader will become acquainted with the high-level platform breakdown of a distributed user-visible application. The reader will learn criteria for separating functionality and designating it to a particular tier within the architecture, and the reasons behind those. Risks to application performance and integrity within each layer and at its borders are exposed, and techniques for preventing or mitigating those risks will be explored and explained.

Client-side logic

There are considerations to make when determining whether to locate code on a server-side platform, including cloud services, or as part of the local client application. This section discusses general principles for isolating functionality to any one platform and then describes several use cases that call for client or server-side deployment.

Avoid multiple sources of truth

Significant behavior should be encoded in one place. For example, if the logic that defines how to determine which offer a shopper is eligible to receive is encoded in the **eligiblePromotions()** method of a class named **PricingAdjustor**, that set of rules is encoded there and only there in the codebase. The reason for this is simply stated: relying on more than one source of truth invites discrepancies between them, resulting in *no* reliable source of truth. This relates to a basic algebraic practice, that of simplifying polynomial expressions with a common factor. In this case, the redundant code implementing the same operation in multiple locations can be viewed as a common factor, and the refactoring performed to extract and isolate the operation is the equivalent of simplifying the expression.

In an application with a single runtime environment, wherever this function is needed, the invoking code can simply import the **PricingAdjustor** module and then perform a simple method call to utilize it. The static or compile-time location of the code is the primary consideration, as there is only one dynamic runtime location. Any and all invocations will use the same logic and experience roughly the same performance.

Within a distributed, multi-tiered system, there is a further necessary consideration of the *physical*, or more accurately, the *topological* location of the code at runtime. As well as the static location, the package, module, and class in which an operation is encoded, the developer must also decide on which runtime platforms to instantiate instances of that code.

The common and easily understood designs are the decision to deploy code as a common non-client-specific server component or to run it locally on each and every client that runs the application's frontend.

There are several forces to consider when deciding on which side of the client-server divide a component should reside. The remainder of this section enumerates and describes some of the major use cases where this decision is relevant, and relevant considerations to each of them.

Presentation of the user interface

The output that the human user sees, hears, and feels is presented on the client hardware platform and by software running on that platform. That much is inevitable.

How much of the preparation of that visual and audio content occurs on the client, the rendering of the user-visible output, can vary. The typical default action is to render on the client, but this should not be a binary decision, all or nothing, client or server. Let us consider the advantages of performing more or less of the user interface rendering on the client versus the server.

Client side rendering provides the user interface that takes the greatest advantage of local client UI elements. The most responsive changes to layout and the arrangement of user interface components will happen when the user interface is observed and controlled by local code. However, there are factors introduced by the use of cloud-based resources that provide counterweights or opportunities that do not exist for the client. We will now examine a couple of examples to illustrate these use cases.

In the first example, an image from a gallery stored in the cloud is viewed in any of several client platform applications. The image must be scaled, and the color depth and palette must be adjusted to match the viewing pane and display characteristics of each specific client, for example, a smartphone.

An obvious approach is for the server to provide the image in some reasonably high-quality format, agnostic of any particular client platform, and let each client adjust the image to match its own presentation capabilities. This technique maintains the strongest boundaries between the platforms. The client alone has knowledge of its display capabilities and of its intended use of the image, i.e., a thumbnail, icon, or full screen. There are costs and practical concerns that make this principled approach less attractive.

An image of higher quality consumes more network bandwidth, taking longer to transfer. Network bandwidth is not free or infinite; both cellular and landline networks have limited capacity and incur costs, both in fees and in performance degradation.

The client is likely going to take longer to resize and resample the high-quality image than the server would have, further increasing latency and increasing power consumption on the client. The additional time to transfer the higher-quality image was truly wasted, as we then spent additional time throwing away some of that image quality.

This is a case where some knowledge of the client being *leaked* to the server is a reasonable compromise. The client can, at a session scope or when requesting an image, advertise a capabilities profile, including preferred image size and resolution, color depth, and audio quality. The server can then provide content that is suitable to the client's capabilities, removing the excess data transfer and costly, redundant resampling on every client.

Another technique that is used in web applications is known as **server-side rendering (SSR)**. A web application that uses SSR executes any JavaScript on the server and sends a fully rendered HTML page to the client. The advantages of SSR are mostly in client-side performance; the browser only displays HTML with no JavaScript or CSS execution delays on the client. This is of the most benefit to users with older or less powerful client hardware and has important side benefits for those using assistive technology such as screen readers. Screen readers often have trouble correctly interpreting JavaScript and CSS, but can properly parse a fully rendered HTML page.

SSR is offered or is used transparently by many JavaScript frameworks, including Angular and React.

Capturing user input, selection and entry

Similar to the more precise use and control over display elements, the user interface controls for obtaining user input have arguments for and against greater isolation within the client platform.

On the one hand, data validation, such as ensuring that all required or corequisite fields are entered, is well suited to code running on the client. There is little to be gained by sending individual fields in round-trip envelopes to the cloud for validation and construction of error messages, and the delay would be noticeable and unacceptable in practice.

On the other hand, consider a case where the user enters a text field for lookup against a known set of values, such as a product ID. If there are a small number of product IDs to choose from, the list could be downloaded to the client for local code to use to validate user input. However, what if there are a very large or unbounded number of IDs, perhaps 200,000 of them, each up to 50 characters long? Downloading 10 megabytes of product IDs will introduce a noticeable delay and take a large portion of the memory available to a mobile app. In this case, some form of server-side validation is more feasible, or a hybrid approach where a narrow list of candidate product IDs is fetched from the server as the user types into the text field.

Client-side validation can provide a richer and faster user experience, but relying on it incurs a risk. If server-side components rely on the client to ensure that all data is of the expected types and ranges, this opens the risk of security vulnerabilities. A client application that fails to fully validate values sent as parameters to a cloud service API could cause that service to become corrupt or be open to an intentional exploit. In a more insidious scenario, a malicious actor could reverse engineer the client/server protocol and inject their own traffic, bypassing the client application's data validation.

The best practice is a two-tiered approach to validation. In this, the client application employs interactive input validation, and then the server API methods perform their own validation of all input sent to the cloud. This way, the application can give fine-grained low-latency validation and prompts to the user, the network is spared from round-trip traffic for intermediate field or form submissions, and the server-side components are shielded from unexpected, potentially corrupting input. To ensure consistency, both the client and server-side validation should use the same validation rules and values, but instantiated and invoked from components on their respective platforms. The design for this double use of common validation rules is illustrated in the following class figure with some code snippets to illustrate their usage in each location:

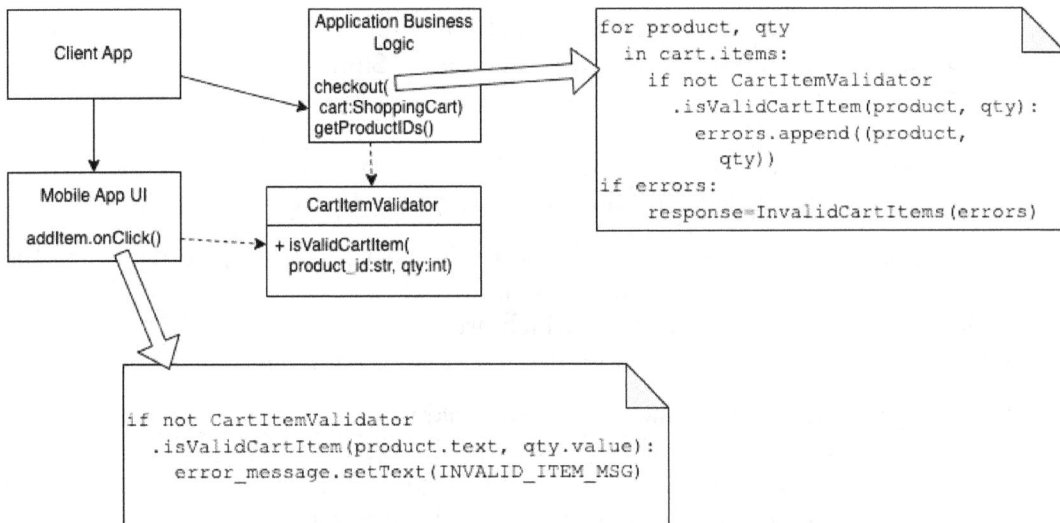

Figure 7.1: Client and server use of common validation code

The code that determines if a specific quantity of a product is written only once is part of the **CartItemValidator** class. That validation is performed in the Mobile App UI as the user attempts to add each item to their cart, providing them with immediate and obvious feedback if there is an error in their selection.

When the mobile app is ready to close out a cart, it invokes the **checkout()** method of our server-side business logic. The checkout operation applies the same validation rules to each item in the cart as items are added to the client, accumulating all validation errors. If there were any validation errors, those are sent back in the response to the client who will act, presumably including displaying the list of errors and perhaps moving those items out of the active shopping cart.

With this set of input validations in place, we have satisfied our goal of responsive feedback and business logic that is protected from an erroneous or malicious client. We have also maintained one source of truth: a canonical encoding of our data validation rules. The set of such rules should be the responsibility of experts in business logic, and any regulatory or contractual requirements rather than left to parallel interpretation by frontend and backend engineers.

Hiding sensitive logic from observation

The previous section introduced the separation of business knowledge from platform-specific and user experience expertise. While a small or tightly integrated development team may result in the same person being *the engineer* and maybe also the *product manager*. Isolating these specializations in code location has benefits to the ability of the product and the team to scale up, and in application stability and correctness.

The implications of regulation are often unrealized until a problem introduced by an unaware engineering team leads to non-compliance. Similarly, there are marketing and product strategy decisions behind policies that may be unknown to the engineers implementing features from a set of specifications. Gathering all business logic into dedicated modules or packages allows the implementation of policies to be reviewed by their subject matter experts: legal, product marketing, or industry specialists.

These preceding reasons are generally wise strategic considerations when designing the architecture of an application. There are more immediate and practical gains from tightly encapsulating key application behavior, which are easier to achieve with a distributed cloud-backed system: the protection of market advantage and intellectual property.

Consider an application with a unique, groundbreaking feature. This can be anything: a placement algorithm, data transformation technique, or ranking method. The point is that your application's code does *something* different that gives your application an edge over the competition. Imitation is the sincerest form of flattery, but it would be better for your business if this unique advantage remained yours for as long as possible.

In an architecturally simple one platform application, the code that implements this new feature is installed on every mobile and desktop client. That presents the opportunity to dissect your runtime application, iteratively probe identified internal modules and, in the end, reverse engineer that unique feature behavior.

By offloading sensitive business logic to dedicated modules, we introduce ways to mitigate this exploit. It is unlikely that your algorithm or internal process can remain secret forever, but like the use of bicycle locks, it will benefit you to put as many speed bumps as possible in the thief's way.

To reduce these risks to our application and the business, we can take advantage of design patterns that have already been discussed. A relevant design pattern was described earlier in this chapter in the section *Capturing user input, selection and entry*. Isolating business logic to specific policy modules or *Policy Engines* can isolate the code for a specific domain, such as the placement of advertisements on a page or regulatory mandates for certain combinations of items. With the code now isolated, another design pattern, discussed in *Chapter 6, Cloud Services at the Backend Border* in the section *Visibility levels to the client* can be employed to relocate this policy to a cloud-based service which presents as opaque a public face as possible. The following figure shows a design that includes such policy engines for two domains: item layout and retail sale regulations:

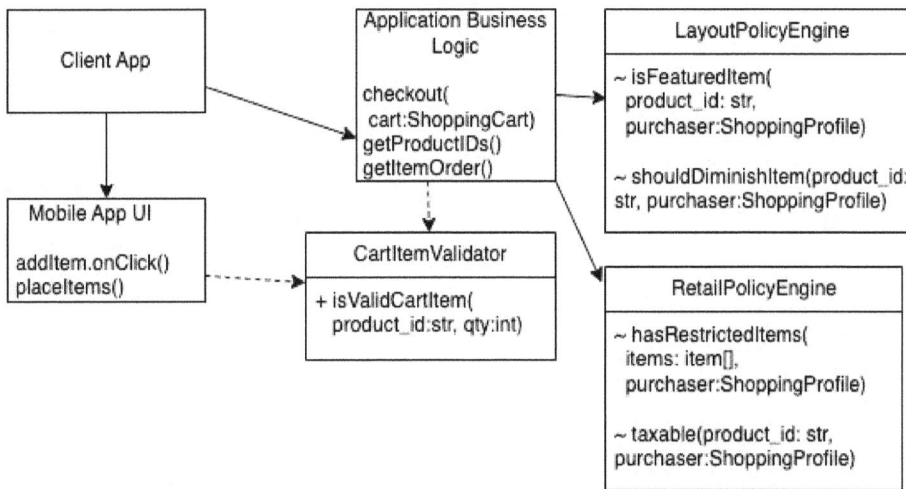

Figure 7.2: *Use of domain-specific Policy Engines*

As well as the concentration of business domain knowledge, this pattern empowers us to place barriers in the way of efforts to reverse-engineer our application. Code in cloud-based components can be protected from direct dissection or decoding by restricting access to narrow APIs. A cloud service can be placed behind load balancers and proxies that detect and block irregular or suspicious access patterns, such as automated repeated method invocations.

Making frequently changed code easy to deploy

An application's stability is not only based on consistent, expected behavior while in use, but also by the visible release cycle of the software. A user will quickly tire of being prompted or forced to install new versions daily. When someone launches your application, they want to use it *and*, not wait for your system to do its housekeeping.

It is inevitable that some changes will require a client software update, but in a well-designed distributed application, functionality that is expected to change frequently should be removed from the client as much as possible. This will allow the release team to push new versions and updates exclusively to the cloud-based components. To maximize the opportunity to do so, keep the client focused on client-side work and keep client-visible APIs of server-side components as narrow and platform-agnostic as possible.

In the most straightforward design, this practice incurs constant back-and-forth between the client and server as the client invokes server-side business logic to guide the user's navigation through the application's features. The conflict between the dynamic distribution of software and minimizing in-session network traffic is one that is addressed by another design pattern, the downloading of internal components for offline use. This design pattern is used in latency-sensitive applications, such as the dynamic selection of language in speech recognition products like the Google *Speech to Text* service. This allows a client to use an installed recognizer or download a new one if a previously uninstalled language is detected.

In this application of the design pattern, a well-defined interface exists for the business logic component, in this case, an abstract speech recognizer class. Any number of language-specific implementations of this interface may be available on the cloud, but a given client installation cannot include recognizers for all languages and dialects. There are several reasons that this is impractical. There is not enough space on a phone to include them all, the list of recognizers is regularly expanded, and improvements to existing recognizers are introduced.

Rather than a client installation being bundled with a language-specific recognizer, the application is installed with a small set of default recognizers and a minimal classifier to manage the installed recognizers. If speech is not recognized, or a new language is specifically requested, the classifier will download the recognizer from the cloud that is determined to be the best match for the newly encountered language. Since the client-side components that are hard-coded or *baked into* the application only require an implementation of the abstract recognizer interface, the existing client app continues to work after a relatively brief delay to download and install the new language support. The presence of a local speech recognition service minimizes cloud access during a user session, and the isolation and dynamic installation of recognition engines avoid the need to update the entire client application to access new language support.

This pattern can be employed for many use cases in business: a navigation app could download local traffic rules, and a shopping application could download a rule engine for shopping session management. These are both scenarios where the presence and application of rules are fixed within a user's session, but the encoded rules themselves are subject to change over time based on client or external factors.

Defining client requests to the backend

The set of client requests to the backend services should not emerge, appearing to be a collection of the operations that came up during frontend feature implementation. A backend should be defined with intent, based on a set of well-understood functional requirements, and the frontend application should make use of these published backend services.

Planning is important enough that it is never over. It is likely that some improvement or shortcoming in a backend will become apparent during development. This is fine and working as intended; change the plan, do not abandon it.

Backends for Frontends

The goal of a popular cloud design pattern, *Backends for Frontends* is to avoid muddying the purpose of a backend service to make it fit multiple clients with different requirements. In this pattern, a specific backend service is developed for distinct frontend client applications. The main advantage of this practice comes in an architecture where multiple clients have different requirements of the backend. A single backend service would become unwieldy as it converged on being all things to all clients. The complexity of this monolithic backend grows, which slows down development, increases the breadth of needed testing, and introduces a common choke point for the development of otherwise independent client applications. The development of the web client may require changes to the common backend service, which will necessitate changes or at least testing and verification by the mobile client development team.

The trade-off to consider when deciding to implement this design pattern is the potential explosion in the number of overall components and the possibility of redundant code amongst the peer backend services. The former concern is an unavoidable consequence of the pattern, but the effect is limited to the number of client applications. The latter concern can be mitigated and often completely removed by well-designed inheritance and decomposition of common functionality.

The following component figure presents an ideal, albeit somewhat abstract, use of this pattern in the running example of a shopping application:

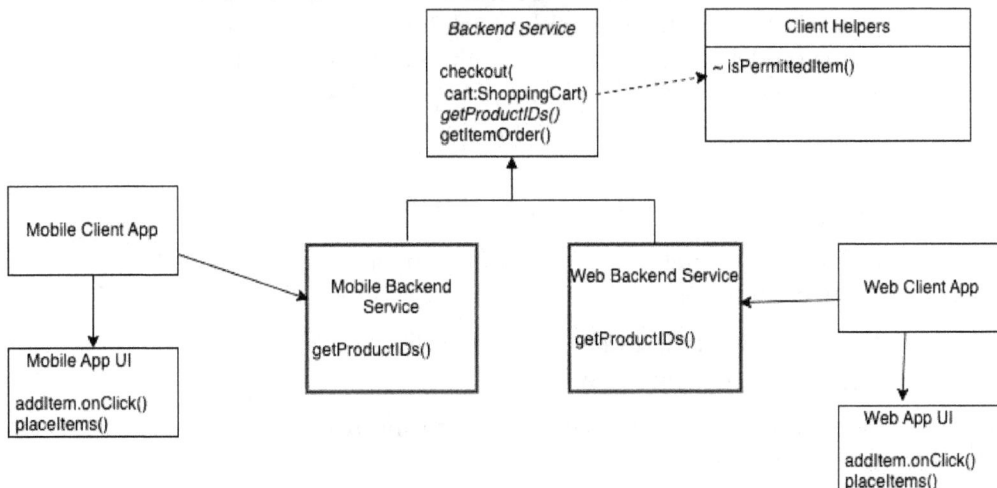

Figure 7.3: Use of the backends for frontends pattern

Deploy backend services on as lightweight and flexible a cloud service as possible.

Backend services are a useful piece of infrastructure, and as they are focused on specific client apps, you can configure them to best serve the number of expected users and usage patterns for each platform. It is a good practice to use the same **Google Cloud Platform (GCP)** product for all of an application's peer-backend services. The use of backend services introduces architectural complexity, and architects should avoid compounding that with different deployment models within the tier.

An ideal backend service is stateless, with each method call having no side effect on the service itself. While Cloud Run is recommended as a platform for a service that requires large scalability and development tool flexibility, the App Engine Standard Environment is a good choice to start with as it provides the same deployment support of version management, rapid scaling, load balancing, and traffic splitting when rolling out a new release of a service. The fully managed standard environment allows a developer to easily and seamlessly deploy serverless stateless servers, and if your case outgrows the App Engine's capabilities, then there are well-documented processes for migrating from App Engine to Google Cloud Run.

Blocking and non-blocking request responses

Blocking or synchronous method calls are the basic function call that all programmers learn early on. In *Chapter 5, Client-side Technology Choices*, the section *Asynchronous Message Handling* briefly describes the synchronous method call in which the invoker of a method is suspended, entering a wait state while the invoked method is executed. Only when the invoked operation *returns* control to its caller does that invoking method resume execution.

The asynchronous model is one in which the invoker dispatches a method but then resumes execution. In this model, the method call initiates the invoked method, whereas in the synchronous model of execution, the method call executes the invoked method in its entirety. The design pattern for this is fairly simple and well understood, and there are a multitude of implementations for different use cases.

Identifying asynchronous methods

The need for asynchronous methods is determined by a two-part litmus test determined by the following two questions:

- Does the invoked method take longer than it is acceptable for the client thread, invoking it to do nothing but wait?

- Is there anything else the client can do to improve the user experience while waiting for the invoked method to complete?

   Note: **This could include updating a progress indicator, if useful.**

If the answer to the first question is yes, then the operation under scrutiny should be examined critically with an eye towards improving its performance. If that is not practical and/or the answer to the second question is yes, then asynchronous method invocation is a good option. We will now discuss and contrast different methods for implementing such asynchronous execution.

GCP provides support for distributed, scalable asynchronous processing with several features that support error handling of errors in asynchronous processing, such as cloud functions triggered by logging activity and the trace analysis tools of Cloud Observability.

Google Cloud Pub/Sub is a product that can be used to implement a form of this at a large scale and with invokers completely decoupled from the invoked methods. GCP also provides Google Cloud Tasks, a queuing service for GCP that can invoke to App Engine handlers or HTTP requests to target URLs.

There are client-side language and framework-specific techniques for invoking methods asynchronously.

The choice of whether to use a service dedicated to asynchronous processing or to implement asynchronous method calls in the client is a judgment call in the design phase, based on the specific use case. The former, using a service such as Cloud Tasks, offers the scalability and failover of a GCP-managed service but adds hard dependencies on specific vendor products, a learning curve, and the ongoing administration of an additional product. Using a client-local mechanism carries the complementary advantages and drawbacks: less automatic scaling and failover but no added vendor lock-in and product administration. These considerations should be weighed for an application's use case where it is determined that asynchronous processing is needed.

In the specific use case of *Backends for Frontends* described earlier in this section, the invoked backend service that will be executed asynchronously is already on a scalable, managed service such as Google App Engine. The backing service is behind a load balancer. If the traffic spikes are within the standard environment's capabilities, there is little reason to add another layer of complexity on the server side.

Client technologies for asynchronous processing

Clients can choose from language, framework, and platform-specific mechanisms for asynchronous execution.

JavaScript provides *async* functions, which are used with *Promise* objects to dispatch and later wait for completion of methods. These JavaScript features are used within JavaScript frameworks' own asynchronous processing features such as *useEffect* hooks in React. The Go language includes goroutines and channels as primitives for concurrent (asynchronous) programming but with a different programming model than JavaScript's. C# provides support for typed *Task* objects with the *async* and *await* keywords.

Android mobile developers can make use of the *AsyncTask* class to implement any task, including calls to server-side methods, in the background in a dedicated thread. The background task can signal its completion status, resulting in shared memory to the main execution thread.

Swift iOS developers can use a *Task* block, *async* functions, and the *await* keyword to create background functions and poll, or wait, for their completion.

If endpoints on the backend service are long-running, they can be dispatched from the client and tied to Promises, goroutines, Tasks, or another client-side technique for asynchronous method execution. The choice should be made based on the specific development environments and tools used and the desired reuse of code across client platforms.

Pushback and handling unexpected responses

The response from a server method is often treated as binary: success or failure. In this view, success is the desired outcome. We requested a list of product IDs and received one, a username was presented for authentication and was confirmed, or the application requested that an item be added to the user's shopping cart, and it was. Failure is defined as a catch-all for everything else. The shortcomings of this approach can be described from two points of view. The user's and the application's opportunity for robustness.

In this generic error handling scenario, the user is given an error message with as little information as *something went wrong*. This mystifies the user and undermines their confidence in the application's reliability.

The application internally ignores the fact that there are two types of failures: operations that the application did not allow due to internal rules or constraints, and unexpected states such as a network error, a write failing due to a device out of space, or an uncaught overflow error. If the application discriminated between these, it could recover or provide workarounds in some cases, improving overall robustness.

We will label the first category of failure, the caught violation of application rules, *pushback*, and the second category will be referred to as *unexpected*. We will discuss how these can be handled differently, saving the user or at least maintaining their confidence in our system's reliability.

Pushback can often be anticipated and avoided. Adding more items to your cart than there are in inventory or that are permitted by trade regulations can be prevented before a checkout request to the server. However, in a multi-user system, the potential for a race condition, where two competing users collide, could lead to a checkout failing due to insufficient inventory. This can be anticipated, and an explanatory message, sometimes with a proposed workaround or alternative action such as reducing the items to the available quantity and asking the user for approval, can be executed.

The unexpected response is harder to handle effectively. To present the details of an infrastructure failure to the user is not useful, and there is no action for them to take based on the information. There is also a risk in revealing details of your infrastructure; this is useful information for attackers.

While not showing details of an unexpected failure to the user, there are actions the application can take based on the nature of the failures. In the case of a transient failure, such as a network or other resource timeout, a few retries can be attempted. In the case of a resource shortage in the cloud, saving the client's current state locally on the client and an option to retry the failed operation at a later time can provide user value, when presented with well stated description of the situation and giving the user a reason to believe that the situation will be resolved. If a data store ran out of disk space, saving the current cart on the client, internally sending an alert to the operations team or administrators, and telling the user that both of these actions have been taken is a good response. Having the client application receive some notification when the situation has been resolved and telling the user to resume is an additional convenience that instills user confidence in the robustness of our system, the application, and the organization behind it. To find a balance between keeping the details of the system's infrastructure and its failures private and providing enough information to be useful to the client, the server response should carry as much information as needed to inform the client of the nature of the failure.

Consider some of the errors that may be encountered in the cloud while executing a client request. A transient infrastructure failure could be specific, such as a network error, or a timeout on a call to an external service or operation or an error that GCP itself labeled with its generic *TransientError*. The client app would take the same action in response to any of these, so the only needed level of detail in the server response is that of a *TransientServerError* being encountered, with an optional hint as to when to retry the request.

For the server method failures described in previously in this section, the following set of responses provide the needed precision to the client without leaking server implementation details:

Response code	Payload	Retriable by client
OK	Method's expected return value	Not applicable
TransientServerError	Delay for retry	Yes
ServerError	Handle to resolution event	No
InsufficientInventory	List of items and available quantities	User action required
InvalidContents	List of items, quantity affected and messages	User action required

Figure 7.4: Server method responses

The mapping of responses on the server side, such as in a method of the *Backend for Frontend* discussed earlier in the chapter, into one of these five classes of response allows the server-side method closest to the specific client to supply the detail with as much sensitivity as possible to that client. For example, it makes sense to specify different durations for the *Delay for retry* value for phones than for desktop computers.

Defining and handling non-user-initiated actions

The normal flow of events in a computer application is fairly simple. The user of the application makes a request, and the application responds to the request. In a distributed, multi-tier application such as one backed by Google Cloud Platform, the response may be generated by a complex sequence of interactions and state changes across many platforms, but in the end the user experience remains *I request that the application does something and the application indicates that it has done so.*

We have already seen some scenarios where actual practice differs from this model. If the user requests an action that is not allowed, such as purchasing more of an item than we allow, the application does not take the action that was requested, but still generates a response. Similarly, if some internal failure interferes with the fulfillment of the user's request, the application's response indicates this. The request/response interaction still holds up, but it is now generalized to *I request that the application does something and the application indicates what has been done.*

Use cases for server-initiated actions

The individual user is not the only active agent in a distributed system. Other concurrent users, processes not initiated by a specific user request, and side-effects of external processes and systems can all change the state of our system. Changes to the shared state of the system may have direct consequences on users, and an application should have a way to incorporate, resolve, and inform the user of such imposed state changes.

Before going into the details of how this non-response traffic can be implemented, we will first categorize and describe the types of traffic that is delivered to the client in this manner, and some examples.

A server initiating an interaction with the client, in effect inverting the expected roles, is outside of the most typical interaction, but not uncommon. An application that is unable to handle requests from the server, in effect, ignores the fact that there is a real and complex machine behind the API calls and persistent state that backs our client application. This limited view of a distributed system may work for some applications, but it is likely to present some situations that are cul-de-sacs to the users. So, the following use cases should be considered as part of an application's requirements:

- **Limited or unavailable application availability**: The collective set of cloud-based services may be unavailable or only partially functional. The server should be able to inform client applications of this, if possible (i.e. assuming any connection to the cloud is working). The alternative would be some mix of successful or failed individual operations, leaving the users confused, frustrated and perhaps compromising any stored application state.

- **Broadcast alerts**: Some message, special feature state, or impending event is present in the cloud, and there's no preexisting, coded knowledge of this on the client.

- **Result of an asynchronous method call or operation**: The asynchronous processing discussed in the prior section, *Blocking and non-blocking request responses*, effectively decoupled a client request from the server response. This leaves the server response as a *free agent*, which can be presented at any time, with no strict association to the request that triggered it. This is a special case of a server generated traffic. While the client *did* request it, that request was in the past, and the response is delivered independent of that requesting operation.

Mechanisms for receiving server-generated traffic

There are two ways for software to receive a notification, also known by the synonyms a message, a signal, or an event. The receiver can pull, or the sender can push, a notification. Some other terms that are used when describing this topic are polling as a synonym for pull notifications and callbacks for push notifications.

Pull notifications are retrieved by the client with a dedicated polling request. This model can be described by the following sequence of events:

- The server adds notifications to a queue of notifications and goes on with other work

- Clients send a pull request to the server, which equates to return a queued notification.

- The server returns a notification from the queue, removing it from the queue:

    o If there are no enqueued notifications, the server returns null or None.

Pull notifications are, in fact, the traditional client request-response mechanism. The distinguishing characteristic is that the request is not an imperative **doSomething()** invocation by the client, but rather an interrogative **isThereAnything?()** to which the server may simply, accurately, and expectedly reply **no**.

Push notifications invert this relationship, placing the server in control of the timing of delivery notifications. In effect, the client acts in the role of the server, providing a target for the server to send notifications to. This target could be a reachable HTTP endpoint or a continuously open connection or *channel* such as a WebSocket. There are also mobile client-specific protocols: Push Notifications for iOS and Google's Firebase Cloud Messaging, which supports many client platforms.

The sequence of events of a Push notification is as follows:

- The client registers a notification channel or endpoint with the server and goes on with other work

- The server sends a notification to the registered notification means
- Client receives the notification as a method invocation of the endpoint or an incoming message with a payload on the open channel.

Inverting the control or initiation of notification delivery implies a tradeoff of costs. In the case of pull notifications, there are potentially many requests that yield null responses. Push notifications only generate a cross-platform message when it is needed. Balanced against this is the fact that push notifications require a constantly open connection, which can potentially be idle for much of the time. Polling only requires a connection to be available when a pull is sent by the client.

The sequence of events between the client and the server are well defined for both the push and pull interaction models. An implementation of either of these should follow the basic pattern of interaction.

The following figures illustrate the pattern of interaction in both the push and pull models when delivering two server notifications from a server task to a client:

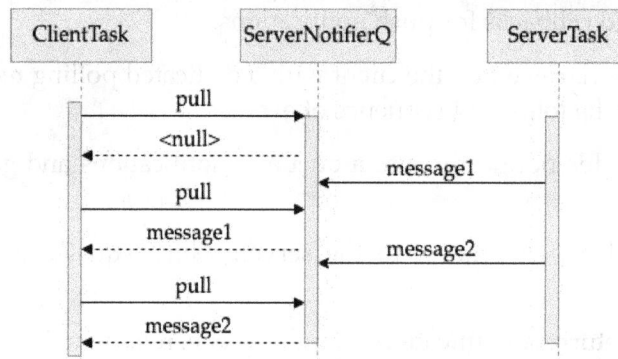

Figure 7.5: Polling/Pull notifications

Refer to the following figure for more details:

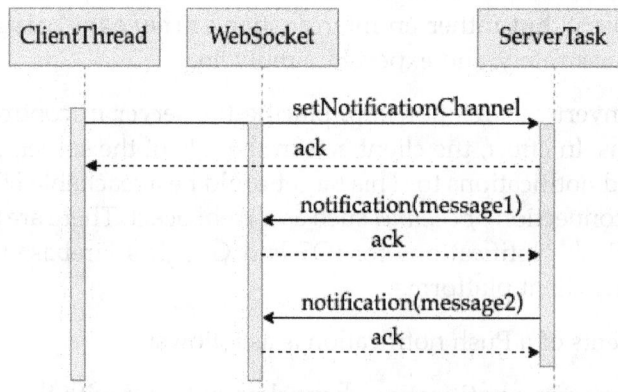

Figure 7.6: Push notifications

One set of key differences between the two is the presence of extra pull operations in the pull implementation and the decoupling in time of the *ServerTask* creating messages from the *ClientTask's* receipt of them. These can be summed up as a lack of efficiency and immediacy in the polling model. A difference that serves as a counterargument is the additional requirement for the persistent client WebSocket in the push implementation. This long-lived object implies a long-lived network connection between the two endpoints.

Special considerations for client or cloud interfaces

The tradeoffs between push and pull notifications described previously are true for all use cases, but there are considerations to make that merit special interest when designing the architecture of a client application that rests on cloud-backed infrastructure.

The requirement of keeping a connection open for the notification channel in a push model consumes some resources on the client, some on the cloud, and depends on a stable, reliable network connection between the two. We will now evaluate the cost of each of these.

The local connection resources on the client are not large, and so are not a significant consideration. A WebSocket or platform framework reserves some reference or handle to the lower layer connection along with some library code: such handles are small, and we will assume the code is well optimized.

The connection resources on the cloud are not necessarily large *per client*, but the cloud platform must provision one connection for *each* concurrently active client. It is likely that resources needed to hold this connection are paltry, alongside other resources already reserved for the client, so the resources on the cloud are also not a significant cost.

The network connection itself, the lower layer that the client and cloud both hold references to, is a different sort of consideration. Unlike the client and cloud resource cost, which are allocated and then available, the network connection is a constantly challenged resource, dependent on other systems outside of our control. Phones go in and out of service, intermediate network paths become congested, and **Internet Service Providers** (**ISP**) have outages. Obtaining a connection used for always available push notification is not a guarantee of the connection being there when the server tries to push a message to a client.

When a push channel is down, the client *may* or *may not* be missing attempted pushes from the server. A greater risk to the integrity of the application's state is presented by the fact that the client may not even be aware that the channel is down at any point in time.

Pull notifications or polling models are as vulnerable to the fragility of a network path as push notifications; there is no avoiding it. Polling models, however, have an advantage in that their nature confers an awareness of the connection state: a client makes an explicit attempt to reach the server with a polling request, and it is known if the attempt fails. While push models can implement keep alive or heartbeat probes to emulate this advantage, it is inherent in a polling model, and the state of the connection is known at the time of the poll, rather than as of the most recent heartbeat, which is disconnected from any attempted pushes from the server.

Conclusion

This chapter explored the design of client applications as both a frontend or user portal and as an integrated part of the system's functionality. Reasons for executing logic on the client platform were given, alongside the drawbacks of doing so. The practice of encoding statically included platform-agnostic policy modules was presented to address the potential introduction of multiple sources of truth, leading to out-of-sync implementations of common logic.

Portions of the user interface that can be prepared in the cloud were identified with examples illustrating reasons to do so. The chapter then described accepting and validating user input and the use of double validation to provide responsive and effective feedback while providing data validation in server-side components consistent with the user experience.

The opacity of server-side components is critical for both reusability and to guard against malicious actors. The level of abstraction of server-side responses is an important factor in isolating server infrastructure while still providing sufficient information to the client. A model for finding that balance was presented.

Finally, the chapter described the two models for handling server-side requests: push and pull notifications. The advantages and appropriate use cases for each were described along with their tradeoffs.

In the following chapters, we will apply practices and patterns that have been presented in the development of a real-world application. We will develop a voting system for televised talent competitions with a mobile client frontend and a scalable, reliable cloud-backed backend. The next chapter will describe the voting system in detail and discuss the critical features and challenges that it presents.

Join our Discord space

Join our Discord workspace for latest updates, offers, tech happenings around the world, new releases, and sessions with the authors:

https://discord.bpbonline.com

Section 3:
End-to-End: A Global Voting System

CHAPTER 8

Making a Voting System Available and Reliable

Introduction

This chapter begins the next section of the book and introduces our case study: a real-time online voting system. The world's largest digital democracies, televised talent competitions, are excellent candidates for a useful case study of the practices that have been laid out in the preceding chapters. High surges in user demand, a strong requirement for data integrity, and accessible frontend applications are all critical features of a popular voting system and exercise the strengths of a cloud-backed system. This chapter introduces the features of our voting system, and the major concerns and challenges presented by each of these features.

Structure

The following topics will be covered in this chapter:

- Digital voting system overview
- Overview of an online talent competition
- Voting system performance requirements
- Usage models
- Data aggregation

- Accessibility
- Creating the package and directory structure codelab

Objectives

This chapter will explore the real-world forces that challenge the reliability and availability of a distributed system, specifically in the context of our voting application. We will identify aspects of these challenges, such as geographic and temporal distribution of demand. We will then conduct detailed analyses of demand and identify ways to mitigate risk to the integrity of the system posed by the factors that are isolated and examined.

The codelab for this chapter will setup the initial high-level package and component hierarchy for the voting system's codebase.

Digital voting system overview

Before delving into the design of our system, it is important to clearly state the problem we are solving. So first, let us recap the scenario, the process, and then the scale.

Overview of an online talent competition

A series of rounds is used to represent each tier of the competition, with fewer rounds composing each of three successive tiers: quarterfinals, semifinals, and finals.

Prior to the quarterfinals are auditions, which are participated in by an undisclosed number of contestants. Selection of quarterfinalists from the auditions is done by panels of judges, not by popular vote. Unlike the voting process, the audition selection considers the type of act, to ensure, for example, that the initial competitors voted on include some number of singers, athletes, comedy acts, etc.

Twelve contestants appear in each round of the voting competition, with a global audience casting votes for their top picks. Each vote is cast by a registered user, or voter. A voter may cast six votes in a round, which is half of the number of contestants in a round.

The top half of the contestants from each round, ranked by the number of votes they receive, are selected to go on to the next tier, and the remaining contestants are eliminated from the competition.

The rounds progress, each pitting different winners from a previous tier against each other until the single final round. In the final tier of one round, the top 3 acts are chosen and designated as first, second, and third-place winners of the competition.

Counting backward from the final round, we determine that 48 acts participate in a total of seven rounds in three tiers, illustrated in the following figure, depicting a tree diagram:

Quarterfinal rounds

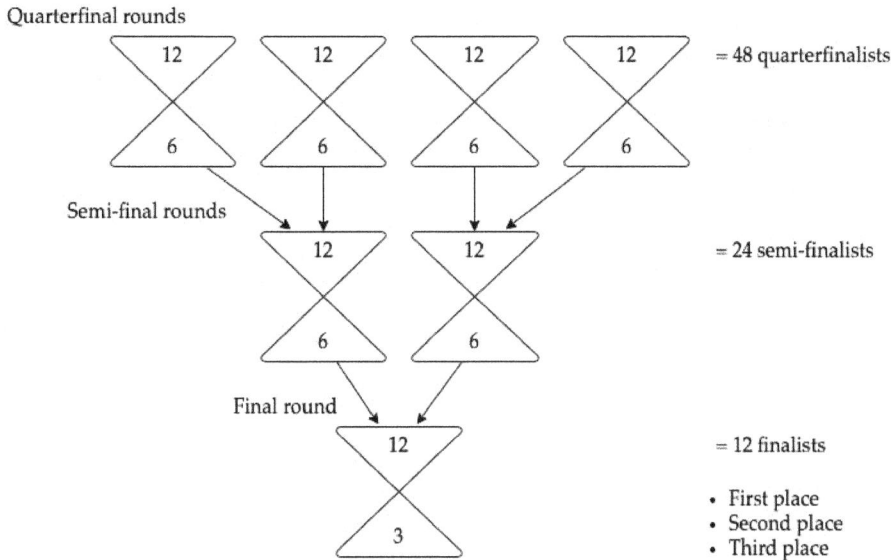

Figure 8.1: Competition tiers and rounds

Voting process

The process of voting follows specific rules and constraints which are enforced by the system. These rules are matters of policy on which the trust of the viewing public is established, and so it is mission critical that the application visibly adhere to them and be secure against exploits and misuse that could allow violation of the published voting rules.

As an act airs, viewers are expected to be watching the act. This is enforced by only allowing votes to be cast for a given act once that act is marked as eligible by the program administrators, who use a separate application to do so. The administrators do this for each act as it is airing in the first official broadcast of the act.

At the end of a round, the administrators leave the acts in that round eligible and open for voting for a given period of time, after which they mark them as no longer eligible for voting. This enforces a time limit for a round's election.

A voter is given a budget of six votes to cast in each round, of which they may cast any portion: a voter may vote for no acts in a round, one act, and up to six. A voter may only vote once for a specific act in a round, casting multiple votes for an act in a round is not allowed.

Once a vote is cast, it cannot be recalled or undone: there is no way for a voter to second-guess themselves in cases of voter's regret. An expected and observed side effect of this rule is that many voters defer voting at all until a large number, or all of the acts in a round have been seen.

Scalability requirements

There are several aspects of scalability to consider in the design and configuration of the deployment of a distributed application. The first step in designing scalability is identifying and describing each relevant aspect in the context of our voting system for each relevant feature. In this case, the Cast Vote feature is the only request we will concern ourselves with.

The scalability aspects due to consideration for the casting of votes are as follows:

- The floor or *idle request rate* is how many votes are attempted when the fewest people are voting.

  This is the *normal* or sustained rate when there is no exceptional demand. The plateau from which demand spikes depart. This is useful to plan a minimum online capacity for server-side resources.

- The *maximum request rate* is how quickly votes are being cast when voter participation surges.

  This is the expected theoretical maximum user demand, the number of requests per second that could be made if every eligible user were active and voting for the same act.

- The *traffic peak slope*, aka rate of acceleration, indicates how rapidly the voter community starts voting when participation surges.

  This is how quickly users start voting in a **high demand** or traffic spike situation. Do we ramp up from **idle** to **maximum** within 10 seconds, within a minute, or over the course of 5 minutes?

- The *trigger for a traffic peak* is the event that precedes a surge in user demand.

  This is the event that causes the most users to start voting. Is it the conclusion of an act, more people vote for an act right away or at the end of a round's episode, more people wait to vote until all of the acts are done?

- The *sustained peak rate window* is how long surges of voter participation last.

  There is a duration for the maximum rate of voting participation. Do most people vote within a minute of the peak trigger or do they get around to it, distributed over the course of several minutes? How long is the maximum rate of voting sustained?

- The *distribution of traffic origin* reflects where people vote from concurrently.

  When large numbers of people vote, it can be from one region, from a set of regions or globally all at once. This can be a function of a tendency for regional bias towards acts or different local broadcast times for episodes.

Voting system performance requirements

Having enumerated the above six aspects of user demand with regard to the voting feature, we can assign some informed values to each of them. As experience with usage accumulates over time, it is expected that these will be changed due to new or more precise information or, even better, due to organic growth or other changes in user behavior.

As well as user functionality, it is important to consider reliability and performance as first-class requirements. An application's design must take these into account, along with, not after, the functionality that is specified in user requirements.

The aspects of user behavior driving system performance are as follows:

- **The idle request rate is a measure of user demand at periods of relative rest**: Episodes are aired weekly, and we assume that after a round has aired and voting has ended, no more votes will be cast. This would indicate an idle request rate of zero. There may be non-user sources of traffic, such as monitoring and maintenance tasks, but these will be nominal in scale and easily identified.

  However, the real world is more complex than the ideal situation. Even after the last broadcast has aired and the contest administrators have ended voting for a round, there are other sources of viewers to consider. Some broadcasters may repeat the airing of an episode. If our contest episodes or individual acts are available on a streaming service, there is no way to predict when a viewer might mistakenly try to vote for an act that they see via that service. Personal Video Recorders can be used to record a broadcast show for later viewing. In any of these cases, while the system will not accept and count votes being cast outside of the prescribed time window, the system still must respond to the request in some fashion, such as with a status code of `429 Too many requests`, so the frontend should be ready to accept those *attempts* to vote.

  Given the global audience and our product team's emphasis on user trust and responsiveness, we must always be able to service some small amount of voting attempts. Our product team has set the expectation that we should expect at least 500 votes per hour, or approximately 0.2 **queries per second** (**QPS**).

- **Maximum request rate**: The maximum number of votes being cast at a time is a straightforward value to determine. We can assume that a massively appealing act would cause every single registered voter to cast a vote. So, the maximum rate of votes being cast is reached by having every eligible viewer vote at that climactic moment in the performance. With a global audience, this is less than the total number of potential voters; it is the number of voters in the largest regional viewing audience plus the number of viewers outside of that region who may watch the act through other venues like live streams, asynchronous streaming services, or remote access services. The expectation from market researchers has set this to be up to 20 million concurrent viewers. We have a working assumption of a two-minute window of time over which the immediate voters will cast their votes, which means that our frontends must be able to scale up to handle 20 million requests in two minutes, which is an average of 167K QPS.

- **Traffic peak slope**: A two-minute spike will have a steep slope on both the increase and decrease sides of the peak. There is, however, a ramp-up of demand; votes will be cast as soon as an act is introduced, due to either anticipation and predisposition for the contestant or to early positive reactions to the act. There is a tail of votes: voters who debate with family and friends or do not take their attention from the performance itself.

Market analysis and examination of prior art yields a model for voting demand around the airing of a popular act that resembles the following figure:

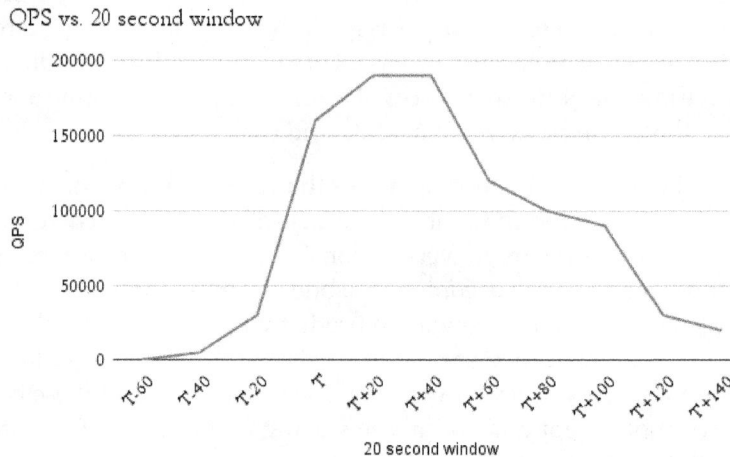

QPS vs. 20 second window

Figure 8.2: Shape of a traffic spike

A few explanations of the graph, shown in the preceding figure, are in order as we will refer to this graph in several of the following analyses:

- The X-axis represents a 3-minute and 20-second window of time, anchored at T, which is the conclusion of an act. Each X-axis tick mark is the beginning of a 20 second slice of that 200-second observed window.

- The Y axis is the average Queries Per Second during a 20 second window. For a plotted value of 150,000 QPS, the 20-second slice included 3 million total queries.

  Not shown on the graph but worth noting is the total number of queries received in this period, which is 18.7 million. Also noteworthy is the overall average request rate during this observed period, which is 93.5K QPS.

- **Trigger for a traffic peak**: The expectation is that viewers cast their vote following some climactic or compelling moment in an act, which is near the end of the performance. As these acts are brief, a few minutes in total length, the viewers who cast their vote immediately following the conclusion of a performance will overlap and merge with those climactic moment votes. This is shown in the demand graph as the sharp climb that begins at T-20, or 20 seconds before the closing of the performance, and continues through the concluding moment, represented by T on the X axis. So, there is a trigger for a peak in demand, which is some non-specific point in time close to the conclusion of a performance. In the case depicted in *Figure 8.2*, **the trigger occurs during the 20 seconds** preceding the conclusion, during the slice starting with T-20.

- **Sustained peak rate window**: The highest rate of votes being cast begins, as discussed, a brief time before the conclusion of a performance and is observed to continue for close to a minute after the conclusion. In *Figure 8.2*, the demand peak is the period from T to the 20-second window starting at T+40 for **an effective peak window of 1 minute**. We do not consider the peak to include only the literal apogee of the graph; the rate of 160K QPS at T is close enough to the absolute peak to be considered.

- **Distribution of traffic origin**: It is necessary to consider the distribution of demand across our global audience. While the total number of votes cast is the sum of all voters across the globe, not all viewers see the performance and cast their votes at the same time. So, we can expect multiple periods of peak demand, centered in different regions, as a round is broadcast by different regions' primary venue. There are larger and smaller markets and different viewer profiles in each region, which must be understood to predict demand and provision resources to maintain system availability in all regions.

Network resources, load balancers, frontend servers, and backend processors are all resources that the Google Cloud Platform allows us to configure at a regional level. The number of instances, scaling strategy, and the number of instances to keep warm on standby are all relevant to the shape and size of demand peaks that were described earlier in this section. The analysis illustrated in *Figure 8.2* should be performed for each major regional audience. The shape of the slopes is likely to differ in different regions: for example, in some markets where the audience is mostly broadcast television viewers, demand will have the sharp, well-defined peaks shown in *Figure 8.2*. In a market where most viewers use streaming services, the demand will be flatter as people watch the acts on their own schedule, their collective actions not synchronized by their provider.

Usage models

The previous section was an in-depth analysis of peak demand for our voting system, the highest rate of user requests to cast a vote across the entire global user community. Our episodes are broadcast live in North America by one provider and concentrates the largest single voting response among all regions. This is the roughly 20 million voters that were the subject of discussion in the previous section.

Google Cloud Platform regional boundaries

We will now enumerate the major geographic regions that are served by GCP and the expected voter participation and traffic profiles within each of those regions.

GCP represents geography in a hierarchy of Continent groups, Regions, and Zones. Continent groups are the major geographic landmasses of the globe. Regions are locations where GCP services are hosted. Each Region contains many Zones, which are specific serving sites such as datacenters. Not all products are available in all Regions, but all GCP runtime infrastructure products are offered in every continent and by more than one Region in most continents.

There are other geographic entities, such as network Points of Presence, but they are outside of most developers' consideration when configuring an application deployment.

The continent groups and a brief description of their offerings are as follows:

- **Americas—North, Central, and South America**: GCP has many Regions within the American continents, like Canada, the USA, and South America. Several of the Zones are *low carbon* locations, which means that those sites have low grid-carbon density. For specific information on the low-carbon value, the reader is referred to the current Google Cloud documentation.

- **Europe—The UK, North Europe, Southern Europe and Eastern Europe**: GCP coverage of Europe, including the UK, is like that of North America, with the majority of Zones being low-carbon sites.

- **Asia Pacific (APAC)—Australia, South and North Asia, East Asia**: GCP offers multiple zones within each major landmass of this region. Network connectivity is the most constrained between Zones of this region due to the large number of disjoint and distant land masses included (for example, Australia). None of the Zones in the APAC region are low-carbon sites at the time of writing.

- **Middle East—North Africa and Southeast Asia**: GCP offers a few Regions in the Middle East, with one region being offered exclusively through a regional partnership with a local reseller. There are restrictions on both account location and the availability of GCP services from that Region. Some products are not available within the Middle East continent, such as Bare Metal and Firebase Storage.

- **Africa—Central and Southern Africa**: GCP currently offers one Region on the African continent. Not all services are currently available in the African region, determined largely by local customer demand.

Voting system demand by continent

To be able to design our voting application to gracefully scale to meet demand, we must understand where and when that demand will be made. The selection of cloud techniques, such as asynchronous request funneling, requires us to know where stress points will be.

We can make a safe assumption that usage in each of the continent groups can be considered independently. With that assumption, the following table of demand summarizes the peak usage analysis performed in the previous section for each of the five continent groups identified by GCP and described previously in *Google Cloud regional boundaries*:

Continent	Peak window	Max QPS	Total requests per voting window	Average voting QPS
Africa	100 seconds	70K	7M	34K
Americas	60 seconds	190K	18.7M	93K
APAC	45 seconds	110K	11.1M	27K
Europe	150 seconds	90K	15M	40K
Middle east	120 seconds	80K	5M	16K

Figure 8.3: Peak voting demand by continent

This preceding table reveals a few important points:

- The largest number of votes are in the **Americas, Europe and Asia-Pacific (APAC)**. When we are designing the locality of whatever mechanism aggregates votes, it will be best to keep that service local in those continents.

- The highest rate of **queries per second (QPS)** is in the Americas, for a burst of one minute. The second APAC is not close, but it is still very high and for a shorter burst. This guides the scalability of voting request handlers.

These insights are valuable input to optimizing the deployment of our system, and our design must support that deployment model. We will discuss the design of our vote request processing in detail, and how it incorporates this knowledge of regional demand in the next section.

Data aggregation

The number of votes requires an equal total number of requests to record them. This resource demand is for workers, but unless we are permanently recording every individual vote (we are not), it does not affect the size of our datastore: one vote or 20 million votes still fit inside of a long integer field. However, these votes, while ephemeral, still require some resources to represent them until they have been added to the total. These resources can be request handlers, asynchronous messages on a queue or some other artifact, but they must be robust, and quick to create, given that our system will be creating 190K of them every second in one instance. We should design the lifecycle of a Vote to be as simple and efficient as possible, striving to shorten the required lifespan of each vote by quickly delivering it to the process that applies it to the total votes, after which time we no longer need each of these millions of votes.

We now must apply some topographical considerations to our design. Requests that cross regions are more expensive than intra-region requests, and crossing continents is still more expensive. Expense is not just material cost or service charges, it is also evident as higher latency and reduced reliability, so keeping as much traffic local as possible is a high priority for our application.

Aggregating distributed votes in a global system

Our voting system does not require us to ally all votes in real-time or even during a broadcast. It would not be useful, given how widely distributed our voting community is, in both space and time. Recall the Eisenhower matrix in *Chapter 3, Determining the Infrastructure to Build Features Upon* and the separation of importance and urgency. It is not important to tally all votes, it is not urgent. So, we can introduce some latency in the process of counting all votes as long as we guarantee that they will all be counted.

With that in mind, there is no strict requirement to ever cross the continental boundaries for requests at the fine granularity and large scale of individual votes. Summing up votes within a set of local or regional domains lets us avoid costly (as defined in the preceding section) requests and each of our regional domains can then synchronize their small set of tallied votes into a merged global election result.

With this architectural precept in place, our design focuses on how to design that regional vote tallying pipeline, favoring reliability and user responsiveness over the window of a vote being counted. Viewing this regional process as a black box to be defined later, our distributed system architecture is illustrated in the following figure:

Note: **Several regions are elided, they are duplicates of the ones explicitly shown.**

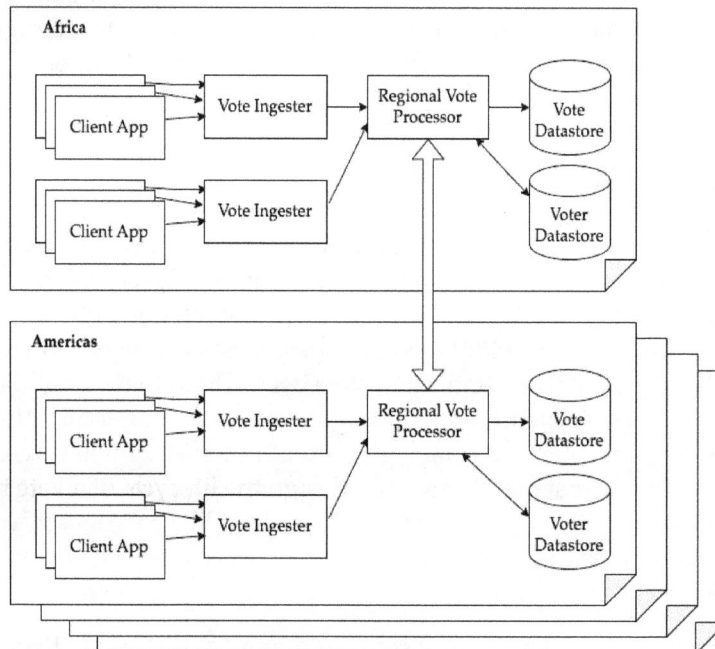

Figure 8.4: Distributed vote processing architecture

This architecture introduces tiers that can be scaled independently and appropriate to demand under load. The clients are the ultimate drivers of demand and are subject to the largest and least constrained horizontal scaling. The number of users is not only beyond our control, but also is the resource that we do not wish to constrain: the more voting, the better for us. We wish to take the voting request from the client as quickly and efficiently as possible, so we connect the clients to some ingesting frontend optimized to take the vote, pass it on and respond to the user as quickly as possible. This optimization should allow us to handle as many clients as possible with each Ingester frontend able to maintain hundreds of concurrent connections and hold several thousand QPS. Allowing GCP to horizontally scale the Ingester frontend to hundreds of instances serves several hundred thousand client requests per second.

The Regional Vote Processor has no real-time latency requirement and the number of clients it serves is under our control: it is the number of Vote Ingester frontends that we start up. This number will be orders of magnitude lower than the number of clients and is subject to a configured cap. As long as the mechanism for delivering vote requests from the ingesters to the Vote Processor is reliable, it can be asynchronous. Pub/Sub is an excellent choice for decoupling these two processes in time. It can take votes from Ingester frontends in tens of milliseconds, placing them on a durable message queue to be retrieved by a Vote Processor whenever it has available cycles. Our backend application logic detects and prevents the counting of duplicate votes through the enforcement of vote budgets.

A quick confidence check is useful at this point to determine the feasibility of this approach to the highest-demand scenario we have identified in *Figure 8.3*. The votes cast as a popular act is broadcast in North America. This will not guarantee a satisfactory performance in all regions and scenarios but is the most likely to strain the capabilities of our infrastructure and is the best place to start looking for and eliminating failures.

The following table relies on reasonable assumptions for frontend server performance:

Concurrent client requests	190,000	Given
Vote Ingester frontend latency	50 milliseconds	Assumed
frontend instance concurrent requests	20	Assumed
frontend instance QPS	400	(1 second / 50ms) * 20 concurrent)
frontend instance count needed	475	190,000/400

Table 8.1: Performance and scaling of peak demand scenario

The key numbers to evaluate in this table are the latency of the frontend and the number of frontend instances. The following questions are relevant to determining if our performance requirements can be met:

- Is 50ms latency of the frontend achievable?
- Is 50ms latency of the frontend acceptable to our client app?
- Can we scale to 475 frontend instances in the North America group of regions?

Accessibility

The availability of sufficient resources to service regional demand is convenient but cannot safely be assumed. While Google Cloud Platform is always revising the service offerings and availability based on customer demand, there are both external constraints, such as available space and power and insufficient overall demand, that could result in a needed service being unavailable in any region close to an area of high user demand.

How does an application architect address this situation?

At a high level, there are a few approaches that will be discussed in detail after listing them here:

- Strategically relocate some resources to the nearest available location in a manner that best preserves user latency and data integrity.

- Attempt to further optimize the application to perform acceptably with regard to response SLOs within the available resources at critical locations.

- Redesign the application to fit within the available services at critical locations.

These are ordered from the least disruptive to the most disruptive approach, which is the most to least desirable changes for an application architect to make.

We would prefer to make the infrastructure resources fit the application, rather than have the application written to accommodate the available platform resources. The reasoning behind this preference is twofold: the application should serve the user and the product, the infrastructure is ideally a means to that end; and the platform provider *will* change the regional distribution of resources, and changes we make fitting the application to the infrastructure resources may be quickly and frequently obsolete.

With that directive in mind, we will describe these three approaches to handling regional service shortfalls.

Strategically relocating resources

Let us refer to *Figure 8.4*, our high-level voting system architecture. It relies on the regional presence of our datastore. If we have decided that Spanner is our ideal storage service for any number of reasons, we look at GCP's service map and find that there are several regions in South Asia, part of APAC, that provide the Spanner service to address the situation where Spanner is not offered in any region in (for example) the Middle East group of regions? We look at GCP's service map and find that there are several regions in South Asia, part of APAC, that provide the Spanner service. At a naïve first reaction, we would simply configure the Regional Vote Processor in the Middle East to use a dedicated Spanner instance in those APAC regions. This is not a strategic decision as the latency between the Vote Processor and the Spanner datastore is high and would introduce unacceptable latency and failed RPCs to the Vote Processor.

A more considered reaction is to move both the Vote Processor and the Spanner datastore for the Middle East to an APAC region. This shifts the inter-continental traffic to the connection between the Vote Ingester frontends and the Vote Processor. This is not problematic, recall that the connection between those components is through Pub/Sub, the asynchronous nature of which makes it an ideal buffer for the higher latency of this traffic flow. This consideration of where to introduce distance and latency is what is meant by the *strategic* relocation of resources.

Optimizing the application to fit available resources

When we implement an application, the first concern should be satisfying the functional requirements–the users' needs. A computer system exists to serve a business or entertainment function, not an inherent self-defined need of the computer itself.

This practical and human-centric point of view leads to one of the most famous sayings among software developers:

Premature optimization is the root of all evil.

Its source is credited to *Donald Knuth*. Here is the full quote from his seminal book *The Art of Computer Programming*:

The real problem is that programmers have spent far too much time worrying about efficiency in the wrong places and at the wrong times; premature optimization is the root of all evil (or at least most of it) in programming.

The reason for this is that fixating on the optimization of a specific algorithm or module may speed up that portion of an application, but the time spent doing so may distract or preempt the software developer from more important concerns, such as the completion of a critical software feature.

> Note: **Developers can use profiling tools to identify profitable targets of performance optimization, when the need for such optimizations is clear.**

For example, suppose the list of items in a shopping cart takes 200 milliseconds to refresh. A clever software engineer realizes that they can rewrite the entire cart representation in the database and in-memory cache in only a week and speed this up to a 10-millisecond refresh delay. This is outstanding, a 20x speedup.

The counterargument to this work is that no one cares or notices. Most people will not perceive this difference of less than a fifth of a second, and with that week of intense effort, the engineer could have been adding the function *Move all items to wish list* from the feature request queue. The users *would* have noticed that.

The time to optimize for runtime considerations, such as time (response latency) or space (memory or worker count), is when they are needed for the users or by the business. That is the situation we may find ourselves in when deploying a distributed application to a region with insufficient resources for our regional user demand.

This is not premature optimization; this is optimization at the right time and in the right place. Suppose we wish to deploy our voting system in the African continental regions. The following table summarizes our resource requirements based on the breakdown of global demand given in *Figure 8.3*:

Concurrent client requests	70,000	Given
Vote Ingester frontend latency	50 milliseconds	Assumed
Frontend instance concurrent requests	20	Assumed
Frontend instance QPS	400	(1 second / 50ms) * 20 concurrent)
Frontend instance count needed	175	70,000 / 400

Table 8.2: Performance and scaling of demand in Africa

This is straightforward, but suppose that when we configure our application in African regions, we find that there is a constraint: a maximum of 100 instances of our Ingester frontends can be provisioned. That may change, but for now, that is a hard limit.

We need to serve 70K QPS from 100 frontend instances, a 42% reduction in resources.

We could do this through a number of means: reducing the frontend latency by 42% to 29 milliseconds, increasing the number of concurrent requests by 42% to 28, increasing the latency tolerance of our client, or any combination of these. The target improvement may or may not be achievable, but there are a couple of factors in our favor: most software has room to improve, and the lack of early optimization implies latent optimization waiting to be realized if needed.

Redesigning the application

Let us look at a scenario: You find a performance challenge that can neither be routed around (the first strategy) nor improved away (the second). You may have found that your proposed architecture is fundamentally incompatible with the chosen infrastructure and performance requirements.

Let us suppose a situation such as this, one in which the datastore, Spanner, cannot process updates to voter activity from the Regional Vote Processor at the expected peak rate. We first examine other persistence products capable of a high rate, such as Bigtable, but none offer the global consistency among regional data stores that our design relies on. We have hit a fundamental design flaw and must return to the proverbial drawing board.

This is a problem, the solution for which we can find prior art. A common solution is adding an in-memory cache in front of the Spanner database, which would bring the performance of the Vote Processor back within requirements. Looking for side-effects, we determine that the relatively infrequent write-throughs from the cache to Spanner are well within Spanner's performance guarantees. Since the global synchronization between regions is not latency sensitive, the delay in propagating voter activity between regions is not an issue.

The last concern is one of durability. Since Memcached is an in-memory datastore, we will use the GCP product *Memorystore for Memcached* which provides fully managed Memcached clusters in multiple zones for guaranteed high availability.

The high-level architecture with this addition is shown in the following figure:

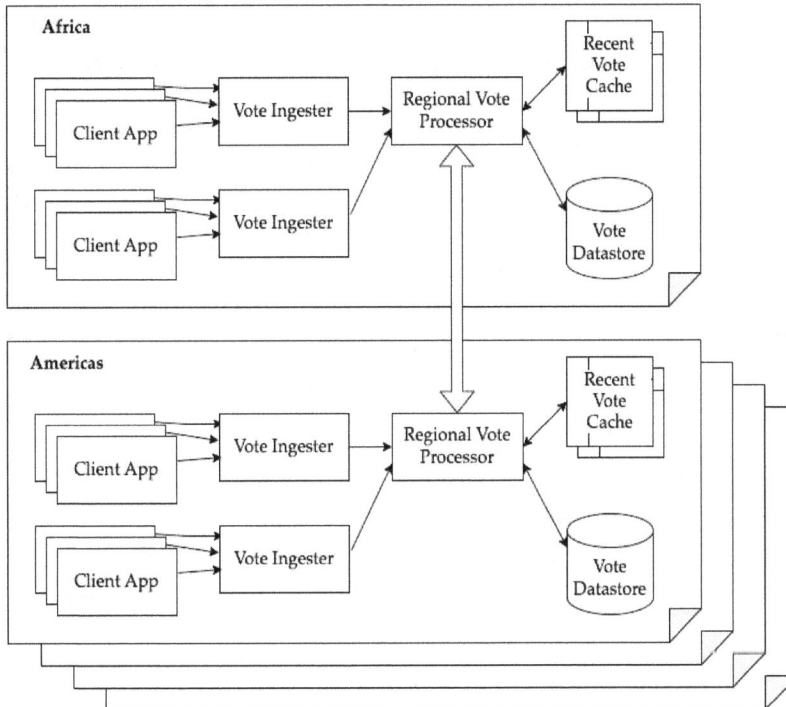

Figure 8.5: Distributed vote processing architecture with caching

We described three possible challenges that could arise in deploying our application to our global audience and addressed each with a different strategy to give some insight into the applicability and application of each technique. In general, the architectural practices presented can be employed to address *any* scenario, assuming that some bare minimum of needed infrastructure capabilities is available.

Creating the package and directory structure codelab

The voting application has been described with regard to functionality and our distributed deployment plan. This section of the book will present codelabs in each chapter, illustrating portions of the voting application implementation. These codelabs will present GCP configuration and program code implementing that chapter's theme.

This codelab lays out the directory and package structure, allowing client and server-side code to reference each other and common library and declarative definitions.

Platform components and initial files

These are the components that this codelab will declare. The color coding separates the components by platform, which we will strive to reflect in the application's package hierarchy as supported by our programming language, in this case, Python 3.

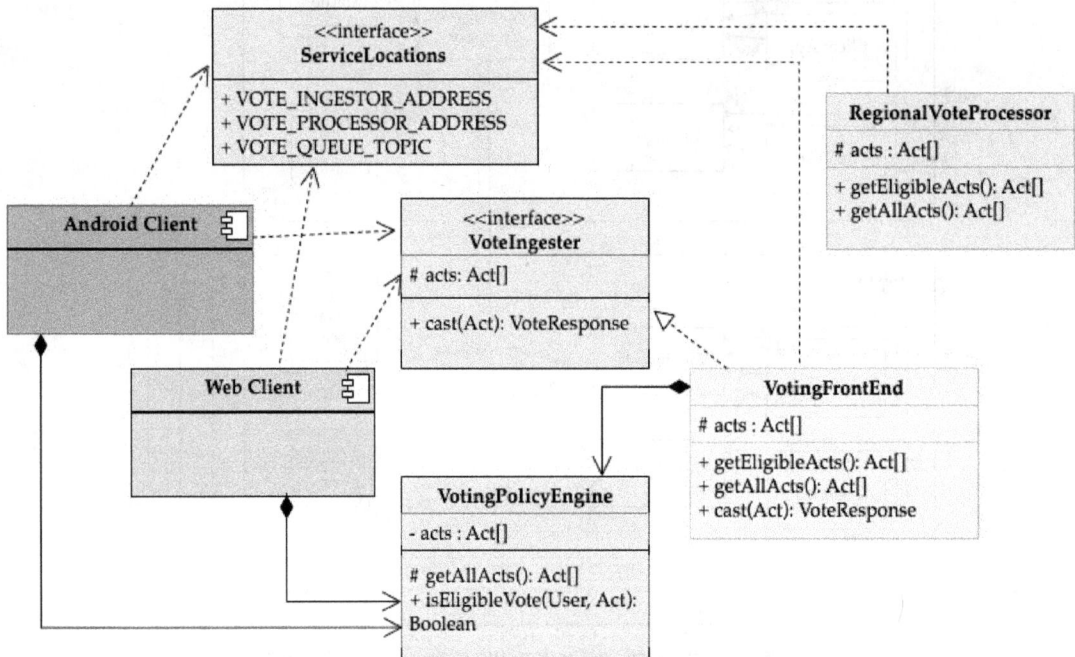

Figure 8.6: Component packages and dependencies

The codelabs will use Visual Studio Code to edit a GitHub repository. The VS Code project's Explorer pane showing the files used to implement Figure 8.7 is as follows:

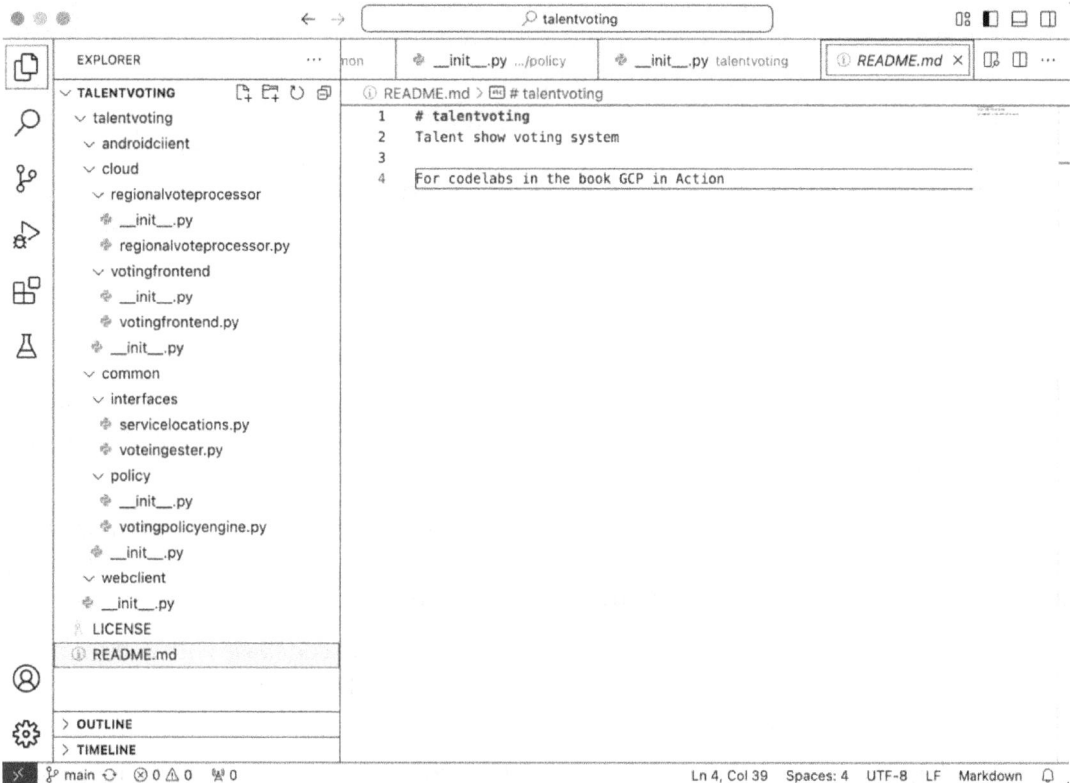

Figure 8.7: VS Code Explorer for our main package files

Codelabs in the coming chapters will add files and illustrate the code contained within them.

Backends for frontends

The distributed system design pattern *backends for frontends* was described in *Chapter 7, Frontends at the Client Border.* It is appropriate to consider employing this at the border of a client platform and server or cloud component to isolate non-client-specific code from multiple clients, concentrating client dependencies in as few locations as possible.

This pattern is embodied in the **VoteIngester** interface which is implemented by the **VotingFrontEnd** server. The various client platforms, including those defined within the **webclient** and **androidclient** packages, will rely on the remote implementation of **VoteIngester** methods rather than independently implementing the actual **cast()** logic.

Voting API

The API for our voting service is defined as abstractly as practical, decoupling the clients of this API from the actual provider of the service. This is a common low-cost step to future-proof our system by limiting the hard dependencies on any concrete component to as few places as possible. In this case, rather than having each client encode a hard dependency on our Voting frontend implementation, this dependency has been concentrated into the files that are contained within the `talentvoting.common` family of packages.

Conclusion

Our voting system is used to select a winner from a large number of contestants, relying purely on the majority popular vote. This chapter illustrated the process of analyzing and documenting the usage of a distributed system, from the business/product model.

The reader was guided through the planning of major components' deployment, related to their regional affinity to users. Likely, shortfalls specific to regional platform resources were identified, and different techniques to mitigate these were explored.

The first codelab laid out the arrangement of our voting feature codebase with a description of the API design and related it to the design best practices that were described earlier in the book.

The next chapter identifies the narrowest points in the voting system, where the system is most susceptible to fail under load. The established ways to forestall and, more importantly, detect and mitigate such failures will be described. That is the goal of **site reliability engineering (SRE)**, a crucial part of any engineering culture and organization.

Join our Discord space

Join our Discord workspace for latest updates, offers, tech happenings around the world, new releases, and sessions with the authors:

https://discord.bpbonline.com

CHAPTER 9
Identifying the Stress Points of our Voting System

Introduction

This chapter examines the bottlenecks or stress points of the voting system. By this, we mean those parts of the voting system which fail to meet our performance expectations under heavy load before their adjacent modules fail to.

In identifying these weak points, it is also necessary to determine what conditions bring these to their breaking points. For each of these bottlenecks, we will then conduct an effects analysis: Identifying the specific failure when critical thresholds are passed, i.e. what goes wrong? With an understanding of root causes and impact, we can plan preventative detection and mitigations for the failures that hopefully will not, but typically will occur as our voting system is put to the test of popular and trusted usage.

Structure

The following topics will be covered in this chapter:

- Types of failures
- Assessing impact
- Monitoring, detection and notification
- Incident response

- Matrix of failure modes and appropriate measures
- Implementation and monitoring of the Vote Ingester API codelab

Objectives

There is a diverse set of ways in which a system can fail, with different root causes, impacts, and approaches to mitigation. This chapter will guide the reader through each of these dimensions of a potential outage, describing the techniques and indicators used to categorize a specific incident. The reader will finish this chapter prepared with a methodology for categorizing these failure modes and measures for mitigation, which can be applied to any highly available distributed system.

Types of failures

Before looking into specific potential points of failure in our voting system, it is useful to clarify exactly what we mean by the term failure in these discussions and to give body to the concept through examples.

Not all failures deserve equal notice: In an example that should be fairly self-evident, if the indicator light in an automobile that signals when a door is open fails due to a broken lamp, it would not get the same attention as the intermittent failure of the indicator lamp that indicates that the engine is overheating, and neither of these would get the immediate response that the failure of the brake pedal should receive.

Just as the failures of an automobile's systems vary in severity, we rank failures in a software system by two aspects of the failure: It is scope and progression. Understanding these two aspects of a potential outage, or failure, of our application is crucial to help identify strategies to prevent these failures, select techniques to detect them in production, and to plan effective means to quickly mitigate their effects on our users.

Scope of a failure

The scope of a failure is the reach of the problem, often referred to as the failure's blast radius. In a distributed application, with clear regional runtime boundaries such as our voting application, the scope is likely to be isolated to one of a few scopes:

- A local failure affects a group of users with some affinity to a per client aspect of the user; such as a client host version, a certain type of connection or a specific browser.

- A regional failure impacts a collection of regions which probably share some cloud resource.

- A global failure affects all users of the application.

While a local failure may seem the least of the evils, it is most likely to be an indication of a chronic condition: A failure that recurs, becoming the subject of conspiracy theory and the basis of memes. In the voting application, if a specific group of users cannot vote, that will be interpreted to be prejudicial to those users or to any common interest of the affected users, such as a certain performer.

Some examples of local failures are a bug specific to a particular client application and platform, e.g., an iOS mobile app on an *iPhone 13 mini*. Another client-specific affinity that could introduce a local failure is all users relying on 3G connections in a locale where the frontends are experiencing peak demand and are in the process of horizontally scaling up. We classify a failure as local if the failure is not uniformly affecting users across a large geography or topological area, but rather is associated with pockets of users. We presume in that case that the trigger or underlying cause for the failure is also local, specific to a user.

Let us turn our attention to regional failures, those that affect users within a geographical or topological boundary. The distinction between geography and topology as used here is that geography refers to neighbors in a region of physical space, whereas topology could also include neighbors in a network, parties who share a point of presence, network peer, load balancer or other point in cyberspace, not physical space.

Examining a failure experienced by users of our voting application in one place, while users elsewhere can vote without a problem, leads us to a logical assumption: It is nothing about the individual user that is causing the problem. We can apply a similar argument from the other side, the fact that users in other places are able to vote tells us that the application is essentially capable of working as intended somewhere, so it is not the overall system that is broken.

If the blame lies with neither the individual nor with the overall system, there is a cause somewhere in the middle. A regional failure usually has a regional cause.

The third, most obvious and potentially catastrophic failure domain is that of global failure or total system outage. If no one can vote, the failure is not triggered by any difference between distinct regions or users. The failure is due to something shared by all users in all places. A global, system-wide constant is to blame for the outage. That global constant could be a shared program code, a single shared runtime resource such as a global datastore, or a common configuration artifact or value.

Progression

The scope of a system outage may differ over time to affect additional users of a given feature or to impact more users through the failure of additional features. If the number of users for whom the application fails is graphed over time, it will usually conform to one of the following timelines:

- A failure may manifest as a constant set of affected users who cannot cast their vote.

- There may be a steadily increasing number of users experiencing voting failures as time goes by.

First, let us describe the steady state or constantly scoped failure. In this failure mode, the stream of failures that we first observe remains statistically constant set of failures in the following seconds, minutes, and hours. In absolute terms, if we see approximately 2% of iOS users encountering an error, or all users in the *Northeast US* cannot vote; whatever the scope of the failure is, the same scope remains true as the outage persists. This is a steady stream of failures.

A failure with a creeping or expanding scope is a one in which the affected set of users increases as the outage persists. In an example, perhaps 2% of iOS users initially receive an error, but after five minutes that has grown to 25% of iOS users. Another example of a failure with expanding scope is one in which the users in the Northeast US cannot vote, but 10 minutes later, users in the *Southeast US* are also encountering errors.

A creeping failure may be a cascading failure in which the effects of the failure spill over into adjacent regions, or it may be a failure whose underlying cause is spreading throughout the system.

An example of a cascading failure is one in which traffic spills over into adjacent and inadequate regions. We will follow the progression of a simple cascading failure in the following diagrams and text.

As a precursor to any failure, we begin with a moment when demand in *Africa* and APAC is at their expected peaks and all is well:

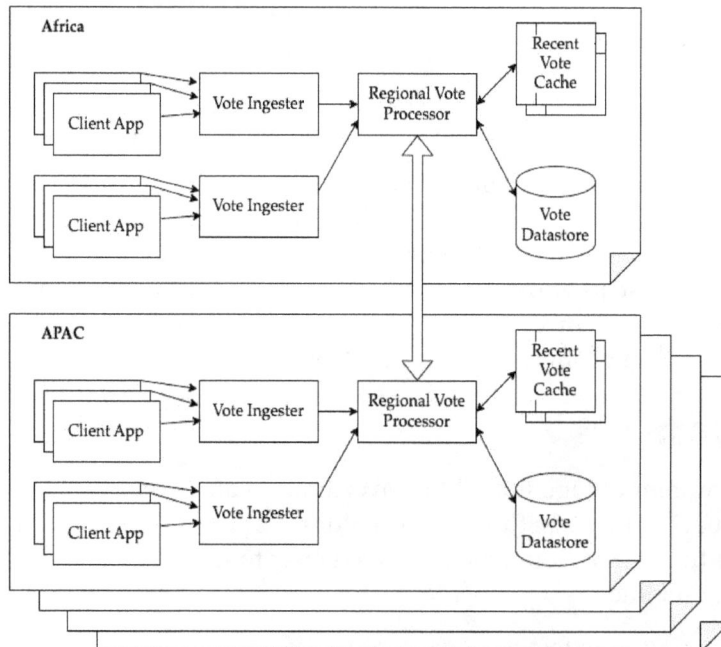

Figure 9.1: Precursor to cascading regional failure

While the system is performing well and users in both Africa and APAC are voting without incident, that is all about to change. The world is complex and will sometimes present an unanticipated situation, leading to unexpected system behavior.

In this case, we will present the hypothetical situation that a local African hero act has made it to the semifinals and that they are performing adjacent to a popular Asian act. The timing of these performances guarantees that the peak demand in their home continents will coincide. An additional consideration is that the **Google Cloud Platform (GCP)** does not have the resources to instantiate an exceptional number of our Vote Ingester frontends. The load balancers for our African network regions are configured to send requests to Vote Ingesters in APAC, if no frontends in Africa are available. There are resources in the APAC regions to start additional Vote Ingester frontends if needed.

This stage of our failure scenario is illustrated in the following figure:

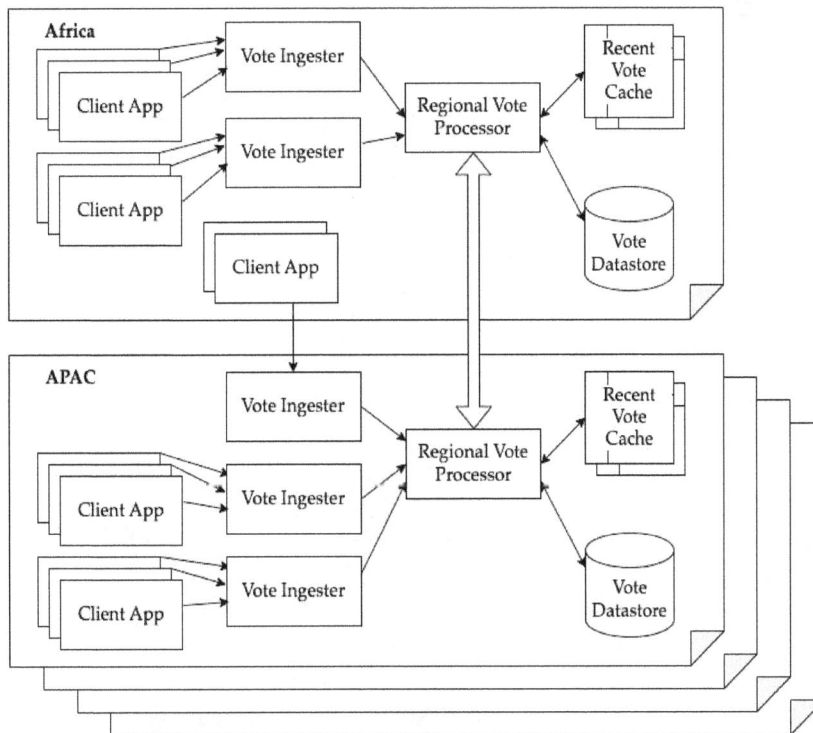

Figure 9.2: Spillover of client traffic to adjacent continent

At first, the chosen approach seems to work; we had available resources elsewhere and routed requests to utilize them. We have tested our client application with cross-regional requests, and it worked, so we believe that this scenario was covered in our deployment plan.

There is, however, an external condition that we could not test with. As our cross-regional requests are coming to the APAC frontends, they are experiencing high demand from the local clients who are voting for their favorite act. While all this voting is going on, the underlying network fabric in the APAC region is delivering video to all of those millions of viewers.

The GCP network is robust and capable, but it is not infinite. The competing demands for bandwidth result in increased latency, in some cases past the limits of a timeout for our client requests to the frontends. The clients in Africa who are routed to Vote Ingesters in APAC start to see a mix of high latency responses and request timeouts. This final stage in the evolution of a cascading failure is depicted in the following figure:

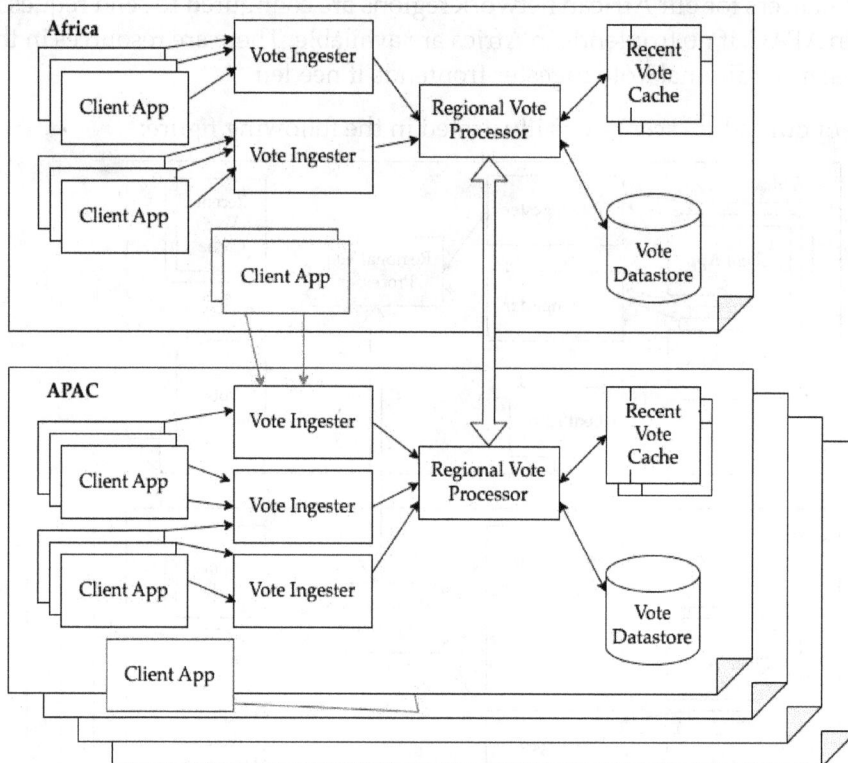

Figure 9.3: Beginning of series of cascading failures

The clients illustrated at the bottom of the Africa region are connected to a Vote Ingester in APAC, crossing various network boundaries to send requests and receive responses. They are depicted in red to indicate the failure state that they are experiencing. This is not the end of the failure; the term cascading indicates that this is part of a series or sequence, which is represented by the red clients at the bottom of the APAC region. The introduction of Africa-based clients has fully saturated our local Vote Ingester frontends, and at this time of peak demand, additional voters in APAC are casting votes for their favorite act. The same spillover logic is in effect for APAC demand as in Africa: When no more frontends can be instantiated in APAC, the requests prefer to be sent to the nearest neighboring region, in this case, Africa.

Of course, Africa is already oversubscribed, which is what led to the problem in APAC. With no resources in Africa, our spillover logic sends these APAC clients to European regions. This is sub-optimal under the best circumstances, and those APAC clients begin to experience similar errors as their continent-crossing counterparts in Africa. The possibility exists for the same situation to emerge in European regions, indeed a failure such as this often propagates across most or all the globe.

Causes of a failure

We have now identified, codified and described the two aspects of a failure that we will use to categorize the failure: it is shape in space and over time. These describe how the failure persists among our user community once it has manifested, but there is one missing feature of an outage we should consider in the end: its trigger.

The origin of a failure is the seed or trigger of the problem. Every outage starts somewhere and sometime, and those values are obvious attributes of the origin of the failure. When and where a failure occurs are evident. What is more basic and sometimes less obvious is why a failure manifested at that place and time.

Here, we will enumerate the categories of failure origins which are the third and final aspects of an outage that will be considered in prevention, detection, and mitigation:

- **Latent failures incurred by the passage of time**: Staleness of resources, obsolescence of components or dependencies and inattention to capacity versus current expected usage are all variations of this. Bit rot is an instance of this sort of failure, one which is particular to storage systems.

- **Force majeure events**: This means greater force and refers to an event for which no party can be held accountable. An unpredictable yet always possible act of God or nature, such as an earthquake, flood, or solar storm, can cause failures in the most carefully planned systems.

- **Failures caused by ignorance or malevolence**: These types of failures are rooted in process deficiencies: Either operational processes or security processes respectively.

- **Failures due to usage in unanticipated operation sequence or volume**: These come about because users acted in ways that were not anticipated by the architects and operators of the system. These are usually the result of planning deficiencies.

- **Failures resulting from flaws in systems or their components**: While the presence of some defects is accepted as inevitable, bugs and a lack of isolation or a means to contain them can lead to runtime failures that have greater impact than they need to. Deficiencies in quality assurance and release processes lead to these having a significant user or operational impact.

Failure categorization

In this section, we have identified three facets of a failure: scope, progression and trigger or cause. A given failure will have at least one value for each of these three attributes, so the potential failures can be visualized as a matrix, shown in the following figure:

Cause	Scope	Progression
Introduced over/by time	Local	
Force majeure		Constant
Ignorance or malevolence	Regional	
Unanticipated usage		Creeping or expanding
Defects	Global	

Figure 9.4: Failure categorization matrix

According to this matrix, a comprehensive view of risks to our application should take up to 30 *(5 * 3 * 2)* different failure modes into account. An effective plan for gauging and ensuring system robustness must include either a means to detect and mitigate each of these possible failure modes or acknowledge the presence of unaddressed risks.

The likelihood and impact of these different failure modes must also be quantified in some way and considered. No matter how large or small the effect of a given failure might be, we should recognize that cost and use that to prioritize how we allocate resources for improving the performance and reliability of our voting application. That projected cost of a failure and its impact is the primary factor to consider when prioritizing addressing that failure among the others we foresee.

Assessing impact

The ultimate impact of a failure is its cost to the business over time.

Note the over time part of that sentence. A failure of any system has both short-term and long-term costs, some of which are direct and some which are indirect. The impact of a failure on a business is the sum of all of these. This costing exercise is complicated by the fact that the further away in time, or less direct an effect is, the more guesswork and estimation will be used in determining the cost of that effect. So, the cost may not be quantifiable for every failure mode but the order of the magnitude, or if nothing else, a stack ranking of the different potential failure modes by cost should be possible to devise and may be enough to direct a system owner's reliability efforts.

Determining short-term cost of an outage

Suppose we have a regional failure due to underprovisioning the number of instances for a given service. The mitigation for this is obvious and immediately effective: We can increase our scaling ceiling, quota, and billing limits for the affected component.

The cost to the business is also straightforward and can be quickly determined using several factors. The following list is not intended to be exhaustive or universally applicable, but presents a reasonable set of factors in our scenario of voting frontend failure:

- The number of failed requests before the situation was mitigated. Each of these requests incurs some infrastructure cost. A failed request is often more taxing on many resources than a successful one is, e.g., a request that times out ties up a client thread and a connection for the longest time possible, whereas the average request that succeeds released those resources in less time.

- If the window of time of the failure is significant, it will extend the peak demand window. This adds usage based fees for products that are scaled up during peak load.

- There will be additional resource fees charged by GCP for the additional instances.

- Some expense is incurred in damage control—writing and publishing communications explaining the outage.

- Any compensation or rebates to advertisers or sponsors as contractually specified.

The long-term cost of an outage

Suppose there is a different sort of an outage: A software bug that causes us to lose data, in our case, votes. What if we discover that some significant portion of the votes that were cast were not recorded or tallied? This failure incurs a longer-term cost to the business that will not be fully realized until well after the situation is resolved.

The major impact of this outage in the long-term is rooted in a loss of reputation. As a result, it is projected that fewer people will be tuning into or participating in our competition.

This affects our bottom line in the medium to long-term as endorsement and product placement fees in future competitions will be reduced and our show will be less appealing to top tier advertisers. While the short-term outage incurred some expenses at the time, this failure had lingering effects has reduced future revenue. While this impact is difficult to quantify, it has the looming potential to change the future of our business whereas the cost of a brief service outage can be known and accounted for soon after the incident window has closed.

No outage is good but the difficulty in determining and containing the impact increases as the effects of the outage persist. An unknown or open-ended cost presents a great risk. When deciding what failure modes to focus on preventing, the ones whose effects cannot be quickly undone are those on which the owners of a system should focus their attention and effort. The reasoning behind this is simply stated by a popular idiom *better the devil you know than the devil you don't*. This means that it is better to deal with a difficult situation one knows than with a new situation that could be worse.

Monitoring, detection and notification

It is as important to understand why a distributed system must be monitored as it is to understand what about the system should be monitored. We will first address this question of why before discussing what and how monitoring should be applied to an application.

Observing first and then controlling

In more general system and business practices, predating distributed software, the principle of *you cannot control what you are not monitoring* has been accepted for many decades. In a very relatable example, take the case of a doctor whose goal is to keep a patient's blood pressure within a healthy, expected range of values. The doctor can exert control by prescribing treatments which have one of two effects on the patient: To raise their blood pressure or to lower their blood pressure. The doctor can control the blood pressure of the patient, but no responsible physician would prescribe either treatment without first establishing a routine of measuring and charting the patient's blood pressure over time. Once the doctor knows what the patient's blood pressure is, and perhaps varies over time, they can confidently exert control over it, steering it towards the desired range's boundary.

If the control that the doctor had was absolute: Bring the pressure to 130 over 80, it would be possible to bypass prerequisite monitoring. However, in this example, as with most feedback loops, the control is not absolute, they do not set a value, they steer it. Rather than a treatment that sets the patient's blood pressure to a specific value, the available treatments raise or lower blood pressure by some hopeful predicted value. Ongoing observation is needed to determine the actual effect of the treatment and advise further application of control.

Monitoring terminology

The field of monitoring is wide and complex; before diving deeper into it, we will define some of the most encountered terms in the domain's vocabulary:

- **Monitoring**: The collection, aggregation, and displaying of quantitative data about a system in real-time. Some examples of the data elements we may include in monitoring a distributed computing system are query counts, processing times, and server instance counts.

- **Metric**: A metric is a value that is collected from the system being monitored and used to evaluate or measure the system and its performance. Examples of metrics are request processing time or latency, error count, and requests per second.

- **Dashboard**: An application that provides a summary of a system's metrics. The metrics are the data collected from the system or are data derived from the metrics collected. An example of a derived value is the maximum server instance count observed during the last 24 hours.

- **Alert**: A notification directed and intended for human notice and consumption. An alert is the system's way of informing a human of some specific condition that has arisen within the system. Alerts are typically delivered to humans using one or more channels, depending on their urgency. Tickets or bugs, email, and pages are the most common classes of delivery channels in ascending order of urgency.

- **Root cause**: A defect in software or processes that the elimination of would prevent a consequential failure from reoccurring. Put another way, a root cause is the thing to fix to prevent a repeat of a problem. A failure may have multiple root causes and only occurred when each root cause was present. An example of such a compound root cause is an increase in demand due to a regional database failure and a billing account used to scale up additional resources that is tied to an expired credit card.

- **Node**: A node is generically used to refer to an individual instance of something that is being monitored. For example, if we are monitoring the Vote Ingester service, a node refers to a specific Vote Ingester server or task.

- **Push**: A change to a running system's software is referred to as a **push**. This is related to the push notifications that were described in *Chapter 7, Frontends at the Client Border*, as they are generated from a source outside of the recipient and forcefully delivered to the receiver at an unscheduled time. Software in this context can include code, configuration files or both. A replacement of the code running by an App Engine service with a new version of the application is a typical code push.

Types of metrics

Metric is an appropriately vaguely defined term: *A value that is collected from the system being monitored.* Before applying the term in practice, we will provide more concrete definitions and classes of metric. The metrics used to monitor the performance of a distributed system are one of the following types of metrics:

- **Counters**: A counter is a value that can only increase over time as the system operates. Some examples are rate per second and delta in a time window.

- **Gauges**: A gauge is a derived value that can increase or decrease over time. Some example gauges are maximum over time and open connections.

- **Summaries**: Summaries are accumulated absolute counters. Example summary metrics are request count and total bytes streamed.

Key reliability metrics

There are many metrics that can be revealed by and monitored for a distributed system. Any set of metrics is associated with a specific aspect of service: Revenue generation, reliability, and specific resource utilization are all potential objectives of a service. The most common service objective that this and subsequent chapters will be concerned with is reliability, which includes the availability of the system.

There are four metrics of reliability that serve to indicate the health of the system under observation. We will identify and briefly describe those as follows:

- **Errors**: The rate of requests that fail, either explicitly by the application issuing an intentional failure response, such as an HTTP 500, or implicitly, as in the case of a timeout.

- **Latency**: The elapsed wall time it takes to service a request. Calculated by the time between a user issuing a request, by clicking some functional equivalent of a submit button, and the application responding to that user with the result of their request. The latency of failed and successful requests should be monitored separately.

- **Saturation**: The portion of your system's resources that are in use. Saturation is the aggregated effect of different measures. How much disk space, memory, network bandwidth, instance quota, and anything that your system consumes, and for which you have a budgeted amount, is subject to saturation.

- **Traffic**: It is the demand being placed on your system by its users. The measure of traffic is based on what it is that your service provides. A web service measures traffic in requests per second; a storage system measures traffic in bytes to store and retrieve per second.

Monitoring distributed systems

Bringing these concepts to our immediate use case, a distributed voting system built on GCP, we can view the rate at which the Vote Ingester frontends can process votes being cast. Our desired value is to process votes at the same rate at which they are being cast by users. We will refer to that rate as **votes cast per second**. To restate this, if at a given point in time, users are casting 500 votes over the course of one second, we would like the system to ingest those 500 votes over the course of that second, so that the set of Vote Ingesters is available to process the next second's 500 votes. We wish to achieve a steady state in which supply or capacity equals demand. Like the physician's limited set of controls, a system architect has no way to set the absolute latency and processing rate of an application. What can be done is to horizontally and vertically scale various components of the processing pipeline to converge the pipeline's rate with our desired value.

Monitoring GCP applications

Google Cloud automatically captures metrics from many Google Cloud services and makes the metrics described in this section available via predefined dashboards. Notifications can be configured to escalate a condition that has been defined as a potential indicator of a problem, such as Cloud Storage disk space usage is at 90% of configured capacity, or cloud service billing for your project has reached $1,000 in the current billing period.

GCP includes an operations suite, products that provide an integrated set of products, including observability tools that support GCP application monitoring. The three main services in this suite are Cloud Monitoring, Cloud Logging, and Cloud Trace. This section will briefly describe each of these products and present applications of each in our voting system.

Cloud Monitoring provides visibility into the availability and health of your cloud-based application. Automatic metric collection is reflected in out-of-the-box dashboards. Beyond the supplied dashboards, Cloud Monitoring's query language can be used to research and identify deeper trends and derived performance data. Alerts can be defined to send notifications based on alerting policies with user-specified thresholds, such as send notification to the primary on-call channel when the 90th percentile request latency is over 200 milliseconds for 5 minutes.

When a GCP service is added to a project, a default monitoring dashboard specific to that service is added to the project's Cloud console. For example, deploying the App Engine service for the voting service frontend added this dashboard to the project owner's Google Cloud console.

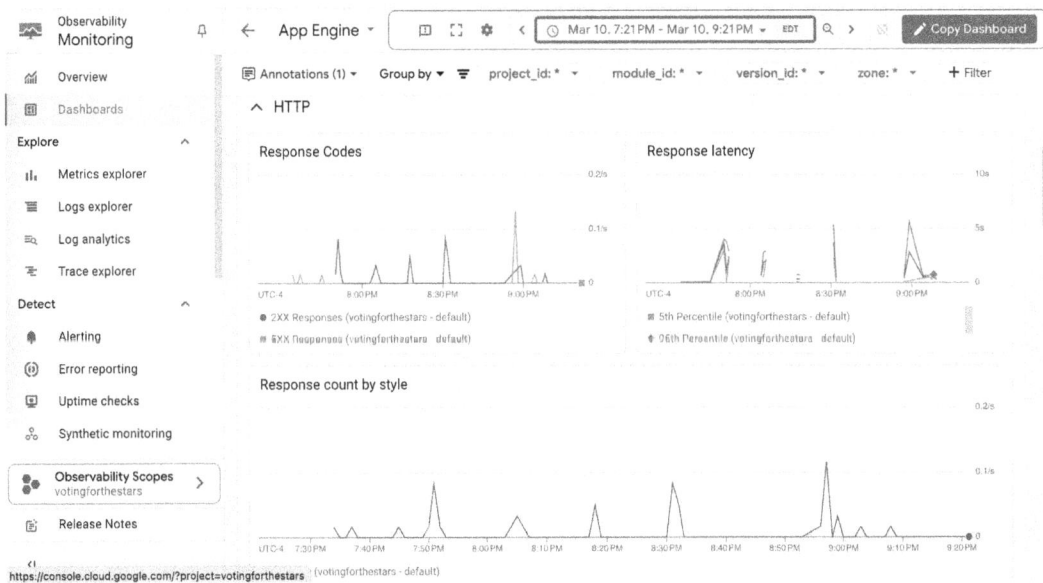

Figure 9.5: *Default App Engine service monitoring dashboard*

As well as the default dashboards, a developer can configure custom dashboards using a library of GCP supplied components and integrate monitoring by Prometheus, a popular third-party provider of service monitoring.

Cloud Logging can be used to manage and analyze application and infrastructure logs for troubleshooting and auditing support. Logs Explorer can be used to view and analyze log entries. Log Analytics integrates log data with BigQuery to enable integration of logs with other business data. Log Analytics can be used to process and analyze higher volumes of detailed data, such as network telemetry logs, than is practical with other tools. This can help troubleshoot widespread problems or those that exist at several degrees of separation from an application's own components. Log Analytics can also be used to gain business insights from system-wide application usage. Log Explorer and Log Analytics are available in the Cloud console alongside the monitoring dashboard and alerts for a project. An example of the **Log Explorer** showing some of the available filters is as follows:

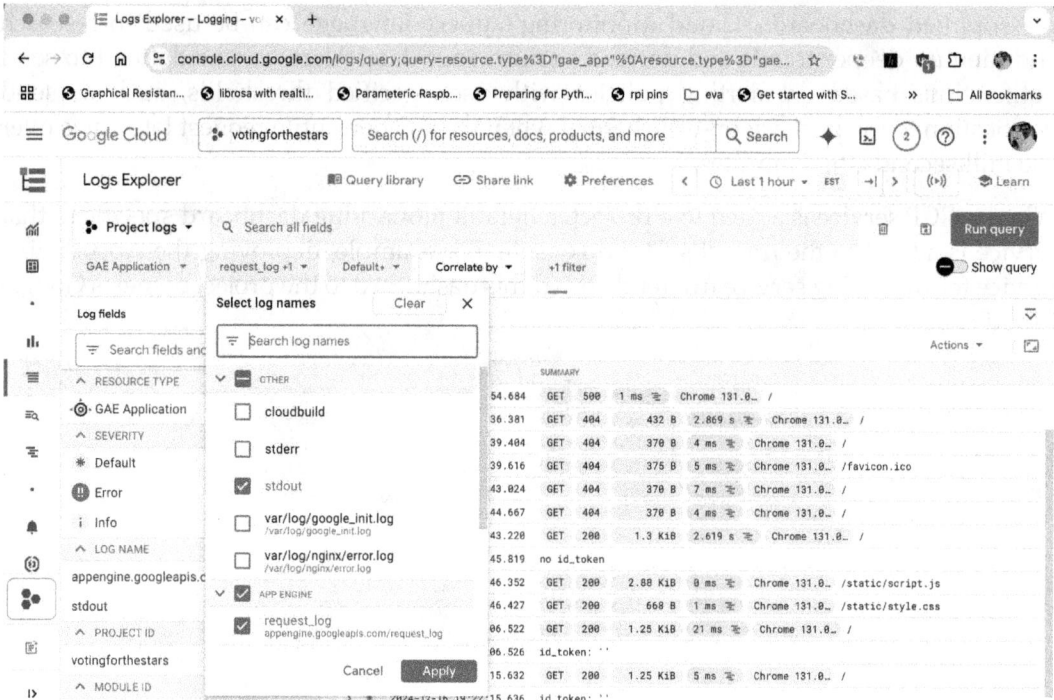

Figure 9.6: GCP Logs Explorer with filters

Cloud Trace is a distributed tracing system. It gathers latency data from GCP applications and displays it in predefined dashboards in real-time. Cloud Trace is invaluable to provide an extra means to monitor system performance during a component push or an anticipated demand peak. The Cloud Trace system can be accessed in the Cloud console through the default Trace Explorer, as shown in this figure:

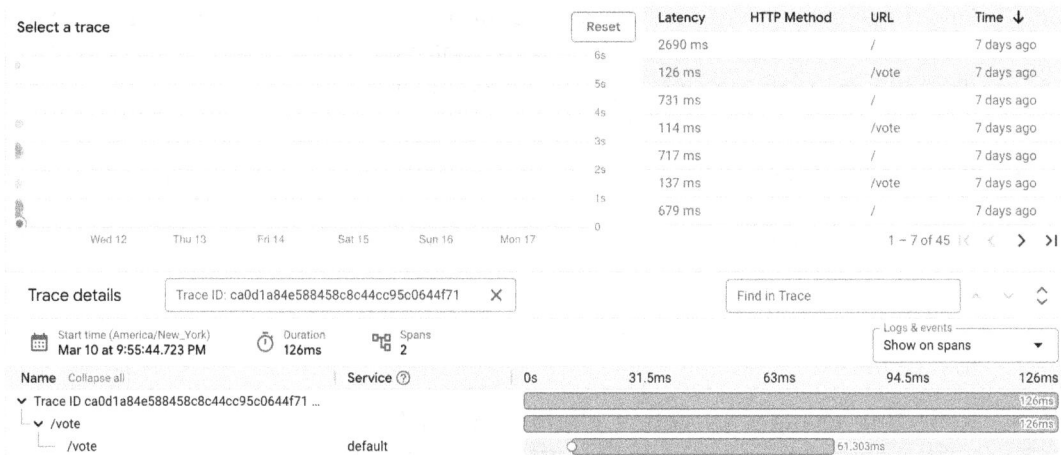

Figure 9.7: GCP Trace Explorer

Performance watchpoints in the voting application

The voting application has a well-defined set of user visible features. We will enumerate those features which are critical to the core functionality of casting a vote for a selected act. For these features, we will identify the reliability metrics that must be monitored to ensure that this functionality is reliable and performant to meet user expectations.

Casting a vote occurs in real-time and is perceived as the most critical feature of the application. However, this feature is dependent on several other prerequisite functions and incurs some follow-up activity. The smooth execution of the user's **vote** button cannot happen without the success of all these tightly coupled features.

The following is the sequence of events that results in a satisfied user of our voting application:

- **User authentication**: Authentication is the key that unlocks the rest of our application features. The user login must have completed before voting can commence. While a user may already be logged in from authenticating in an earlier session, and can proceed directly to casting a vote, there are a few situations in which an enthusiastic voter will find themselves redirected to login. These situations that will redirect the user are an earlier session having expired, an application component push that replaced or invalidated the previously acquired credentials, or simply not having authenticated previously on the current client application and specific device. This will place some load on the system at the time of peak demand. For some number, n, of people who wish to cast a vote at any given time, we can assume that there will be n logins occurring during the first acts of that round, as each voter sees the first performance for which they wish to vote.

- **Fetching current eligibility**: Voting in a round requires fetching information about that round's contestants. As each user initially launches their client application, there will be a quick round-trip message to determine if the client has the current information for acts in the current round.

- **Refreshing state**: Some number of the connected users will be found to have obsolete information about the round's acts and will then fetch the current list of acts and their statuses from the cloud.

- **Voting**: The casting of a vote is the driving factor for this chain of events and is the one feature guaranteed to be exercised by every user for every act that they wish to vote for.

- **Reflecting changes in voting eligibility**: Finally, as acts are made eligible for voting, push notifications will be sent to each user, updating the status of those acts. Voting can also be closed for acts at some point in time following their conclusion, and push notifications will be sent for these changes as well.

A flowchart of the preceding functions, that may be executed at the time a vote is cast, is presented here to help identify what may present a choke point at times of peak demand. The functions with a shaded background are those which include traffic between the client and cloud platforms:

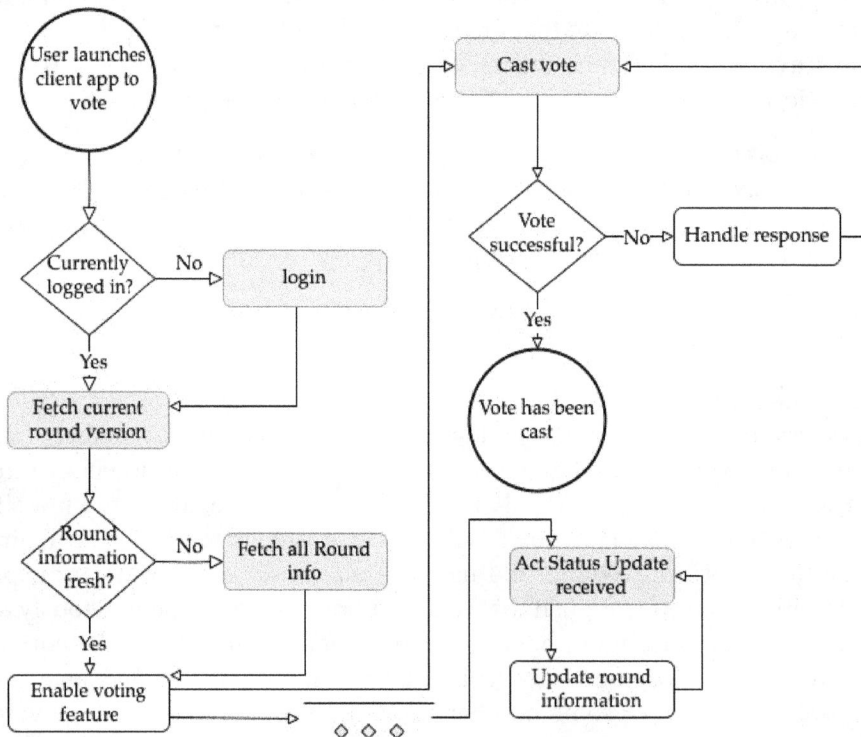

Figure 9.8: Voting feature flowchart

Walking through the possible paths in this flowchart reveals that the most frequently executed functions that rely on the cloud are those of fetching the current round version and casting a vote. Casting a vote executes every time that a user decides to vote for an act, and fetching the current round version is executed every time a user launches the app and is logged in. Since these are most frequently executed, monitoring those and quick scaling of the underlying cloud services, are the highest priority in ensuring the availability of our voting application at peak demand. While each of these functions are needed by some users at voting time, these two are required by every user when they wish to vote.

Incident response

The goal of mechanisms such as auto-scaling of resources, redundant servers, and automatic failover is to prevent an incident (incident being a general term for service degradation or outage). Proper use of these techniques and tools will reduce the impact of the events and situations that work against the continuous availability and desired performance levels of a system; reduce but not completely prevent. Things will go wrong.

Thorough monitoring and alerting practices will make these emergent situations apparent to the operators of an application system. If a metric is predictive of a user facing outage, rather than indicative of one, an alert and quick notification can prevent a problem from ever affecting the users. Consider an alert such as disk usage is 80% of available space and climbing in contrast to a counterpart alert out of disk space. Responding to the former should prevent the latter from ever materializing and heads off any user impact.

In either case, whether an outage occurs or not, monitoring and notification have to be coupled with a documented, communicated, and rehearsed incident response plan. There are several components to this that we will list here:

- **An on-call rotation**: At any time, someone should be designated as the first responder or point of contact for both automated notification channels and internal human stakeholders.

- **On-call escalation tiers**: People are fallible, trains break down, and phones have dead zones. If the primary first responder does not respond, a secondary backup person should always be designated and ready to act.

- **Playbooks**: Figuring out what to do under pressure is unwise, inefficient, and error-prone. Establish and maintain a set of easily navigated documents describing how to diagnose and identify a problem and guidance on how to mitigate it.

- **Empowerment of incident commanders**: Save the user should be the most important action a product supporting team performs. Incident responders should have both organizational power and system permissions needed to act with as little delay as feasible.

- **Incident response testing**: Do not try out a process when your business is on the line. Rehearse the entire process: Introduce a condition, verify that the expected monitoring is triggered, notifications are sent, and that your on-call rotation is reached and knows how to respond. Google conducts periodic tests of the entire production environment, known as **disaster recovery testing (DiRT)**.

- **Postmortem analysis**: During an incident, keep careful notes. After the problem has passed and everyone has gotten some rest, conduct a postmortem analysis of what went wrong, what went right, and what would be done differently.

- **Postmortem induced change**: The result of a postmortem is not blame; it is improvement. Lessons learned should lead to changes in the system to lessen future incidents and changes to response processes to increase the effectiveness of responses.

Further reading on these is recommended, there are many learning resources for SRE principles published by Google and others.

Matrix of failure modes and appropriate measures

For every outage, there is a most effective mitigation, which will conform to one of several known patterns. The optimal response can be determined based on specific aspects of the outage; certain situations call for certain responses. When viewed from a general perspective, the dominant root cause for a service outage can be classified as being one of several known types.

Earlier in this chapter, *Figure 9.4* associated failure mode with scope and progression. Building on that table, we will end this section on incident response with a table that associates the category of failure with the most commonly effective type of response. The following figure showcases the table:

Cause	Response
Introduced over/by time	Scale resources
Force majeure	Drain and failover
Ignorance or malevolence	Rollback
	Temporary unavailability
Unanticipated usage	Scale resources
	Drain and failover
Defects	Rollback

Figure 9.9: Matrix of root cause and response

The general responses or mitigations from *Figure 9.9* are described briefly here. The topic of incident response is well covered in industry literature and the community on the topic of site reliability:

- **Rollback**: If a failure is rooted in a defect, presumably the defect was not present in the last known working state of the system. So, rollback or revert changes that either correlate to the outage in time or that affected the failing functionality. Do not spend time trying to fix the bug on the fly, first restore the system to a working state, then analyze, devise and push a fixed version of the reverted change.

  Note: **These are immediate responses, more involved mitigation specific to the incident are expected once the system is out of immediate danger.**

- **Drain and failover**: If a resource or component is not working but siblings or counterparts are, redirect the load from the failing components to the working ones. Draining a resource means to divert requests upstream away from that resource, draining it of all work (and potential for doing harm).

- **Scale resources**: If a worker is slow or a distributed database cannot keep up, scale the over-taxed component either vertically or horizontally, or both.

- **Temporary unavailability**: The least desirable response is to make the system unavailable for a period. This can be surprising and may seem drastic, but telling users that the system is unavailable can be preferable to presenting a non-functioning application or one in which the users' data is possibly compromised.

Implementation of the Vote Ingester API codelab

The implementation of a service, such as the voting service we have described, can be viewed as having two sides: Implementing the deployment and interaction between the various components, and implementing the specific business logic. The former, which defines the shape or form of the system, is the side that is more tightly coupled to the infrastructure on which we build the system. For that reason, we will first, in this codelab, implement a voting service client and cloud service that offer the core features that have been identified for the service, without the functionality; in other words, the user will be able to cast a vote for an act, the voting service will accept votes but there is not yet any actual tallying of those votes which are cast.

Part of the definition of the service is the configuration of GCP and Firebase projects that we will deploy our service to. The codelab will describe the definition of those projects. Lastly, the codelab will identify GCP monitoring for the cloud service.

Project considerations in setting up the repository

First, we will review the directory structure of the application, which we modify slightly from the logical package structure that was presented in the previous chapter, to more naturally fit our implementation choices of a JavaScript web client using Firebase Auth and a Google App Engine service written in Python. The entire application will be contained in a single GitHub repository, which will also be reflected in the directory and file structure that evolves. Our repository for this stage of the voting system can be found at **https://www.github.com/raygeeknyc/gcp_9**

Top level directories: **webclient**, **cloud** and **common**.

At the highest level, we separate the code into three partitions: cloud-based code, client code and code common to the entire voting system. The top level directory structure of the **talentvoting** repository looks like the following:

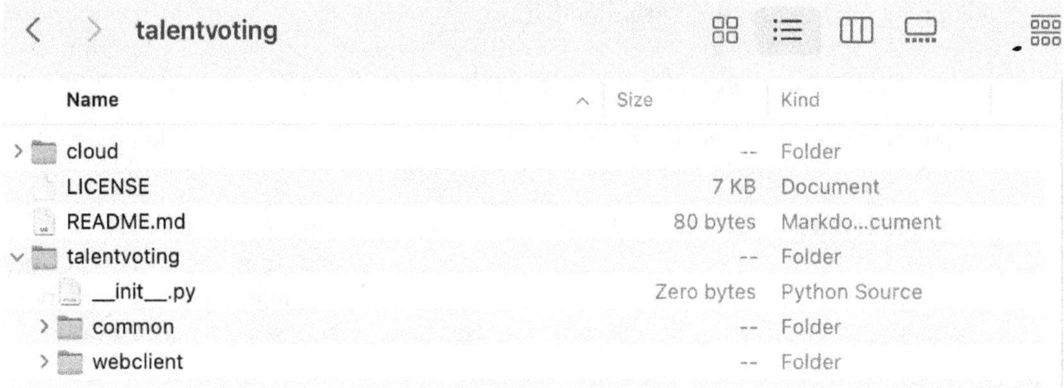

Name	Size	Kind
> ■ cloud	--	Folder
LICENSE	7 KB	Document
README.md	80 bytes	Markdo...cument
∨ ■ talentvoting	--	Folder
__init__.py	Zero bytes	Python Source
> ■ common	--	Folder
> ■ webclient	--	Folder

Figure 9.10: *Top level directory structure of the repository*

We will describe each of the high-level folders and their internal structure in the following sections:

Web client and common code

The web client is composed of HTML and accompanying file types such as **.js** files and static content. There may be other types such as Python files in the eventual implementation but at this initial definition, we use those browser native file types. In addition, the choice of Firebase to host the client imposes some Firebase specific files.

The planned mobile client apps will be siblings to the web client and so we place the **common** package at this same level, under a parent **talentvoting** package to make it easier to share common code in all client packages.

Using Firebase client authorization includes placing some private information in our web client application. It would be a quickly exploited security leak to upload these authorization secrets to GitHub, so we create a **.gitignore** file which will prevent the secret files from being uploaded to our repository.

The fully expanded common and web client package directories contain the following files and folders:

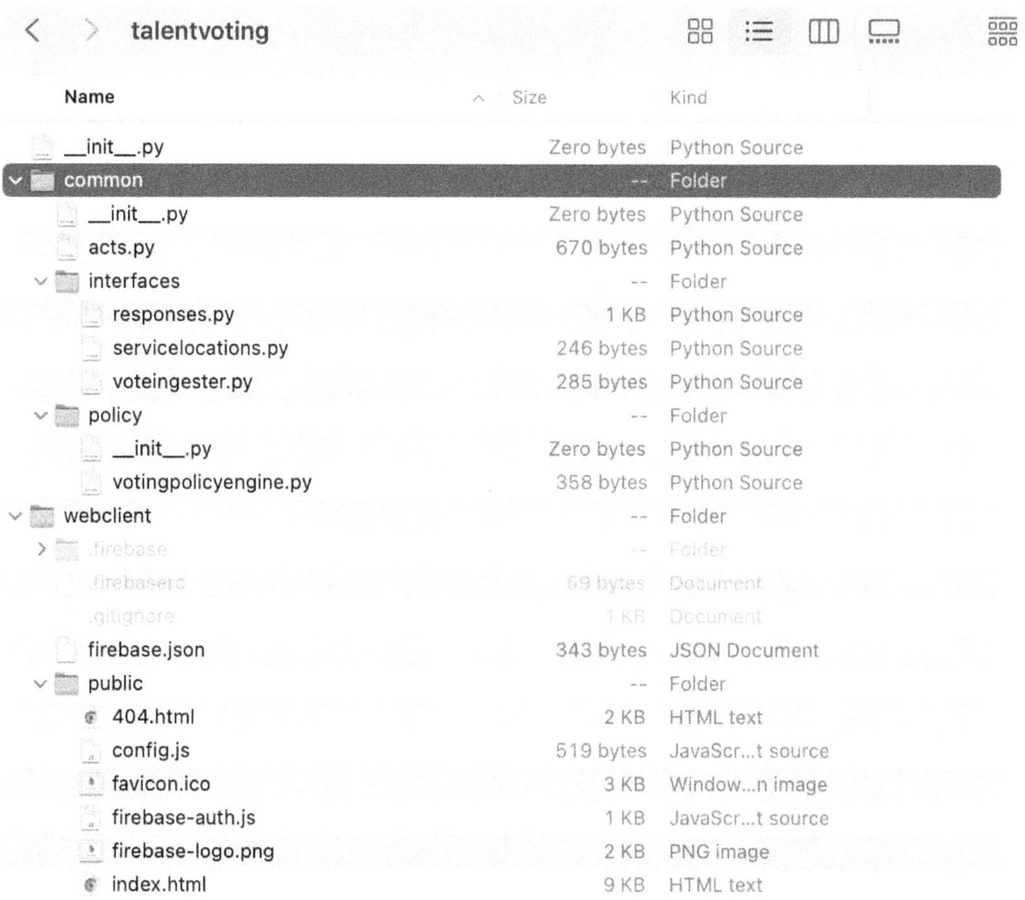

Figure 9.11: Folder structure of common and client packages

Our initial web client will use Firebase authorization with only the Google identity provider, via a popup window. The code to support this is largely contained in the file **firebase-auth.js**. The aforementioned secrets, which are copied from the Firebase, develop console into our application are isolated in the file **config.js**. Isolating the secrets in this way allows our **.gitignore** file to omit the smallest necessary amount of code from the GitHub repository.

As was mentioned, we initially will implement a service that does not include a complete backend. To still allow testing and demonstration of the service, we include a hard coded set of acts in the dedicated **acts.py** module in the common package. This file contains the following Python code:

```python
from typing import List, Dict


# For now an Act is a JSON object with no stricter definition enforced
Act = Dict[str, any]
```

```
# Any number of Acts are often referenced as a group
Acts = List[Act]

# This is a helper stub to use until we define backing storage services for
Acts
def example_acts() ->Acts:
    act1 = {"season": 1, "act": "S01A001", "name": "Crazy good rock",
            "voting_eligible": True}
    act2 = {"season": 1, "act": "S01A002", "name": "Serious Wizardry",
            "voting_eligible": True}
    act3 = {"season": 1, "act": "S01A004", "name": "Acrobatic comedy",
            "voting_eligible": False}

    acts  =  list(
        [act1, act2, act3]
        )
    return acts
```

Cloud-based code

The vote frontend is implemented as an App Engine service written in Python 3. The Google Cloud development tools place the required App Engine configuration and resource files under the home directory of an App Engine application, as well as impose an expected directory structure for the application.

Similarly to the Firebase authorization secrets, our App Engine service includes a service account key, which must be kept private. At runtime, this is protected through the use of a private directory in the application hierarchy, but we must also ensure that this account key is not revealed on GitHub. The **.gitignore** file at the top directory prevents this file from being uploaded to GitHub with the last line of the following specifications:

```
talentvoting/webclient/public/config.js
talentvoting/webclient/private/**
**/serviceAccountKey.json
```

The folder and file hierarchy of the **votingfrontend** package is shown in the following figure:

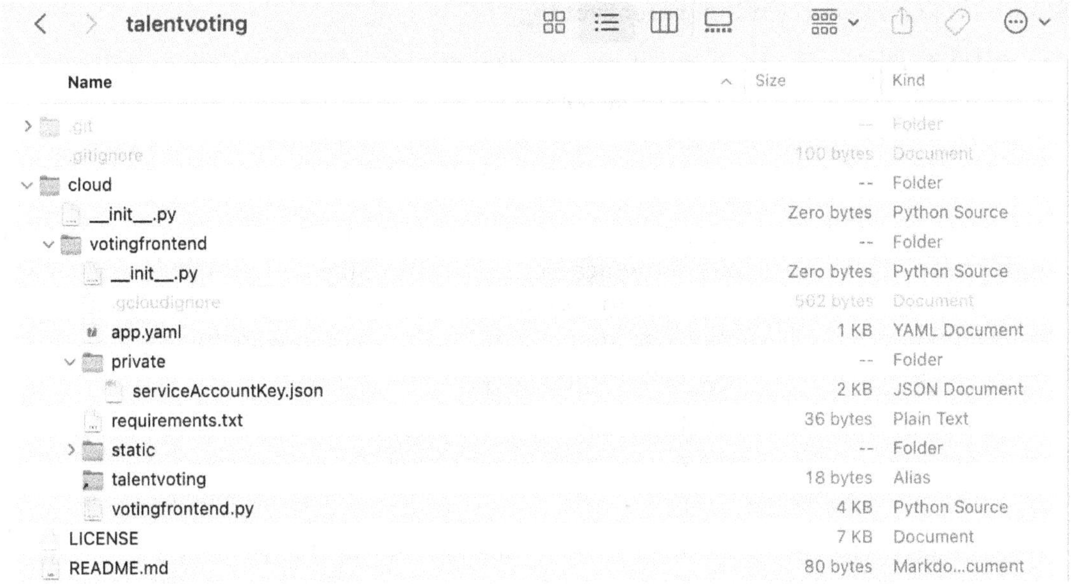

Figure 9.12: Folder and file structure of cloud packages

There is a problem with the application's directory structure when deploying an App Engine application. The **gcloud deploy** command, which will be illustrated later, only works on folders and files rooted in the base directory of our application: In this case the **cloud:votingfrontend** folder. Although we wish to include files in our **talentvoting:common** folder, which is a sibling of the **cloud** folder, those files would not be deployed to App Engine by the **gcloud** tool, which would result in errors like the following in our App Engine service:

```
from talentvoting.common.acts import Act, Acts
ModuleNotFoundError: No module named 'talentvoting'
1
```

This is a common enough problem to have an easily described and widely employed solution. Notice the presence and type of the **talentvoting** folder, highlighted in this detail from *Figure 9.13*:

Figure 9.13: Detail of cloud folder

In the base folder of our App Engine deployment, the **cloud:votingfrontend** folder, we have made an **Alias** or **symlink** to the **talentvoting** package folder that encompasses the **common** package. In Linux or MacOS this is done with the following **ln** command from the **votingfrontend** directory:

```
$ ln -s ../../talentvoting talentvoting
```

The **gcloud deploy** command will see this **Alias** in the base folder, and traverse and upload the files enclosed in the original source folder when uploading to App Engine.

Google Cloud project configuration

The voting frontend server running on App Engine must be associated with a Google Cloud project. This is the entity for which permissions, billing, and available services are configured. The details of navigating to specific web pages change and can be googled by the reader when ready. However, one might navigate, the following are the required terms to reference and entities that must be setup to deploy GCP services:

- **The Google Cloud developer console**: This page serves as the home page or base for a Google Cloud developer account. From this page, one can define projects, enable APIs, setup billing accounts, and access monitoring dashboards.

- **Project settings**: All runtime services, such as an App Engine server or database table, are part of a Project. Roles and permissions can be defined and managed at this level and then inherited by services that are associated with the project. The billing account which will be used to pay for charges incurred by services under the project is associated with the project. Quotas and usage limits can be defined for a project, to isolate the cost accounting of a project from other projects.

One important part of the project configuration is the definition of service accounts and the creation of service account keys. Service accounts are accounts that represent a Google Cloud service identity, as opposed to a logged in user. A service account key is a private key that is used to authenticate to Google Cloud APIs and establish the identity of the runtime component as one that is known and trusted to act as that service account.

A service account key is stored as JSON and has the form of this redacted example:

```
{
  "type": "service_account",
  "project_id": "PROJECT_ID",
  "private_key_id": "KEY_ID",
  "private_key": "-----BEGIN PRIVATE KEY-----\nPRIVATE_KEY\n-----
END PRIVATE KEY-----\n",
  "client_email": "SERVICE_ACCOUNT_EMAIL",
  "client_id": "CLIENT_ID",
  "auth_uri": "https://accounts.google.com/o/oauth2/auth",
  "token_uri": "https://accounts.google.com/o/oauth2/token",
  "auth_provider_x509_cert_url": "https://www.googleapis.com/oauth2/v1/
certs",
  "client_x509_cert_url": "https://www.googleapis.com/robot/v1/metadata/
```

```
x509/SERVICE_ACCOUNT_EMAIL"
}
```

Since the service account key contains the private part of a public/private RSA key pair, it should be protected and kept secret from all unnecessary viewers.

Note: Do not upload a service account key to GitHub and use service specific features such as a private folder in App Engine to prevent browsers from accessing their contents.

If a private key is uploaded to a public GitHub repository, cooperative security features in GitHub and GCP will inform the owner and disable the service account to prevent the account from being exploited by others.

Firebase project configuration

Firebase hosting provides a reliable, globally available site on which a developer can host web applications. Firebase hosting offers release management, standard subdomains for your application, custom domain support, identity management, and usage monitoring.

Sign-in methods, such as Google authentication, Facebook logins, email/password, and phone login, are enabled at the hosting level, and user activity is tracked there as well.

A Firebase app is a specific application that is associated with a Firebase hosting site. Firebase apps can be an Android app, iOS app, web app, Unity app, or Flutter app. These apps use the Firebase resources, such as authentication, that are associated with their hosting site, which provides a convenient means for the same user to authenticate on various client platforms for your application.

Similar to the service account information for Google Cloud projects discussed in the preceding section, Firebase generates configuration information used to identify and authenticate Firebase users to operate as a Firebase service account. An example configuration JavaScript snippet for a web application, redacted, follows:

```javascript
// Import the functions you need from the SDKs you need
import { initializeApp } from "firebase/app";
// TODO: Add SDKs for Firebase products that you want to use
// https://firebase.google.com/docs/web/setup#available-libraries

// Your web app's Firebase configuration
const firebaseConfig = {
  apiKey: "XXXXXXXXXXXXXXXXXXXXXXXXXXXXX",
  authDomain: "your-hosting-site.firebaseapp.com",
  projectId: "your-hosting-site",
  storageBucket: "your-hosting-site.firebasestorage.app",
  messagingSenderId: "###########",
```

```
    appId: "1:########:web:XXXXXXXXXXXXXXXXXXXX"
};
```

```
// Initialize Firebase
const app = initializeApp(firebaseConfig);
```

This information should be hidden from direct observation by users: GitHub **.gitignore** files and Firebase ignore and rewrite features can be used to prevent exposing these in the repository and from being served to HTTP requests. The **hosting.ignore** element of the **firebase.json** configuration file prevents Firebase hosting from serving a file, as follows:

```
  "hosting": {
    "public": "public",
    "site": "votingforthestars",
    "ignore": [
      "firebase.json",
      "**/.*",
      "**/node_modules/**",
      "**/config.js"
    ]
  },
```

GCP Monitoring

At the base page of the Google Cloud developer console is a link to the user's dashboard. This convenient link brings the viewer to an overview dashboard that has panes for usage summaries of deployed services, such as App Engine, and comprehensive breakdowns by service and API. These usage summaries link to detailed, service specific dashboards with filtering by time window, breakdown by URI, and response type, such as Application and Server errors. The dashboard hierarchy presented here is generated by GCP automatically and requires no configuration or request by the developer.

Conclusion

The scalability and reliability of a distributed system must be planned for in the design of the system. While it is possible to correct an inherently unreliable or unpredictable system, it will be much easier and straightforward to adjust a system designed with reliability in mind.

Understanding the types of potential failures and their impact is critical to prevention and mitigation of those types. The size or blast radius of a failure and its progression or advancement over time are the key aspects to be considered.

The impact of a failure is helpful in determining an appropriate level of response. The more costly an outage is, the more urgent its mediation. Appropriate means of notification and incident response should be defined before any incident might occur; following a plan while under stress is far better than writing a plan under stress.

Observability was also discussed, as it is difficult to control a system when its state cannot be easily determined. This principle of observe then control is rooted in real world practices, such as medicine, and in software development practices like test-driven development.

The chapter concluded with a codelab that described an initial implementation of a voting feature: A web app client and App Engine service. The configuration of the hosting services and tips to understanding the contents of the GitHub repository that contains this initial application implementation were presented.

In the next chapter, the voting application will be extended to the next tier: The asynchronous processing that will provide scalability and reliability of many concurrent voting requests.

Join our Discord space

Join our Discord workspace for latest updates, offers, tech happenings around the world, new releases, and sessions with the authors:

https://discord.bpbonline.com

CHAPTER 10
Securing All User Votes

Introduction

A distributed application is subject to demand that demonstrates sudden, steep changes in rate. In our voting scenario, many users respond to the same events in a short time, and each expects the system to accept and **acknowledge (ACK)** their vote quickly. Users should not be affected by the level of other users' activity. A predictable and consistent experience builds user confidence in the system, so they continue watching the competition and participating.

One of the goals of a capable infrastructure layer is to provide services and tooling that enable systems to easily deal with rapidly changing workloads.

Structure

The following topics will be covered in this chapter:

- Demand modeling
- Load balancing
- Employing message queues to pool requests
- Asynchronous processing of requests
- Dispatching user requests to asynchronous work queues via Pub/Sub codelab

Objectives

Google Cloud Platform (**GCP**) can automatically scale resources in different dimensions in response to changes in user traffic. In this chapter, the reader will learn the advantages and disadvantages of the available alternatives for adaptive scaling of an application.

As well as resource scaling, GCP includes products that can be used to reduce the impact of sudden increases in demand by shifting latency away from the user. The reader will learn design patterns to make use of these products and how to apply different types of auto-scaling to shape system capacity to match demand.

Demand modeling

Demand is the product of the aggregated effect of several cycles. The end of a performance will trigger a flood of votes, which trail off and perhaps overlap with the next act, which generates a similar cycle. The conclusion of an act may trigger votes for earlier acts that were being withheld until later acts were seen. This is a complex set of behaviors, and while we can forecast the theoretical maximum total number of votes cast, we can predict only the general shape of the multiple demand factors.

Independent cycles of demand

The factors that contribute to the total user demand are those which trigger a user to make a request, in our specific case casting a vote, with no direct dependency between them. By direct dependency, it is meant that a specific request is not generated by a previous request, either of two requests can be issued independently of the other.

First, we will enumerate the factors that compel a user to cast a vote for an act:

- An act concludes, or nearly concludes, and generates and enthusiastic response in a viewer. The viewer sees an act and immediately wants it to win. This is the most simple and direct cycle of demand; votes go up as a popular act air.

- An act concludes which failed to live up to some expectation or anticipated aspect. This trigger votes for other, previously seen acts from users who are conserving their quota of votes; remember that a user may only vote for a smaller number of acts than appear in each round.

- The conclusion of a round will unleash votes that were held in abeyance for reasons similar to the previous point. 35 viewers withhold voting until they have seen all acts, to not exhaust their budgeted vote count while unknown acts remain to be seen.

Each of these 3 factors will be present and can be modeled in our demand forecast for a round of our competition. What we cannot predict is the actual size of each of these effects: How many votes will be cast due to each of these 3 factors, in each instance. Accurately forecasting that degree of specificity would be close to predicting the outcome of the competition, and practically impossible.

The aggregate number of votes cast over the duration of a round, broken down into the 3 contributing categories of vote for a hypothetical round of 12 acts is depicted in the following figure:

Vote factors, aggregated

▨ Concluding round ▦ Previous acts ▪ Concluding act

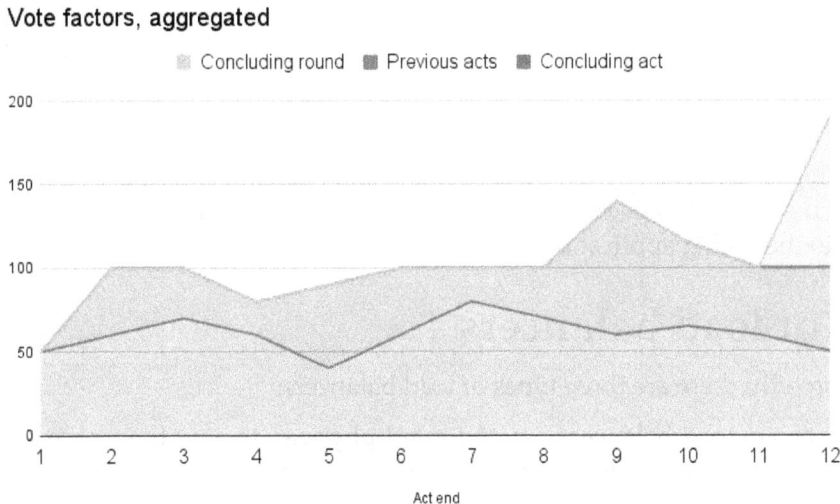

Figure 10.1: 3 cycles of demand vs. round timeline

The precise number of votes shown previously, and the individual ups and downs of the counts are only hypothetical. However, there are a few key points to take away from this diagram for the purpose of demand forecasting.

First is that there are no votes for previous acts until the second act is underway, and that there are no votes triggered by the conclusion of a round until the final act of the round has begun. These are self-evident and inherent in the definition of those factors.

A less obvious pattern is that a popular act, shown in the high number of votes at the conclusion of acts 3 and 7, is followed by a drop in the number of cast votes that had been withheld for the following few iterations. This holds up on some consideration: if an act generated immediate enthusiastic voting, there were fewer voters who were holding back, hedging their bets for that act.

A counterpart pattern in the relationship between unpopular acts and withheld votes exists. A relatively unpopular act releases voters to cast their votes that they had been withholding until they had seen more of the competition. This pattern is shown in *Figure 10.1* at the conclusion of acts 5 and 9.

The exercise of demand modeling in this manner provides valuable insight, forcing the application architects to reason through the forces that drive user demand and may dispel some false assumptions about the shape of traffic. In particular, the fact that votes cast following popular and unpopular acts net out to similar amounts of traffic may be a surprise; a naive assumption would be that a popular act generates clearly greater demand on the system than unpopular ones.

Load balancing

Load balancing is the process of distributing work across multiple servers to optimize system performance in terms of total time and other resources spent in completing that work. It ensures that no single server is overloaded, relative to its peers, and that no request competes unfairly for resources.

The following sections briefly introduce some load balancing concepts and nomenclature before discussing GCP specific services and then focuses on the application of load balancing to the voting application.

Types of load balancers

Speaking broadly, there are three types of load balancers:

- Hardware load balancers are dedicated physical devices that serve as the initial recipient of user requests which then redirect that traffic to the actual services.

- Software load balancers are software that run on the existing servers as other components, dividing up and distributing the incoming traffic.

- Cloud load balancers are cloud services that resemble hardware load balancers but run on the existing cloud hardware. They are more easily scalable than hardware load balancers and more isolated from side-effects of other software than software load balancers.

Load balancing algorithms and considerations

Load balancing can be performed using a number of techniques, each of which is a better or worse performing choice based on several application-specific considerations:

- **Size of tasks**: More than the exact execution time of each task, knowing the variability of the execution times helps to reach an optimal load configuration. The greater the mean deviation from the average execution time, the more unpredictable a task's execution time is.

- **Dependencies**: If some of the tasks depend on each other, or if groups of tasks share common dependencies, the distribution of such groups will affect overall performance.

The more information that is known about the tasks being balanced, the better a choice of load balancing algorithm can be made. Load balancing algorithms are of two classes: Static algorithms, which are well suited for balancing work which is relatively stable or uniform;

and dynamic algorithms which are better able to balance tasks which are unpredictable or highly variable in their resource consumption.

If the execution time and distribution of the task demand is not known ahead of time, static load distribution is always possible. The most common and straightforward load balancing algorithm is a static one known as **round-robin scheduling**.

In a round-robin load balancer, there are a certain number, n, of servers available, each of which gets equal consideration over time. The first request is sent to the first server, the next request is sent to the second server, and so on. When each server has been sent work, the $(n+1)^{th}$ request is assigned to the first server, then the next to the second in an ever repeating cycle.

A round-robin algorithm's simplicity allows it to be modified to fit many situations. For example, if some servers have more capacity than others, those servers can be weighted to receive a larger number of requests or to receive them first.

A dynamic load balancer requires some communication from the servers back to the load balancers about the state of the servers. One of the common and simplest dynamic load balancing algorithms is a master-slave algorithm. In such a scheme, each server pings the load balancer when it has capacity to accept a request, the next pending request is directed to that server. This type of algorithm works well in ensuring that all dispatched requests are executed efficiently, and that no server is overloaded but it introduces the possibility of requests being starved when no server calls in its availability to take on more work. To address this vulnerability, a master-slave load balancer is best used along with the ability to horizontally scale the pool of servers as the queue of pending requests grows or as latency increases in the frequency of server call ins.

These are only two of many load balancing algorithms that exist and are meant to give the reader an introduction to and appreciation for the many considerations and choices that are made by GCP when managing traffic for a running service.

Load balancing in Google Cloud Platform

GCP provides a set of load balancer options that encapsulate combinations of the many decisions to be made in load balancing: type, strategy, and algorithm. What is offered is tailored to fit the nature of a GCP application and the specific relevant aspects Google's cloud architecture and network. Google Cloud Load Balancing can scale to support and distribute 1 million+ queries per second and can be configured to automatically scale the pool of application frontend servers to match demand trends.

At the highest level of classification, GCP provides two types of load balancer: Application Load Balancers, which operate on **Hypertext Transfer Protocol/ Hypertext Transfer Protocol Secure** (HTTP/HTTPS) requests and requests, and Network Load Balancers which work with any **Transmission Control Protocol (TCP)**, **Universal Datagram Protocol (UDP)** or other **Internet Protocol (IP)** network traffic.

Another attribute that distinguishes GCP load balancers is that of domain:

- Regional load balancers distribute requests originating within a GCP region among servers in the same region.

- Cross-region load balancers can accept requests from within a given region and distribute them among servers located in a set of multiple regions.

- Global load balancers can accept requests from within a given region and distribute them among servers located in all regions in which the target server is configured to have a presence.

A third distinguishing characteristic of GCP load balancers is that of traffic origin. Internal load balancers distribute requests that come from clients within your cloud network, whereas external load balancers can manage requests that come from anywhere on the internet.

Another consideration of a different nature that determines the choice of a load balancer is of service level or cost. GCP offers different tiers of network service: Premium, Standard and a specific combination of load balancer type and load balancing scheme may not be available in all tiers.

Reviewing all load balancer options in GCP is a large task, beyond the scope or need of this chapter. Google publishes a summary table at **https://cloud.google.com/load-balancing/docs/choosing-load-balancer - summary-gclb**. This table enumerates 14 different load balancers and for an exhaustive exploration the reader is advised to read the encompassing documentation of that page.

Selecting voting system load balancers

In this chapter, we will choose a load balancer that is a good match for our application, based on the scalability requirements that were described in *Chapter 8, Making a Voting System Available and Reliable*, and the reliability concerns identified in *Chapter 9, Identifying the Stress Points of our Voting System*.

The voting application works with only HTTPS requests and responses, so the first choice: Application vs. Network Load Balancer is simple. An Application Load Balancer will fill our system's requirements and is simpler to configure and operate.

The next choice, domain, can be made by referring to the requirements shown in *Figure 9.2*, spillover across continents. Due to the potential for mismatch of relative demand and capacity within specific locales, we plan to send spillover traffic between regions; thus, a cross-region load balancer will be used for the voting system.

The identification of traffic origin requires a deeper exploration of Google's networking model. Understanding the concept of a Google **Virtual Private Cloud** (**VPC**) is necessary to fully identify the boundaries of internal load balancers. While a VPC can be used to extend the applicable domain of an internal load balancer, it would be relatively costly and complex to apply this to our voting frontends which must be accessible to clients of many types using many different types of network connections and providers. So, an external load balancer is our optimal choice for the voting system.

To restate the load balancer choice that has been arrived at through the preceding section, the voting frontends will be managed by a cross-region, external Application Load Balancer.

Employing message queues to pool requests

The voting frontends have the main responsibility of accepting user requests, in this case, casting a vote, and getting that vote into the system as quickly and reliably as possible. The two requirements of speed and durability, which is the expression of reliability in this case, are in competition from an engineering point of view: persisting and verifying an update to the vote tally is a slow operation. As we explored in *Chapter 3, Determining the Infrastructure to Build Features Upon* and illustrated in *Figure 3.5*, we can decouple the persisting of a vote from the application of that vote to the totals for each act through the use of a durable asynchronous mechanism: A message queue. We will define a Pub/Sub topic for the delivery of each vote from the voting frontends to the downstream vote processing. The voting frontend will consider a vote to be complete when it has successfully published that vote to this topic, trusting that the infrastructure will perform as expected. The Vote Ingester has done its job once the vote is in the system permanently.

Creating Pub/Sub resources for votes

The use of Pub/Sub requires the definition of a topic and at least one subscription. We will define a topic named votes and a subscription named votes-sub in the Google Cloud console. The following steps will define these Pub/Sub resources:

1. First ensure that Pub/Sub is enabled for your project:
   a. Open the Google Cloud console and log in.
   b. Select your Google Cloud project.
   c. Click on the **Dashboard** tab.
   d. In the **Getting Started** pane, click on **Explore and Enable APIs**.
   e. Click on +**Enable APIs and Services**.
   f. In the search box type **Pub/Sub** and press *Enter*.
   g. From the results list, click on **Cloud Pub/Sub API**.
   h. If the status **does not say API Enabled**—click the **ENABLE** button.

2. Now, create the Pub/Sub topic named votes and a companion subscription:
   a. From the navigation menu at the top left of the console, choose **Cloud overview | Dashboard**.

    b. In the search box at the top of the dashboard, type **Cloud Pub/Sub** and click the **Search** button.

    c. Click on **Cloud Pub/Sub** in the results list, not **Cloud Pub/Sub API**.

    d. Click on the **Go to Cloud Pub/Sub** button.

    e. Click on **Topics** in the left nav bar.

    f. Click on the **Create topic** button.

    g. Type **votes** in the **Topic ID** field.

    h. Make sure that **Add a default subscription** is checked/selected.

    i. Leave all other default selections and click the **Create** button.

You should see a message confirming that a new topic and a new subscription have been created.

Publishing votes to Pub/Sub

With a topic in place, our next step is to add the publishing of messages to the topic. This will take place in the **votingfrontend.py** module's handler for the **/vote** method.

The **vote** method currently simply checks for the presence of a request field named **votedAct** and accepts the value of that field to be an act ID. We will add some validation to the method, as a redundant check to any client-side validation. If the act ID is not valid, an error response will be generated.

Here is where Pub/Sub comes into play. Once we have a valid act ID and a valid user, which we do from the auth code presented in the previous chapter's codelab, we have all the information needed to record a vote. To do this, the frontend will construct a JSON object encapsulating the vote and publish this as a Pub/Sub message to the vote's topic.

Votes are written to the Pub/Sub topic, and acceptance of them is confirmed by a successful response from the Pub/Sub client library.

There are two steps to this process, shown in the following example code snippets. The full code will be included in the codelab later in the chapter:

First, we setup a publisher and a topic address or topic path in our Python code. When a vote is received, the create a vote JSON object and publish it as a message to this topic:

```python
# import JSON support
import json


# Import the Pub/Sub Python client library
from google.cloud import pubsub_v1
```

```
project_id = "votingforthestars". # The project-ID shown in the Cloud
console
topic_id = "votes".  # This is the name used when creating the Topic

# Create a Publisher
publisher = pubsub_v1.PublisherClient()

# Create a path to the votes topic
topic_path = publisher.topic_path(project_id, topic_id)

# Create the JSON object
vote_json = {"vote": {"act": actId, "user": userName}}

# Pub/Sub messages must be a bytestring, so we serialize and encode the
JSON object
vote_str = json.dumps(vote_json)
message_data = vote_str.encode("utf-8")

# When you publish a message, the client returns a future
future = publisher.publish(topic_path, message_data)
# The result method blocks until the message has been successfully
published or
# it raises an exception
try:
  print(future.result())
except Exception as e:
  print("vote for: {} failed with: {}".format(vote_str, str(e)))
  raise
```

Asynchronous processing of requests

Moving votes from user actions to messages on a queue completes one part of our objective: We have decoupled the user from the processing of votes. To accomplish our goal, we must implement the remaining part of the requirement, to actually process the votes.

Processing votes published to Pub/Sub

Recall the discussion of a message queue in *Chapter 4, Choosing Between GCP Options*, section *Asynchronous message handling*. Based on that description, the following figure illustrates our intended use of Pub/Sub in the voting application:

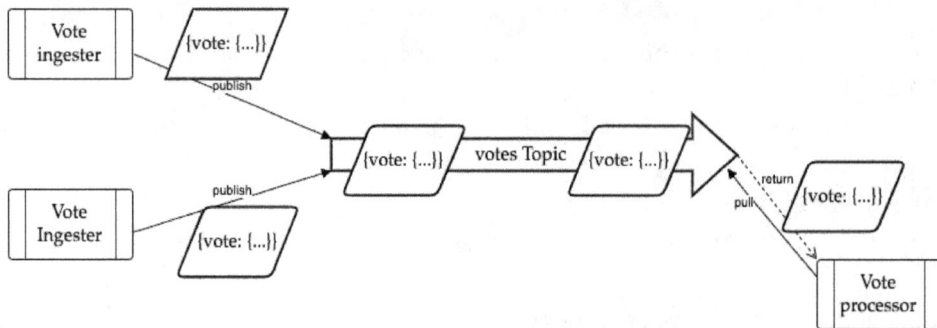

Figure 10.2: Use of Pub/Sub in voting

The role of Pub/Sub is to decouple the low latency requirements of the user from the high latency operation of processing (recording) votes. Pub/Sub for our purposes is embodied by the votes Topic in *Figure 10.2* with the publish and pull operations which are the interface between the two decoupled components and the topic. The preceding section has described the choices and implementation of the publisher side, now it is time to examine the subscriber side, represented by the pull operation in *Figure 10.2*.

Messages on a topic are received via a subscription to that topic. Pub/Sub offers three types of subscriptions:

- Pull subscriptions in which a subscriber calls to the topic to pull the next messages from the queue. Messages stay on the queue until explicitly pulled.

- Push subscriptions resemble push notifications which were discussed in Chapter 7, *Frontends at the Client Border*, in the section *Client-side request handlers*. A push subscriber is called asynchronously by Pub/Sub, passing a message from the topic when it is published.

- Export subscriptions automatically forwards published messages published to their topic to a BigQuery table or to a Cloud Storage bucket.

Each of these have their relative uses and strengths. For our specific case, we have already addressed the requirement for low latency in our design, and this part of our architecture is focused on reliability and permanence. We will use a push subscription,n which is well suited for our use case: A Cloud Run service that handles bursts of high traffic with long periods of inactivity. The reason for this selection is that push subscriptions can be used to automatically scale Cloud Run instances to match demand, whereas a pull subscription would have to manage its own scaling of processors and would require a worker to always be on to poll the topic throughout periods of inactivity.

We will setup the described Pub/Sub resources for this in the Cloud developer console. A Pub/Sub topic and then a default push subscription, which will automatically send the topic's published messages to our Cloud Run service as an HTTP POST request. The **Topic** and **Subscription** summaries in the Google Cloud console are shown in the following two figures:

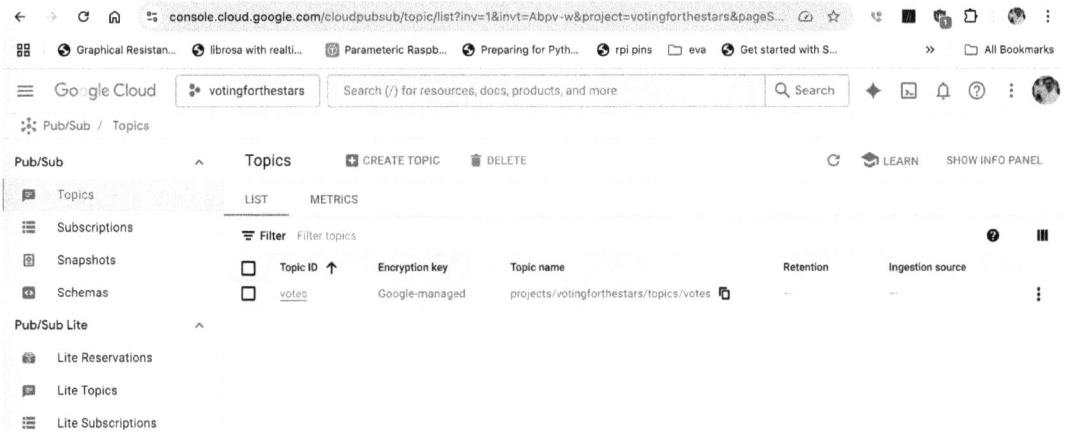

Figure 10.3: Pub/Sub topic in the Google Cloud console

Refer to the following figure for more details:

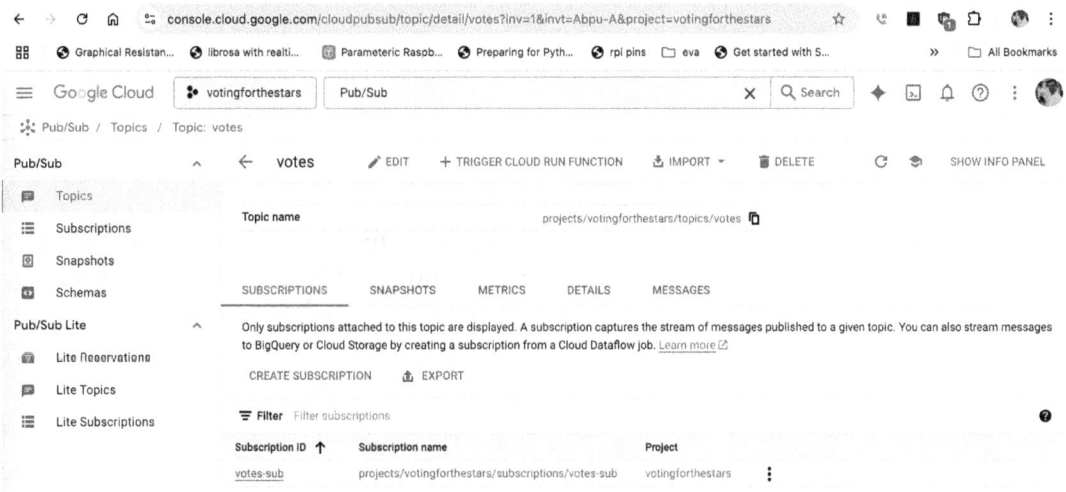

Figure 10.4: Pub/Sub Subscription in the Google Cloud console

When the subscriber detects a published, **negative acknowledged** (**NACK**) message on the topic, it places the message in a pending state and sends it as the body of a POST request to the push endpoint defined for the subscription.

An instance of an HTTP server at the defined push endpoint will receive the message that was sent by the subscription. The HTTP status code returned by our handler tells the subscription if the message is ACK or should be considered unprocessed and redelivered in a subsequent POST request.

A minimal implementation of this push endpoint is shown in the following code snippet. The full details and code are included in the codelab later in this chapter:

```
@app.route("/", methods=["POST"])
def index():
    """Receive and parse a Pub/Sub message which should contain valid
JSON."""
    message = request.data

    print("incoming message!")
    if message:
        print("data: {}".format(message))
    try:
        vote = json.loads(message)
        print("vote: {}".format(vote))
    except ValueError as e:
        print("Invalid JSON received: {}".format(e))
        return ("Invalid JSON", 400)
    except Exception as e:
        print("error: {}".format(e))
        return ("", 500)
    return ("", 204)
```

Scaling backend processing

What we now have shown are the overall design and the implementation details of a voting system that provides low latency to the user, and a highly durable transient storage of users' votes. The actual processing of the votes, considered a backend task, can be done without the need for user-perceived low latency. The Vote Processor is not without latency considerations; they are just not directly tied to any user or client requirement.

Some considerations that do affect a latency requirement on the Vote Processor are based on infrastructure constraints and some are based on user requirements, aside from the immediate ACK of a vote being cast. We will enumerate some of these considerations as follows:

- There is a maximum number of messages that a topic is configured to hold at one time.

- A message has a maximum **time-to-live** (**TTL**) that it can remain on a topic before being consumed by a subscriber.

- The audience expects the votes to be tallied and the results of a round to be announced within a certain period of time after the conclusion of voting for that round's acts.

We must satisfy each of these requirements, or the system or the business will fail. The failure of the system will erode the value of the business and over repeated outages; the business will fail. So, it is important to have a plan that guarantees that the system meets all these requirements as close to always as possible.

Let us explore the consequences of failing to meet each of three requirements listed previously:

- If messages are left on the topic for too long, or too many messages accumulate on the topic, votes that we confirmed as recorded will be dropped. We have then not fulfilled our contract with the user community to count all votes. We have also not held to the guarantee that we gave each user when they cast their individual votes, that the vote was recorded.

- If we take 4 days to announce the winners of a round when we had promised to announce them within 2 days, we have lost credibility with the audience. Crossing another threshold with more severe consequences, if it takes a week to determine the results of a round, we will not be able to select the participants of the next tier of voting if that starts a week after the round whose results were delayed.

None of the preceding situations should arise and we can build our system to avoid them. We can also adhere to site reliability best practices and put monitoring in place to detect and notify us when the state of the system is trending towards any of the preceding problems, before we cross a point of no return and can mitigate the situation.

The failure that could lead to any of these scenarios is when our rate of vote processing is insufficient to process the pending votes in the required window of time.

Applying GCP scaling

There are ways to control the rate of vote processing, the most direct of which is to increase the number of Vote Processors that process votes from the topic. This is simple horizontal scaling, and it has several strengths that we will now discuss.

Horizontal scaling is easy to configure, observe and control in GCP. Most GCP compute products can be configured to automatically increase or decrease the number of workers running in a service in response to current demand.

Pub/Sub supports and works well with multiple concurrent push subscriber instances receiving messages from topics.

The effect of horizontal scaling on throughput or the rate of vote processing is predictable and roughly linear. If one Vote Processor can process 25 votes per minute, two Vote Processors can process approximately, but not quite 50 votes in a minute. Approximately, because there is going to be some overhead internally in Pub/Sub, managing lock semantics and load balancing among multiple clients.

Another way to increase throughput is through vertical scaling, increasing the processing rate of each Vote Processor. This can be done by increasing resources, such as memory and CPU cores, used to run each server. This is a good choice when the workers being scaled are bound by any of these resources. The existence of such a limiting resource can be determined by profiling a worker when it is under load. Profiling with a tool such as Cloud Profiler can reveal which, if any, resource is the underlying bottleneck, for example, if the process is occupying all available memory or using 100% of its CPU cores' capacity. GCP can be configured to automatically vertically scale server instances in response to reaching certain utilization thresholds on these resources.

An advantage of vertical scaling is that the number of connections to shared resources, such as a target database table, remains constant, unlike horizontal scaling.

With a more intricate design, both scaling techniques could be employed in tandem. For example, when CPU utilization in workers is high, the workers' CPU resources can be increased to a certain limit to enable them to keep up with the demand. If the current pool of workers fails to keep up with the rate of message publication, even with additional CPU cores and memory, then new instances can be created to take on the additional load. This technique is not needed in most situations, and if used, it shifts much of the scaling logic from GCP configuration to application-specific code. It is best to avoid unnecessary complexity and rely on existing, tested features whenever possible.

Vote Processor deployment

The functional requirements of the Vote Processor backend server have been described at a sufficient level of detail that we can use them to form a set of technical requirements.

Briefly, some of the key requirements are:

- The service should not be directly reachable from the public internet or any endpoints outside of our application. The reason for this lies in a principle of cybersecurity best practices, the least visibility principle. This principle limits visibility to sensitive data and operations to minimize the potential surface area of a system that is vulnerable to attack. To implement this principle as comprehensively as possible, since there is no requirement for the Vote Processor to be accessed by any external endpoint, we do not make it even possible for it to be. Making the service invisible to external endpoints has no impact on our intended use cases, thus any potential access that we have removed would be unintentional or malicious.

- The service should scale horizontally to keep up with spikes in demand, followed by long lulls of activity. As demand increases, more system resources should automatically be brought to bear in response, and as demand drops, underutilized resources should automatically be released.

- The Vote Processor service does not have any dependency on external services, outside of our application. The only dependencies we have identified are sibling Vote Processors and our data persistence services, all of which are GCP services within the same application.

We will use Cloud Run to deploy the Vote Processor. It can connect to our internal services, perform automatic horizontal scaling of instances under load, and interoperates with Pub/Sub as well as any other GCP service.

Monitoring of backend performance

As well as scaling resources, monitoring and notification should be employed whenever demand is trending towards any critical situation. For example, if the maximum number of pending messages in the topic is configured to be 10,000, an alert when the message count has been over 85% of that for five minutes would be useful so that system operators can be verify that the system operates as intended and that auto-scaling kicks in and is effective. An additional alert that is triggered if our auto-scaling is not effective in reducing a backlog, such as if the number of pending messages in the topic ever reaches 95% or more of our limit, is also advisable. We trust that auto-scaling and our application design work as intended, but also plan for the worst.

Regular reviews of historical performance are also a good practice. A weekly review of demand, auto-scaling, and system resource utilization will reveal if assumptions about performance are still true. For example, if auto-scaling is starting up more new instances than expected, the workers might be starved for CPU, or some other resource, and it might be effective to raise the CPU allocation to increase each worker's processing rate.

Dispatching user requests asynchronously via Pub/Sub codelab

This chapter's codelab will define the implementation of the Vote Ingester frontend and the Vote Processor. The tallying of votes will be described and implemented later in *Chapter 11, Guaranteeing Data Permanence*.

On the frontend, this codelab adds code to publish valid votes to Pub/Sub, incorporating that operation's success or failure into the client response.

The Vote Processor will receive votes from the Pub/Sub topic, and invoke a stub processing method which will be expanded upon in *Chapter 11, Guaranteeing Data Permanence*. The success or failure of that method will determine if the vote is ACK and thus removed from the topic or left on the topic for repeated retrieval and processing.

Asynchronous vote processing components

The following runtime components will be implemented in this codelab:

- **votingfrontend**: The service that was deployed in the previous *Chapter 9, Identifying the Stress Points of our Voting System*, will be augmented to publish votes to Pub/Sub and indicate the success of that operation in their response to the client.

- **RegionalVoteProcessor**: This is a service we will deploy using Cloud Run. It is written in Python. The initial implementation will receive messages from the topic and ACK them as processed if they can be parsed as valid JSON. Logging the success and failure of each message will allow us to later verify the Vote Processor's behavior.

- **Pub/Sub topic**: We defined the votes topic earlier in this chapter. This topic is the conduit between the frontend and backend services. We will configure the topic's maximum number of pending messages and message maximum TTL.

- **Pub/Sub subscription**: A push subscription for the votes topic, named **votes_sub** was created earlier in this chapter and will be reviewed here:

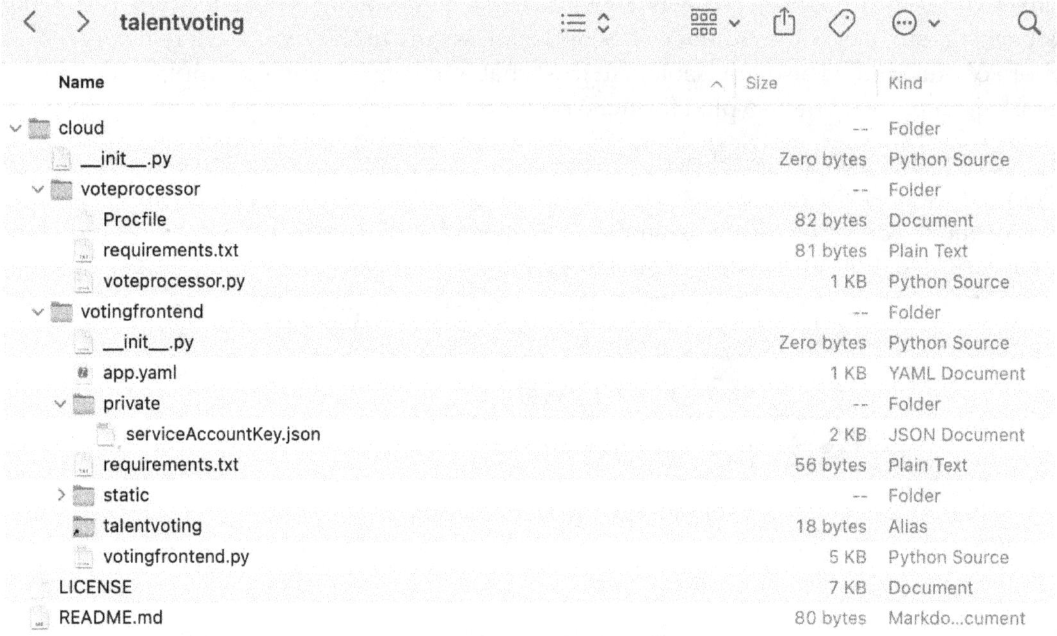

Name	Size	Kind
⌄ 📁 cloud	--	Folder
📄 __init__.py	Zero bytes	Python Source
⌄ 📁 voteprocessor	--	Folder
📄 Procfile	82 bytes	Document
📄 requirements.txt	81 bytes	Plain Text
📄 voteprocessor.py	1 KB	Python Source
⌄ 📁 votingfrontend	--	Folder
📄 __init__.py	Zero bytes	Python Source
📄 app.yaml	1 KB	YAML Document
⌄ 📁 private	--	Folder
📄 serviceAccountKey.json	2 KB	JSON Document
📄 requirements.txt	56 bytes	Plain Text
> 📁 static	--	Folder
📄 talentvoting	18 bytes	Alias
📄 votingfrontend.py	5 KB	Python Source
📄 LICENSE	7 KB	Document
📄 README.md	80 bytes	Markdo...cument

Figure 10.5: Folder and file structure of cloud packages

- **Cloud Run service**: A Cloud Run service named **vote_processor_service** will be deployed to Cloud Run from source.

Top level directories with new cloud code

There are no new or removed files in the **votingfrontend** package, but the cloud package now has a second subdirectory: **voteprocessor**. We will review the contents of these files later in this codelab.

Code additions to the Vote Ingester

The Vote Ingester, implemented in the **votingfrontend** module, has a function named **vote** that parses a client request, returns error responses for several possible problems, and then simply echoes the details of the vote that was requested back to the client. We will extend that method and add a new helper method to publish the vote to Pub/Sub.

The following code is excerpts of the updated **votingfrontend.py** module. There are minor refactoring and style changes throughout the module, but we will call out the relevant portions for this chapter's functionality in the following the code:

```python
import json
import sys

from talentvoting.common.acts import Act, Acts
from talentvoting.common.policy.votingpolicyengine import
VotingPolicyEngine
from talentvoting.common.interfaces.voteingester import VoteIngester
from talentvoting.common.interfaces.responses import FrontendError,
IneligibleVote, InvalidUser, InvalidLogin, MalformedRequest, VoteCastError
from talentvoting.common.interfaces.servicelocations import VOTE_WEB_
CLIENT_DOMAIN, VOTE_QUEUE_TOPIC, PROJECT_ID


from google.cloud import pubsub_v1

policy_engine = VotingPolicyEngine()
publisher = pubsub_v1.PublisherClient()
# Create a path to the votes topic
topic_path = publisher.topic_path(PROJECT_ID, VOTE_QUEUE_TOPIC )

def _getActs() ->Acts:
    return _policy_engine.getAllActs()



    except auth.InvalidIdTokenError:
        raise InvalidLogin(str(id_token))

def _recordVote(act:Act) ->any:
    try:
        log("_recordVote({})".format(act))
        # Message data must be a bytestring
```

```
            message_data = act.encode("utf-8")
            future = publisher.publish(topic_path, message_data)
            _ = future.result()

        except Exception as e:
            logError(e, "_recordVote()")
            raise VoteCastError(str(act))

@app.route('/vote', methods=['POST'])
def vote():
    form = request.form
    uid = __validateUser(form)

    try:
        actId = form['votedAct']
        vote = {"user": uid, "act": actId}
        vote = json.dumps(vote)
        log("vote({}".format(vote))
        _recordVote(vote)
        response = make_response(vote, 200)
        _fixResponseHeaders(response)
        log("response data: {}".format(str(response.get_data())))
        log("response headers: {}".format(str(response.headers)))
        return response
    except BadRequestKeyError:
        error = {"error" : str(MalformedRequest("votedAct").response()
[0])}
        error = json.dumps(error)
        logError(error, "error:vote()")
        response = make_response(error, error.response()[1])
        _fixResponseHeaders(response)
        log("response data: {}".format(str(response.get_data())))
        log("response headers: {}".format(str(response.headers)))
        return response

    except FrontendError as e:
        error = {"error" : str(e.response()[0])}
        error = json.dumps(error)
        logError(error, "error:vote()")
```

```
response = make_response(error, e.response()[1])
_fixResponseHeaders(response)
log("response data: {}".format(str(response.get_data())))
log("response headers: {}".format(str(response.headers)))
return response
```

First, at the beginning of the file, there is now code to import and initialize the Pub/Sub library and create a **PublisherClient** that will be used with our Pub/Sub topic.

The **vote** function now invokes a new method **_recordVote**. We also add user authentication to the **vote** method, identical to code in the **getActs** method that was defined in the codelab of the previous chapter.

The new **_recordVote** function is where the actual work takes place. This publishes the JSON from the client request in a new message on the Pub/Sub topic. If any error occurs, it is logged for later forensics and a new application defined exception, **VoteCastError**, is raised. This new error class is appended at the end of the **responses.py** module and follows the same pattern as other error classes in that module:

```
class VoteCastError(FrontendError):
    def __init__(self, act):
        self.__act = act


    def response(self) ->any:

      return ("error:vote not recorded. "+
          "act:{}".format(str(self.__act)),
      500)
```

The new error class returns a 500 HTTP status code to the client which indicates an internal server error. Details of the failure are not sent to the client to prevent reverse engineering and help protect against potential exploits by malicious parties. Our engineers will access the server logs via GCP monitoring to see the exact error that was encountered.

We have also added new endpoint definitions to the **servicelocations.py** module. The complete contents of that module follow.

```
_VOTE_INGESTOR_ADDRESS = "https://votingforthestars.ue.r.appspot.com"
VOTE_URL = _VOTE_INGESTOR_ADDRESS + "/vote"
GETACTS_URL = _VOTE_INGESTOR_ADDRESS + "/getacts"
VOTE_PROCESSOR_ADDRESS = "https://votingforthestars.run.app/processor"
VOTE_QUEUE_TOPIC = "votes"
VOTE_WEB_CLIENT_DOMAIN =  "https://votingforthestars.web.app"
PROJECT_ID = "votingforthestars"
```

Pub/Sub configuration

Pub/Sub topics have several configuration options that should be understood when defining a topic, as they have a bearing on the suitability of a topic for a specific usage pattern. For most of these options, the default setting is applicable to most applications and other settings are for specialized use cases.

This following figure shows the **DETAILS** tab of the **votes** topic configuration in the Google Cloud console:

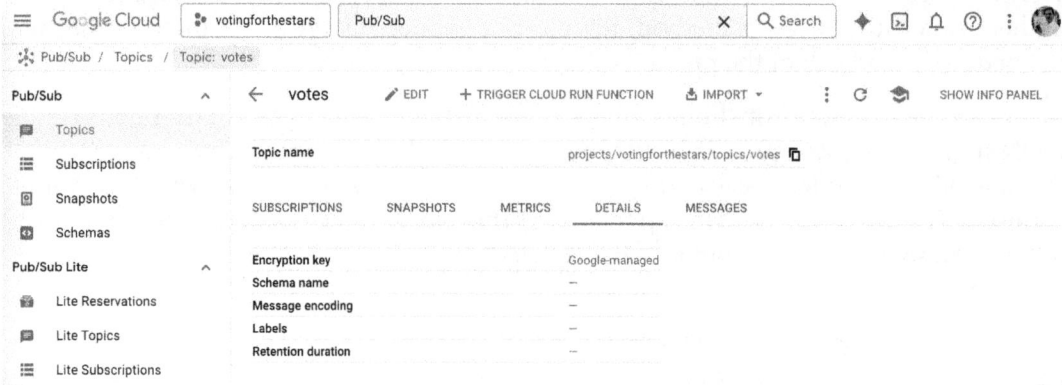

Figure 10.6: Pub/Sub topic details

The values shown are all defaults when creating a topic. The most relevant and commonly changed settings are the **Schema name** and **Retention duration**, for which we will discuss the default values and their relevance.

Schema allows you to define a strict format that Pub/Sub Publishers will enforce when publishing messages to the topic. A schema is a record definition that may be specified in either JSON or protocol buffer format. The advantage of schema enforcement is the guarantee that all messages will be of an expected form when consumed from a topic. The drawbacks of using a schema are the additional configuration work and a performance cost, as each publish operation must invoke the validation logic for its message. For our application, with only one source of messages and a strong latency requirement, schema enforcement offers no real advantage.

Retention duration is the maximum time a published message will be stored on the topic queue before potentially being deleted. Once a message is published, it will be consumed by a regularly run process: Either real-time, periodic, or on demand. Since pending messages take up storage space, they incur charges, and if allowed to remain forever, orphaned messages would continue to accumulate disk usage and charges back to the owner. ACK messages are typically deleted immediately, but this setting is the maximum time that a message will be stored on the topic, whether or not it has been delivered to the subscriber and ACK.

The default retention period is 7 days, which is meant to accommodate messages that are consumed either in real-time, or by daily or weekly batch pipelines. The retention setting can be set to any duration from 10 minutes to 31 days.

As well as a topic, a **Subscriptions** is needed to consume Pub/Sub messages. The following figure shows the **DETAILS** tab of the **votes-sub** subscription configuration in the Google Cloud console:

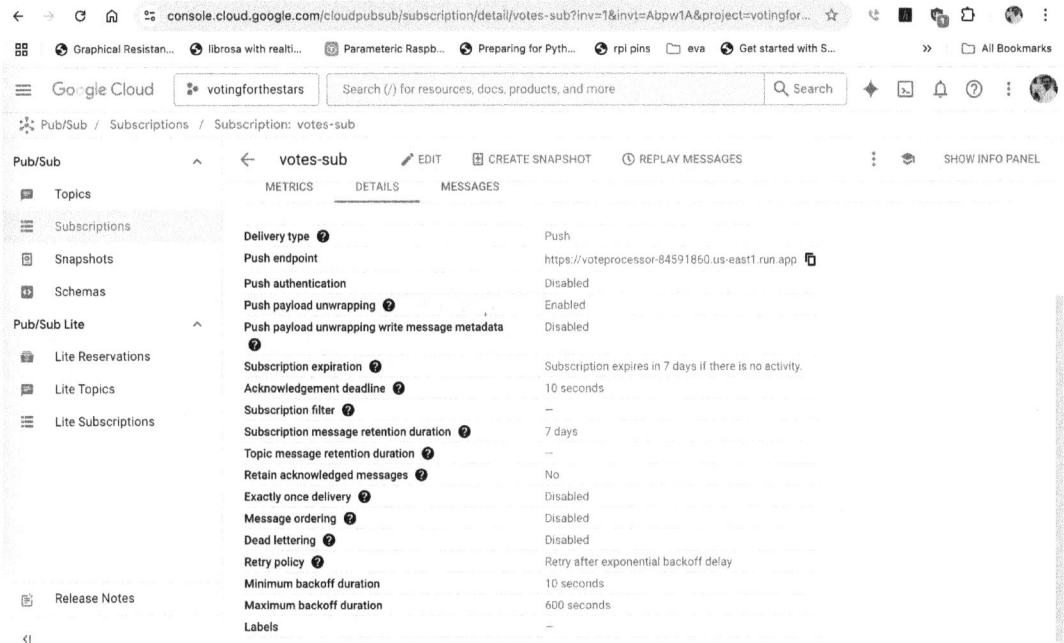

Figure 10.7: Pub/Sub subscription details

The settings most relevant to our application are **Delivery type**, **Push endpoint**, **Push payload unwrapping**, **Retain acknowledged messages**, **Retry policy**, and **Dead lettering**.

A **Delivery type** of **Push** specifies that the publishing of a message will trigger an action by this Pub/Sub subscription. The subscription will issue a POST request to the **Push endpoint** with this message data.

The **Push endpoint** is the URL at which the Vote Processor Cloud Run service is deployed. That will be displayed by the `gcloud` command when deploying the service. For now, you can enter any value and edit the subscription later, or you can wait to create the topic and subscription until you have deployed the service.

Push payload unwrapping instructs the subscription to send the message raw data as the POST request body. If this is disabled, the message is wrapped in a Pub/Sub-specific JSON object with several metadata fields. We have this disabled as the message data is the only content we need at this point.

A **Retain acknowledged messages** value of **No** directs Pub/Sub to delete messages from the topic as soon as a subscriber has consumed the message and ACK the message delivery. Our Vote Processor will only ACK a message once it has been successfully processed and we have no other use for the messages, so we set this to no to release message storage as quickly as possible.

The **Retry policy** controls how the subscription handles messages that are not ACK by their consumer endpoint. The subscriber can try to resend a message immediately after an error response or timeout, or it can wait for an exponentially increasing delay. The latter is useful to recover from a transient problem that is likely to correct itself over time, such as an external service being temporarily unavailable. The **Dead lettering** option of the **Retry policy** specifies an alternate message queue to which messages which remain NACK past a specified threshold are transferred.

Vote Processor code

The message handler for our push subscription is a relatively short piece of code. Most Pub/Sub-specific work is done by the subscription, leaving only a basic HTTP REST endpoint to be implemented. The complete code for our Cloud Run based **voteprocessor** is as follows:

```
import json
from flask import Flask, request
app = Flask(__name__)


def _processVote(message:json) -> bool:
    """
    Process a JSON message containing a vote.
    args:
        message: A JSON dict
    Returns:
        True if a message was processed, False otherwise
    """
    if not message:
        return False
    if not isinstance(message, dict):
        return False
    if "user" not in message or "act" not in message:
        return False
    return True


@app.route("/", methods=["POST"])
```

```python
def index():
    """Receive a Pub/Sub message which should contain valid JSON and issue
HTTP response."""
    message = request.data

    print("incoming message!")
    if message:
        print("data: {}".format(message))
    try:
        vote = json.loads(message)
        if _processVote(vote):
            print("Processed vote: {}".format(vote))
        else:
            print("Invalid vote: {}".format(vote))
            return ("Invalid vote", 400)  # Invalid content error status
    except ValueError as e:
        print("Invalid JSON received: {}".format(e))
        return ("Invalid JSON", 400)
    except Exception as e:
        print("error: {}".format(e))
        return ("", 500)  # Internal server error status
    return ("", 204)  # No content OK status
```

This basic Flask app has one handler, the root path **"/"**. The request is validated as containing JSON using the **json.loads()** function, which will raise a **ValueError** exception if invalid JSON is found.

If the request body contains a JSON object, this is passed to the **_processVote** function. This function currently guarantees that the JSON has the expected elements for a vote message and returns **True**, otherwise **False**. Based on this return value the handler either ACKs the message with an OK status code or NACKs the delivery of the message with an error status.

In the next chapter, the **_processVote** function will be expanded to tally votes, but for the purpose of asynchronous processing using Pub/Sub, this function is feature complete.

Cloud run configuration and deployment

To deploy the Vote Processor service to Cloud Run, we will initially use a feature called deploy from source. This feature allows you to specify the contents of your Cloud Run service with some configuration parameters and allow the **gcloud** build service to create a Docker container from a preexisting supplied image which includes you your package built from your source files and configuration specifications.

The configuration for our Cloud Run service is contained in two files, **requirements.txt** and **Procfile**.

The **requirements** file is identical in purpose to the one used for the Google App Engine **votingfrontend** service. It lists the packages to be installed in your service's runtime environment. The contents of our **requirements.txt** file are shown as follows:

```
gunicorn==23.0.0
Flask==3.0.3
Werkzeug==3.0.3
google-cloud-pubsub
google-api-core
```

The second file, **Procfile**, specifies how your service is to be started when Cloud Run has finished setting up the runtime environment and is ready for your service to begin execution. The contents of our **Procfile** follows:

```
web: gunicorn --bind :$PORT --workers 1 --threads 8 --timeout 0
voteprocessor:app
```

These two files and the source file for our service, **voteprocessor.py**, are all that is needed to deploy a Cloud Run service from source.

In the directory where these files are located, the following command deploys the service:

```
gcloud run deploy --allow-unauthenticated --source .
```

The **--source .** parameter specified that this is a source deployment from the current directory, refered to as **.**

The command will confirm the service name and prompt for a region. Once that is done, it will invoke the Cloud Build service to create a container and deploy the service. The URL of the Cloud Build service logs will be displayed where status and error messages about the build can be viewed.

When a deployment completes, the service URL of the deployed service is displayed. This is the URL to use as the push subscription endpoint, referred to in the earlier section *Pub/Sub configuration* of this codelab.

Configuring Vote Processor auto-scaling

Cloud Run deployed services are set to allow horizontal auto-scaling by default. When a push subscription is used to send messages to a Cloud Run service, the service will start new instances if no existing instance is available to receive a message. When an instance has been idle for some time, Cloud Run will automatically scale down, that is, shut down the idle instance to conserve resources and cost.

To prevent unexpected high costs during traffic spikes, there is a maximum number of instances that auto-scaling will start. By default, the **max** instance count is 100 but this can be overridden when deploying a revision of the service by adding the `--max-instances=n` flag to the `gcloud run deploy` command, where n is an integer between 1 and the number allowed by your region and CPU and memory configurations.

It is important to note that every concurrent request does not require its instance of the service. Cloud Run services dispatch multiple concurrent requests to each instance and only start up new instances when the existing instances' CPU utilization is high or the concurrent request limit per instance has been reached. By default, Cloud Run sets a limit of 80 concurrent requests per instance. This can be set to a different value using the `--concurrent=n` flag of the `gcloud run deploy` command, where **n** is an integer between 1 and 1000. It is advisable to start with the defaults and monitor CPU and memory utilization of your service instances, raising the limit if instances' usage of these resources remains low when under load. Monitoring the instance resource utilization is described in the following section.

Monitoring for service resource usage

The dashboards automatically provided for a Cloud Run service, display all the metrics needed to check on how well instances are provisioned to handle their demand. In the Cloud console, navigate to **Cloud Run** and select the service, in our case **voteprocessor**, which is the service name that was provided by the `gcloud run deploy` command. In the dashboard that opens, scrolling down will reveal graphs of CPU and memory utilization, as shown in the following figure:

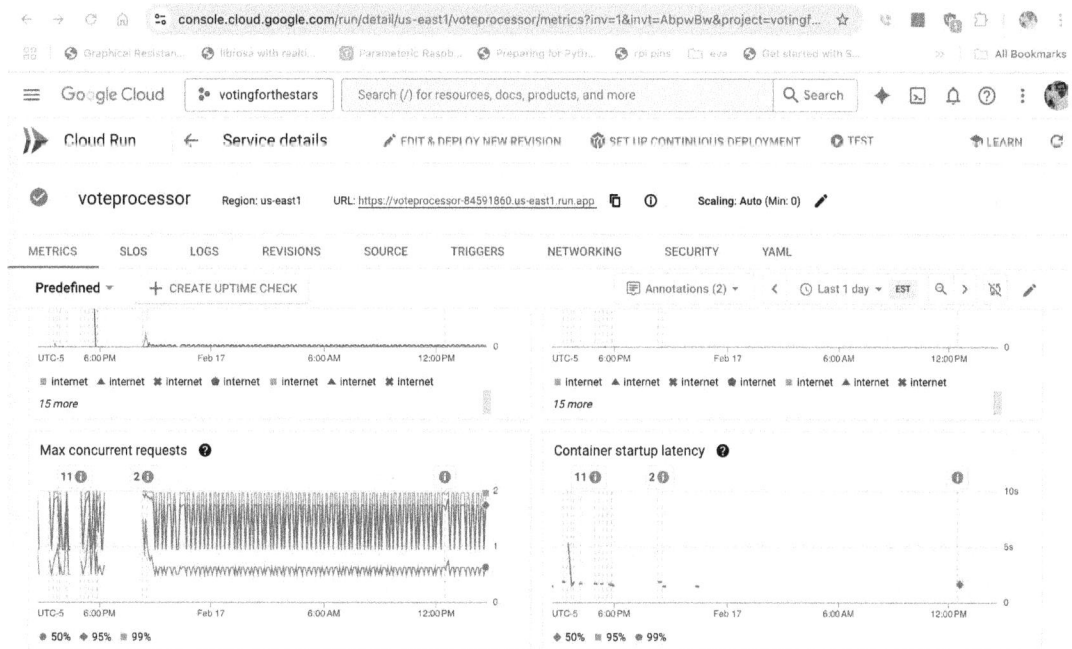

Figure 10.8: Cloud run instance resource graphs

This shows that our one instance was always using below 20% of both CPU and memory resources during the window shown. Ideally, this will be checked for a window that included a heavy load of requests.

The number of concurrent requests that was handled by each instance can be confirmed by scrolling to reveal an additional graph in the same dashboard, shown in the following figure:

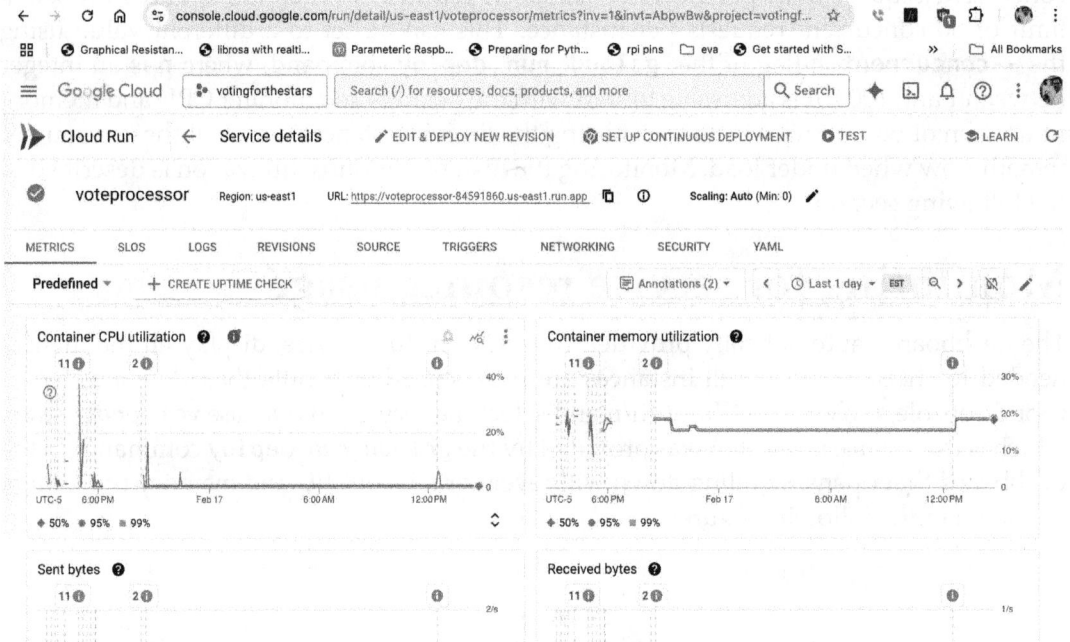

Figure 10.9: *Cloud run instance resource graphs*

We can see that in the window shown, there were never more than two concurrent requests for our instance. Different time ranges can be selected until a period of heavier load is found. Once a period of high demand is found, use the resource graphs to gauge the resources used by an instance and project how many concurrent requests an instance could possibly serve.

Monitoring for Pub/Sub topic backlog

Apart from dashboards, GCP offers alerts, which serve a complementary role. A dashboard is an excellent way to take in a large amount of information, over arbitrary windows of time. Alerting, on the other hand, delivers one piece of information, a single data point, at a single point in time: Right now.

Typical usage is to setup alerts for conditions which can be expressed as a single statement, such as there are more than 8500 votes queued in the topic that is true at the current time. The alert should be a condition that requires action, and a recommended response is to view a relevant dashboard to see the larger picture, to understand why the condition that triggered the alert has come about.

To setup alerts require two definitions: A notification channel—where to send the alert, and a policy—what the triggering condition and metric are.

First, setup a channel with the following steps:

1. From the **Google Cloud console | Observability | Monitoring** page click on **Alerting** in the **Detect** section of the left navigation bar, shown in the following figure:

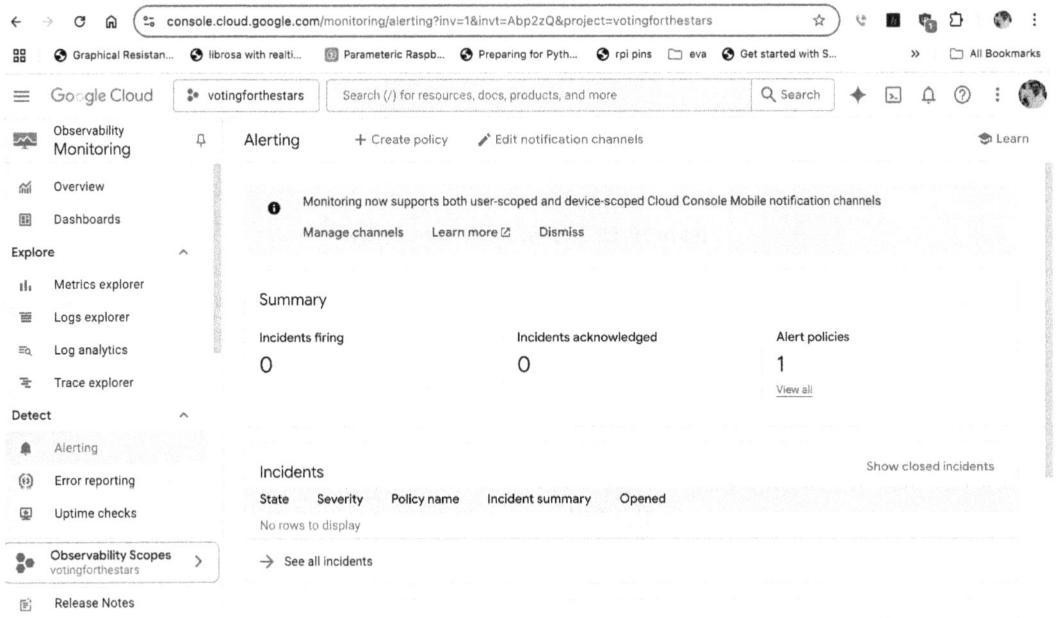

Figure 10.10: *Main Alerting page*

2. Click on **Edit notification channels** which will display the page shown in the following figure:

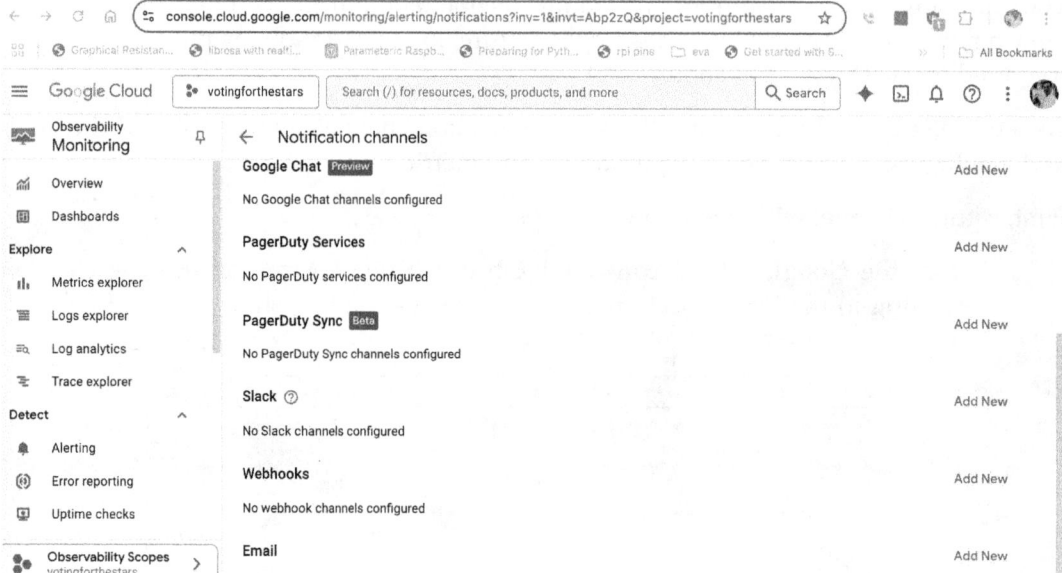

Figure 10.11: Notification channels page

You can add as many channels of as many types as you wish. Email, SMS, and Slack are common ones depending on the preference of the party being notified.

At least one channel is defined so you can define an alerting policy. This typically involves three components: A metric, a resource, and a threshold.

3. On the **Monitoring** page, shown in *Figure 10.10,* click on **Create policy** which will display the page shown in the following figure:

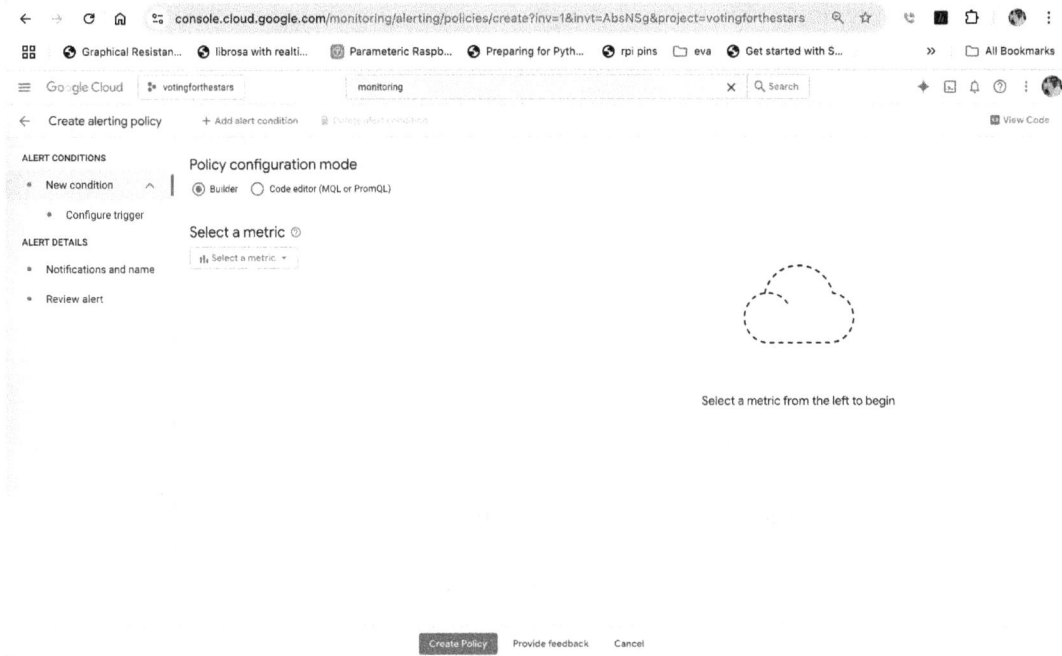

Figure 10.12: Alerting policy page

4. Select **Builder** as the **Policy configuration mode**.

5. First, we have to specify a metric. Click on the **Select a metric** pulldown and select **Cloud Pub | Subscription | Subscription**. Then, select the submenu item: **Unacked messages**.

6. Click the **Apply** button.

7. Now, we restrict the alert to our vote topic. This is done to preserve the integrity of this alert if we should add other topics to the project in the future.

8. Click **Add filter** then select **subscription_id = votes-sub** from the controls and click **Done**. The filter expression should appear under the **Add filters** button.

9. Click **Next**.

10. To define the alert trigger, select and enter these settings:

    a. **Condition type** = `Threshold`

    b. **Alert trigger** = `Any time series violates`

    c. **Threshold position** = `Above threshold`

    d. **Threshold value** = `9999`

11. Click **Next**.

12. Now in the final step we select the notification channels to be used when this alert is triggered.

   Select at least one of the notification channels you have defined, and enter a **Notification subject line**. Then, enter an **Alert policy name** such as `large pending vote queue`.

13. Finally click **Create policy**.

   A graph will be displayed, showing how many times this alert has fired over time; currently none.

Monitoring for Pub/Sub old messages

Another alert worth setting up is for messages that remain NACK for an excessive amount of time. A message may be in this state due to a processing backlog, a transient failure in the **voteprocessor** or due to a problem with the message itself. Recall that our **voteprocessor** NACKs all messages with an invalid vote format which leaves them on the topic for later redelivery attempts, this is intentional, as such a message would indicate either a bug in the voting frontend or that some other source is publishing messages to the vote's topic. This alert will be used to get our attention on the matter.

If a message has been NACK for more than a few retries, it is likely to be the third reason given: an invalid or corrupt message. When receiving this alert, a good response is to check the Vote Processor service logs to find the message that accompanied the message being rejected.

The metric name for this alert policy is defined on subscriptions, not topics, and is called **oldest_unacked_message_age**. Use a threshold value of two minutes which is 120000 milliseconds, the unit used in the metric.

After investigation and analysis of the problem is complete, the offending message should be pulled and ACK or deleted. There is a Pub/Sub feature that is useful in this situation called **dead letter topic** that could be added to the votes-sub subscription if desired.

Monitoring for frontend latency

The third alert to setup is one that fires if the voting frontend latency is high, that is it takes longer than a specified amount of time to return responses to users. A good starting point for acceptable frontend latency is 300 milliseconds. We will set this up in the same way as the alert policies for Pub/Sub.

Make the following selections and entries in the alert builder dialog:

- Select the metric **GAE Application | Http | Response latency**.
- No filter should be specified.
- Set the trigger to be a value above 300.

Responding to notifications

When an alert fires, an incident is opened. This is an issue tracking artifact that is useful for tracking resolution, including assignment of tasks to different people. For now, simply marking an incident as closed when appropriate is recommended. Incident management is highly specific to a team and product, and training and establishing protocol should be completed before any business-critical system is deployed.

Conclusion

This chapter explored many aspects of scaling an application to anticipate and service user demand, with regard to responsiveness and reliability. Using the voting portion of our system, the reader was taken through the exercise of modeling demand. With these forecasts of load on the system, architectural choices were described that minimize the portion of the system that must scale with user demand. Load balancing techniques and deployment schemes for our global community were described.

The chapter then focused on the use of an asynchronous processing model to detach user responses from large portions of vote processing. Pub/Sub was described in detail and then specific features and options applicable to our use case were identified.

The codelab for this section developed the Pub/Sub conduit or pipeline from the application frontend to the backend Vote Processors. Monitoring of critical points of infrastructure performance was added, along with monitoring of end-user responsiveness.

In the next chapter, the backend processing to actually store votes will be discussed and implemented. Several GCP products will be compared for suitability along with techniques for synchronizing work across regions.

Join our Discord space

Join our Discord workspace for latest updates, offers, tech happenings around the world, new releases, and sessions with the authors:

https://discord.bpbonline.com

CHAPTER 11
Guaranteeing Data Permanence

Introduction

In this chapter, the permanent and consistent recording and replaying of user activity will be explored and implemented. Data integrity is the most important feature of a system in preserving user trust, and a lapse in data integrity is the surest and most lasting way to lose that trust. Data integrity has a brief definition: What you write is what you read. Following the establishment of data integrity is the requirement of data availability, which can be summed up in the statement, you can read what you wrote whenever you expect to.

This chapter describes the data storage products that are included in GCP and the types of information each one is specialized to contain. The reader then walks through the storage systems that will be used in the voting system and the considerations that go into these selections. With the technology identified, we then describe the data reliability features of our selected storage systems and the failure modes that they prevent and mitigate.

The codelab for this chapter will define the storage services used to persist votes and user activity, and the code used to implement persistence features in the voting system backend, accompanied by code in the web client to reflect the persistence of user activity. Monitoring of these services for reliability and performance will also be described and defined in the codelab.

Structure

The following topics will be covered in this chapter:

- Types of data
- Relational and non-relational databases
- Binary large objects
- Access patterns
- Guaranteeing data availability
- Permanence goals of snapshots and archives
- Persistence of votes and voter activity codelab

Objectives

The reader will explore the different types of data, aspects of the data that are independent of the information content. These are modeled as the shape and form of the data as opposed to its meaning. Specific storage services are better or worse suited to host a given datastore based on these structural aspects of the data, rather than suitability being based on the information represented within.

After these static facets of data, the dynamic aspects: Actual usage in practice, play a major role in determining the storage service best suited to host data. Frequency of access, reads, and writes can be examined and categorized into typical access patterns. The chapter will demonstrate this categorization and guide the reader through the process of applying it.

The chapter will then lead the reader through consideration of the need for data permanence and the different scenarios that term may refer to. Practices to guarantee each of those will be identified and explained to the reader.

The codelab for the chapter will illustrate the practical application of the principles discussed in the chapter, using specific **Google Cloud Platform (GCP)** tools and features. The codelab will build on the application developed in previous codelabs, adding updates to votes and user activity to the system.

Types of data

As well as function, data has form. Let us define these two often used terms in the context of data in an information processing system.

The function of data is the pure information content, the meaning that the data is representing or meant to convey. The current temperature in *London*, the attendees of a conference, and the image of the *Mona Lisa* are all examples of the function or information content.

> **Note: There was no mention of the form or representation such as Celsius, list, or JPEG.**

The form or structure of data is the physical bits and structures used to represent the information's content. Here is where specific implementation details are encountered, using terms such as *a decimal number set to the degrees in Celsius of the current temperature* and *a high resolution 24-bit color JPEG file of a painting*. The form of data is how it is represented, whereas the function or content is what is being represented.

The form of data is what most often guides the selection of a storage service and method. We focus on two aspects of data's form: The degree to which it possesses internal structure and the depth or layers of internal dependence and abstraction within the data.

Structured and unstructured data

Some information adheres to a common, predefined format across many instances. Such data is organized and arranged into identifiable, nameable components. An example of this is a date in the Gregorian calendar. A date is one item of information but always consists of three components that we can name: The year, the month, and the day of the month. You can examine a date from before the social use of electricity: April 3rd, 1832, and a date in the far future: February 18th, 2433, and the format and the process for interpreting the information remains the same.

A great strength of structured data is the predictability in many dimensions. For every date, it will always occupy the same amount of space, it will take approximately the same amount of work to interpret and process and the significance or amount of information that is encoded is the same.

Let us turn the discussion to unstructured data.

Unstructured data is something that is difficult to break down into consistently relevant constituent parts. A transcript of audible speech is a good example. All three of the following are unsurprising examples of transcribed speech:

- *What do you want to eat? Surprise me. I do not want to choose for you. Well, no matter what you make, I will be happy to have it as long as it is with you.*

- *I see a tree on the road ahead!*

- *"blah blah blah"*

Aside from containing words, which is the basic element of speech, these three have little in common. The length of the text, the number of subdivisions, sentences, and the amount of information contained varies greatly between the three examples. In addition, there are inferences that can be made, such as the participation of two speakers in the first transcript which cannot easily be made without analysis of the entire transcript's text.

Certain types of storage systems are optimized for storing structured data while others are ideal for storing unstructured data. The difference between the two is so significant that when information contains both structured and unstructured components, a common solution is to save these in separate storage systems with a reference (link) to the unstructured data's location stored as part of the structured data. The following figure illustrates a schema of this sort:

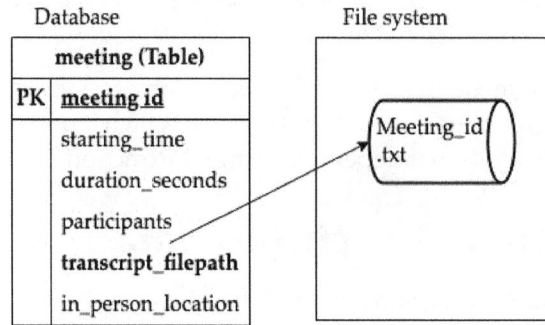

Figure 11.1: *A two system storage schema*

This is a common case, one which is worth describing in detail as it occurs frequently enough so that database vendors have added features to support it.

The general use case is of a set of data fields that describe a meeting, some of which are suitable for definition as database column and some which are not. In this case, the database transcript. The transcript is a single text field of arbitrary size; it could be the four words this meeting is cancelled or the text of the spoken words by 10 participants of a 3 hour summit. This is a good fit for a text file. Files are optimized to efficiently store data of widely varying size. File systems provide efficient direct access to individual files through their filename. So, it is a simple matter to store the filename of a meeting transcript as a proxy for the actual transcript and then resolve one additional reference to open the file located at that filename. Some database systems offer a **binary large object** (**Blob**) datatype which is implemented using different techniques, some of which are similar to the separate file and reference that is described previously. There are advantages and disadvantages to each approach: Using Blob datatypes simplifies your application design, and managing separately stored files allows more freedom in file size and disk usage.

Deep vs. flat data

A specific and unique type of structure that data might contain is one which is deep. Deep data is that which contains an internal hierarchy or layers of data. Flat data is that in which any constituent parts are at an equal level of significance and visibility. The date example previously used in this section is an example of flat data. The three components of a date: Year, month, and day are all of equal visibility and there is no containment of one of these field's value within another. You can determine June, the 3rd, and 1976 each independently of the other.

An illustrative counter example of deep data is that of a department or team in an organization. The department data can be arranged into nested structures; the constituent parts of a department themselves have sub-components. A department has, for example, an arbitrary number of team members; each of the team members has an employee ID, a name, and a start date.

The following figure illustrates a typical representation of this data structure. This does not dictate any platform-specific implementation but will be used to determine how well suited each storage service is for storing this data:

department	
PK	**dept_id**
	manager
	+employee_id
	+email_address
	+name
	cost_center
	dept_email_address
	in_person_location
	team_members[]
	+employee_id
	+email_address
	+name

Figure 11.2: *A deep data element definition*

The key elements that indicate classifying this data as deep are the presence of an array, the set of employees that are referred to collectively as the **team_members**, and the existence of sub-fields for the **manager** and **team_members** fields. Each of these data items is not one atomic employee value but rather a compound set of values that each have independent meaning but also contribute to the entire specification of an employee.

Voting data definitions

There are two bodies of data that application must access in the voting function we are developing. The tally of votes for each act is the most obvious one, but there is another that is implied by the rules of the election. Each user has a budget of votes that they may cast in each round and must not be allowed to exceed that. An additional constraint is that each user may vote only once for a specific act in each round. To support this, we will have to maintain a durable record of the number of votes cast by each user for as long as the round remains open for voting. Whether or not we keep these counts outside of the eligibility of each round is inconsequential to the competition.

The following figure shows the data we will store for act votes:

Votes	
PK	**round_id**
PK	**act_number**
	voting_opened_at
	voting_closed_at
	total

Figure 11.3: Act vote stored data

The key for a vote is a two-part identifier: An **Act_ID**, which is the identifier for the round, concatenated with the **act_number** within that round. This is a unique identifier for the performance, which is what the vote is being cast for. The same performer in different rounds may have different act numbers, the association of performers and their act IDs is made elsewhere in the system and not germane to the voting process. It is worth noting that this compound key has been seen earlier in the **acts.py** module included in the codelab for *Chapter 9, Identifying the Stress Points of our Voting System.*

Votes are written to much more often than they are read. A popular act may be voted for by every viewer of a given round, so a vote can potentially be updated that many times. This is where the use of asynchronous processing by the Vote Processor shows its benefit. The updates can be spread across an arbitrary window of time, rather than being attempted in the narrow window during which viewers cast their votes.

The following figure shows the data definition for tracking users voting activity:

votebudget	
PK	**round_id**
PK	**user_id**
	last_voted_at
	total_votes_cast
	voted_acts[12]

Figure 11.4: Eligible round user vote budget data

This data is used to track each user's voting activity for a specific round and to enforce the user's voting budget. The access of the **Votebudget** and **Votes** datastores is tightly coupled and follows this sequence of operations:

- Each vote must first be checked against the users **Votebudget**
- If the budget allows for this vote, the **Votebudget** is updated to include this vote
- If the vote was allowed, the total for this round and act's **Votes** is incremented

The preceding three operations must take place in a transaction. If an update to either a **Votes** or **Votebudget** were to fail, any update to the other datastore must be rolled back.

Votebudget are read as often as they are updated. While there is a read a potential update to a **Votebudget** for every potential update to **Votes**, the operations on **Votebudget** are spread across many more records or rows: Each user accesses their own corresponding **Votebudge**, whereas all updates to **Votes** converge on a total of only 12 records.

As there are different scopes of concurrency and locking between the two datastores, minimizing the time spent in the transaction must be a focus of our design. This optimization is why the **total_votes_cast** and fixed array field **votes_acts** are both present. It is faster to check the value of the **total_votes_cast** than to calculate the length of a variable length array of votes already cast. In a similar optimization, since the show rules guarantee 12 acts in a round, we can use direct array element access, indexed by act number, into the **votes_acts** field to check and set the voted status of an individual act.

Relational and non-relational databases

There are many different types of databases available for storing data with varying degrees of structure. By type, we do not mean product but rather databases that implement a specific paradigm or model of how data is arranged and accessed. The most prevalent and widely used databases are those that follow a relational model, known as **relational database management systems** (**RDBMSs**). Since such databases are the majority, we will describe what differentiates an RDBMS from the other categories, including what makes a relational database an optimal choice and what aspects of data make it worthwhile to investigate alternatives.

In a relational database, data is arranged in a matrix: A 2-dimensional array of rows and columns, similar to a spreadsheet in structure. The columns are the declarations of the data, the names of the fields, their data types and precision. The rows are the actual values for those fields that are associated with the same entity. The entire matrix, the column definitions, and the rows of values are referred to as a table.

The following figure illustrates a small relational table of employee data:

employee_id Integer NOT NULL	first_name String	last_name String NOT NULL	email_address String NOT NULL	start_date Date NOT NULL	end_date Date
103	Raymond	Blum	raymond@nosuch.com	09/18/2007	NULL
2	Tarana	Abdulla	taranaa@nosuch.com	03/16/2002	NULL
5	William	Wither	willw@nosuch.com	04/01/2002	05/30/2003

Figure 11.5: A table of employees

The preceding table does not offer any features other than those offered by a simple text file or spreadsheet of data. There is nothing about the table so far that explains or deserves the term relational. The basis of a relational database is in how the data in a table is related to other data.

Let us add another item of data that we wish to store: The manager | report relationships in the organization. In our company, a manager may have any number of direct reports and an employee report to only one or no manager. We describe this relationship as managers having a one-to-many relationship with their direct reports, and employees having a one-to-zero or one relationship to managers. This can be efficiently encoded in our employee table through the addition of one column that represents the relationship. The following figure shows this extended version of the employee table:

employee_id Integer NOT NULL	first_name String	last_name String NOT NULL	email_address String NOT NULL	start_date Date NOT NULL	end_date Date	manager_id Integer References(Employee.employee_id)
103 Raymond	Blum		raymond@nosuch.com	09/18/2007	NULL	2
2 Tarana	Abdulla		taranaa@nosuch.com	03/16/2002	NULL	NULL
5 William	Wither		willw@nosuch.com	04/01/2002	05/30/2003	2

Figure 11.6: A table of related employees

This relationship is declarative, we define it for the column **manager_id** and the database system enforces that relationship with every modification to a row in the employee table. The fact that we allow **NULL** values for the **manager_id** permits the one-to-zero case in which an employee has no manager.

The same sort of relationships can be defined between two or more tables, allowing a schema to model complex relationships directly in the database declarations.

Relating data is what a relational database specifically excels at. There are other structures and types of data than relations, and it is important to recognize where another type of database is a more appropriate choice than a relational database.

Non-relational structures

Support for repeating fields is one feature where the relational model is not the leader. Take the case of a table of engine tests in which each row represents a test run of a motorcycle engine. We wish to record the times that the throttle was applied and then released during the test.

In code, this would be declared with an array like in the following C++ snippet:

```
typedef struct {
  std::time_t startTime;
  std::time_t endTime;
  } Duration;

typedef struct {
```

```
  std::string driver;
  int max_speed;
  std::vector<Duration> throttles;
  } engine_test;
```

This array structure is straightforward and efficiently declared in a programming language, but the columns of a relational table are scalar: They hold only one value. To represent a set of values, such as these multiple pairs of throttle times in a relational database, requires the introduction of a new table to hold the array values with a reference back to the key of the row of the test in the first table.

Some non-relational databases, such as Bigtable, provide direct support for repeated fields in a column, the storing of an array within a column's data. This is a simpler and more direct design, and more efficient at runtime as well. If your data contains repeating values, a non-relational database may be a more appropriate choice.

Searching through large amounts of unstructured text is a weakness of relational databases and the specialty of another type of database system: A document database such as Firestore. There are vendor and third-party extensions for several relational databases to address this shortcoming.

There are other types of databases, each with their own strengths. These were discussed in greater breadth in *Chapter 4, Choosing Between GCP Options,* in the section *Where to store your data*. It is possible that your data will contain some elements that are ideal for one type of database and other elements better suited for another. In such a situation, you can choose to store data in multiple services or make compromises for a best-fit unified solution.

Storage models for voting data

Now, that we have described the types of data stores available and some of the advantages of each, let us select storage products for the two data stores in this chapter's scope: **Votes** and **Votebudget**. Let us recap major considerations discussed earlier in this section about the access of these two data stores:

- **Votes** are subject to single updates from many concurrent separate requests.
- **Votes** are identified by a compound primary key.
- A **Votebudget** is subject to a read and potentially an update.
- Many **Votebudget** are accessed concurrently.
- A **Votebudget** is identified by a compound primary key.
- A transaction will include one **Votebudget** and one **Votes**.
- **Votes** will be part of many transactions concurrently.

- A **Votebudget** will usually be part of one but no more than 6 transactions concurrently.

- **Votes** are global in scope. Updates to an act are likely to happen in multiple regions concurrently, and those must all be resolved into one globally applicable source of truth.

- **Votebudget** are typically local. While it cannot be ruled out, a specific voter is not likely to be casting votes that are processed in multiple regions.

In addition, there is a design consideration: **Votebudget** contains an array field.

Considering these requirements, we select Spanner as a storage product for **Votes** and **Votebudget**. Spanner provides high availability and guarantees of eventual consistency in distributed databases. Spanner supports repeated fields through the use of the array datatype.

While Bigtable would seem to be an ideal choice for **Votebudget**, it does not support distributed transactions across multiple data stores.

Binary large objects

The word Blob is both a noun that describes the form of the data typically contained in a Blob. Let us explain each of these terms.

A Blob, as a noun, is defined as a lump or drop of something, or as something shapeless. This is consistent with the data stored in a Blob, which can contain anything, with no expectation of structure or metadata being present. A Blob can store data for an image, an audio recording, a Word document, or a spreadsheet. The storage system for a Blob does not impose any constraints or structure. In this way, a Blob is a shapeless lump of data.

Blob, acronym:

- **Binary**: The contents of a Blob are stored as binary data, ones and zeroes, with no requirement that the data be encoded as **American Standard Code for Information Interchange (ASCII)**, Unicode, or other higher-order data formats.

- **Large**: Blobs can contain large amounts of data; they are of arbitrary size. Large does not imply a requirement or a minimum size, but the data can be of an undefined and large size.

- **Object**: The data in a Blob is viewed as one object, as opposed to a struct, array or other defined set of constituent parts. The Blob is a single object, and the storage system has no way to recognize or isolate sub-parts.

Storage systems that are optimized for Blob storage are usually modeled after file systems. None of the following are explicit requirements of Blob storage, but in practice, they are features of most Blob storage systems.

In a file system, Blobs are referred to as **files**. Files are directly addressable by unique names and filenames. Individual files are independent; new files can be created, and existing files can be modified or deleted without affecting the other files in the file system. The size of a file is not imposed by the file system, but there is often a maximum size that is a limitation of the implementation. For example, the number of bits used to store the size of a file, or the capacity of the supported devices that a file system stores file data on.

Blob storage is usually associated with applications that have complex internal processing of data, such as parsing text, manipulating images, or playing audio. The reason for this association is that the amount of data processing performed by the storage infrastructure and the application code is complementary. The reason that Blob storage systems have little to no metadata about Blobs is that there is large or complex metadata and processing inherent in the application. On the other hand, an application that relies on a structured data storage system, such as a table of employee data, must do relatively little work to interpret the data. Parsing the table into individual fields, guaranteeing internal dependencies, and determining the cardinality of the data is managed by the storage system itself, using the metadata encoded in the table and column definitions.

The voting system is largely a bookkeeping system: **Votes** are credited to a performance, these are debited to a voter's account, and all of the books are eventually reconciled. The system can be defined by the static structure of its data, with very simple atomic operations being applied to that. There is no place where the application performs complex or compute-intensive operations on highly distinguished pieces of data. In other words, none of the qualifying aspects of Blobs are present in the system.

Access patterns

The access patterns of a given datastore are a major factor in designing to meet latency requirements. Access patterns are a widely used term, and in this context, it refers to the ratio and ordering of reads vs writes. Consider some contrasting examples:

Write an immutable item of data once, such as a legal acknowledgement; read this data element many times, whenever it is needed to check if a party has signed a contract.

Write transient or ephemeral data frequently; read it many times, not coupled to the write operations. An example is the cache of the current stock price, which is updated as the price changes and is constantly queried to determine the symbol's current value.

The first case has no special latency requirements on either the write or read operation aside from those imposed by the performance requirements of applications that access the data.

The second is more interesting: there is a critical need for low latency on the write operation, if a security changes value, that information must become canonical as soon as possible. The read operations should not take too long, but the greater impact would be if a stale price were returned, so the critical latency consideration is on the write.

When designing a datastore, the access patterns described previously should be considered when deciding the persistence service to use and designing the physical schema. Some services may be optimized for fast writes or for many concurrent reads. Some schema designs may be optimized for reads, when in fact writes are the frequent operation.

In schema design, the colocation of fields in a record or row is typically decided by logical groupings: Data for a person goes into a row of a **Person** table. However, what if distinct subsets of the fields are updated frequently while others are typically static. It may make sense to break the logical record into separate physical records to avoid locking and reloading large rows when only a relatively small amount of data is changing.

Guaranteeing data availability

Data availability is a measure of how much of the time information can be read within what is considered an acceptable threshold of latency. For example, the percentage of the time that a read of any **Votes** record can be completed within 50 milliseconds. If the data takes too long to read, it is essentially the same as the data not being available to read at all.

Spanner includes built-in features to raise data availability in a distributed application system. The Spanner system scales both compute and storage resources in response to the size of the data and the requests and access patterns being applied to the data. Spanner automatically creates synchronous replicas for a database, removing dependence on any single machine resource. In addition, as Spanner databases are brought to multiple regions, Spanner uses this redundancy to provide load balancing and failover of the database.

Spanner's guarantee of strong consistency allows our application to utilize transactional updates to global data stores, such as **Votes**, without concerns about the order of operations or concurrency updates among replicas. Spanner can order transactions across the globe in true time and perform locking in a time-sequenced order. With this guarantee of one global transaction context, the application's primary consideration is one of performance: minimizing the amount of time spent in each read-write transaction. The management of those transactions and the underlying locking of resources is entrusted to the Spanner service.

Permanence goals of snapshots and archives

Data permanence is the guarantee that what you read is the same as what was written. There is another aspect to permanence: Preserving the state of a dataset at a specific point-in-time. These two are not the same, as the first guarantee implies what you read is the same as what was last written.

There are two techniques for achieving data permanence: Snapshots and archives. Both will be discussed in this section, but first, we will describe a more fundamental technique that is used to guarantee continuous system operation: backups and restores.

Backups for recovery

Every running system should have a regular schedule of backup and a tested recovery playbook.

The loss of data is the most potentially catastrophic outage that a business can experience. Most service outages, such as availability or high latency, are transient and go through the following stages or steps:

1. The service cannot be reached or is taking too long to respond.
2. The users are frustrated.
3. The service operators are notified.
4. The outage is mitigated.
5. The service is restored.
6. Users resume using the service.
7. Apologies and guarantees are issued by the service owner.

The outage is over, and it is likely that the business and users will be wary, but as time goes by, the outage will have no lasting effect.

This is not the case for an outage that introduces data corruption or data loss. Such an outage has side-effects that can last for years. Here are the stages of one such possible scenario:

1. The datastore containing user documents is affected by a software bug that empties all user files saved before January 1st.
2. A few users find their recent files empty, and file support tickets.
3. The service operators are notified of the large number of such tickets.
4. System administrators check and find many empty user files.
5. Developers are alerted and identify the software bug.
6. A fix for the bug is rolled out at urgent priority.
7. A list of affected files and users is given to the company's legal and public relations staff.
8. Apologies and guarantees are issued by the service owner.

The bug may be fixed, but the lost files are still gone. The effects of this outage can fan out for years. What if some of the files were needed for tax filing or for legal compliance?

There is one way to prevent this: System operators must have the ability to restore any or all data. Any means that selected items, such as a list of files or database rows, can be restored. All means that the entire state of a datastore can be restored. A restore operation must be able to be completed in a reasonable time, and to tell a user that their lost emails will be restored to their inbox in 2 weeks is not acceptable.

Restoring data is a feature, and backups are a way to enable that feature. Not all restores require backups: For example, if a given piece of data can quickly and safely be recreated on demand, there is less need to make a backup. This is preferable to restoring from a backup, as a restore does not recover the data as it was when it was last written, it only recovers it as it was when it was last backed up.

There are two factors to consider when planning a backup strategy, known as **recovery point objectives** (**RPOs**): Backup cadence and backup retention.

Backup cadence is how often a backup is taken. This, in turn, sets the maximum amount of data loss that can be experienced. If we backup our data every 12 hours, and a data loss occurs 1 minute before the next backup, all data written in the last 11 hours and 59 minutes is lost as it was not present in the most recent backup we have.

Backup retention is how long we keep our backups. This sets how long we allow for a data loss to be noticed and a restore to be initiated. Let us assume a scenario where we backup our data every 12 hours and save only the last two backups. If a data loss occurs at 3:00 AM on Sunday and users report the loss starting at 8:00 AM on Monday, there is nothing for us to restore. The two backups we have are both copies of the data that existed after the loss. We do not save backups for more than a day.

We could save backups for longer, perhaps a week. However, this would require enough space to hold 14 extra copies of our entire datastore and would also tie up system resources, such as memory and network bandwidth, with this constant copying of our entire datastore. There is a way to reduce both concerns: incremental backups.

To make the restore process timely and space-efficient, there are two types of backups: Full backups and incremental backups.

Full backups are complete copies of a datastore's contents. It is as large as the original and will take significant time to complete. It is a guarantee, there is another complete copy of the data if the original is corrupted.

An incremental backup is a copy of the changes only: Additions, updates, and deletes, since the last full backup. Since it is very likely that not all data is updated within the backup cadence. This will allow these incremental backups to be much smaller and, consequently, much faster to complete than a full backup.

Using these two techniques, we could establish a cadence such as:

- A full backup weekly, on Saturday at 3:00 AM, when the system is fairly idle

- Incremental backups on Saturday at 3:00 PM and every other day of the week at both 3:00 AM and 3:00 PM

We now have a maximum amount of data loss of 12 hours and a maximum time to notice of one week. If an average incremental backup only has to include 5% of the entire datastore, the space we require to hold a week's backups is *(100%+13*5%) = 165%* of our datastore's total size. For safety's sake, we will keep the entire set of backups until the next full backup has been completed successfully, so we will actually need 265% of our datastore size for that period, while the full backup is running and before it is verified as completed successfully.

Cloud Spanner allows the developer to configure a backup schedule for databases, specifying cadence and retention duration. We will describe this in detail in this chapter's codelab.

Snapshots for continuity

If you wish to recover the state of your system as of a point-in-time, you can accomplish this by taking a snapshot.

A snapshot is a point-in-time copy of your data, capturing its current state at the time of the snapshot. It is meant for a quick restoration of the data to that state, usually as part of recovering from a corrupt state. A snapshot relies on internal mechanisms of the **database management system** (**DBMS**), such as transaction logs, and thus resides in the same environment as the primary or live database. An important point of snapshots is that they are a point within the live database rather than an external or independent copy of its state. This is desirable as it provides the fastest means to both take a snapshot and to restore the system to a snapshotted point-in-time, not having to copy or transform data to and from external destinations and formats.

Archives for posterity

In contrast to snapshots and backups, an archive is a portable, standalone copy of the data in a system. An archive is frozen in time and detached from the running system; it may not even be in a form that the live system can use.

There are reasons for preserving the state of a system other than disaster recovery. In a regulated industry, you might be required to preserve the contents of a system at the end of each reporting period. In a system involved in litigation, the state of the system at a specific time might be required.

A regular use of an archive in business operations is for research. There are several advantages to performing research against a separate archive rather than querying the main database. Let us enumerate several of these:

- Complex queries for market or performance analysis would affect the performance of the live system.

- The queries used for such analyses might require different indexing than the live system.

- Analysis for a specific window of time may be difficult or impossible to perform against live data which is always changed by normal system operations as you query it.

Snapshots and archives of voting

Every running system should have a regular schedule of backups and tested recovery. The following discussions are meant to be in addition to, or on top of, such recovery plans. Establishing regular backups is described in the GCP Spanner quick starts and tutorials.

The **Votes** datastore contains the actual permanent state of our system, whereas the **Votebudget** data is largely inconsequential after each round is closed. **Votebudget** data might be used for analysis of user behavior, for example: Aggregating and correlating how often two acts were both voted for. There is no need to recover the state of **Votebudget** within the live system after a round has been processed. So, an archive of **Votebudget** data when each round is closed is useful.

Votes are continuous over the life of the system, the contents of **Votes** at the end of a round are needed to recreate the contents at any later point. For this reason, a snapshot of the **Votes** data should be taken when the **voteprocessor** have completed processing the **Votes** message queues in Pub/Sub.

Cloud Spanner allows snapshots to be taken manually from the Cloud Spanner console or the **Google Cloud Command Line Interface (gcloud CLI)**.

Archives of Spanner databases are commonly created by exporting the database into a Cloud Storage bucket, in either **comma separated values** (**CSV**) or Apache Avro format. These can also be done using the console or through the `gcloud` command.

Persistence of votes and voter activity codelab

This chapter's codelab will create the Spanner artifacts and application code to implement the actual tallying of and the enforcement of users' vote budgets to the voting application. A more detailed outline follows.

Codelab components

These database resources will be created in this codelab:

- A Cloud Spanner instance and database
- Two Spanner tables: **Votes** and **Votebudget**

The codelab implements the following runtime components:

- **Voteprocessor** will update **Votes** and users' **Votebudget**
- **Votingfrontend** will mark acts as eligible, or ineligible based on the user's **Votebudget**
- The web client page will enforce the vote budget policy as votes are cast

Additionally, the codelab will describe the following procedures:

- Inspecting the backup schedule of the Cloud Spanner database.

- Adding an incremental backup schedule of the Cloud Spanner database.

Enabling billing for the project

Before Spanner is enabled in a project, the project must be associated with a billing account. A billing account specifies how payment will be made for charges incurred by GCP service usage above the free usage quota that is included for most GCP products. Spanner is one of the services that cannot be used without a billing account.

To create a billing account, refer to the following steps:

1. Open the Google Cloud console and choose **Billing** from the left-hand navigation menu.

2. Select your project if it is not already selected.

3. Create a billing account by clicking on the **Manage billing accounts** and **Create account** links.

4. Follow the prompts to create an account.

5. Copy the **Billing account ID** that is displayed for the new account, you will need to paste it into commands in subsequent sessions.

6. Also, take note of the **Project ID** for your project. It is usually the same as the project name you specified when creating the cloud project.

To protect yourself from any surprising charges while developing a project, it is advisable to enable billing for your project when you begin a development session and then disable billing when done. Commands to do this are presented later in the codelab.

GCP admin interfaces

Most GCP administrative functions are available via three mechanisms:

- A service API and client libraries.

- **A CLI**: The `gcloud` command.

- The GCP Console web page UI, which we have used before this. To exercise a different administrative interface than we have used so far, we will now use the `gcloud` command when defining our Spanner resources.

Defining Spanner components

Before issuing Cloud Spanner commands, billing must be enabled for the project.

In a Linux or MacOS Terminal, the commands and responses will look like the following:

Note: **The lines beginning with # are comments for the reader.**

```
# Ensure that you are logged in and using the correct account and project
$ gcloud auth login
Your browser has been opened to visit:
…
You are now logged in as [XXXX@gmail.com].
Your current project is [votingforthestars].  You can change this setting
by running:
    gcloud config set project PROJECT_ID


# Link your billing account to the project
# Replace votingforthestars with your project ID and [BILLING_ACCOUNT_ID]
with your billing account
$ gcloud alpha billing projects link votingforthestars \
    --billing-account=[BILLING_ACCOUNT_ID]
billingAccountName: billingAccounts/BILLING_ACCOUNT_ID
billingEnabled: true
name: projects/votingforthestars/billingInfo
projectId: votingforthestars


# Create a spanner instance
$ gcloud spanner instances create talentvoting-instance
--description=Talentvoting-instance --config=regional-us-central1 --nodes=2
API [spanner.googleapis.com] not enabled on project [votingforthestars].
Would
you like to enable and retry (this will take a few minutes)? (y/N)?  y


Enabling service [spanner.googleapis.com] on project [votingforthestars]...
Creating instance...done.

# Create a database in talentvoting-instance
$ gcloud spanner databases create talentvoting-database \
  --instance=talentvoting-instance
Creating database...done.
```

```
# Create two tables in this database
$ gcloud spanner databases ddl update talentvoting-database --ddl='CREATE
TABLE Votes ( Round_id INT64 NOT NULL, Act_number INT64 NOT NULL, Voting_
opened_at TIMESTAMP, Voting_closed_at TIMESTAMP, Total INT64) PRIMARY KEY
(Round_id, Act_number)' --instance talentvoting-instance
Schema updating...done

$ gcloud spanner databases ddl update talentvoting-database --ddl='CREATE
TABLE Votebudget ( Round_id INT64 NOT NULL, Userid STRING(128) NOT NULL,
Last_voted_at TIMESTAMP, Total_votes_cast INT64 NOT NULL, Voted_acts
ARRAY<STRING(1)>) PRIMARY KEY (Round_id, Userid)' --instance talentvoting-
instance
Schema updating...done
```

Confirm Spanner resources in the console

Now, that we have defined our tables, let us use another GCP admin interface, the Cloud console, to view the resources we have defined. In the console select the **votingforthestars** project, and in the search box, enter **talentvoting-database**, and you will be able to click through to the following database overview page:

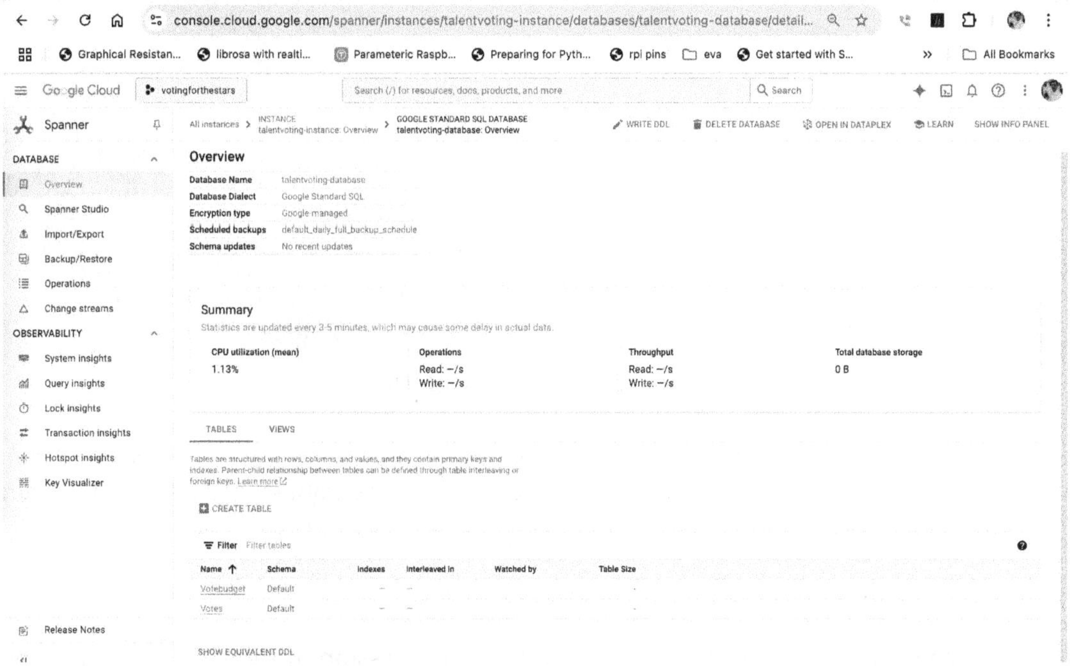

Figure 11.7: GCP console database page

On this database page, you can see that when the database was created, GCP configured a default backup schedule descriptively named **daily_full_backup** we will see how to view and change the backup schedule later in this codelab.

You should note the very low CPU utilization and 0 bytes of storage reported on this page. These are appropriate as the instances compute resources have only executed a few **data definition language** (DDL) commands, and we have not inserted any rows into the database tables.

At the bottom of this page, notice the names of the two tables we created in the database: **Votebudget** and **Votes**. Click on the **Show Equivalent DDL** link to bring up the following page:

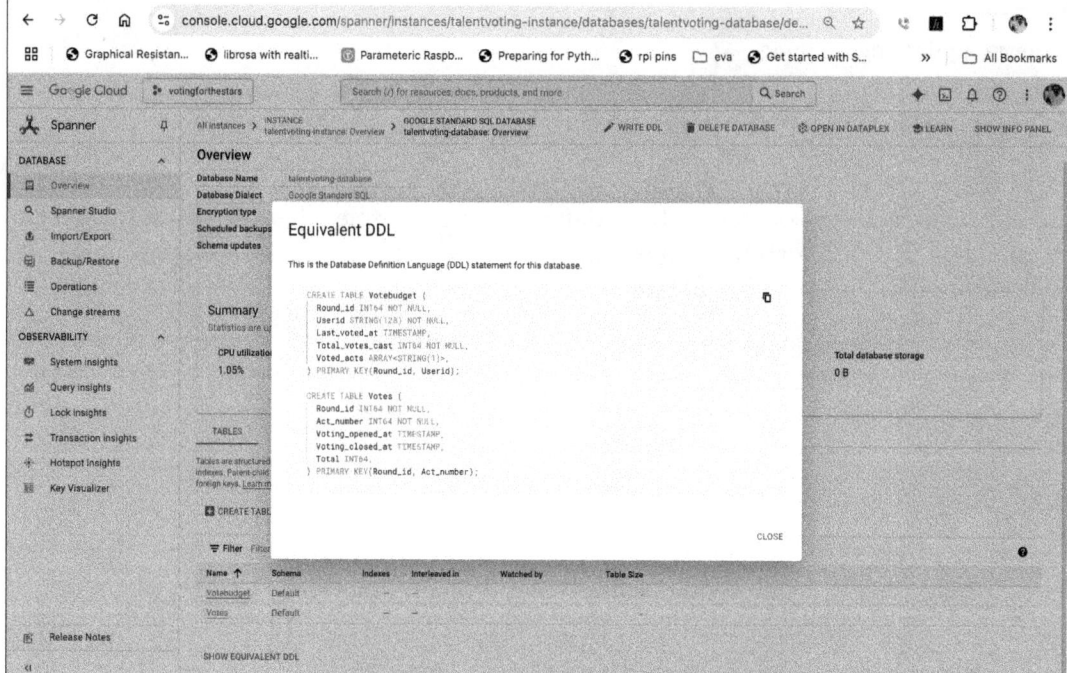

Figure 11.8: GCP console table DDL

Reviewing this and comparing it to the statements we executed to create the tables confirms that the `gcloud spanner` commands ran successfully. Our database and tables have been defined.

Disable billing for the project

Whenever you are done working in the project for a session, disable billing using the gcloud CLI:

```
# Unlink the billing account from this project
# Replace votingforthestars with your project ID
```

```
$ gcloud billing projects unlink votingforthestars
billingAccountName: ''
billingEnabled: false
name: projects/votingforthestars/billingInfo
projectId: votingforthestars
```

Code to connect to Spanner resources

A common function to return a connection to our Spanner database is defined in the module **talentvoting.cloud.common.votingdatabaseutils.py**. This will be used by all cloud components that require a database connection:

```
from google.cloud import spanner
from talentvoting.common.interfaces.servicelocations import SPANNER_
INSTANCE, \
    SPANNER_DATABASE


def get_database():
    "Create a database connection."
    spanner_client = spanner.Client()
    instance = spanner_client.instance(SPANNER_INSTANCE)
    database = instance.database(SPANNER_DATABASE)
    print("Created database connection")
    return database
```

The **get_database()** function returns a database object which provides an open connection to the Spanner database. The connection is used to execute **Structured Query Language (SQL)** statements and generate transactions which are used as containers for multiple SQL statements executed on the databased.

Accompanying definitions have been added to the common **talentvoting.common. interfaces.servicelocations.py** module:

```
SPANNER_INSTANCE = "talentvoting-instance"
SPANNER_DATABASE = "talentvoting-database"
```

Code additions to the Vote Processor

The Vote Processor backend service, implemented in the **voteprocessor** module, has several additions and reflects the bulk of the relevant changes for persistence. The full source of the module follows, along with a description of some features of the implementation.

First, all of our dependencies are resolved, and we create the web service object:

```
import json
from flask import Flask, request
```

```
from talentvoting.common.policy.votingpolicyengine import
DefaultPolicyEngine
from talentvoting.cloud.common.votingdatabaseutils import get_database
from talentvoting.common.acts import parseAct

app = Flask(__name__)
```

Next, several internal helper functions are defined:

Note: The Pythonesque visibility convention of prefixing function names with one or two underscores to indicate the function as respectively protected or private.

```
def __is_vote_in_budget(transaction, user_id, round_id, act_number):
    """
    Get the voting history for the round if user has remaining votes in
their budget
    and has not voted for this act.
    In a transaction, insert a new Votebudget if no Votebudget exists.
    Returns: Array of string if a vote can be cast for this act, False
otherwise
    """

    result_rows = transaction.execute_sql(
        "SELECT Total_votes_cast, voted_acts from Votebudget "+
        "WHERE Round_id = {} AND Userid = '{}'".format(round_id, user_id)
    )
    result = result_rows.one_or_none()
    if result:
        prev_total = result[0]
        prev_votes = result[1]
        if DefaultPolicyEngine.is_eligible_vote(round_id, act_number, prev_
votes):
            return prev_votes
        else:
            return False
    else:
        new_votes = DefaultPolicyEngine.DEFAULT_VOTE_HISTORY
        print("creating votebudget for user {} round {}".format(user_id,
round_id))
        print("new_votebudget: {}" .format(str(new_votes)))
        sql = ("INSERT INTO Votebudget "
```

```
                "(Userid, Round_id, Last_voted_at, Total_votes_cast, Voted_
acts) "
                "VALUES('{}',{},NULL,0,ARRAY{})".format(user_id, round_id,
                str(new_votes))
            )
        row_ct = transaction.execute_update(sql)

        if row_ct != 1:
            raise ValueError("Error inserting, {} rows for round {} act
{}".
                             format(row_ct, round_id, act_number))

        return new_votes


def __update_vote(transaction, act_number, round_id):
    "In a transaction, increment the votes for this act by 1."
    row_ct = transaction.execute_update(
        "UPDATE Votes "
        "SET Total = Total + 1 "
        "WHERE Act_number = {} ".format(act_number) +
        "AND Round_id = {}".format(round_id)
    )
    if row_ct != 1:
        raise ValueError("Updated unexpected {} rows for round {} act {}".
                         format(row_ct, round_id, act_number))


def __update_votebudget(transaction, user_id, round_id, act_number, vote_
budget):
    """
    In a transaction, update the vote history to show this act as voted
for.
    The vote history is 0 indexed, act numbers start at 1 so adjust the
index
    into the history array.
    """
    vote_budget[act_number-1] = 'Y'
    print("vote_budget set to: {}".format(str(vote_budget)))
    sql= "UPDATE Votebudget "+ \
    "SET voted_acts = ARRAY{}, ".format(str(vote_budget)) + \
        "Total_votes_cast = Total_votes_cast + 1, " +\
```

```
                "Last_voted_at = CURRENT_TIMESTAMP " +\
                "WHERE Round_id = {} AND Userid = '{}'".format(round_id, user_id)
        print("UPDATE '{}'".format(sql))
        row_ct = transaction.execute_update(sql)

        if row_ct != 1:
            raise ValueError("Updated unexpected {} rows for round {} user {}"
                            .format(len(row_ct), round_id, user_id))

def _apply_vote_if_allowed(transaction, user_id, round_id, act_number):
    """

    In a transaction, check the eligibility of this vote
    and update the votes and votebudget tables.
    """

    vote_budget = __is_vote_in_budget(transaction, user_id, round_id, act_
number)
    if not vote_budget:
        print("vote_budget: {}".format(vote_budget))
        print("vote out of budget, user {} round {} act {}".format(user_id,
                                                                  round_
id, act_number))
        return
    __update_vote(transaction, act_number, round_id)
    __update_votebudget(transaction, user_id, round_id, act_number, vote_
budget)
    return
```

Then, we define the expanded vote processing function and handler for incoming Pub/Sub messages:

```
def _process_vote(message:json) -> bool:
    """

    Process a JSON message containing a vote.
    Create a transaction and update the database if the user and act
    are in the message.
    args:
        message: A JSON dict
    Returns:
        True if a message was processed, False otherwise
    """

    if not message:
```

```
            return False
        if not isinstance(message, dict):
            return False
        if "user" not in message or "act" not in message:
            return False
        round, act = parseAct(message["act"])
        get_database().run_in_transaction(_apply_vote_if_allowed,
                                          user_id=message["user"], round_
id=round,
                                          act_number=act)
        return True


@app.route("/", methods=["POST"])
def index():
    """
    Receive a Pub/Sub message which should contain JSON
    and issue an HTTP response.
    Process the vote if the message contains valid JSON.
    """

    message = request.data

    print("incoming message!")
    if message:
        print("data: {}".format(message))
    try:
        vote = json.loads(message)
    except ValueError as e:
        print("Invalid JSON received: {}".format(e))
        return ("Invalid JSON", 400)
    try:
        if _process_vote(vote):
            print("Processed vote: {}".format(vote))
        else:
            print("Invalid vote: {}".format(vote))
            return ("Invalid vote", 400)   # Invalid content error status
    except Exception as e:
        print("error: {}".format(e))
        return ("", 500)   # Internal server error status
    return ("", 204)   # No content OK status
```

The major points of the **voteprocessor** implementation to highlight are the creation and usage of a database transaction, which begins in the **_process_vote()** method. A database provides a method, **run_in_transaction()**, which can be used as a database connection to execute SQL, just as a database itself can. The mechanism is somewhat different in its semantics: **run_in_transaction()** accepts a reference to a callback method, along with parameters for that callback. The callback method, in this **case _apply_vote_if_ allowed()** is passed a transaction, which can be used as a database connection to execute SQL statements.

If the callback method completes and returns successfully, the transaction is committed, and the SQL that was executed through it is finalized in the database. If the callback does not return, usually through an exception being raised, the transaction is rolled back, and the effects of the contained SQL statements are undone and not reflected in the database.

During a transaction, the effects of the SQL being executed are isolated and not visible outside of the transaction, so the effect of a rolled back transaction is that it never happened as far as any outside process or observer can detect.

Code additions to the voting frontend

The **Votingfrontend** now fetches a copy of a user's **Votebudget** when a list of acts is requested by the client. This **Votebudget** data is used to set the eligible flag for each act that is returned to the client.

The method that looks up the voting history follows, for the full source of the **talentvoting. cloud.votingfrontend.votingfrontend.py** module, the reader is referred to the GitHub repository for this chapter:

```python
def __get_user_vote_history(db_connection, \
                            user_id:str, round_id:int)->Tuple[int,List[str]]:
    "Return the array of voting history for this user in this round."
    result_rows = db_connection.execute_sql(
        "SELECT Total_votes_cast, voted_acts from Votebudget "+
        "WHERE Userid = '{}' and Round_id = {}".format(user_id, round_id)
    )
    result = result_rows.one_or_none()
    if result:
        log("votebudget(total,history):{} [1]:{}".format(result[0], result[1]))
        prev_total = result[0]
        prev_votes = result[1]
    else:
        return (None, None)

    return (prev_total, prev_votes)
```

This is the only SQL statement executed in this module and is read-only. For this reason, a transaction is not needed and this function is executed without any transaction, through a connection provided directly by a database using the following statements:

```
with get_database().snapshot() as db_connection:
    _, fetched_vote_history = __get_user_vote_history (db_connection,
                                                       uid, round_id)
```

Code in the voting policy engine

The voting policy engine has changed substantially. It encodes the rules of a vote budget, the maximum number of votes a user may cast per round and constrains a user to vote for a specific act only once in a round.

The interface for the policy engine is now implemented through a singleton instance **DefaultPolicyEngine** which clients import and access constants and methods through.

The full source for the **talentvoting.common.policy.votingpolicyengine.py** module follows:

```
from talentvoting.common.acts import Act, Acts, exampleActs, parseAct
from typing import List


class VotingPolicyEngine(object):
    "This is meant to be used through its provided instance (see bottom of
file)."
    MAX_VOTES_PER_ROUND = 6

    DEFAULT_VOTE_HISTORY = ['N','N','N','N','N','N','N','N','N','N','N','N']

    def __init__(self):
        self._acts = exampleActs()

    def get_all_acts(self) ->Acts:
        "Return all current acts as retrieved."
        return self._acts

    def get_current_round_id(self)->int:
        "Parse out the round_id from the first act in the current round."
        first_act = self._acts[0]["act"]
        return parseAct(first_act)[0]

    @staticmethod
```

```python
    def is_eligible_vote(round_id:int, act_number:int,
                         prev_votes:List[str]) ->bool:
        """
        Determine if this vote is within the vote budget.
        The vote history is 0 indexed, act numbers start at 1 so adjust the
index
        into the history array.
        """

        if not round_id or not act_number or not prev_votes:
            return False
        prev_total = prev_votes.count('Y')
        if prev_votes[act_number-1] == 'Y':
            return False
        if prev_total >= DefaultPolicyEngine.MAX_VOTES_PER_ROUND:
            return False
        return True


# Provide a singleton for clients to use
DefaultPolicyEngine = VotingPolicyEngine()
```

Code in the web client page

The web client now updates the table of acts to enforce the vote budget rules that are encoded in the **DefaultPolicyEngine**. The vote history is extracted from the **GetActs/** response and stored within the document. As votes are successfully cast, this local vote history is updated, and the rules are applied to the table of acts. This is performed locally within the page to avoid additional server traffic with every vote.

The JavaScript functions that set and enforce the policy follow. For the full source of the **talentvoting.webclient.public.index.html** page, the reader is referred to this chapter's GitHub repository:

```javascript
// Count all 'Y' votes in vote_history array and store that as our tally of
votes
function countVoteHistory(vote_history) {
  let vote_tally = 0;
  for (let voteIdx = 0; voteIdx < vote_history.length; voteIdx++) {
    if (vote_history[voteIdx] == 'Y') {
      vote_tally = vote_tally+1;
    }
```

```
  }
  document.getElementById('voteTally').value = vote_tally;
}


// This duplicates knowledge in the Python policy engine,
// kept local for performance.
// If we have reached the limit on votes, disable all vote buttons
// After a vote has been cast for an act, disable its vote button
function enforceBudgetForVote(voted_act) {
  let voted_count = parseInt(document.getElementById('voteTally').value);
  voted_count = voted_count + 1;
  document.getElementById('voteTally').value = voted_count;
  let vote_limit = document.getElementById('voteLimit').value;
  const actsTable = document.getElementById('actsTable');
  const rows = actsTable.rows
  for (let i = 0; i < rows.length; i++) {
    const row = rows[i];
    if (i > 0) {  // The first row is a TH
      const rowActId = row.cells[0].children[0].value;
      if (rowActId == voted_act || voted_count >= vote_limit) {
        row.cells[1].innerHTML = '';  // Removes all children
        row.cells[1].innerHTML = '--';
      }
    }
  }
}
```

Deploying the Cloud Run service

The **voteprocessor.py** module now has dependencies on the **talentvoting.common** package hierarchy. To deploy this service from the source requires us to make a copy of the dependencies into the Cloud Run service base directory, similar to the link that was created in the voting frontend Google App Engine base directory. Having to rely on these two hacks to fix our deployments indicates a mismatch between our package hierarchy and our deployed components. This will be addressed in subsequent codelabs when we use the python packages and repositories. For now, we will use the following commands to deploy the Cloud Run service from the **voteprocessor** base directory:

```
# Make local common directories and copy the common directories into them
$ mkdir talentvoting/common;mkdir -p talentvoting/cloud/common; \
  cp -r ../../talentvoting/common/ talentvoting/common/; \
```

```
  cp -r ../common/ talentvoting/cloud/common/; \
  gcloud run deploy voteprocessor --allow-unauthenticated --max-
instances=10 \
  --source .
```

Inspecting the backup schedule

We will use the gcloud CLI to view the default backup schedule created for our instance. Remember that billing must be enabled before any Spanner resources can be accessed:

```
# List all backups for the spanner database
$ gcloud spanner backup-schedules list --instance=talentvoting-instance \
  --database=talentvoting-database


NAME                                BACKUP_TYPE  CRON
RETENTION_DURATION   ENCRYPTION_TYPE
KMS_KEY_NAME   KMS_KEY_NAMES
default_daily_full_backup_schedule  FULL         42 22 * * *  604800s
USE_DATABASE_ENCRYPTION
```

The main fields of interest are the **BACKUP_TYPE**, **CRON**, and **RETENTION_DURATION**. A type of **FULL** indicates that the entire contents of the tables in the database are copied. **CRON** is a schedule in the **CRON** expression format. The value of **42 22 * * *** indicates 42 minutes after the 22nd hour (10:42 PM), and the three asterisks indicate, respectively, every day of every month and every day of the week. For more information on this format, Google cron spec or cron expression format. The **RETENTION_DURATION** states how long these backups will be retained in seconds; the **604800s** is 7 days.

Adding a backup schedule

This full backup schedule represents a maximum amount of data loss of 24 hours and a maximum time to notice of one week. For our system, we will assume that losing up to a day of updates is too high a risk and would accept 12 hours at most. To do this, we will inject an incremental backup at the midway point between every two full backups.

Using the gcloud CLI again, this command adds an incremental at 10:42 AM on every day:

```
# Add a new backup schedule for the spanner database
$ gcloud spanner backup-schedules create  daily_incr_backup_schedule  \
--project=votingforthestars    --instance=talentvoting-instance    \
--database=talentvoting-database    --retention-duration=604800s    \
--cron="42 10 * * *"    --backup-type=incremental-backup    \
--encryption-type=USE_DATABASE_ENCRYPTION
```

This command fails against our database as we are using the lower service tier of Spanner, Standard edition. The incremental backup feature is only available to users of the higher and more expensive Enterprise edition.

For now, we will add a 2nd full backup every day at 10:42 AM. Until the database grows to a much larger size, the cost and time of a full backup vs an incremental is not prohibitive:

```
$ gcloud spanner backup-schedules create  daily_incr_backup_am_schedule  \
--project=votingforthestars    --instance=talentvoting-instance    \
--database=talentvoting-database    --retention-duration=604800s    \
--cron="42 10 * * *"    --backup-type=full-backup    \
--encryption-type=USE_DATABASE_ENCRYPTION
```

Listing the database backup schedules again shows both schedules:

```
# List all backups for the spanner database
$ gcloud spanner backup-schedules list --instance=talentvoting-instance \
  --database=talentvoting-database
NAME                             BACKUP_TYPE  CRON
RETENTION_DURATION  ENCRYPTION_TYPE
KMS_KEY_NAME  KMS_KEY_NAMES
daily_incr_backup_am_schedule       FULL         42 10 * * *
604800s                 USE_DATABASE_ENCRYPTION
default_daily_full_backup_schedule  FULL         42 22 * * *
604800s                 USE_DATABASE_ENCRYPTION
```

We can now rest assured that we can recover our database contents to any state within the past 7 days with a maximum of 12 hours of data loss.

Conclusion

This chapter discussed different shapes or forms of data, structured versus unstructured and deep hierarchies versus flat data. The types of data most suitable for relational databases, other non-relational databases, and data stores for raw artifacts, Blobs, were described. Having identified these categories, the relevant classification of our voting data was made.

The performance goals of data persistence, like availability and permanence, were then discussed with techniques to measure and ensure them.

Finally, the codelab for this chapter reviewed the implementation of data persistence in the voting application. The codelab concluded with the creation and backup of Spanner resources for the system to ensure this functionality is supported.

In the next chapter, the focus will shift to the more immediate user experience: Client application architecture. Decisions on what functionality to implement on the client platform versus in the cloud will be discussed along with techniques for implementing those to find an optimal balance of the user experience and the demands placed on the distributed system. We will further develop the web client and introduce a simple mobile app for the voting system.

Join our Discord space

Join our Discord workspace for latest updates, offers, tech happenings around the world, new releases, and sessions with the authors:

https://discord.bpbonline.com

CHAPTER 12

Developing Voting Frontends

Introduction

The backend and overall architecture can make or break an application's long-term survival in real-world use, but without an engaging frontend no one will ever find out how good your system holds up. This chapter describes the features of a good frontend, one that complements the capabilities that we have built into our cloud-based backend. Frontend expertise includes more than **user interface** (**UI**) design. The separation of responsibilities between the client and backend platforms should allow the client application to exploit the backend so that the frontend developers can focus on the **user experience** (**UX**) rather than design around distributed performance considerations.

Structure

The following topics will be covered in this chapter:

- Client application's responsibilities
- Not in scope
- Our voter's client application
- Voter's web interface
- Voter's mobile application

- Refactoring the codebase
- Building multiple client applications codelab

Objectives

The chapter will examine the composition of a user-visible feature, specific implementation details of the implementation of a feature's functionality. Each of these constituent parts of the feature's body will be categorized in several dimensions that add to the strengths and weaknesses of a typical client platform when compared to a cloud-based service. The affinity between these parts is a consideration and this binding force is a factor in the representation of these components.

With this table or graph defined, the reader will be guided through the evaluation of an optimal location for each of these detailed internal components. The result will be a detailed design of user-visible features that clearly identifies the scope of a client application's responsibilities and dependencies. The codebase will be refactored to facilitate the independent development of multiple related software products.

The codelab for this chapter will illustrate a minimal implementation of a mobile client application that follows from the methodology described in the chapter.

Client application's responsibilities

The client application, regardless of the platform, is the user's window or gateway into the entire system. By platform, we refer to an application-independent vehicle on which our application, presumably alongside others, resides. That could refer to a specific piece of hardware, such as a given model of a smartphone, tablet, or laptop computer.

Modern end-user computers are much better at providing platform independence, and for client applications, there is no reason to distinguish between specific models of iPhone or the Android phones of different manufacturers. Likewise, we do not design for a model or brand of laptop computer but rather for the capabilities shared by a type of device.

Identifying client application platforms

For application developers, the client platform is the layer of software that defines and supports a consistent UX. iPhones 13, 10, and 15 are not client platforms; iOS, the mobile operating system that defines the common capabilities of these devices, is the platform. Likewise, browser-based client applications are a platform, rather than individual browser and host operating system combinations. To complete the reach of these examples, Linux and Windows are desktop client platforms rather than Ubuntu on *Asus laptops* and Windows 11 Home on *Hewlett Packard desktop computers*.

For this chapter, and consistent with earlier discussions throughout the book, we consider client platforms to be among the categories in the following table:

Specific hardware	Client platform	Client metaplatform
iPhone 11	iOS	Mobile app
iPhone 15		
iPad Air	iPadOS	
iPad Pro		
Samsung Galaxy Tab S10	Android	
Google Pixel 9 Pro		
HP Desktop running Ubuntu	Linux desktop	Desktop client
Dell laptop running Windows 11	Windows	
Mac Pro running macOS	macOS	
Linux Chrome browser on Asus laptop	Web page	Web app
Safari browser on Macbook		

Figure 12.1: Partial hierarchy of client platforms

Although not exhaustive in its samples, the preceding community of devices provide examples of all the platforms and Meta platforms that we will consider in the taxonomy of client platforms. By Meta platforms, we mean the set of characteristics that group a set of platforms which users might consider functionally equivalent. The boundaries between the capabilities and consumer expectations of a powerful smartphone and a tablet are blurry, as are those between different desktop operating systems.

Client application's responsibilities

In short, the client application is responsible for interacting with the user. While that description is convenient and accurate, it is also too broad to be measured or provide guidelines for action to the developer. Let us break it down into more clearly defined expectations.

A client application reveals the relevant state of the system to the user.

The client application keeps the user informed of the information contained within the system that is relevant to the user in their interaction with the client application. There are different levels of relevance, so we will offer and explain several examples and counter examples as a means of explanation. These examples will be extracted from the voting feature that was developed in previous chapters and specifically the web client implemented in *Chapter 10, Securing All User Votes*, and *Chapter 11, Guaranteeing Data Permanence*:

- The list of acts that are competing in the currently open round is a piece of internal state that is relevant to the user, who in this use case will be selecting from among those acts. So, the set of the currently competing acts is relevant to each user and presentation of that list is the responsibility of the client application.

- The eligibility of a specific act to have a vote cast by the current user is very specific state that is relevant to only the current user and potentially changes with every action the user takes. The information is very tightly coupled to the individual user and the current moment in time and is best delegated to the client application.

- The current tally of votes for each act, the in-flight results of the competition, is peripherally relevant or perhaps of interest to the user but not required for the voting feature or practical to provide to the client application. This would require a broadcast to each client application, with some high cadence. The value of this broadcast is dubious as the voter is presumably already watching a real-time broadcast, the competition itself. Presentation of this information is better assigned to some centralized component and display mechanism, handling this in the client application adds no value and incurs a high cost.

- The window of time during which the current rounds acts are eligible for voting is a case we have not explored. Recall the rules of the competition, the acts of a round are eligible for voting from the first broadcast of the round until some declared point in time after the last act has aired. This was represented in the votes Spanner table defined in the codelab of *Chapter 11, Guaranteeing Data Permanence*, by the table columns *Voting_opened_at* and *Voting_closed_at*.

While we have not yet implemented any features that reflect this functionality, we can design and place it within the application now. The voter may be looking at a live broadcast while voting but there is no expectation of that. A broadcast recording, a video clip from a friend, or simply a delayed action can decouple a potential vote from the time that a round is open. So, the presentation of the voting window, the time when the most recent round is open to voting is relevant to the act of voting and is good to present in the client application, regardless of any other display of this information, as these other displays may be recordings or not available when the user wishes to vote.

A client application provides controls for the user to initiate a feature's actions.

Our voting feature is an interactive one. Interactive here means that two things, in this case, the user and the application system, have an effect on each other. The system informs the user of the acts from which they may choose to vote, and the user casts votes which change the standing of acts in the competition that is stored within the system.

Not all applications are interactive: Dashboards are full featured applications that present the state of information that is known by the system, but the user cannot in any way use the application to influence that state. In an extreme and obvious example, a dashboard that displays the local weather can present many views of weather information but cannot offer the user a button to stop the rain or make the wind blow.

In the portion of the voting system that we have focused on, there is one critical user action: voting for an act. The web client that was implemented in previous chapters' codelabs also provides a button to load the list of acts, but this could be relocated to an automatic feature of the application when the page is first opened.

With the one user action of our feature identified, casting a vote for a specific act, we can consider where this feature is best located. The controls for refreshing the set of candidate acts and indicating an act that the user wishes to cast a vote for require direct input from the user, directed at specific data elements. This implies that the controls for specifying the act of voting must be in the client application, how else could the user indicate their request? As we have seen, the actual fulfillment of that user request can involve many backend components, but the specification of a user's choices resides in the domain of a client application. The user must be able to indicate their preferences with the necessary precision both in space (which of the set of acts they are voting for) and in time (the moment at which they wish to cast a vote). This precision requires direct communication and interaction with the user, only available from the client platform.

A client application provides a means for the user to identify themself to the application system.

This is increasingly difficult to implement and critical for any business system to do well, as both the challenges to application security and the cybersecurity techniques used to combat those challenges become more sophisticated and carry higher stakes.

The standard mechanism by which a user's identity was established for several decades was the combination of two pieces of information, one public and one private: A username and a password. As the incentive for hijacking or forging user identity has increased, with the rise of finance and social capital presence on the internet, increased levels of social engineering (scams) and technical resources (site credential thefts, password spraying campaigns) have reduced the safety offered by the username/password mechanism. The chief vulnerability in the classic mechanism is that a username and a password are not all that different: They are both strings of characters that are something the owner knows.

Modern authentication schemes supplement confirming the knowledge of the owner with the proven presence of the owner. There are different popular ways to do this: biometrics such as Touch ID or face recognition and **multi-factor authentication (MFA)**. Each of these rely on either a known person being present, or corroboration of a person's identify by requiring proof of some other physical token that the user is known to have possessed in the past. The common characteristic is that neither relies solely on knowledge held by the user, there is an additional and different aspect of the user that is challenged and must be proven, in these examples, one tied to the physical world.

The key point is that these security devices all live in close physical proximity to the user, and so are best or even only suited for implementation on a client platform. A cloud service has no direct means to take a user's fingerprint or verify that they are in possession of their security key.

There are other replacements or supplements to the reliance on user and password combinations: Captchas and behavioral risk analysis are both used to further prove a user's presence but are generally considered as effective in user authentication as the physical mechanisms we have described preceding.

A client application adapts or allows the user to customize its features to the individual user's needs and preferences.

There are many attributes of an application that contribute to its ease of use. Some factors of usability are centered around the system and its data, such as how much information is presented at once and the appropriate level of detail and order of presentation. Other factors that determine how easy or difficult to use a user finds the application are centered around the user and their environment. Capturing the attributes of the local UX and adapting to best accommodate those attributes is a responsibility of a well-designed client application.

The first category of client-specific factors is environmental. Light levels, ambient sound and time of day are easily determined, relevant considerations that should steer the behavior and appearance of an application. A recent popular development reflecting these concerns is the adoption of night mode by many applications and browsers. It is important to let the user opt in to such changes in the application or to easily opt-out, rather than assume that everyone prefers a dark screen after 10 PM.

Accessibility requirements are those considerations that are focused on the individual user, rather than their surroundings, although the same environment may affect individual users differently. The ability to adjust contrast and brightness are two obvious well known usability features but vision is not the only consideration. The use of haptic feedback, scrolling speed, cursor size and tracking speed, and click patterns are all important and necessary features that must be adapted to the user's needs.

The range of options that an application can support for both types of adaptive behavior is determined by the client platform and underlying hardware, and thus are appropriate to implement in the client application.

The following table summarize these features of an application that most clearly require the strengths and lie within the domain of a client application:

Client application feature	Reasoning
Display currently relevant information	Irrelevant or not timely information distracts from immediate user action
	Fetching and holding irrelevant information consumes client resources without adding value for its locality
Provide direct controls for feature activation	Low latency and precise controls depends on direct user interaction with the application
Authenticate the users identity	Multi factor and biometric authentication are coupled to physical presence
Adapt to the environment	The ability to detect environmental factors most resides on the local platform
Adapt to users' accessibility requirements	The capability to detect and range of adaptive features are particular to the client and depend on specific client platform control

Figure 12.2: *Summary of client application responsibilities*

Not in scope

We have highlighted certain features of an overall application that should be included in the client facing, local to the user components of the system. Now we will explicitly call out the counter-cases, those functions which are most suited to reside and to be implemented on the backend.

First a brief recap of scope. The following figure of an abstract distributed application architecture recreates an earlier one seen in *Chapter 6, Cloud Services at the Backend Border* and will serve as a reference for this section:

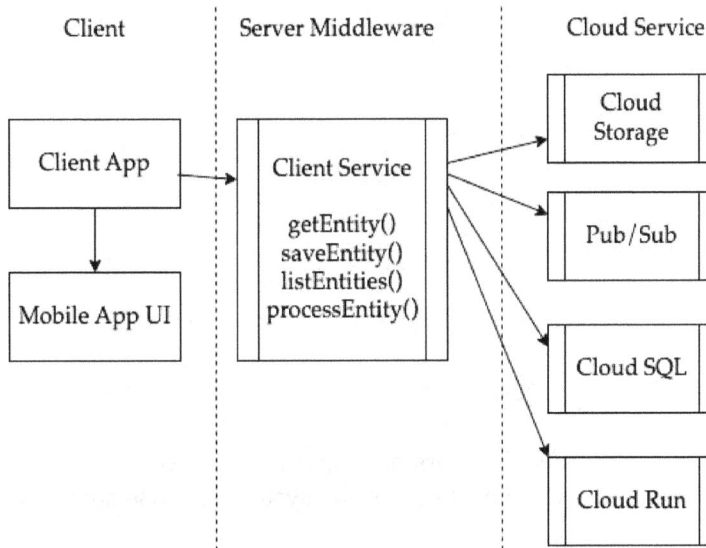

Figure 12.3: *Architecture of an n-tiered distributed application*

The backend refers to every component and supporting infrastructure that is not resident on the frontend client platform. For our discussion the components in the server middleware and cloud service tiers are backend components.

However, there are other constituents of the system that are implicit backend components. The infrastructure and services that support the operations between tiers such as networking and discovery services are also considered backend supporting components of the architecture.

The process followed in the preceding section to identify frontend components works well and will be used here to designate and describe the backend functionality of an application.

Backend tiers' responsibilities

Foremost, the system backend represents a portion of the system as an independent entity, supporting the existence of the application, but existing above and beyond any individual user's visibility or client platform's reach. The approximate relationship between the system as an entity and its various users is depicted in the following Venn diagram:

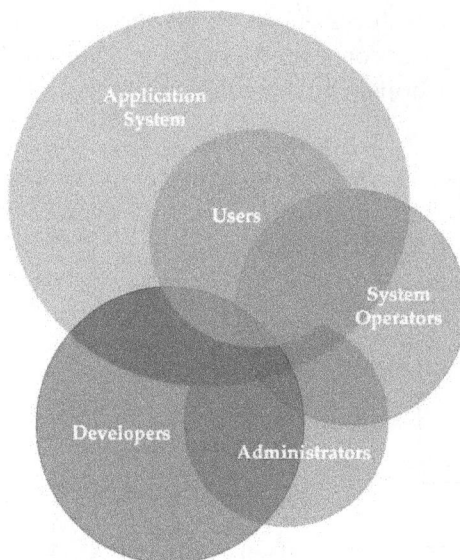

Figure 12.4: *Usage of a distributed application*

Developers have both the largest overlap with the system and use the largest number of external tools and services in their roles, such as compilers, code editors, debuggers and repositories. System administrators and operators are similar to developers in that they directly interact with larger portions of the system and use some external tools and services in their roles.

Users of the system are unique in that their interaction with a well-designed system can be completely through features provided by the system itself.

What is important to note is the area of the application system that is not overlapping with any of the other roles illustrated. There are parts of the system that exist independent of any direct use by a developer, operator or administrator, but without this independent portion of the system, they would not exist to interact with these other parties.

There are two classes of functionality that fall into this scope. There are features and artifacts of the system that are not directly visible from any user's point of view. There is also functionality that exists to support or materialize user-visible features. While user-visible features depend directly on this functionality, it does not pass the test for implementing on the client platform.

We will describe several categories of backend features and use examples from our previously established voting system to illustrate them.

The backend should perform functions that merge or aggregate the actions of many users over time.

A function such as tallying votes from all users is an evident example of a function of the voting system that meets this qualification. The collection and application of votes to the centralized database is done for many users over the entire voting window for a round. Locating this with strong proximity in the cloud allows us to place the involved components as close as possible in terms of network topology. This reduces network traffic and thus latency, and potentially reduces bandwidth charges incurred. Additionally, placing these components in the cloud enables us to exercise control over resource scaling that is only possible from a vantage point that can see total user demand, something that an individual client has no visibility into.

Functions whose effects persist in the system beyond the context of the initiating user request should be implemented in the backend for as much as is feasible.

This statement is somewhat lengthy, but we have a good example that can help to clarify its intent. Firstly, the separation of registering a user's vote from the actual processing of that vote is a good example of this. When a user casts a vote, that action affects the state of the information stored in the system even after the user has moved on to their next action. This is what occurs in the votingprocessor's Pub/Sub handler. The goal is to move permanent or persistent changes to the state of the system out of the client, which is a relatively ephemeral environment, into the larger system residing in the cloud, as quickly as possible. This increased reliability is because server-side technologies are more robust, providing richer support for retries and failover of in-flight requests when a component fails.

Preprocessing or postprocessing of data for clients should be performed on the backend, with only the user-relevant levels of detail present in the client application.

The preprocessing of data for clients is an overhead, and most likely does not involve much information from the user context. An example of this is the sending of acts from the voting frontend to the client. We do not send all acts for all rounds to the client and then leave it to each client to filter out the current round's acts. We do this selection of user-relevant data in the cloud components and send the client only the data that will be shown to the user. The alternative approach, leaving filtering and possibly transformation of data to the client application, would increase network traffic to each connected client and move the execution of this filtering to the slower, more expensive client hardware. In addition, the filtering and transformation logic would be executed once in a frontend instance that serves potentially hundreds of clients, in a client-resident design this logic would be executed hundreds of times, repeated on each of those clients.

Our voter's client application

Now that we have described the portions of an application system's features that are suitable for implementation on client platforms and some counter examples for contrast, we can design the voting application, agnostic to any specific client platform.

The first step will be to decide on the requirements for our client. The following is not a complete **product requirements document** (**PRD**) or full technical design, but enough of a statement of intent to guide our development and to checkpoint the product against.

Voting client application requirements

There are aspects of a client application that reflect the platform on which they are developed, showcasing the strengths of that environment. There are also a set of functional requirements that must be fulfilled in some way by each client implementation. These requirements are stated in platform-agnostic, business-centric terms. Our requirements for the voting client are as follows:

- **Abstract**: The voting client application (hereafter voting client) is the means through which a registered voter can select a set of acts in the current round of the competition for which they wish to vote.

- **User authentication**: The voting client allows a user to login as a known user. Establishment of a user identity is not in scope.

  User registration is through existing identity providers. To avoid the same user voting using multiple accounts from different providers, such as their Apple ID and Gmail accounts, we will limit logins to Google accounts.

  While not logged in, the only function available is the control to login.

  When a user is logged in, the login control is replaced with a logout control.

  Logging in and logging out are to be handled through the specified authorization system API calls.

  A logged in user remains logged in, until the underlying authorization system might force a change to their logged in state. The voting client must recognize asynchronous changes to the logged-out state and switch to the logged out state described above, with the only function available being the control to login.

- **Logged-in display**: The logged in user is presented with a list of acts in the current round. There may be any number of these and the voting client provides a way to traverse or scroll through the list. The order of acts is determined by the server and the voting application should preserve this order.

  Any number of these acts in the current round are eligible for the current user to cast a vote for. This eligibility is determined by voting policy, defined externally. Eligibility is a Boolean state per act; each act is currently either eligible or not.

  Eligibility of all acts must be reevaluated after every act of voting (below).

- **Voting**: For each eligible act, the voting client provides a control to cast a vote. There is no parameter or secondary control. A vote is cast for an eligible act with no other information being relevant. Votes may be indicated as a group or individually by the user.

If a voting client allows for a selection of multiple acts to be voted for, the voting client must enforce the voting policy as each selection is made. This is due to the policy provision that while two or more acts may be eligible for voting, the combination may not be.

Voting frontend API

The voting frontend service provides the only access to the voting system for client applications. The **application program interface** (**API**) that it presents must be well documented and remain agnostic to the preferences of specific clients, such as client language.

We present a set of overarching API guidelines and the details of each available method call in the following section.

Server-side API usage

The voting client must make use of the methods provided by the voting frontend service REST API.

The voting frontend method URIs are provided in the following client language symbols and their values should not be reverse engineered to any observed base URL:

- The API only accepts POST methods.
- HTTPS is required.
- Method parameters are specified by element name on the request form.
- Parameter values are all strings.
- Response types are specified by the Content-Type header.
- HTTP status codes of 2XX, 4XX and 5XX are returned.

The voting frontend provides 3 methods for the voting client:

- **getActsURL**:
  - Parameters: `idToken`
  - Response: `application/json` (`acts_bundle: {acts: [], vote_history: [], vote_limit: str`)
- **voteURL**:
  - Parameters: `idToken, votedAct:actId`
  - Response: `application/json ( {user:str, act:str})`
- **getPolicyRulesURL**:
  - Parameters: `idToken, clientLanguage:('JavaScript'|'python')`
  - Response: `text/(JavaScript|python) (budget_enforcement_function_src)`

Voting client performance

Any implementation of the voting client should strive for the following, common set of performance objectives. This is needed to avoid biasing either installation or usage of the client to a particular platform, preserving the concept of equal access: an important consideration in a voting system:

- **Connectivity**: The connection to the internet, and thus our cloud services, is outside of the scope of the voting client. Whatever native or other client platform connectivity mechanisms exist should be the only provider of internet transport, and no third-party or custom connection controls or libraries are incorporated into or bundled with the voting client.

- **Latency**: Responses to the user are highly latency sensitive. A perceptible (meaning visual, audible or haptic) response should be presented within 100 milliseconds $(1/10^{th}$ second) of the user triggering any action. This may not be the ultimate or total response to the user's request. For example, clicking a **vote** button could generate a tone, a haptic buzz or a screen flash to indicate when a backend request was sent, even if the pending response is needed to display the confirmation and update the local state.

- **Error handling**: Errors can be classified in two dimensions: Expected or unexpected and local or server-originated. The classification of a specific error when it is encountered determines how useful and descriptive the application's response can be.

   Offering the user the options to retry or abandon/cancel a failed operation is always recommended. If the error is one that is anticipated by the application developer, guidance or corrective measures can be offered before retrying.

   In the case of locally generated errors, the specific technical root cause or origin should not be revealed to the user. Displaying a framework or component name in a message, such as an error returned by `<Document.body.scrollview>`, does not inform the user of anything relevant or actionable and reveals information that can aid reverse engineering attempts and application exploits.

   In the case of server generated errors, such as 400 or 500 series HTTP status codes, the fact that a server error occurred is recommended as the only level of detail to reveal. A 400 series error in the backend may be due to an internal permission or access problem, but not one that a user is empowered to affect or address. The full error details should be logged for server-side debugging with enough information to tie the logged error back to the failed request.

- **Accessibility**: Accessibility features are valuable to achieve the goal of equal access for all voters. Such features vary by platform and their use may require certain configuration options or practices be included in an application. Some, such as alt-text, require active implementation by an application developer. The voting client should make use of all applicable available accessibility features.

Client-side policy rules

The rules used to determine which votes are eligible are a case worth special consideration. The policy itself can be encapsulated into a single function, operating on a set of acts and their current status. This was seen in the codelab of *Chapter 11, Guaranteeing Data Permanence* in the **is_eligible_vote()** method defined in the **voteingpolicyengine. py** module.

Recall that the logic of this function was duplicated in the web client, in the JavaScript function **enforceBudgetForVote()** defined in the **index.html** file. The reason for this was that we if we were to rely on a server call to enforce the policy rules, it would double the number of calls to the voting frontend service from a client and add a significant increase in the number of bytes being sent across the network.

The drawback to the chosen approach is that we have coded the same logic in two different locations. If updates to one of these were released out of sync with the other, the rules being enforced would be difficult to guarantee, and the end result would probably be inconsistent with both definitions.

There is a middle ground. We can define the rules in one place and still avoid the constant server calls as policy is enforced on the client. We will securely fetch a new policy function from the server and install it in the client when a user logs in. The voting client will then execute that installed policy engine locally throughout a user's session. The execution of remotely provided code can open up the possibility of a type of exploit known as an injection attack and the authentication protocol and safeguards in our application and service configuration are needed to prevent malicious exploitation of this feature.

This implementation is provided by the voting frontend method at **getPolicyRulesURL**.

Requirements summary

That is the set of requirements that we will meet when implementing a mobile client application. We will also be refactoring the web client to converge on these requirements.

Voter's web interface

A web implementation for the voting client has been developed in the previous chapters' codelabs, but does not yet meet the requirements above. We will present the specifications for a web voting client here identifying and addressing the differences between the existing web client implementation and those specifications.

Web client language and framework

For a combination of considerations, we make the decision to implement the web client in plain JavaScript. The choice of platform is influenced by a number of factors: Technical, organizational and market driven. In this case, we decide that organizational factors: An engineering team with JavaScript experience and market research indicating the largest potential user community being web/browser based outweigh the technical considerations advantages of cross-platform or higher-level framework development.

Web client login and logout

The login and logout through a Google popup, fills the requirements of user authentication that were presented in the preceding section. There are a few changes to the web client that are needed to match the required behavior of the logged in display.

The login display should always present the current set of acts, with voting controls reflecting the voting policy applied to the user's current state. The **Get Acts** button is not represented in the requirements, the information that it presents should always be displayed while the user is logged in.

There are already places in the code where we take actions when a user login occurs. The **setView()** function is invoked to swap the visibility of the HTML sections labeled signed-in and signed-out. There is also code that retrieves the ID token from Firebase Auth when the user is authenticated. We will invoke the same functions as the **Get Acts** button does when the user has been authenticated, since we need the ID token to make calls to the voting frontend.

The following callback in **index.html** is invoked when the user's login state changes and is already used to fetch the ID token:

```
// Listen for the auth state to change and store the user info on the
document
firebase.auth().onAuthStateChanged(async function(user) {
    if (user) {
        // User is signed in.
        document.getElementById("userName").innerHTML = user.email;
        user.getIdToken().then((idToken) => {
            document.getElementById("idToken").value=idToken;
        });
```

Also, on **index.html** is a click handler for the **Get Acts** button:

```
// Listen for clicks on the Get Acts button
$('#actsButton').click(() => getActs());
```

We can remove the **Get Acts** button from the page and the click handler above; adding to the Firebase callback function which now contains this:

```
firebase.auth().onAuthStateChanged(async function(user) {
    if (user) {
        // User is signed in.
```

```
    document.getElementById("userName").innerHTML = user.email;
    user.getIdToken().then((idToken) => {
        document.getElementById("idToken").value=idToken;
        getActs();
    });
```

Error handling

Error handling in our initial web client was inconsistent. Expected points of failure are non-200 HTTP response codes from the voting frontend. Successful responses result in the desired effect being evident in the client display: Logging in displays the current acts, voting displays an alert and updates the list of eligible acts. Error responses yield messages logged to the browser developer console and are evidenced by the lack of the request's expected effect, but we do very little to handle or inform the user of expected failures. Best practices recommend collecting and forwarding such errors to the server, for detection and analysis of trends in user errors.

We can adopt a consistent technique for informing the user of error responses. There are two categories of response issued by the voting frontend: A 500 series response status, indicating an internal server error, and a 400 series status, indicating a bad or unauthorized request sent from the client.

In the case of internal server errors, the problem is on the server-side and is more likely to be client agnostic. The nature of these makes the root cause more likely to be visible to GCP monitoring and thus to get attention and mitigation. The server condition may also be transient, such as a momentary resource shortage while auto-scaling takes effect. For these reasons, a message advising the user that an error occurred in the system and suggesting retrying their request is appropriate.

The root cause of a 400 series response is likely to lie in the client or in a bug in the code handling the specific client request. For example, a missing expected parameter of a request, such as the act ID of a vote request, indicates either a bug in the client code that failed to include the act ID field, or less likely a bug in the server-side handler that extracts the act ID from the request parameters. In either case, retrying is not likely to yield a different result and the data on the client should be considered to be in a dubious or inconsistent state.

There is another type of failure, the unexpected error. While we anticipate the server sending a 400 response, we cannot plan for failures generated outside of our control. The separation of these can be seen in this elided snippet of the current web client code:

```
// Send a form to a remote service.
// Pass the json response to a callback
function getResponse(form, url, callback) {
    console.log('getResponse URL: ', url);
```

```
fetch(url, {
    method: form.method,
    body: new FormData(form)
})
.then(function (response){
    if(response.ok) {
    …
    }
    else {
        console.log('HTTP-Error: ' + response.status);
        …
    }
})
.catch(function(error) {
    console.log('Error: ', error);
});
}
```

The code for handling a non-200 response, the expected errors, is the scope following the statement **console.log('HTTP-Error: ' + response.status);** The code for handling unexpected errors thrown by the different frameworks that are used to fetch the response asynchronously is in a catch-all scope that follows the statement **console.log('Error: ', error);** Discriminating between expected and unexpected failures and then finer distinguishing between different classes of expected errors will be implemented and discussed in the codelab for this chapter.

Web client accessibility

There are well-defined guidelines for web content accessibility, defined by the **World Wide Web Consortium (W3C)**. Known collectively as **Web Content Accessibility Guidelines (WCAG)** these guidelines are internationally recognized to help content creators and developers make web content accessible to people with disabilities. The full list of guidelines is published at **https://www.w3.org/TR/WCAG21/**

Our web client application supports the WCAG guidelines in several ways:

- We provide text labels for all buttons.

- Our layout uses nested standard container types which ensures that elements receive the focus in a logical order when using the keyboard.

- The use of standard button click handlers ensures that keyboard activation of controls is supported.

- All visible content is rendered using standard HTML document elements, providing compatibility with screen readers and visibility preferences such as high contrast settings.

- Operation and interpretation of the UI is understandable, that is relevant to the users' vocabulary and free of technical jargon.

Client-side policy rules

The **votingpolicyengine.py** module contains rules for determining which acts in the current round are eligible to receive a vote from a specific user. As described earlier throughout the book, it is best practice to encapsulate business logic, such as the policy for voting eligibility, to a single point of authority in an application.

We deferred from making calls to the backend to evaluate the current round's acts with the voting policy rules after every vote as it would more than double the network traffic between each client and the voting frontend. Instead, we implemented a local equivalent of the policy engine in our web client's JavaScript: Trading potential application integrity for performance.

This was addressed in the voting client requirements through the specification of a local policy engine that is fetched from the backend. An additional endpoint on the voting frontend provides the actual code for a client to execute when determining acts' eligibility for votes.

The implementation of this service on the backend will be given in this chapter's codelab. The JavaScript mechanisms to dynamically add functions to the current page will also be described in the codelab. Here, we will review how this is incorporated into the existing web client.

First, we refactor the function **markVoteCast** which is the callback invoked when a vote has been successfully cast via the voting frontend. We add code to this function to invoke a function named **updateEligibleVotes**, which takes parameters for all values needed for this operation that are stored elsewhere on the page:

```
// Process the response from a remote "vote" call.
// confirm to the user
// Call the voting policy engine downloaded from the server to
// update the act table to enforce the votebudget
function markVoteCast(responseJson) {
    const act = responseJson['act'];
    alert('you voted for ' + act + '!')
    updateEligibleVotes(act, document.getElementById('voteTally'),
        document.getElementById('voteLimit').value,
        document.getElementById('actsTable')
```

```
    );
}
```

The function we are invoking, **updateEligibleVotes()**, has not been defined. In JavaScript there are a number of ways to define a function, one of which is dynamic declaration through the **Function()** object constructor. This is how we will define the **updateEligibleVotes** function, through the execution of a function constructor, before the **markVoteCast()** callback is ever invoked.

The source for the body of this function will be fetched from the voting frontend, at the new endpoint that was specified earlier in this section, in the voting client requirements document. Since we are making a call to the voting frontend, this will have to be done after the user has been authenticated, as we must restrict access to the service to authenticated users.

The timing requirements of the policy engine construction is like that for the loading of the acts list. After user authentication and before any voting activity. We will add code to the same **firebase.auth** callback that was modified for the **getActs** function. This callback now contains the following code:

```
// Listen for the auth state to change and store the user info on the
document
firebase.auth().onAuthStateChanged(async function(user) {
    if (user) {
        // User is signed in.
        document.getElementById("userName").innerHTML = user.email;
        user.getIdToken().then((idToken) => {
        document.getElementById("idToken").value=idToken;
        getActs();
        fetchPolicyEngine();
    });
```

Note: Storing the ID token in a document element in this manner is not recommended practice in a production app and is done here for simplicity. More secure alternatives include storing the token in the browser's session storage or in browser memory.

The **fetchPolicyEngine** function issues a call to our frontend's REST API using the same techniques as our existing calls to the **/getActs** and **/vote** endpoints:

```
// Fetch the policy engine implementation
function fetchPolicyEngine() {
    console.log("Fetch policy", new Date().toLocaleString());
    getResponse(document.getElementById('actsForm'),
        getPolicyURL, setPolicyEngine);
}
```

This section has reviewed the different parts of the remote policy engine implementation and the timing of these in the execution of the features of the voting client. The handling of the server response and the dynamic registering of the new **updateEligibleVotes()** function will be described in this chapter's codelab.

Voter's mobile application

As well as a web client, we have a requirement to deliver a mobile app for one platform, iOS or Android, with the other platform to follow. Unlike the urgency to deliver our first client, we can spend some time considering cross-platform development. We also have one team working on both mobile platforms, so as much reuse as possible between the two products is highly desirable.

Mobile application development tools

In *Chapter 5, Client-side Technology Choices* the advantages and trade-offs of development strategies such as native platform, cross-platform mobile, and cross-platform including desktop development. Several examples of popular products were reviewed for each of these, but the alternatives discussed were not exhaustive and no list could be complete in a constantly evolving, and improving, landscape.

To briefly restate the parameters of our evaluation:

- Cross-platform mobile development is ideal.
- The application will make use of GCP APIs, with associated JSON data interchange.
- Firebase auth support is required.
- The development team is heavily invested in Python.

Two products in popular use that meet these requirements are Kivy and BeeWare. The major difference between the two is that Kivy produces Kivy applications, that is, applications that use Kivy toolkits and features, whereas BeeWare leans towards unifying other existing libraries as part of the product.

Either of these meets our requirements; we will use BeeWare **https://beeware.org/** as our application itself is fairly narrow and it is a better fit with our use of our own and third-party Python libraries and features. BeeWare does not offer integration with Visual Studio Code, but a series of repeated commands in an embedded terminal session work well with BeeWare's tooling.

BeeWare mobile applications

We will implement a standard BeeWare application implementing a native UI that presents displays and controls similar to those in the web client. Firebase Authentication support for user authentication will be performed with the platform agnostic Firebase Auth REST

API. Calls to our voting frontend service will be made using the standard Python **httpx** package.

Once we have an application defined, we will build and deploy for iOS with the BeeWare Briefcase utility that builds and deploys BeeWare applications on specific platforms.

Mobile client-side policy rules

The distribution of runtime modules to a client is a common pattern, and the solution for a Python application is similar to the solution implemented in JavaScript for the web client in the preceding section of this chapter. Mobile runtime environments have safeguards to block the replacement of code in a running application, which can be circumvented in a use case such as ours.

However, the need for this in the web client was introduced by the inability of a JavaScript application to easily use a Python module directly. With the proper use of abstraction and packaging, the mobile client written in Python will be able to invoke the same policy engine as is used by our cloud components. The additional complexity of runtime client module distribution can be avoided, which is the design decision made in the mobile client architecture.

A Python implementation of the installation of remotely defined methods is included in the repository archive for this chapter in the **talentvoting_policy.ruleinstaller. py** module. This is not used in the application but is included for completeness and comparison with its JavaScript counterpart.

The complete BeeWare client application, and its deployment to iOS will be described in the codelab for this chapter.

Refactoring the codebase

Early on, the package hierarchy was defined from a purely logical, implementation and language-independent point of view. In practice, our language and framework of choice is a consideration in the package and module taxonomy and may not align well with that earlier abstract definition. Symptoms of this mismatch were seen when we added some clever hacks to our two Python cloud deployments: The creation of symbolic links and the copying of source subtrees into our deployment base directories for the *Google App Engine* voting frontend and the Cloud Run voting processor.

Python package portability

The package hierarchy in Python is top-down, a source module can import other source modules relative to the importing module's directory. There is no way to reference some higher-level **anchor** package at a directory outside of the current path's subdirectory tree or parent. This forced us to use symlinks and copies to make our **common** package appear as subdirectories below the source directories of our cloud modules.

The Pythonesque way to handle this situation is to create a Python package of the needed modules and then place that package in a known package directory that is visible to all source within the environment. This is how built-in packages such as **time** and **os** as well as installed third-party packages such as **firebase_admin** and **flask** are accessible with the following source statements, which are not concerned with the packages' directory paths:

```
import time
import os


from firebase_admin import credentials, auth
from flask import Flask, request, jsonify, Response, make_response
```

There is a package tree: **talentvoting.common**, that spans the cloud and client trees. This is an ideal candidate to be published as a portable hermetic package, sealed and self-contained, which can be imported as easily as the **time** and **flask** packages in the source example above.

Use of a Python package involves three steps: Creating the package, distributing the package, and installing the package. The interested reader can learn more in-depth at **https://packaging.python.org/**; the basic steps for our project will be described here and then will be implemented in this chapter's codelab.

Isolating the source

The following figure illustrates our source tree at a high level:

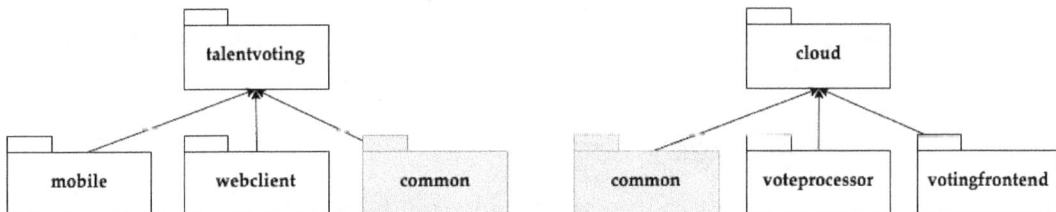

Figure 12.5: Top-level source package hierarchy

There are three problematic relationships in this hierarchy. The first is that both of the **common** packages are siblings to their clients. An extension of this is that the higher-level **common** package, the one under **talentvoting** is referenced in the cloud package hierarchy. While this is not insurmountable, reference to a relative parent directory in Python is brittle and can be confusing to the reader. This led us to create links and copy source directories when deploying our cloud services.

The second issue is that of component rank or equivalence in the system architecture. The cloud components: **voteprocessor** and **votingfrontend** are grouped together under cloud as they share a common environment, but the **mobile** and **webclient** applications are as significant as either cloud component, and it makes sense for these deployable components to appear as siblings or equivalents.

An alternative package taxonomy that facilitates the use of Python packaging and addresses these concerns is shown in the following figure:

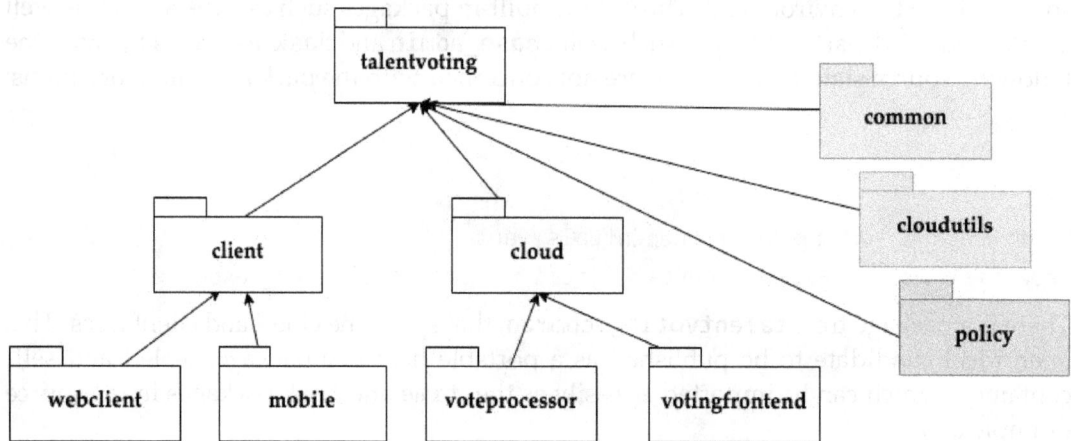

Figure 12.6: *Revised package hierarchy*

With the new directory structure in place, we will define the three shaded packages **common**, **policy** (formerly known as **common.policy**), and **cloudutils** (formerly known as **cloud:common**) to be contained in Python packages which we will build and distribute independently of the modules that use them.

Once these packages are portable, meaning that they have no external dependencies or references which are relative to their own boundaries or location, they can each be addressed as a top-level independent entity. We can import and use them from any number of modules each of which can be located at any point in our source tree.

Defining the package

A Python package, for purpose of importing source modules from other source modules in the same directory tree, consists of a directory whose name is the package name and the presence of a special empty file named **__init__.py** in that directory.

When defining a package for independent distribution and installation, there are additional requirements which are defined by your choice of build backend tool. We will use the set of requirements that are centered around a [project] table for metadata, a format supported by several popular build backends. Most importantly, we will be using GCP Cloud Build to store our packages in a Google Cloud Artifact Registry, which uses the tools and format we have selected.

The file **pyproject.toml** located in the root folder of our package source tree tells the build frontend tools which backend to use for our project and what external dependencies our package has. Additionally, project metadata such as the project homepage and license type are specified in this file.

A **README.md** file is a markdown file that is the root level of your package's documentation.

The **LICENSE** file contains the text of your chosen license. If the URL of a known license is specified in **pyproject.toml** this **LICENSE** file will be automatically fetched by the backend tools when you build your package.

Identifying a package repository

Python packages can be stored at and installed from local directories or from a remote repository. The Python Package Index at **https://pypi.org** is the de-facto standard or default repository for public package distribution. For the voting application, we will use a Google Artifact Registry associated with our project to store our Python packages. The steps to do this are included in the codelab.

We will use the standard Python installation tool, pip, to install the packages in our local development environment from the Artifact Registry.

The deployed versions of our cloud services: **votingfrontend** and **voteprocessor** will be configured to automatically install the latest versions of our published packages from this registry.

Creating or building a package

Distribution packages are built from the source files, including the packaging files described above under "Defining the package." To build a distribution package, the Python build utility is used to create package archives. Two types of archives are generated by build: source distributions, which have a filename extension of **.tar.gz**, and built or binary distributions with a filename extension of **.whl**.

Package distribution

Google Artifact Registry supports APIs and requirements of the existing Python distribution and installation tools. The standard Python twine utility uploads Python packages to supported registries, and so we will use this to upload package archive files to our Google Artifact Registry by supplying the registry's URL to the command.

Installing packages

The packages in our Artifact Registry can be installed using the Python standard utility **pip**. Much like the twine command previously, the **pip install** command can accept the URL of our registry as a parameter specifying the location of the packages being installed.

When we deploy our Google App Engine and Cloud Run services, we will add our relevant package names to the **requirements.txt** file for each of those services and specify the registry's URL as an additional index in the same **requirements.txt** file.

Building multiple client applications codelab

In this chapter's codelab, the various steps necessary to produce a mobile client application that is consistent with the voting client requirements will be described.

There are many steps to this, each of which will be covered. Sections of source code relevant to points being made will be included here; the full source is available in this chapter's GitHub.

The delivery of a consistent client application is broken down into the following sub-tasks in this codelab:

- Refactoring the package hierarchy.

- Building and distributing Python packages to a Google Artifact Registry.

- Modifying the deployment descriptors to use the Artifact Registry.

- Setting up a BeeWare development environment.

- Writing the BeeWare client application.

- Deploying the application to an iOS simulator.

The result will be independent release cycle for common code and each deployed component. Our mobile client application will be deployable for iOS devices and can be extended to Android and other target platforms supported by BeeWare.

Refactoring the package hierarchy

The rearrangement of the package hierarchy is accomplished in three steps. First, we simply rename and move directories and modules to their new locations, regardless of referential consistency between modules. Then, we can use on the facilities of our IDE, Visual Studio Code, to identify problems in the workspace. These problems will include import statements that cannot be resolved. We will visit and correct each of these problems, albeit the imports of our three portable packages will not be resolved until we have completed building and installing those. The third step in refactoring the hierarchy will be building the three Python packages and installing them locally and deploying them to a Cloud Artifact Registry, which will resolve the workspace problems and cloud deployment issues introduced in the refactoring.

The new directory structure is that which was illustrated in *Figure 12.6*. To move folders and files to their new locations, we should use the **git mv** command which ensures that GitHub tracks the folder and file moves and renames. Without using **git mv**, GitHub would see these moves as deletes of the old files and additions of new ones.

Note: **Be sure to close your IDE or editors before moving files that they may have open.**

The following table lists the from and to folders and files to perform moves of. These should be executed in the order shown in the following figure to ensure that parent folders are present when required:

Original folder or file	New folder or file	Note
cloud/__init__.py	talentvoting/cloud/__init__.py	Copy to the existing alternate location of the cloud directory
cloud/common	talentvoting/cloudutils	move and rename
cloud/votingfrontend/talentvoting	none	remove link
cloud/voteprocessor/talentvoting	none	remove directory and its contents
cloud/voteprocessor	talentvoting/cloud/voteprocessor	
cloud/votingfrontend	talentvoting/cloud/votingfrontend	
talentvoting/cloud/common	none	remove link
None	talentvoting/client	create this new directory
talentvoting/webclient	talentvoting/client/webclient	
None	talentvoting/client/mobile	create this new directory
talentvoting/common	talentvoting/common	no change
talentvoting/common/policy	talentvoting/policy	

Figure 12.7: Package folder and file moves

Once the folders and files are rearranged, references to old source package locations need to be updated. An example is shown in this message displayed in the VS Code **Problems** tab for the file **votingfrontend.py**:

"Import "talentvoting.cloud.common.votingdatabaseutils" could not be resolved … [Ln 12, Col 6]"

To fix this, update the **Import** statement to reference the new folder location, as seen in *Figure 12.7*:

```
from talentvoting.cloud.common.votingdatabaseutils import get_database
```

The preceding is replaced by the following:

```
from talentvoting.cloudutils.votingdatabaseutils import get_database
```

The same change is needed in the module **voteprocessor.py**.

Look through each **.py** file for such broken references to imported modules and update them to the three new package names.

Building and distributing Python packages

The source code of our system is now in a directory structure that reflects the compartmentalization of components by platform, such as subpackages of cloud, and also affinity by role, such as the subpackages of client. The directory trees whose use spans different subtrees of our directory structure: **common**, **policy**, and **cloudutils**, are now independent of any of their clients.

This last point is the focus of this section. Having detached those three subtrees, we can make them available to all clients, with the same visibility and using the same standard mechanisms.

Package naming

We will make three Python packages: **talentvoting_common**, **talentvoting_policy** and **talentvoting_cloudutils**. There is a packaging practice, the use of namespace packages, that could be used to allow our package names to be logically grouped into a common namespace, for example **talentvoting.common**, **talentvoting.policy** and **talentvoting.cloudutils**. Using namespace packages has several caveats and offers little benefit in a small collection of packages such as ours. We can recommend and use the following import format to keep the import object short, if desired:

```
import talentvoting_common as common
import talentvoting_cloudutils as cloudutils
import talentvoting_policy as policy
```

Installing Python packages carry not only the source files of the package but also the dependencies of the package. This is the primary practical motivation to split our modules into three packages: the **cloudutils** module depends on Google Cloud packages, which there is no reason to on a mobile client as a side-effect of installation of a single package when only the **common** module will be used. Another reason is the reliance of both policy and **cloudutils** on common: Separating these allows us to explicitly state such dependencies and control releases with finer granularity.

Package metadata and configuration

With the source rearranged, we now create the package metadata that is used by the package build and installation tools. The full contents of the files for each of our three packages are in the repository archive for this chapter, we will list the files and their purpose here.

Before issuing Cloud Spanner commands, billing must be enabled for the project.

In a Linux or MacOS Terminal, the commands and responses will look like the following:

Note: **The lines beginning with # are comments for the reader.**

```
# Ensure that you are in the base directory of the package project
$ ls pyproject.toml
pyproject.toml
# Install the Python build command
$ python3 -m pip install --upgrade build
...

# Build the packages, two archives will be created in the dist/ directory
$ python3 -m build
...

Successfully built talentvoting_common-0.0.0.tar.gz and talentvoting_
common-0.0.0-py3-none-any.whl
```

```
$ ls dist
talentvoting_common-0.0.0-py3-none-any.whl     talentvoting_common-
0.0.0.tar.gz
```

The source and binary versions of this package are now built and stored locally. The next step is to make them available on a distribution source.

Package distribution using an Artifact Registry

To publish our packages to a Cloud Artifact Registry, we must enable the Artifact Registry API for our project. This API requires an active billing project at the time it is used, so we will do that as well. These are the same steps as performed in the codelab for *Chapter 11, Guaranteeing Data Permanence.*

The following section uses a Terminal for several stages of the process. The same Terminal session should be used, to preserve continuity of the session's location and login state.

In a Terminal:

```
# Log in and set the correct credentials
$ gcloud auth default-login
```

Your browser has been opened to visit:

…

You are now logged in as [raygeeknyc@gmail.com].

Your current project is **votingforthestars**. You can change this setting by running:

```
    gcloud config set project PROJECT_ID
# Save the oauth2token in a variable
$ export O2TOKEN=$(gcloud auth print-access-token)
# Link your billing account to the project
# Replace votingforthestars with your project ID and [BILLING_ACCOUNT_ID]
with your billing account
$ gcloud alpha billing projects link votingforthestars --billing-
account=[BILLING_ACCOUNT_ID]
billingAccountName: billingAccounts/BILLING_ACCOUNT_ID
billingEnabled: true
name: projects/votingforthestars/billingInfo
projectId: votingforthestars
```

Next, in the developer console, search for Artifact Registry, click through the prompts to enable the API for your project.

Now return to the Terminal and run the following commands to create a repository for your Python packages:

```
# Create a repository
$ gcloud artifacts repositories create talentvoting-python-repo \
    --repository-format=python \
    --location=us-central1 \
    --description="Talentvoting python package repository"

Create request issued for: [talentvoting-python-repo]
...
Created repository [talentvoting-python-repo].
# List all project repositories and confirm this one is included in the list
$ gcloud artifacts repositories list
Listing items under project votingforthestars, across all locations.
 ARTIFACT_REGISTRY
REPOSITORY                      FORMAT  MODE                   DESCRIPTION
LOCATION     LABELS  ENCRYPTION              CREATE_TIME            UPDATE_TIME
SIZE (MB)
us.gcr.io                       DOCKER  STANDARD_REPOSITORY
us                   Google-managed key  2024-12-08T15:43:52  2025-02-
16T14:58:34  3340.152
talentvoting-python-repo  PYTHON  STANDARD_REPOSITORY  Talentvoting
python package repository                                  us-central1
Google-managed key  2025-04-09T16:04:35  2025-04-09T16:04:35  0
...
# Set this repository as the default for following commands in this
terminal
$ gcloud config set artifacts/repository talentvoting-python-repo
Updated property [artifacts/repository].
$ gcloud config set artifacts/location us-central1
Updated property [artifacts/location].
```

Finally, we upload the package files in our **dist/** directory to the Artifact Registry.

In the Terminal:

```
# Upload the two packages in the dist directory
$ python3 -m twine upload --repository-url https://us-central1-
python.pkg.dev/votingforthestars/talentvoting-python-repo/ --username
oauth2accesstoken --password $O2TOKEN dist/*
Uploading talentvoting_common-1.0.0-py3-none-any.whl
200 OK
Uploading talentvoting_common-1.0.0.tar.gz
200 OK
```

```
# List the packages in the repository
$ gcloud artifacts packages list --repository=talentvoting-python-repo
PACKAGE              CREATE_TIME           UPDATE_TIME           ANNOTATIONS
talentvoting-common  2025-04-09T16:45:00   2025-04-09T17:10:31
```

We now have a Google Cloud Artifact Registry which distributes our common package in both source and binary forms.

The same set of steps should be done for the **cloudutils** and **policy** packages. The package configuration files are in the repository archive for this chapter.

Local Artifact Registry package installation

Now, that the packages are available, we can use the standard **pip** utility to install them in our development environment.

Google Cloud Authentication works with the **pip** command through a number of interfaces: HTTP authentication and keyring. Google Cloud recommends using keyring, which is the most secure and well-supported. To setup keyring in your environment, follow the documentation for setting up Python package repository authentication at:

https://cloud.google.com/artifact-registry/docs/python/authentication

Back in the Terminal session:

```
# Install the common package from GCP
$ pip install --index-url  \
https://us-central1-python.pkg.dev/votingforthestars/talentvoting-python-
repo/ \
talentvoting-common
Successfully installed talentvoting-common-1.0.0
```

You can confirm that the package is installed locally in an interactive Python interpreter.

In the Terminal, execute the following commands that import the installed package, imports a symbol from a subpackage and displays that symbol's definition:

```
$ python
Type "help", "copyright", "credits" or "license" for more information.
>>> import talentvoting-common
>>> from talentvoting_common.interfaces.servicelocations import VOTE_WEB_
CLIENT_DOMAIN
>>> VOTE_WEB_CLIENT_DOMAIN
'https://votingforthestars.web.app'
>>>
```

We have successfully installed the **talentvoting_common** package from our Cloud Artifact Registry. The same steps should be followed to install the **talentvoting_cloudutils** package.

Cloud deployment using Artifact Registry packages

The local installation of packages allows us to compile and build in our development environment. When an application is deployed to either Google App Engine or Google Cloud Run services, these dependencies are not automatically bundled with the source of our cloud component. The dependencies of a GCP service component must be explicitly stated in the component's **requirements.txt** file. When you deploy to these services, the dependencies specified in the **requirements.txt** file will be installed automatically with your deployed app.

Since we use our own package repository for the **talentvoting_common** and **talentvoting_cloudutils** packages, we will also specify the URL for our Artifact Registry as an additional source of packages.

The new contents of our Google App Engine service config in the file **talentvoting/cloud/votingfrontend/requirements.txt** is as follows:

```
--extra-index-url=https://us-central1-python.pkg.dev/votingforthestars/
talentvoting-python-repo/simple/

Flask==3.0.3
gunicorn
firebase_admin
google-cloud-pubsub
google-cloud-spanner
talentvoting_common
talentvoting_cloudutils
talentvoting_policy
```

The new contents of our Google Cloud Run service config in the file **talentvoting/cloud/voteprocessor/requirements.txt** is as follows:

```
--extra-index-url=https://us-central1-python.pkg.dev/votingforthestars/
talentvoting-python-repo/simple/

gunicorn==23.0.0
Flask==3.0.3
Werkzeug==3.0.3
google-cloud-pubsub
```

```
google-api-core
google-cloud-spanner
talentvoting_common
talentvoting_cloudutils
talentvoting_policy
```

When we deploy the Cloud Run service and the app engine frontend, the deployment tools will install our three packages into the services' deployed containers from their repository, located at the **-extra-index-url**.

Note: **The deploy command for the voteprocessor service no longer requires the cp commands that made local copies of our common packages' source. These are now properly installed from the requirements.txt file. Thus, the command to deploy the voteprocessor service is now simply the following command:**

```
$ gcloud run deploy voteprocessor --allow-unauthenticated \
    --max-instances=10 --source .
```

Development using BeeWare

Our client applications should be identical in functionality and as similar as possible in form: Their design and feature set are meant to be parallel, with any deviations imposed or guided by platform-specific guidance and requirements.

The implementation of the three planned client applications is influenced by this expectation of homogeneity, but there is also the technical consideration optimizing development through reuse of code and processes.

One large factor is the choice of as few programming languages as possible, which has impact in two ways.

The first consideration is that the need for engineers to know and switch between multiple languages both restricts the community of developers and imposes a tax or friction on the developers as they context switch between languages.

The second is a matter of risk incurred by redundant code. The use of one language allows us to define values such as the URL of a service endpoint or the number of votes allowed in a round, once. This was illustrated in the **talentvoting_common.interfaces. servicelocations** module, the partial contents of which are as follows:

```
_VOTE_INGESTOR_ADDRESS = https://votingforthestars.ue.r.appspot.com
VOTE_URL = _VOTE_INGESTOR_ADDRESS + "/vote"
PROJECT_ID = "votingforthestars"
SPANNER_INSTANCE = "talentvoting-instance"
SPANNER_DATABASE = "talentvoting-database"
```

A more substantial example is the goal of providing canonical, single authoritative implementations of critical business logic. The **is_eligible_vote** method of the

talentvoting_policy.votingpolicyengine module is an example of this. The methods of this module can be imported and used in different cloud and client applications which are written in Python.

Our concession to this principle was to provide an equivalent JavaScript method. Containing the two methods within one module allows us to offer two separate encodings of the same behavior and reduces but does not eliminate the risk of these implementations diverging.

The BeeWare suite of libraries and tools allows the development of Python applications that can be built and executed on different target platforms, using each platform's native libraries and frameworks. We will develop our mobile application using BeeWare and then build and deploy that application for iOS.

BeeWare overview

BeeWare is a suite of tools and libraries that are used together to define and deploy cross-platform applications with a native **graphical user interface** (**GUI**) in Python.

The BeeWare suite includes:

- Toga, a cross-platform widget toolkit.
- Briefcase, a tool for packaging Python projects for target platforms.
- Cross-platform libraries such as Rubicon ObjC for accessing platform native libraries.
- Python distributions for platforms where Python environments are not supplied.

BeeWare is available on macOS, Windows, Linux, Web clients, Android and iOS.

Installing BeeWare

BeeWare is a series of tools, like Briefcase and dependencies, such as recent versions of Python and Git. These are all installed using the standard installation tools like **pip**, **brew** and platform installation packages.

Writing a BeeWare application

A BeeWare GUI application is largely built around the developer's choice of UI toolkit. BeeWare provides the Toga UI toolkit but a BeeWare application could use other third-party or native UI frameworks. With the basic skeleton application defined for that framework, the rest of the application is largely agnostic to BeeWare: Standard Python facilities and other libraries can be freely employed in the body of the application.

An example of the free use of standard Python features is illustrated in these code snippets from a transient version of the **talentvoting.client.mobile.src.voteclient.app** module, which is the **main** module of our BeeWare client application. The source of the final version is included in the GitHub repository snapshot for this chapter:

```
from talentvoting_common.acts import example_acts
...

    for act in example_acts():
        act_row = toga.Box(style=Pack(direction=ROW))
        act_row.add(toga.Label(act["name"], style=Pack(width=COL1_WIDTH_PX)))
        if act["voting_eligible"]:
            act_row.add(toga.Button(icon=brutus_icon, id=act["act"],
                on_press=vote_button_handler))
        else:
            act_row.add(toga.Button(icon=cricket_icon, enabled=False))
        acts_list.add(act_row)
...
```

Note: The Pythonesque use of the dict that is returned by our `examplesActs()` method.

The development cycle of a BeeWare application is prescribed by a sequence of subcommands and intermediate targets of the Briefcase tool. A full description of the development lifecycle is at the BeeWare tutorial site: **https://docs.beeware.org/en/latest/**

Briefcase can be run on our app as a native client app in our development environment. This is usually preferred and sufficient for trying out changes during a development session.

The following figure shows our main window running on macOS:

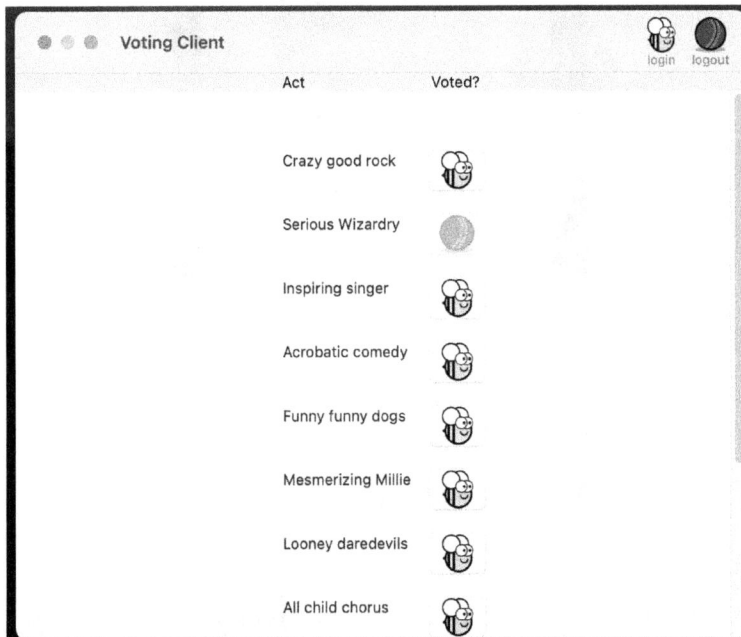

Figure 12.8: The Voting Client on macOS

The basic layout and application behavior is consistent across client platforms and the build and deploy cycle for the development platform is much quicker than packaging, deploying and running on another client such as iOS or Android.

Deploying the application to iOS

To actually publish an application to the App Store involves an account creation and interaction with *Apple Developer Support*, which is outside of the scope of this book. However, iOS development is not blocked on this; Apple's developer tools include simulators for many iOS and iPadOS devices, which can be used to debug and try out iOS applications. The BeeWare Briefcase tool fully supports this, and our app can be brought up in an iPhone simulator, as shown in the following figure:

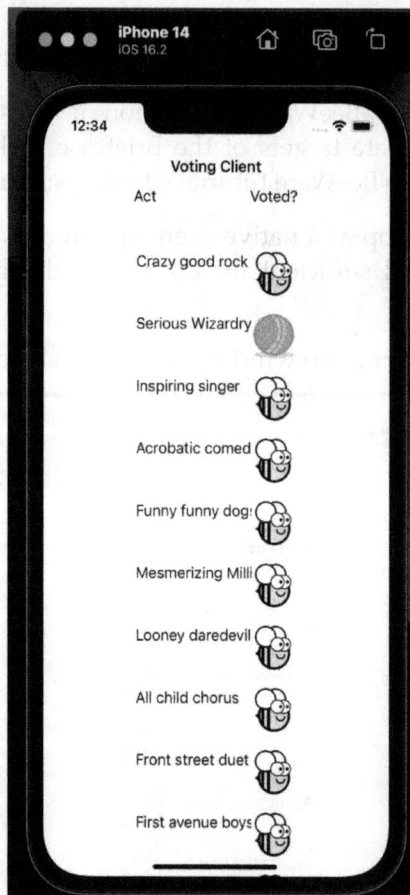

Figure 12.9: The Voting Client in an iPhone 14 simulator

The voting client application is now deployable to iOS and with some further configuration and adjustments to the application, a client application for Android and desktop environments can also be built and deployed.

Conclusion

A client application should have clearly defined responsibilities that complement the strengths of the client platform: A localized connection and configuration for a specific individual. The boundaries of the client and backend tiers should be defined with intent, and the subsequent implementations of each must fulfill their requirements and, thus, trust the other tier's implementation to fulfill theirs. The codebase was refactored to isolate several reusable module hierarchies into portable Python packages which were then deployed to a Google Cloud Platform service: Google Artifact Registry.

Development of client and server-side components can sometimes introduce conflicting directives: The desires to keep voting policy evaluation local and yet share code were at odds in our web client. The reader was introduced to a design pattern that addresses such situations, the remote installation of code at runtime.

The choice of a cross-platform development tool should consider many factors, which in the end led us to use BeeWare. The development of a minimal client application in BeeWare was described to illustrate the use of platform-agnostic frameworks and libraries.

In *Chapter 13, Replacing Components in Isolation,* further explores portability and addresses the inevitable need of a successful system to migrate some components to new infrastructure. The reader will learn forward-thinking practices to ease such maintenance and will be taken through the steps of performing a migration within a running system.

Join our Discord space

Join our Discord workspace for latest updates, offers, tech happenings around the world, new releases, and sessions with the authors:

https://discord.bpbonline.com

Section 4:
Recap: Applying the Case Study

CHAPTER 13
Replacing Components in Isolation

Introduction

Cloud platforms are constantly evolving and growing, adding new capabilities that often supersede your system's existing foundation. Migrating to a new cloud service is justified by demonstrating that the value added by the new service exceeds the cost of the migration. Recognizing the value added by a new service is a matter of critical examination of the vendor's claims. The cost of migration is influenced by the development team at two stages in the life of the system: When we design the architecture of a system, and how we plan and execute the proposed migration.

Earlier chapters throughout the book have discussed design principles that maximize isolation of components from their infrastructure dependencies. This chapter discusses best practices for upgrading to new or counterpart services with a minimal amount of engineering refactoring and rework: The reader will learn how to make the revolutionary, evolutionary.

Structure

The following topics will be covered in this chapter:

- Designing abstractions for infrastructure responsibilities
- Mapping foundation functionality into infrastructure interfaces

- Containing dependencies by converging to black boxes
- Planning a migration
- Changing the tires while the bus is moving
- Designing the migration of a datastore codelab

Objectives

The engineering principles of ways to maximize software reuse have been in place for decades, perhaps first formalized by *Brad Cox* in the development of the Objective-C programming language as a vehicle for creating software components. It is from this work that the concept of plug and play software components has evolved. No complete, ready-made solution exists, but in this chapter, we will describe established practices and available **Google Cloud Platform** (**GCP**) services that maximize the interoperability of our software with as many potential lower-level components as possible. By clearly defining the boundaries between our application and dependent infrastructure and then sharply defining the requirements we make of our infrastructure services, we increase the ability to evaluate appropriate substitutes.

We will conduct a case study of the replacement of an infrastructure component, in this case a persistence service, in a running system. Through this, we will highlight the realized advantages to the relevant design practices and the remaining risks. To avoid harm to the business, we will construct plans for reducing and mitigating the recognized risks.

Designing abstractions for infrastructure responsibilities

A beneficial starting point when designing the application's interfaces with infrastructure to maximize portability is to start from a service or product agnostic point of view. Rather than consider the features of the infrastructure service, instead focus on the needs your own software components have of any system infrastructure that supports them.

This is a classic example of a needs-based approach to specifying the interface between two systems. Rather than respond to the claims and capabilities published by a service provider, instead the consumer or client specifies what their needs are the work is then to identify how a candidate provider can best fulfill those needs, with some way to measure the effort and quality of the solution. In the end, ranking the candidate providers is a straightforward summarization of the solution grades, often weighted by the criticality of each individual requirement.

Requirements-based infrastructure evaluation

This is a process that we perform during the initial phases of our development project, when the architecture is first being designed to fit best with the available choices of infrastructure platform. However, it is something to repeat at later points, when a project is either in maintenance mode or due for a major redesign or forced changes. Changes to infrastructure might be necessitated by market changes or by disruptive changes in technology.

There is a difference in the goals of this evaluation process when it is performed during the initial design versus the later phases. During the initial design, we are looking to shape both the application components and the infrastructure choice to find the best fit, the requirements may be considered fluid to some degree. When we perform this evaluation for a running system to evaluate new or changed infrastructure providers, we consider the requirements to be more rigid and evaluate the infrastructure providers to see how well they can match or improve on the existing services' support of our application.

A template for requirements analysis

To clarify this process, let us execute it for a couple of use cases from the voting application. The first example use case is the selection of a persistence service aka storage system for the voting backend.

First, we will identify the component in our architecture that is the client of a persistence service. From our initial design, it is the Vote Processor, the subsystem that takes votes from the queue of recorded votes and permanently records those votes for both the act being voted for and for the user casting the vote. Our first requirement for the storage system is contained in the sentence *for both the act and for the user*. The storage system must support updating both of these as one single atomic transaction.

Another relevant point is that the queue of recorded votes is isolated, there could be one or many such queues in existence with no difference to the Vote Processor. This is because votes are cast in different regions, and we keep the user-facing service, the voting frontend, local to the users for reasons of performance.

While the queues of recorded votes may be isolated, the permanent record of user and act vote history is not. There is one and only one number of votes that have been cast for an act, and likewise, only one number of votes that a user has cast during a round. There is our second requirement: The storage system must offer a global datastore to more than one regionally isolated client.

Another requirement of our design is that of data addressability. We retrieve and update acts by a unique key and users by their own unique key values. These are our primary methods of access: Direct operations on single entities, but we also perform operations on ranges of entities, such as reading all the acts for a given round to determine their standing in the competition. These are our requirements for the addressability of data, fast direct access to individual entities, and less latency-sensitive access to subsets of entities through some alternate index.

The shape of the data we are storing is another consideration. Recall the discussions in *Chapter 11, Guaranteeing Data Permanence*, distinguishing between structured and unstructured data and deep versus flat data. Our data is all structured and, in some places, can be categorized as deep, most specifically in the existence of sets of votes per user and round. A requirement of our data persistence service is that it supports structured data per entity and data with some depth, sets of values within an addressable entity.

The requirements that we have identified are summarized in the following table, which we will use as a worksheet throughout the process of evaluating several potential storage products offered by GCP. We will revisit and add to this worksheet throughout this chapter:

Application Requirement	<Product one>		<Product two>	
	Effort	Notes	Effort	Notes
Multiple entity transactions				
Globally available datastore				
Fast single entity access				
Address a subset/range of entities				
Supports structured data				
Support for deep data				

Figure 13.1: Initial table of persistence requirements

With this table defined, we will note a few details of this stage of the process.

The number of requirements (rows, named in the leftmost column) is subjectively determined, with no right or wrong size. The requirements in the first column are defined by the nature of the component under consideration, in this case, data persistence products, and the use cases being implemented, as we described in the preceding paragraphs of this section. A general rule of thumb might be that one requirement is too few and more than seven is too many, but even these thresholds could be reasonably challenged in some cases.

The number of products (column pairs to the right of the first column) is determined by the market. When planning an infrastructure migration, it is valuable to include the current service as the first product as a baseline: The migration should improve the application or the development team's workflow overall. Having the current state provides a convenient starting point for discussions of the merits of each replacement candidate product.

We can make a stronger statement advising the number of product columns to include than we could for the number of requirements rows. There must be at least two products in the evaluation: The current product and a candidate replacement. The upper bound in later stages should be open to the products that satisfy the requirements, but limited by the available energy and time of the team performing the research. If an upper bound is to be set, seven is a good number as a threshold of human attention.

For now, we are focusing on constructing the abstraction of our infrastructure's responsibilities, which is captured in the first column and arrived at in the preceding discussion. So, the identification and evaluation of products will be left for a later section of this chapter.

We will next examine the requirements of a second infrastructure role, that of a provider of user authentication and authorization, which we will refer to as an **identity service**.

The first requirement of an identity service is the ability to work with users' existing accounts on well-known and trusted platforms. These can include *Apple, Google, Facebook, and LinkedIn*. We consider Google to be the strongest requirement, that is, the identity service must be able to authenticate an existing Google (aka *Gmail*) account. A secondary, weaker requirement is the ability to authenticate with at least another popular platform.

The third requirement is the ability to authenticate a user using their mobile phone number. While we have not implemented that in the voting system yet, we consider this to be a requirement of a production system in global use, especially as we roll out to regions where cell phones are the most or only popular client computing platform.

The next and strongest requirement we have of an identity service is that it provides credentials that can be used to authorize a user to access GCP services. Now that our service has been developed for GCP, this is a hard requirement unless we plan to migrate all our backend services to another provider.

The final requirement that we have is compatibility with our chosen client platforms. These include Python on iOS and Android and native JavaScript.

Using the same template, we established for summarizing and evaluating infrastructure role requirements, we produce the a table, in the following figure, as our second example:

| Application | <Product one> | | <Product two> | |
Requirement	Effort	Notes	Effort	Notes
Authenticates Google accounts				
Authenticates one other social account type				
Authenticates using mobile phone #				
Provides GCP authorization				
Supports Python (iOS. Android) and JavaScript				

Figure 13.2: Initial table of identify service requirements

Having first specified these requirements clearly, without the mention or consideration of a specific product, allows us to consider the actual needs of the system, rather than the offerings of service vendors.

In the rest of this chapter, we will continue with the process of product evaluation and migration using only the first use case, a persistence service. The same process can be applied to any infrastructure role as the second example illustrates.

Mapping foundation functionality into infrastructure interfaces

After identifying the functional requirements of infrastructure providers, we could evaluate the suitability of a product to our needs. However, this evaluation would largely be based on the claims of the vendor, without hard data. The exact meaning of offers a global datastore might mean very different things in the minds of a database product manager and of an application developer. It is best to map the high-level functional requirements that we have identified to lower-level procedural discrete operations that our application would expect to perform as part of fulfilling each requirement.

Finding appropriate levels of specificity for requirements

At this point, it is important to balance the need to identify legitimate, concrete capabilities against a tendency to rely on what is already known and miss out on or exclude new and novel solutions. The functional requirements should not converge on the level of specificity of code, that is, requirements are not pseudocode, but nor are they simply objectives or statements of principle. The following figure illustrates the range of specificity of good functional requirements with the extremes to be avoided:

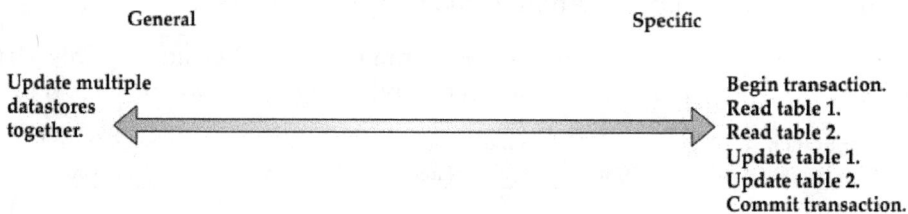

General		Specific
Update multiple datastores together.	⟵⟶	Begin transaction. Read table 1. Read table 2. Update table 1. Update table 2. Commit transaction.

Figure 13.3: Range of requirement specificity

With the extremes spelled out so exactly, it is useful to have the counterexample of an acceptable level of specification. This is dependent on the individual use case but for this example, one requirement statement that is on the spectrum between the two ends is the following:

```
Multiple entity updates:

The service must be able to isolate a set of related operations consisting
of read operations of multiple datastores grouped with updates to those
datastores using values derived from those reads. This set of operations
should be invisible to other clients of the datastores until they are
successfully completed as a group.

If the set is not completed, it is considered to have never happened and
has no effect on the datastores being accessed or on other clients of the
datastores.

From the time that the first operation in the set is executed until the
```

entire set of operations is completed, other clients should be blocked from accessing the individual data elements being updated. This blocking should be invisible to those other clients.

This requirement is typically fulfilled with an implementation of one existing type of database transaction semantic: Multi-table transactions with exclusive locks. However, we have not specified how this should be implemented by the service provider, nor have we left any ambiguity in our requirement.

The lack of implementation details is important in that it does not lock us into an existing, well-known feature. Consider a database vendor that has implemented some novel form of look-ahead that determines which of the read entities might be updated and defines as narrow a set of locks as possible for every set of reads and updates. If we were to specify the pseudocode or the commonly used implementation on the right of *Figure 13.3,* we would be excluding this new and useful feature from consideration. Remember that the requirement is not multi-table transactions with exclusive locks, but rather the capabilities and effects described in the preceding code snippet.

This example presented one appropriate requirement, but the engineering team may find others, either more or less specific or phrased in different terms. There is no one correct solution; if the engineers can understand the terms used and the requirement specification passes the test of not a statement of principle and also not precise enough to be code, then it is most likely a useful and appropriately written requirement.

There should be an expansion, like the one seen previously, for every requirement listed in *Figure 13.1.*

This table and accompanying document are still vendor and product agnostic, these are the requirements of our application. Exploring how each product under consideration can fulfill each requirement is an exercise that will result in the values of the *<Product n>* effort columns of the table in *Figure 13.1.*

Containing dependencies by converging to black boxes

The term black box refers to a component or system where the internal workings are unknown, housed within a metaphorical opaque black box with only the intentional input and output devices exposed. The black box approach focuses on a system's inputs and outputs without delving into or even permitting consideration of the internal mechanisms. Defining the expected inputs and the promised results without understanding how the inputs are transformed into the outputs is the distinguishing characteristic of this principle.

Taking this approach towards specifying our infrastructure components is ideal for enabling us to move freely between providers. With requirements distilled to as pure a set of needed capabilities and the interface defined in terms of the available relevant state, we can identify the largest set of infrastructure candidates that meet our requirements. Any component that can deliver what we need (outputs) based on what we can provide (inputs) is a potential service provider. How the component does this is quite simply not our concern, as long as the side-effects are understood, such as resource cost, performance and sustainability of the working solution in practice.

Requirements as black box specifications

The requirements summary in *Figure 13.1* contains the desired outputs or effects of a component through the aggregated contents of the leftmost column. What is missing for this to be a concise set of black box specifications is a summary of the available inputs: What buttons we would be able to press, or levers we could set, on a literal black box component. While this level of detail is not typically provided, it is a useful exercise to keep in mind when writing requirements: What internal state does a client hold that it could present as parameter values to a service? Determining the relevant items of state and summarizing them in a consistent fashion are the main challenges, but not an impossible task.

Grammar for black box specifications

The essential distinguishing property of black box requirements is that they define what a subsystem should do from the client's perspective, without mentioning the technical details of how it is done.

Well written black box requirements are precise enough to be used to write black box tests—runtime verifications that a system is performing as expected. These requirements are expressed in mathematical functions or well-structured language to reduce the possibility of misinterpretations due to subjective biases or ambiguity.

The following list of guidelines should be considered when writing black box requirements and test cases. They are also useful as a checklist to validate the requirements once written:

- **Focus on functionality**: The specification should clearly state the expected functionality of the subsystem, based on the user's requirements. The benefit or value added by the component should be clear.

- **No knowledge of internal mechanisms**: The specification should not mention how the subsystem fulfills the requirement or what internal structure might exist within the black box. A black box should be magic from the user's perspective, with no evident backing science.

- **Input yields output approach**: The requirement should specify what inputs are provided to the black box and what visible signals or outputs the black box produces in response. It is useful to visualize a true black box with a series of discrete input devices: Buttons, knobs and switches, and discrete output devices, such as lamps, dials or buzzers. For this symbolic black box, a requirement might be: When any two buttons are being pressed in unison for two seconds, a red lamp lights up to indicate multiple buttons being pressed. The lamp stays lit until either button (or both) is released at which point it turns off.

This illustration of a component, literally a black box, serves to remind us of the purpose of the black box designation: The absolute opacity that it confers. All that we, the client, can see are the advertised features, which are there for our use: a switch and two pushbuttons for our system to manipulate, and an indicator lamp for the black box to activate. The rest of the system is featureless and private to the suppliers, the builders of the component:

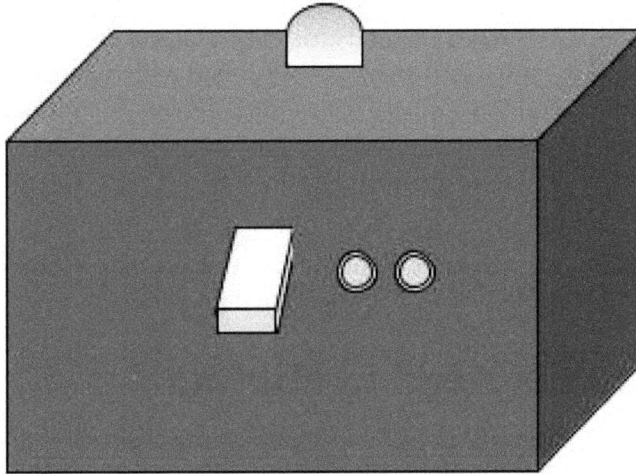

Figure 13.4: A figurative black box component

Advantages of black box specifications

The benefits of black box requirements and testing are primarily the shifting of the burden to the appropriate parties. Understanding the internal workings and semantics of a software component takes time and attention from the client developers and the client development team. In our case, the product and engineering staff designing and implementing the voting application have work to do in that domain and should be allowed to focus on solving those problems, not designing or debugging a storage system. Likewise, the complementary point of view is just as compelling; the developers of a storage system should understand and implement a well-defined and reliable storage service, not become versed in every potential client system's problem domain.

The benefits of black box specification extend through the software development lifecycle, to the testing and continuous verification stage of a system's life. It is more cost-effective to allow test engineers to apply their expertise with the tools of their trade: Unit and integration testing frameworks, continuous testing systems, and chaos injectors, to evaluate the outputs produced by a black box, without any knowledge or research into the component itself.

Planning a migration

Migrating an application from any infrastructure dependency to another should be considered highly risky and expensive. The risk is that of a disruption in system operations or even a major user-visible and business-affecting service outage. The expense is a developer's time and effort in learning the new infrastructure and then planning and executing the migration. There is probably an additional cost in paying for both the old and new infrastructure services throughout the migration period.

Since there are real costs, both known and speculative, the decision to change infrastructure components or providers is a major one and is due both careful consideration and extensive planning. The undertaking must be properly provisioned with regard to staffing, **operating expense (OpEx)** budget, and authority of the project owners. By this last point, it is meant that a migration project must have a high-level sponsor with the authority to, for example, forestall a product release that they deem significantly increases the risk of the migration project failing.

In the following section, we will walk through this process, using the example use case of the proposed migration of the voting application's data persistence service.

Determining the need to migrate

A migration from one environment, a known infrastructure landscape, to a new one requires large changes in your assets and plans. Change in any amount introduces potential chaos and disorder, the likelihood of risk. The safest position is generally to stay where you are: It may not be ideal, but it is familiar, and your position there is established.

To justify the cost and risk of a migration, there must be some compelling advantage, but it is not usually a reduction in risk. We will enumerate and describe several common reasons to migrate in the following list:

- **Improvements in reliability or decreased cost of reliability**: One of the signs of a successful, well received application is the demand for more nines. The term five nines is taken to mean 99.999% and refers to high availability of services, when a service is available for 99.999% of the time, or around 5 minutes of downtime per year. If the users miss an application during its downtime, that is a signal that the application is important to the user community. The reliability of a software component depends largely on the reliability of its dependencies. While an application can compensate for an unreliable infrastructure component through some combination of retry, failover, and local caching, this is a large burden and a distraction from the primary mission of the application. In this case, more inherently reliable infrastructure reduces the cost of application reliability. In cases where the weaknesses of the infrastructure have not been compensated for within its client application, a more reliable infrastructure increases the reliability of the application.

- **New capabilities that are not currently feasible**: Sometimes, a revolutionary product emerges and stands out within a category of homogeneous competitors. A new feature with direct value for the clients of a service can be a compelling reason to switch. The first compute platform to offer auto-scaling or the first relational database that offered transaction log forwarding that could be used to maintain warm standbys and local read-only replicas were beneficial enough to attract many application systems to their infrastructure products.

- **Reduced GCP**: The infrastructure of an application comes at a price. This may be usage charges from a service provider, the cost of machine resources used to run open source or free software, or the combination of software license fees and the cost of machine resources. Regardless of the exact nature of the costs, in a competitive landscape, it is inevitable that some providers will undercut the typical price to gain market share. If the OpEx savings are significant, it is worthwhile to calculate the cost of a migration to see if a net savings exists and is large enough to justify the migration effort.

- **Forced exit**: A well-known cliché *all good things come to an end* can be true in business as much as anywhere else. In the case of software components, it is somewhat easier to terminate a product's lifespan as there is no physical artifact or remainder to worry about. A product can be discontinued for many reasons: sometimes, software that is perfectly good and useful for many is no longer a viable product, or perhaps the owning business has ceased operations, leaving a product in limbo. In some cases, regulatory bodies may order the cessation of a product's use in their jurisdiction. No matter why, there are cases where the usage of an infrastructure dependency must end. This is the most difficult migration scenario as the timeline is usually imposed on the client as an edict and there may not be an obvious, appealing alternative. In other words, the service being migrated from is well-known, but the service being migrated to is unidentified, and it is possible that a good option may not exist.

Let us suppose that our migration proposal is an exploratory one, based on the desire to reduce GCPs. Spanner is very capable but carries relatively high usage fees, albeit appropriate for a premium service. We will investigate if there are net savings to be had by migrating to another storage service within the GCP suite.

Collecting candidate replacements

The possibility of a migration, or in the case of a forced exit, the fact of an impending migration, triggers a surveying operation. The initial set of replacement candidates can be determined by lightweight research of feature claims and reviews, based on the requirements listed in the leftmost column.

The requirements worksheet, which was first presented in *Figure 13.1,* will now include the names of possible alternatives to our current persistence service, as seen in the following figure:

Application Requirement	Cloud SQL		AlloyDB		Bigtable	
	Effort	Notes	Effort	Notes	Effort	Notes
Multiple entity transactions						
Globally available datastore						
Fast single entity access						
Address a subset/range of entities						
Supports structured data						
Support for deep data						

Figure 13.5: Worksheet for persistence migration

The three sets of columns, one for each of the storage products under consideration, are to be filled in without comparison to the current product, Spanner, but rather in relation to each other. The Effort columns are meant to encode a ranking, and one may use a numeric scale, such as 1 to 5, or t-shirt sizes: Small, medium, and large. For this migration, we will use an effort grading of 1 through 5, where 1 is easy and 5 is the highest degree of effort. These grades are purely relative, and the breadth of the scale is meant to allow for sufficient distinction between the candidates. In the absence of other information or experience with the products, a 1-5 scale is a reasonable choice and can be collapsed or expanded later if it is found to be too coarse or if 5 degrees of precision is never needed.

Evaluation of the alternatives

The goal of the evolution is to determine the relative effort for satisfying each requirement, normalized both vertically, relative to other features, and horizontally, relative to that feature's solution in other products. This consistency in both dimensions may not be possible with high fidelity, and the relative effort of a specific feature across multiple products is a more important metric than that of features within a product's solution.

As a first example, the ability to provide transactions that include multiple entities is well supported in both Cloud SQL and AlloyDB. The effort required is not trivial, but is well understood, documented, and popularly used. We will assign this requirement an effort of 2 for both products. Multiple entity transactions in Bigtable are not natively supported, but can be implemented using locks implemented by the application and batched writes to group updates to different tables. This is a high-level of application complexity, although well documented prior art exists. We assign an effort of 5 for Bigtable's support of this requirement.

The migration worksheet now has the following contents:

Application Requirement	Cloud SQL		AlloyDB		Bigtable	
	Effort	Notes	Effort	Notes	Effort	Notes
Multiple entity transactions	2	Small amounts of code, common	2	Small amounts of code, common	5	Application coordinating logic needed
Globally available datastore						
Fast single entity access						
Address a subset/range of entities						
Supports structured data						
Support for deep data						

Figure 13.6: Persistence migration worksheet partially filled in

The same process of investigating how a requirement would be satisfied by a client of each of the three proposed storage services is then carried out for each remaining feature row in the worksheet. It is expected that a significant amount of research goes into each of these gradings, and the researchers should keep a good log of their work for posterity and later exposition. The worksheet is intentionally short, but that does not prevent the existence of easily accessed, copious notes elsewhere. Those notes will be valuable for the engineers who implement the chosen solution, as a guide for what features and usage patterns of the chosen infrastructure product were found to be appropriate choices for this use case.

We will not go through all iterations of the evaluation process but instead will provide the final worksheet:

Application Requirement	Cloud SQL		AlloyDB		Bigtable	
	Effort	Notes	Effort	Notes	Effort	Notes
Multiple entity transactions	2	Small amounts of code, common	2	Small amounts of code, common	5	Application coordinating logic needed
Globally available datastore	4	Application syncs of regional data	4	Application syncs of regional data	3	Eventual consistency features can distribute regional updates, application logic aggregates
Fast single entity access	1		1		1	
Address a subset/range of entities	1	SQL like operator can use existing indices	1	SQL like operator can use existing indices	2	Alternate index creation support
Supports structured data	2		2		1	Protobufs as column types
Support for deep data	3	Sub-relation tables	3	Sub-relation tables	1	Repeated/ARRAY fields

Figure 13.7: Final persistence migration worksheet

An initial observation is that the scores for the first two products—*Cloud SQL* and *AlloyDB*, are identical. This is expected; these are each service that are compatible with PostgreSQL, each with their own extensions and strengths, which are outside of the requirements we have identified. So, the transitive property of equality holds true, and these score equally on our worksheet. Other aspects of these services, such as product cost and specific performance, can be used to select between the two at a later stage of the evaluation.

With the individual features comparatively ranked across the three products, it is worth examining these to see if an easy decision presents itself: the presence of one product that requires the lowest effort in all features. Remember that the scores are effort, for which a lower score is preferable.

Our first evaluation is to see if one candidate is preferred for a majority of the requirements. Comparing AlloyDB and Bigtable, we see that Bigtable has a lower effort on 3 of the 6 requirements, with one requirement equivalent. This is not a clear and obvious win, being close to an even split between the 2, so we move on to a deeper evaluation.

This next stage assumes that the relative efforts between requirement rows are similar, by this we mean that the difference between an effort of 5 and an effort of 2 is roughly the same on different rows. If that is not the case, the evaluating team should attempt to re-score the efforts to normalize the efforts as much as possible.

With the relative scores normalized, we can see which product incurs the greatest relative effort. The delta between effort scores can be calculated from the worksheet and yields a table shown in the following figure:

Application Requirement	AlloyDB Effort	Bigtable Effort	Effort delta (AlloyDB - Bigtable)	(Bigtable - AlloyDB)
Multiple entity transactions	2	5		3
Globally available datastore	4	3	1	
Fast single entity access	1	1		
Address a subset/range of entities	1	2		1
Supports structured data	2	1	1	
Support for deep data	3	1	2	

Figure 13.8: Table of persistence migration effort deltas

The preceding figure shows the relative cost of the more expensive candidate for each requirement. We can see that Bigtable's implementation of multiple entity transactions is the greatest cost of either candidate over the other. However, the total cost delta is the same for each candidate: $(1+1+2) == 4 == (3+1)$

This is where knowledge of the application itself can be applied. The engineers who work on the application can determine if the advantage gained by Bigtable's support for repeated fields outweighs the simpler multiple entity transaction implementation offered by AlloyDB, these being the 2 largest differences in relative effort.

Going through the database usage, the engineering team determines that the replacement of repeated fields with a separate related table is a relatively straightforward feature for them to implement, while implementing the required transaction semantics is a larger effort and harder to test and verify. So, the decision is made to explore a migration to either AlloyDB or Cloud SQL, remembering that these products had equivalent scores in the migration requirements worksheet.

Choosing between the two products, which have been equivalent thus far, requires examination of aspects of the products that distinguish them from each other. Since these are two products sold by the same vendor, we can rely on vendor recommendations for each product's ideal use cases. Some of the comparison points offered by Google are as follows:

- Both products are described as fully managed, and we can infer that neither incurs a significantly higher operational burden than the other.

- AlloyDB offers higher performance and scalability than Cloud SQL, but it is unclear if our application's workload exceeds the comfort zone of Cloud SQL.

- AlloyDB offers advanced analytical capabilities, which are not relevant to our use of the database.

- Cloud SQL is cited as being cost-effective. We can translate that to mean that the usage charges of Cloud SQL are significantly less.

This list leaves us with two questions to answer:

- How much more will AlloyDB cost us to use?
- Is our workload large enough to benefit from AlloyDB's superior performance?

For the first question, the relative cost can be answered through the application of a pricing calculator for each service to our expected usage. Total storage, instance counts, and read and write operations are all values we can model for a migration, based on observed usage, projected demand, and the proposed service architecture.

For the second question, the benefit of AlloyDB is one that weighs or balances against the first question, relative cost. It is a given that the AlloyDB service costs more than the same usage of Cloud SQL, but is that additional cost worth the advantages offered by AlloyDB.

Calculating database service cost

We will work through the cost calculations for both AlloyDB and for Cloud SQL as a way to develop an understanding of the factors and processes. Google Cloud offers online pricing calculators that are kept up to date and should be considered the source of truth for actual fees associated with the products' usage. Each of these products offers add-on features such as automatic backups and snapshots that may incur fees and should be considered in the final cost of each product.

Calculating values for AlloyDB cost factors

The first cost factor to determine is database size, that is, the number of gigabytes stored per month. We can calculate costs on an hourly basis, but our data is not very large, and the more complex per-hour calculations will not save much in storage charges. We will provide resource estimates for the size of a voting database cluster, of which there will be one instance per cluster, and then one additional instance for our aggregated global voting results. As neither AlloyDB nor Cloud SQL provides a unified global database like Spanner, our engineering team has designed a series of regional databases that are updated by Vote Processors and an additional global database instance that will contain the aggregated votes from the regional databases.

The size of all database instances will be nearly identical, as the same acts are represented, just with different vote tallies.

The size of a database row in the votes table is just under 128 bytes with an index entry. A row in the votebudget table and associated rows in a new sub-table to hold the voted acts details, with indices, is estimated to occupy under 1,024 bytes.

The number of rows in the votes table is capped at the number of acts and rounds, which was illustrated by *Figure 8.1* in *Chapter 8, Making a Voting System Available and Reliable* . Based on that discussion, the number of rows in the votes table for a complete competition will be *7*12* or *84* rows.

The votebudget table will have one row for each voting user and round. There are seven rounds, and *Figure 8.3* in *Chapter 8, Making a Voting System Available and Reliable,* estimates our total user count to be 57 million. Let us suppose that usage has shown 40 million users to date, but with a slowly increasing count week over week. It is decided that 50 million users is a realistic expectation for this season's user community.

The calculation of database size using the preceding factors reports that each instance should be expected to contain 330 gigabytes of data at the end of a season.

The next cost factor we will consider is that of network traffic in and out of the database.

Data transfer into AlloyDB is free, or rather, incurs no separate charge. Data transfer out of AlloyDB between regions is charged based on the source and destination regions. Our proposed architecture includes synchronization from each regional database cluster to one global cluster, following each round. There are five planned regional deployments, one of which will be in the same region as the global database. This expands out to each rounds' votes data being sent from four regions to a fifth region throughout the season. Another way to express this is that each of the four regions will send its entire database contents to the 5th region once over the course of the season.

Our billable network traffic per season is *330 GB * 4 = 1.3TB*, shipped between regions.

The third and final AlloyDB cost factor is that for CPU and memory, compute resources. AlloyDB instances are of a specified number of CPUs and memory, which is what you are billed for. AlloyDB offers long-term compute usage discounts for 1 and 3-year commitments, from which we will commit to 1-year. Based on AlloyDB sizing documentation suggestions, we will initially configure each regional instance to have 1 compute node of 64 GB of RAM and 8 CPUs and the global instance to have one node with the same provisions. This deployment configuration includes a total of 6 nodes of 64 GB of RAM and 8 CPUs in various regions.

Calculating the costs of all alternatives

Completion of the cost analysis requires us to perform the same process as described previously for every competing product in the current use case, that is Cloud SQL with a PostgreSQL backend.

When calculating the cost of the alternatives, each product must be examined and have its cost calculated separately from the others. The cost model for Cloud SQL does not have a direct 1:1 mapping of cost factors, so the examination of the pricing calculator and fee schedule for Cloud SQL is needed. Additionally, our deployment configuration of Cloud SQL is not identical to the proposed architecture for an AlloyDB solution. For example, our Cloud SQL architecture 3 includes additional replicas for log forwarding and vote aggregation.

Calculating costs of all alternatives

Once we have fully explored the cost of our Cloud SQL architecture, we find that the cost of our proposed AlloyDB solution by the fees at the time of writing is $11,000 (USD) for a 1-month voting period. This is with applying discounts for committed use in the pricing model.

The cost of our Cloud SQL proposal is $6,000 (USD) and an estimated 2 additional weeks of engineering time.

The decision is made that we have an additional $5,000 (USD) and that the development and operations teams will already be facing a challenging workload without the additional 2 weeks of work.

AlloyDB is the more cost-effective of the two proposed migration replacements for Spanner.

Re-evaluation of the migration decision

When this exercise began, it was declared to be exploratory based on the presumed relatively high cost of the Spanner service. Our Spanner deployment is a multi-region global database for which we subscribed to the Spanner Enterprise edition.

The cost of operating our Spanner database, including the inter-region replication is $8,700 (USD) for the 1-month voting period. While Spanner might carry higher charges, the cost of duplicating its global distributed features in a regional product such as AlloyDB are higher than the cost of using Spanner to achieve the same results. We could save $2,700 per season by migrating to Cloud SQL, but at the cost of 2 weeks of engineering time. Our senior leadership points out that at current staff costs, it would take 6 seasons for the reduced GCP to offset 2 weeks of our engineering and operations staff time.

The migration will not take place, for well-understood and documented reasons. Spanner is the most technically appropriate and cost-effective storage product for the voting application.

Construction of a migration plan

While the outcome of this migration proposal was to do nothing, we will author, schedule, and perform a rehearsal of the proposed operational infrastructure migration. The exercise is valuable as it is nearly inevitable that another situation will arise where either the motivating factors are more critical or perhaps the cost savings are more significant.

An effective way to view an infrastructure migration is as a refactoring. Refactoring code is the rearrangement of the implementation to achieve a more efficient or desirable (by some metric) internal structure without altering the behavior of the refactored module. This definition can be applied almost directly to the sort of service or dependency migration we are describing. The goal is to deliver the same end-product with an altered internal structure, which is superior by criteria that are invisible to the end users of the system.

Based on this definition, we can assert that a successful infrastructure migration is one that is unnoticed by the world beyond the engineering team and maintains and operates the system. End users and even internal product and marketing teams should not see any change to the application system's behavior, features, or user contracts.

Some strategic guidelines for executing a successful migration follow and will be expanded upon in the remainder of this section:

- Hope for the best, plan for the worst
- Choose the least disruptive migration time and place
- Roll out and observe your new configuration gradually
- Do not abandon the old system prematurely
- Have a full fallback plan

The first point, hope for the best, plan for the worst, is an overarching principle that pervades the entire exercise, including the points that follow. Hope for and expect the best. If you plan well, leaving no unresolved mysteries or unknowns, and provide enough resources to do every task on your list well, you should expect everything to go according to plan.

However, the world is complex, and our attention, awareness, and foresight are limited. Complex systems behave in unexpected ways, and the environment often presents situations and inputs that even the best plan failed to anticipate. This is a bigger challenge than any negative factor that we address in our plan. How do you plan a reaction to an unknown? The answer is simple to state, although the actual response may be far from simple. Plan for the worst. The following are a set of questions that your migration plan should answer:

- What will you do if the system throws generic server errors with no useful details once the new components are deployed?
- How will you detect that such errors are being thrown as soon as possible?
- What will you do if your response to the errors does not fix the problem?

Often, a responsible response to these unknowns includes a first action of notifying or escalating. If your database migration was expected to have no more effect than an hour of degraded service on a Sunday evening, but a full outage or a protracted effect is either in progress or expected, make sure that the chain of command is informed. While it is bad for a publicly visible service to be offline, it is far worse for the CEO of the company to find out about the outage on social media or from a reporter. Make sure that the operations lead for the migration has a list of phone numbers and email addresses to send either the celebratory all done, working as intended or we have a problem message to.

The next section will describe the last four items from the preceding list of strategic guidelines in this section, the guidelines that minimize potential impact and provide a path for the migration team to follow.

Changing the tires while the bus is moving

A process of modifying a system that is in use is colloquially likened to changing the tires while the bus is moving. The analogy is as relevant as it is obvious. Imagine a bus with passengers that is driving to its destination. Without disrupting the bus service or missing its schedule, you must replace a tire. This sounds identical in demand and in impact to changing a database provider while a system is running and processing user requests.

We will continue to use this analogy in the discussions for the three strategic guidelines for a migration plan that were listed in the preceding section:

- **Choose the least disruptive migration time and place**: If you could choose the time and locale at which you would change your bus's tires, it would be when there are the fewest people on the bus and when the roads are smoothest and offer the fewest distractions such as traffic lights and intersections. In our use case, this would be when user activity is relatively low and there are few competing events such as system maintenance, offline processing pipeline activity, or IMs from the product team. The reasons for this are twofold. First, we can assume that during the process of switching over from the old infrastructure to the new, tasks will be starting up, and the operations lead will want to collect activity logs and traces to monitor the process. The new task startup will perform better if demand gradually ramps up so that features like auto-scaling can take effect. Ramping up demand implies a relatively low starting point. The second reason is risk mitigation. Simply put, it is better to fail 10 requests than it is to fail 1,000 requests.

  It will also be much easier to recognize and deal with emergent issues if there are fewer other inputs, such as other maintenance processes executing or competing for the operations team's attention.

- **Roll out and observe your new configuration gradually**: This is a recommended practice for all software releases, but with a change as potentially impactful as an infrastructure replacement, this practice should be elevated from a suggestion to mandatory. Referred to as canarying.

  Note: **The reader can Google the term to learn its unpleasant origin.**

  This practice makes the change on some small subdivision of the deployed system, such as one region or one Vote Processor out of many. The changed portion of the system is then allowed to bake in the change for a period and observed closely. If the new components perform well, the scope of the change is increased, and a similar wait-and-see period is maintained. As the new components continue to work as expected, the change is rolled out to the entire system. If the new components raise any surprises, load balancers can redirect user traffic away from the affected components to their counterparts running the previous software, and the change can be examined and mitigated in the affected portions of the system. In a case like ours, where the migration results in different datastores, a post-migration reconciliation plan is needed to merge the updates to the previous datastore with the new one.

- **Do not abandon the old system prematurely**: Do not take the first sign of success as a sure sign that the new system is completely ready and that the previous working system components will never be needed again. The bolts that held the old tires in place have stood the test of time. The nuts and bolts that come with the new tire are untried and may become loose over time due to the vibrations of use and you will want to transplant the old restraining nuts to the new tires. In the storage service case, there might be configuration details that were missed, transaction logs with later useful information or you may wish to use the previous component as part of an A/B test if it becomes necessary to debug unexpected behavior in the new system. In another, more severe case, you may regret discarding the old component if you find you need it again, as described in the following bullet point.

- **Have a full fallback plan**: The top mantra of an incident commander during an outage of a production system is very direct: Save the user a serving system should not double as a laboratory, and if a new implementation does not work, responsible incident management prioritizes getting the system running for the users. If the reasons for the failure are not obvious and rapidly fixed, roll back and debug later. The ability to roll back is predicated on your preserving the old system configuration and dependencies in a state that can quickly and simply be brought back into active service.

Imagine if you replace a balding tire, which was worn but still bearing the weight of the bus, with a new shiny tire of the latest material, and after a few miles, the new tire starts hissing as it rapidly leaks air, or worse, the new tire pops. The old tire was better than no tire, and preparation for this scenario requires you to have put aside the old tire and all of its needed attachments and accessories, without deflating it. You can find the leak in the new tire and patch it later, not while it is attached to the axle, and your passengers' safety is dependent on it.

Designing the migration of a datastore codelab

This chapter's codelab will be a walkthrough of a migration plan for switching the voting application from Spanner to AlloyDB. This plan does not go into the details of the code or configuration file changes, nor does it examine the implementation details of migration tools written for use during this procedure. All of those changes would have been reviewed, tested and approved previously. This plan is an operator's guide, a script for the people who are executing the migration itself.

The migration script

The first part of the plan is a statement of intent and the assignment of roles:

- **Goal of the operation**: To convert voting application frontends and backends to use a set of AlloyDB regional databases talentvoting-local and global database talentvoting-global instead of the Spanner instance talentvoting-instance.

- **Canarying plan**: First, the *South America* regional tasks will be updated. A canary period of 3 hours will be observed, after which time a go/no-go decision will be made for updating the *Western European* regional tasks. After another hour of canarying the Western European tasks, a final go/no-go decision will be made for global deployment.

- **Rollback plan**: If errors are observed during either canary period, both canary regions will be drained of user traffic. South America regional requests will be redirected to the *North America* frontends, and *Western Europe* requests will be redirected to *Eastern Europe* frontends.

- **Migration team**: The migration will be executed by two engineers, working in tandem. The operations lead holds primary responsibility for executing the steps of the migration, and the communications lead holds responsibility for updating the identified communication channels and stakeholders with progress updates and being available for inquiries.

  o **Operations lead**: Joëlle Lin jlin@nonesuch.com, +1555-555-5555

  o **Communications lead**: Raymond Blum raymundo@nonesuch.com, +1555-555-3333

The next section is a checklist of resources to be identified before the operation begins:

- **Prerequisites**:

  Scripts:

  ☐ Script for switching South America Vote Processor and voting frontend to new versions

  ☐ Script for configuring redirects of South America frontends to North America frontends

  ☐ Script for synchronizing AlloyDB datastores from Spanner data after a Vote Processor cutover

  ☐ Script for switching Western Europe Vote Processor and voting frontend to new versions

  ☐ Script for configuring redirects of Western Europe frontends to Eastern Europe frontends

Monitoring:

☐ Dashboard showing voting frontend requests by version and response status for South America and North America

☐ Dashboard showing voting frontend requests by version and response status for South America and North America

☐ Dashboard showing voting frontend requests by version and response status for all regions

☐ Dashboard showing Vote Processor requests by version and response status for South America and North America

☐ Dashboard showing Vote Processor requests by version and response status for South America and North America

☐ Dashboard showing Vote Processor requests by version and response status for all regions

☐ Alert for voting frontend increased error rate for South America and North America

☐ Alert for Vote Processor increased error rate for South America and North America

☐ Alert for voting frontend increased error rate for Western Europe and Eastern Europe

☐ Alert for Vote Processor increased error rate for Western Europe and Eastern Europe

Contacts (fill in list addresses):

o   E-mail and SMS list for outage notification: _____

o   E-mail list for regular progress updates: _____

Versions (fill in version labels):

o   Old version label for voting frontend: _____

o   New version label for voting frontend: _____

o   Old version label for Vote Processor: _____

o   New version label for Vote Processor: _____

- **Permissions**: Confirm operations lead account has the admin role for the following:

  ☐ Vote Processor in SA, NA, Eastern Eu and Western Eu regions

  ☐ Voting frontend in SA, NA, Eastern Eu and Western Eu regions

☐ votes Pub/Sub topic, votes-sub Pub/Sub subscription in SA, NA, Eastern Eu and Western Eu regions

The next section is the sequence of operations, to be followed and checked off with times as completed:

- **Migration script:**
  - **Time done/action:**
    - _____/walkthrough of entire document by operations and comms lead.
    - _____/prerequisite checklist by operations and comms lead.
    - _____/send commencement msg by comms lead.
    - _____/switch SA tasks to new version by operations lead.
    - _____/check dashboard for SA/NA voting frontend to confirm request switch to new version by operations lead.
    - _____/check dashboard for SA/NA Vote Processor to confirm request switch to new version by operations lead.
    - _____/confirm successful switch of traffic, beginning of initial canary period by operations lead, comms lead.
    - _____/confirm successful synchronization of data from Spanner to AlloyDB by operations lead, comms lead.

      _____/send canary progress msg by comms lead.
    - _____/check SA/NA voting frontend dashboard for flat error rate at one hour into canary by operations lead.
    - _____/check SA/NA Vote Processor dashboard for flat error rate at one hour into canary by operations lead.
  - Wait for end of 3-hour initial canary period.
    - _____/check SA/NA Vote Processor dashboard for flat error rate, flat response rate at end of initial canary by operations lead.
    - _____/check SA/NA Vote Processor dashboard for flat error rate, flat response rate at end of initial canary by operations lead.
    - _____/declare go/no-go decision for second canary by operations lead, comms lead.
    - _____/send progress msg by comms lead.

The script continues similarly through the end of the second canary and a global rollout.

Being ready for the worst

The next section is where we address the *plan for the worst* principle discussed earlier:

- **Failure modes:**
  - Elevated errors in voting frontend or Vote Processor during first canary
  - **Time done/action:**
    - _____/ set 10 minutes watchdog timer by comms lead.
    - _____/ send notification of failure to escalation list and progress list by comms lead.
    - _____/ check logs for obvious errors and remedy by operations lead, comms lead.
    - _____/ at 10 min watchdog timer by comms lead (or earlier by operations lead).
    - Execute rollback of Vote Processor to previous version by operations lead.
    - Execute rollback of voting frontend to previous version by operations lead.
    - _____/ send notification of rollback to escalation list and progress list by comms lead.
    - _____/ check SA/NA voting frontend dashboard for return to flat error rate and old version serving requests following rollback by operations lead.
    - _____/ check SA/NA Vote Processor dashboard for return to flat error rate and old version serving requests following rollback by operations lead.
    - _____/ send notification of successful rollback or not to escalation list and progress list by comms lead.

There will be additional similar sections to address failures in the second canary, failures in the post-canary global rollout, and failures in the rollbacks.

An important concept is that of a checklist. Like pilots and surgeons in their critical work, the migration staff should be as explicit and finely grained as possible in their roles and actions. Confirmation of every step is required via a check, initials or such acknowledgement.

Conclusion

The suitability of a particular infrastructure service can change over time. What was once the best fit for an application system's needs may be eclipsed by new competition, obsoleted by changing requirements or deprecated by the provider. Change is inevitable, and we can plan for it and ease our system's adaptation by following design principles that have been described throughout this book.

This chapter discussed the advantages of viewing dependencies as a black box, consisting only of the required effects and the available inputs. A worksheet and process for evaluating dependencies was exercised through two examples from our voting application.

Finally, the principles and a template for executing a storage service migration, free of surprises was described and then illustrated in the codelab for this chapter.

The next chapter presents the voting application as a specific manifestation of more generic business systems and then examines the adaptation of much of the voting application to another specific instance of that abstraction.

Join our Discord space

Join our Discord workspace for latest updates, offers, tech happenings around the world, new releases, and sessions with the authors:

https://discord.bpbonline.com

CHAPTER 14

Voting System as a Reference Implementation

Introduction

In this chapter, voting is a more generally applicable application than most people think. Many applications are a variation of the basic model of an application to register interest in <m> of <n> options and then ranking the popularity of the <n> options to apply to some next stage of processing.

Beyond the applicability of a voting system, thanks to our isolation of responsibilities and containing dependencies, our foundational services can be used as a model for equivalent tiers in applications whose products bear no resemblance to voting at all.

Structure

The following topics will be covered in this chapter:

- Voting systems in business

- Highly scalable request processor case study

- Final thoughts on generic roles

Objectives

The final chapter examines these two extensions of our voting system: The similarity to another business application and the application of one of our foundational tiers to an unrelated product with similar infrastructure requirements. The reader will be presented with insight of how general smaller problems are connected to solve a specific business problem. The reader will learn how a generic technical mechanism can be applied to implement highly dissimilar features in a variety of applications.

By the end of this chapter and the conclusion of the book, the reader will be shown the opportunity for reuse of both the function and the form of the voting application. By reuse of function, it is meant that the solution can be applied to different problems. The form of the application being reused refers to the extraction and use of individual discrete subsystems and components as parts of solutions that bear no resemblance or relevance to a voting application.

Voting systems in business

The first type of reuse that we will discuss is the application of our solution's form to similar problems. There are many examples of systems that go by different names but can be considered a voting system, or that have largely the same goals and face the same challenges as a voting system.

First, we will start with basic principles, what is meant by the word vote.

A popular dictionary gives two definitions, as different parts of speech:

- **Noun**: A formal indication of a choice between two or more candidates or courses of action.
- **Verb**: Give or register a vote.

A voting system is the process and mechanisms used to perform the act of voting.

Systems, which can be classified as voting systems, can be easily identified by their application. Political systems that are democracies rely on some form of voting to determine the will of the people. Popularity contests, such as the online talent voting system that is the focus of this book, are clearly voting systems. However, these are specific applications of voting, ones in which the aggregation of the votes is the ultimate goal. Examining the definition of vote, there is no stipulation that the goal is to determine the popularity of the candidates, just that the choice between candidates is recorded.

Unrecognized voting applications

With the previous definition of voting in mind, there are other use cases that can be explored as possibly being categorized as voting applications. A few of these will be presented here, with the rationale for the reader to consider their being classified as a voting exercise.

The practice of ordering *à la carte* from a restaurant's menu is an indication of which appetizer, main dish, side dishes, and dessert each diner prefers. This is directly analogous to the indication of a preferred mayor, body of councilpersons, and county executive in a local political election.

There are additional considerations in this example, the most significant of which is the budget. While it is a victory for one candidate to receive an overwhelming majority of the votes in a political election, it is very likely to be problematic if every diner orders the same main course in a restaurant. The ingredients that are required to carry out the effects of those diners' votes (aka orders) may not be sufficiently provisioned to feed every patron at the same mealtime. So, while there is no per-vote cost to a mayoral candidate, a restaurant has a per-order inventory to consider. This is typically handled by decisions and rules unique to the system, for example, declaring voting for a specific candidate closed when popularity passes some threshold.

Another common application that overlaps with voting is that of registration for an online or virtual event. The users register their interest in participating and provide an email address at which they will receive an invitation to join the event. This example is closer to the classic political voting application, as there is no supply of ingredients to be exhausted, but it is different from both previous examples, as the candidates are the users' email addresses: The candidates are the voters themselves.

Commonly seen voting applications

Not all instances of a voting system pattern are as subtle as the examples given previously. In business and society at large, there are many times when the distribution of preference is gathered to be used as a factor in choosing a course of action.

Online surveys are available as standalone applications such as *SurveyMonkey*, as separate tools coupled to other collaboration tools, for example, the discontinued *Google Moderator*, or as embedded features like the *Poll* app in *Google Chat*. People often conduct votes without using a dedicated voting application, such as a group text message, *Hey everyone—pizza, dosa or onigiri for lunch?* This can work because with a small enough group, there is less need for a structured voting system: The responses from five people regarding their lunch preferences is easy to see and tally, but if the call for food preference was going out to 50 or 200 people, you had need an application to keep track of the votes for you.

In many matters of business protocol and regulation, voting is required to be controlled and auditable. Shareholder resolutions in publicly traded companies, choosing a board of directors, and advisory voting on executive compensation are all issues where varying degrees of regulation govern different business sectors but all require that the voting be conducted in an approved and secure fashion.

Deriving a similar voting application

Let us examine the adaptation of our voting system to one of the more dissimilar applications described previously, the ordering of dishes in a restaurant. The online talent voting system made several entities visible to the end user, and in the least-effort adaptation of our system, these entities have direct counterparts. The following table presents analogous entities in the two problem domains:

Online talent voting		A la carte ordering	
Entity	Description	Entity	Description
Round	The set of acts that can be selected from for voting	Meal	The set of dishes that can be ordered in the same window of time: i.e. Breakfast, brunch, dinner
Act	An act that can be selected as prefered by a voter	Dish	An item that can be selected as prefered by a diner
Vote	Selection of an act in a round by a voter	Order	Selection of a dish in a meal by a diner
Vote budget	The maximum number of acts that a voter may vote for in the context of a round	Preparation capacity	The maximum number of orders for a given dish that can be accepted in the context of a meal
Voter	A participant in the voting process - one who creates votes	Diner	A presumed consumer of a meal - one who creates orders

Figure 14.1: Parallels in voting and ordering

While there are analogies for the significant entities in the two applications, we can see in the descriptions that it is not a direct, perfect mapping. The most obvious difference is between the vote budget and the preparation capacity. While these are similar in that they impose a constraint on the number of orders that can be placed, those limits are centered on different parties in the order. A vote budget is associated with a voter; we limit the number of votes that a voter can cast in each round. In addition, the voting policy enforces that a voter may only cast one vote for a specific act in a round. On the other hand, a diner may order as many of a given dish as they like, but there is a limit to how many orders for that dish, which is the counterpart to an act, can be prepared during a meal due to a limited amount of ingredients and limited available preparation equipment and staff. These differences do not break the analogy but do highlight the value of containing policy logic to specific components. We can create a clone of our voting system implementation and then apply relatively straightforward refactoring to map the entities and relationships from the original application to the new one. Separately, the business logic that requires the greatest attention in the new application can be the subject of its own requirements, design, and implementation cycle. Since we know the location of this logic in the codebase, in the policy engine package, we can independently pursue these two sub-projects with relatively high confidence in their isolation.

Reuse of voting system components

As well as adapting our voting system to other use cases with a strong degree of similarity, as we have discussed previously, there is another level of granularity in reuse to take advantage of. The principle of black box specification and design produces modules, which have well-defined boundaries and contracts with their partners, whether those are clients or suppliers. When teamed up with the isolation of business logic to separate modules, this produces components with a high potential for reuse.

The reuse of a system can be at a higher level than the actual implementation. In the previous example, which derives a menu ordering system from our online voting application, the reuse is of the architecture and design, rather than implementation-specific artifacts such as code or configuration settings. Reuse at these higher levels can be as profitable or more so than the reuse of a piece of JavaScript code or a Python class.

Just as the reuse of a system can be realized at many stages of development, the reuse of components outside of their role in the original system yields great benefit at different development stages.

Design pattern reuse

The application of a design pattern is eased when a reference implementation is available and relevant. Many example implementations are excellent at illustrating the concepts behind a design pattern, but can be difficult to use as a starting point for implementation. The reasons for this difficulty vary greatly, but it is most often due to a divergence between the example's presumed environment and dependencies and those in use by the local developer. If a reference implementation for a design pattern exists in the developer's local codebase, is in use, and is able to be deployed, the difficulties presented by the environment go away.

Let us look at a specific case for component reuse for which the voting application provides an excellent reference implementation from which other implementations could easily be created. We will start out with a new problem definition and then discuss the existing voting system component whose design pattern applies to the new problem.

Need for classifiers and class-specific processors

We will discuss the design of an ideal, or hypothetical, model for a speech processing application that is highly latency sensitive. Specifically, we will be designing a real-time speech transcription application for mobile devices: One that captures audio from a microphone and converts the heard speech to text with very low-latency.

A major requirement is the need for consistent responsiveness, that is, the application should always complete transcription within a consistent window of time after the speech is heard. Allowing no intermittent pauses or transcription backlogs rules out sending the audio on a round trip to a cloud-based service, as the bandwidth of a mobile connection is unreliable and inconsistent.

The initial design for our application calls for a language and dialect-specific module to be used to tag sets of phonemes as words. There is a library available to us that includes several dozen such **Tokenizer** modules, each specific to a regional or cultural dialect. These modules all implement the same **application programming interface (API)**, and so we could call any one of them interchangeably.

A second requirement of our application is the ability to automatically identify the language being heard. The same library that provides the specific Tokenizers also includes a classifier, a module that can ingest an audio stream and output a set of languages and dialects that are likely to be in use, with confidence ratings for each. The typical use of these is to feed audio to the classifier until it identifies a candidate language/dialect with a high likelihood. Once that is done, the same and subsequent audio is fed to the transcriber, which is set to use the **Tokenizer** for that language/dialect.

This model introduces an initial delay in transcription while the classifier works, but a startup delay incurring a potential one-time per session exceeding our 200ms latency target is considered acceptable.

The design seems to be complete and robust. The following class and sequence diagrams illustrate the modules involved and their interaction:

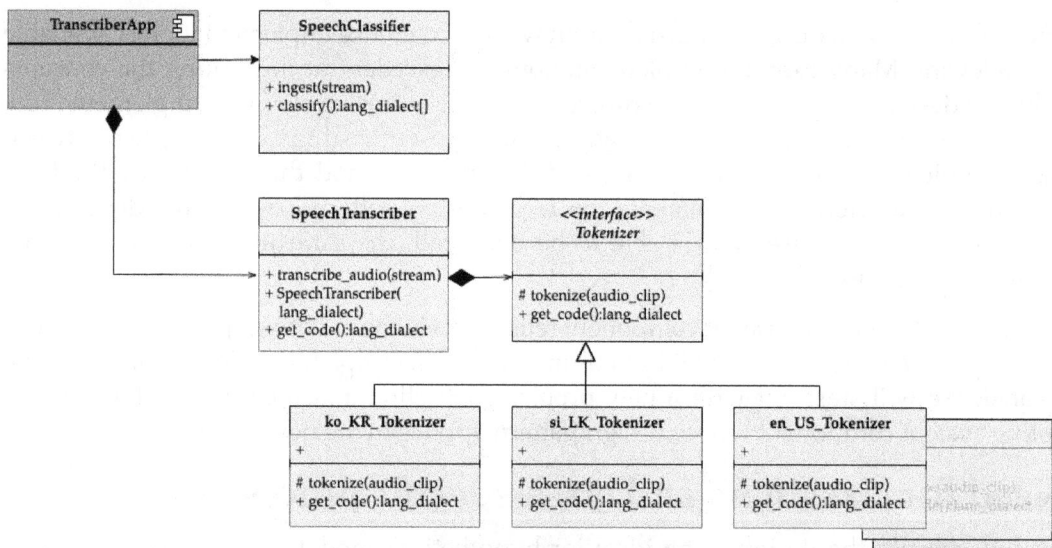

Figure 14.2: Speech transcription class diagram

This class diagram illustrates the relevant modules and relationships from the preceding discussion. Our **TranscriberApp** application makes direct use of a **SpeechClassifier** and a **SpeechTranscriber**. A **SpeechTranscriber** requires an instance of **Tokenizer** subclass. The diagram shows a few specific **Tokenizer** classes with an elided reference to many more.

With those components identified, the following figure illustrates their interactions:

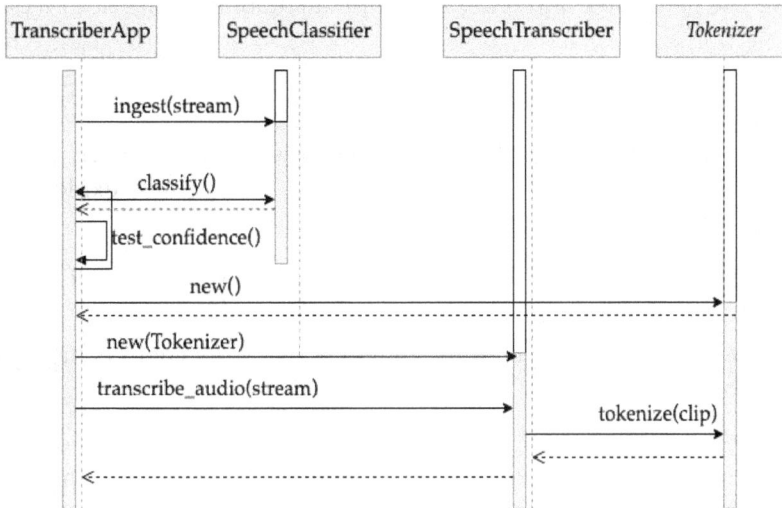

Figure 14.3: *Speech transcription sequence diagram*

The figure illustrates that a **SpeechClassifier** is used and finished with before a **SpeechTranscriber** is created. This is necessary since a dependency of creating a **SpeechTranscriber**, a language and dialect code, is obtained from the **SpeechClassifier**.

As was said previously, the design seems consistent and addresses our requirements. This is a premature conclusion, as we will see in the following section that one of our requirements cannot be met.

Let us address the need to have many alternatives available when only one will be needed.

The problem with this design is the size of the runtime footprint of the entire implementation. As we have said, there are dozens or hundreds of specific language and dialect combinations that the application might have to support. This implies having an equally large number of the **Tokenizer** implementations available at runtime, when only one will actually be needed at a time. If we assume that a **Tokenizer** implementation is large in terms of number of bytes, the runtime footprint of our application balloons past a workable size.

One solution to this problem is to dynamically instantiate only the **Tokenizer** that is needed for the language that has been identified. We have implemented a feature in the voting application that can be adapted to solve this problem. The voting client application fetched the body of an executable function from the server to locally execute voting policy. The same general mechanism that fetches and installs local logic from a trusted source can be used to fetch and install the specific **Tokenizer** for our current language and dialect. In the case of a platform that prevents the execution of any remotely originated code, the logic can be encoded in an interpreted grammar or rules language and evaluated by an embedded interpreter that loads the rules of the specific **Tokenizer** from a remote source.

We have reused a design pattern, which is their nature, and through straightforward refactoring, we can genericize and reuse our implementation of that design pattern in our codebase.

Optimizing the design for performance

This dynamic code installation will incur an increased startup delay, which has been accepted as within the bounds of our requirements. We can also exploit some known aspects of this use case to improve performance.

1. Most clients are used to transcribing only a small number (1 or 2) of language/dialects.

2. The most recently encountered language/dialect on a client is highly likely to be the next one as well.

With these usage patterns in mind, we can introduce a local cache on the client of the most recently used two specific **Tokenizers** and check that cache before fetching a **Tokenizer** from the server. With this in place, our transcriber can handle any supported language and dialect and only transfers a Tokenizer once or twice on most clients.

The class and sequence diagram for this modified design are shown in the following figure:

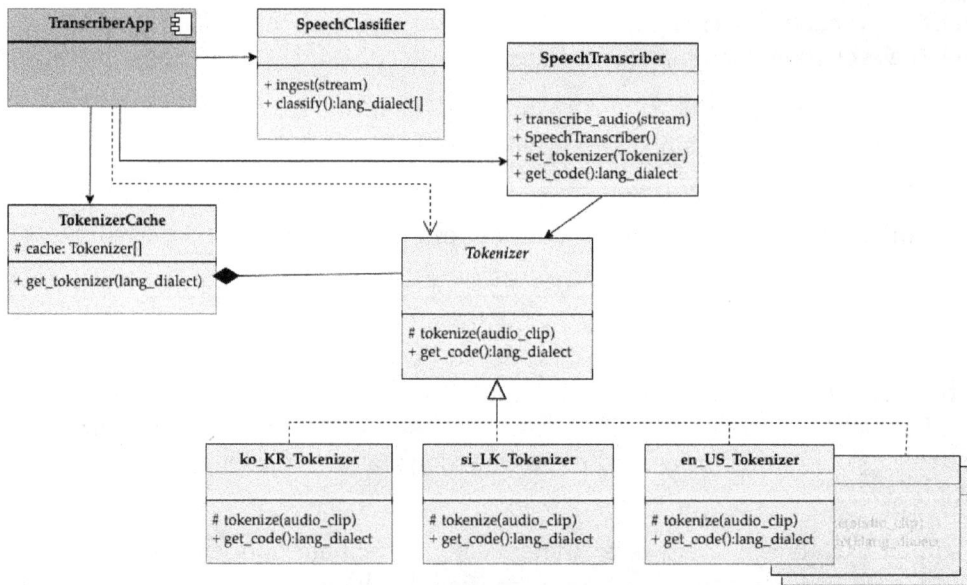

Figure 14.4: Caching speech transcription class diagram

This updated class diagram shows the introduction of a **TokenizerCache** between the **TranscriberApp** and the **Tokenizer** class hierarchy. Rather than holding any number of class definitions and static definitions of **Tokenizer** subclasses, the **TranscriberApp** now holds a reference to a single **TokenizerCache**, which manages the **Tokenizer** classes on the client.

Not included in the class diagram is a cloud-based service that returns a specific implementation of a **Tokenizer**, similarly to how the *PolicyEngine* delivers an executable function to a remote client. This is a method of a REST API and is shown in the accompanying sequence diagram.

The following figure is the sequence diagram for our new design:

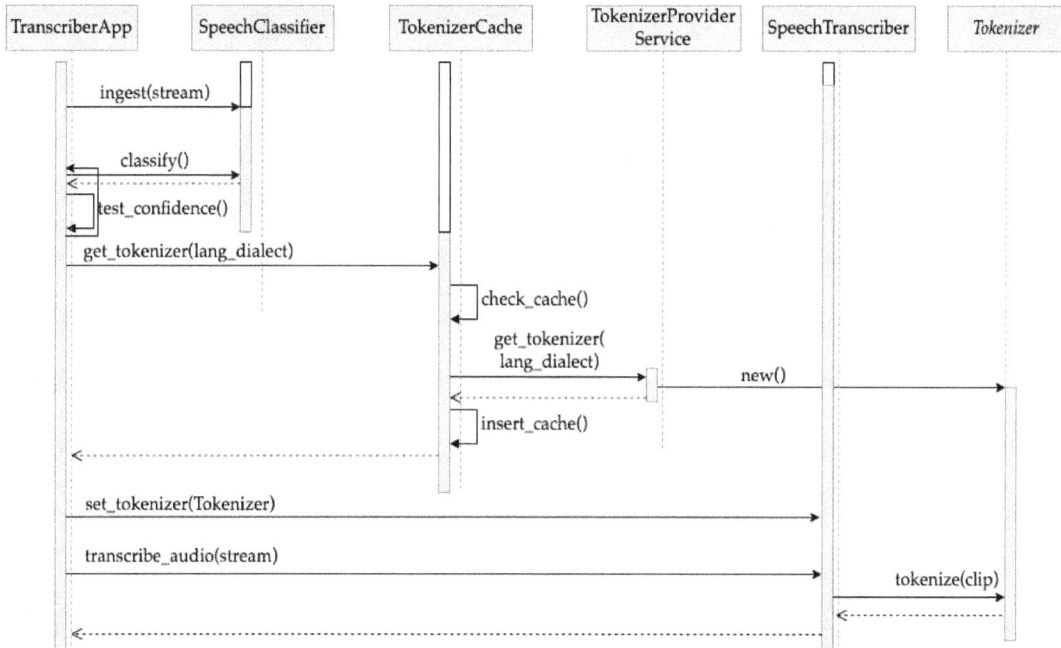

Figure 14.5: Caching speech transcription sequence diagram

The preceding sequence figure illustrates the worst-case scenario use of the **TokenizerCache**, one in which a **Tokenizer** for the requested language-dialect combination is not already in the cache. In most clients' usage, this will be a one-time situation, but it is shown here as the most complete illustration of the involved components.

We have explored the reuse of the voting system assets in several ways and at different levels of reuse. The application itself can be seen in more general terms and either refactored to allow sharing among derived applications or cloned and modified into new applications. When we see the opportunity to apply a design pattern that we have implemented in the voting system in a new application, the voting implementation of that design pattern can be used either as a template or generalized to cover the new use case. Reuse is not limited to code reuse; the application of existing architectures or design knowledge is equally valuable. Any well-designed software system is a valuable resource as prior art for new work if the similarities are recognized.

Highly scalable request processor case study

One issue of contention that emerged from the requirements of the voting application was the requirement for low-latency responses to the voting requests on the client in unison with the need to apply coordinated updates to global-scale datastores to fulfill those client requests. The tension here arose from these requirements being imposed from two very different points of view: The client sees only their own action, the vote that they cast, while the system does not distinguish any one client; but sees a set of database transactions from many sources, all of which must be completed with equal priority and reliability.

The solution that was designed centered around the fact that the urgency of the client was to have their action recorded, that is, for the request itself to be durable, not for it to be completed. The complementary point of view is that the system overall attributes no inherent urgency to any individual request, just an important requirement to fulfill all requests.

This is a common set of requirements: The need for immediate guarantees of eventual consistency. There are systems where the requirement for consistent and final resolution of the system's state is urgent, but these are relatively rare and typically occur in highly specialized domains such as medical applications, real-time systems control, and crisis management and response systems. The *Eisenhower* principle of *the urgent are not important, and the important are never urgent* holds true for most business and social situations.

Generic worker design pattern

The design of our **voteprocessor** backend and its source of work, the votes-sub Pub/Sub subscription is a variation of a well-known concurrent programming pattern, the worker design pattern. The worker design pattern is meant to address problems in which:

- The response time of a **user interface** (**UI**) or API is to be minimized.

- Non-blocking background processing can be tuned to achieve a balance of space (the number of workers processing requests) and time (the latency of a request being fulfilled).

A specialized form of the worker design pattern is the worker pool design pattern, which introduces the central management of a number of workers and decouples the frontend requests from specific workers.

The **voteprocessor** and its associated resources is a straightforward implementation of the worker pool design pattern, but one which takes advantage of **Google Cloud Platform** (**GCP**) services. We will discuss some of these GCP-specific solutions here.

First, we will present a high-level architecture diagram of the generic worker pool pattern:

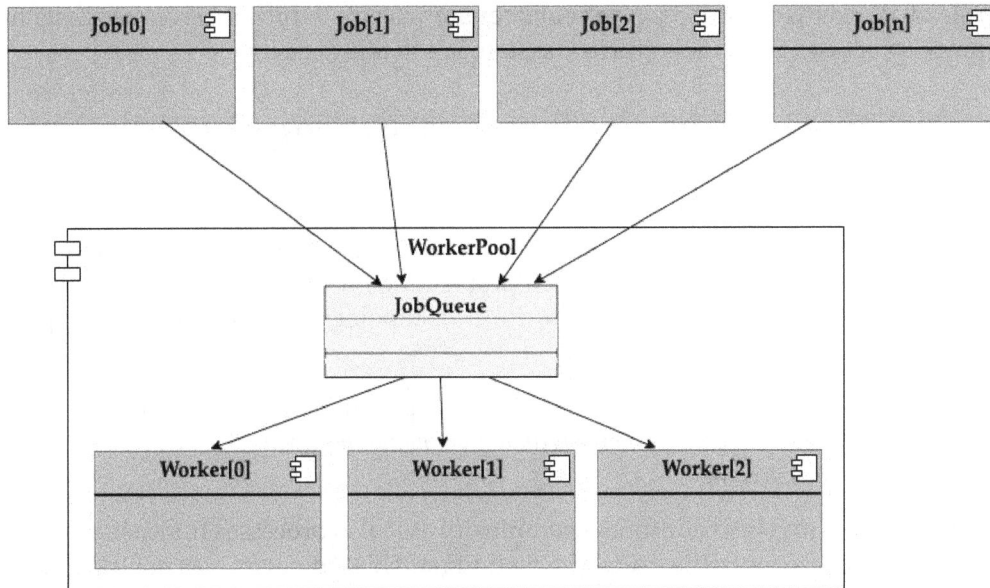

Figure 14.6: *Worker pool design pattern*

Referring to the preceding diagram, the following are brief descriptions of the entities illustrated:

- A Job is an originator of requests, such as a UI client or client-facing API endpoint.

- A Worker is an asynchronous task that processes the requests.

- The JobQueue is the queue of requests that have been issued by the Jobs and that are not yet consumed by the Workers.

- The WorkerPool is the entity that manages the resources of the JobQueue and the Worker instances.

With those roles defined, we will discuss the GCP-specific services that we use to fulfill each of them in the voting application.

The role of a JobQueue is handled well by Cloud Pub/Sub. The set of a topic and a subscription was designed for the purpose of a low-latency job or task queue.

Assuring that the acknowledgement of a vote is reliable or trustworthy relies on the guarantees of the Pub/Sub service that a published message is durable.

The WorkerPool is responsible for managing the lifecycle and number of workers. The voting application delegates this to the combination of a push subscription and auto-scaling of the subscription's endpoint.

A Job in the voting system is embodied by a **votingfrontend** instance that validates and records a user's vote.

The role of Worker is filled by the **voteprocessor** service, which receives requests from the queue, processes them and returns the status of that processing.

Applications of high throughput request processing

Applications with similar problems were discussed earlier in the chapter, such as the à la carte menu ordering use case. Those were problems with similar function, whereas this section explores applications with similar form or topology, technological and logistical challenges.

The general problem represented by the voting application can be stated as follows: *A system which processes transactions that originate from many independent sources over a period of time against a common account.*

The voting system involved additional complexity as it also processes transactions against a secondary set of accounts, the users' voting budget. This, however, was not the challenge with regards to scalability and reliability, and so we will focus this discussion on the accumulation of votes in the global datastore.

If we look for systems that have broad or widespread participation, providing input to a common state or dataset, several come to mind. We will list a few here to expand upon:

- **Real-time contest and registration systems**: These are applications that are used to register interest in a prize, such as goods or event attendance. This is a modern-day update to a classic radio contest paradigm, for the first 100 callers or sometimes to every 10th caller. In these systems, people are rewarded for timely responses. The awarding of the prize to the winning registrants can be a follow-up process, initiated by a backend process that asynchronously consumes the queue of registrations.

- **Telemetry collection systems**: These systems collect and record readings of some sort of instrument in real-time. A specific use is the collection of weather and climate data from many local weather sensors deployed in a city or country. The temperature, barometric pressure, wind speed, and direction readings must be recorded, but aggregation and interpretation of the data is done in the background for some regular cadence, such as on the hour weather forecast updates. The scale of some of these systems is worth calling out. In the *USA*, the *National Weather Service* (*NWS*) collects and analyzes more than 6.3 billion observations per day (4.4 million per minute or 72,900 per second, continuously) and releases about 1.5 million forecasts each year. While not all these observations are from direct sensor readings, the order of magnitude is impressive, especially for a system that must be always-on. This is a use case where the scale and the availability requirements are unmatched in any business sector, with the exception of web search and ad serving.

Evolution of large request processing systems

The need for reliable communication between different parts of a system is common and a compelling enough use case to have given rise to an entire class of products known as **message queue systems**, of which Cloud Pub/Sub is GCP's primary offering. The need for inter-process communication outside of local memory or file systems arose as distributed systems became commonplace. Without distributed systems infrastructure or industry experience, early systems contained homegrown one-off solutions that often were almost good enough for a large portion of their lifetime. Now, cloud infrastructure providers, specializing in addressing these infrastructure requirements, provide these capabilities as accessible and reliable as those of the operating system or those of basic application frameworks.

The availability of reliable distributed inter-process communication allowed application developers to think of new ways to solve business problems, such as processing a very large number of updates to a dataset. Complex multi-stage transactions that propagate updates through a concentrating hierarchy using a successive series of batch jobs were a common pattern in financial and inventory systems before the current type of distributed software architecture became commonplace. In many such systems, the final results of an update were not known for days or weeks, and the true current value of an account could not actually be known in some cases.

Advantages of cloud infrastructure

We have seen that the voting application is an instance of a well-known design pattern, the worker pool. The worker pool design pattern, like all design patterns, is written in an implementation-agnostic manner, and thus, there is no consideration of what might be provided by a cloud service as opposed to being written by the implementing developers.

Examining the details of the voting application shows that the two broadest components of the pattern, the JobQueue and the WorkerPool, were implemented in the voting system with configuration options of two GCP services. Cloud Run and Cloud Pub/Sub were designed to include a use case such as this pattern and offered solutions that required only a small amount of configuration. As well as providing those two roles in the pattern, the combination of Cloud Run and Pub/Sub define the API for the Worker role which is implemented by the Cloud Run **voteprocessor** service; and Pub/Sub defined the API and provides components to enable the Job role to be filled by our **votingfrontend** service.

The following diagram revisits *Figure 14.6*, the worker pool design pattern, but with the GCP-backed specific implementations used in the voting application:

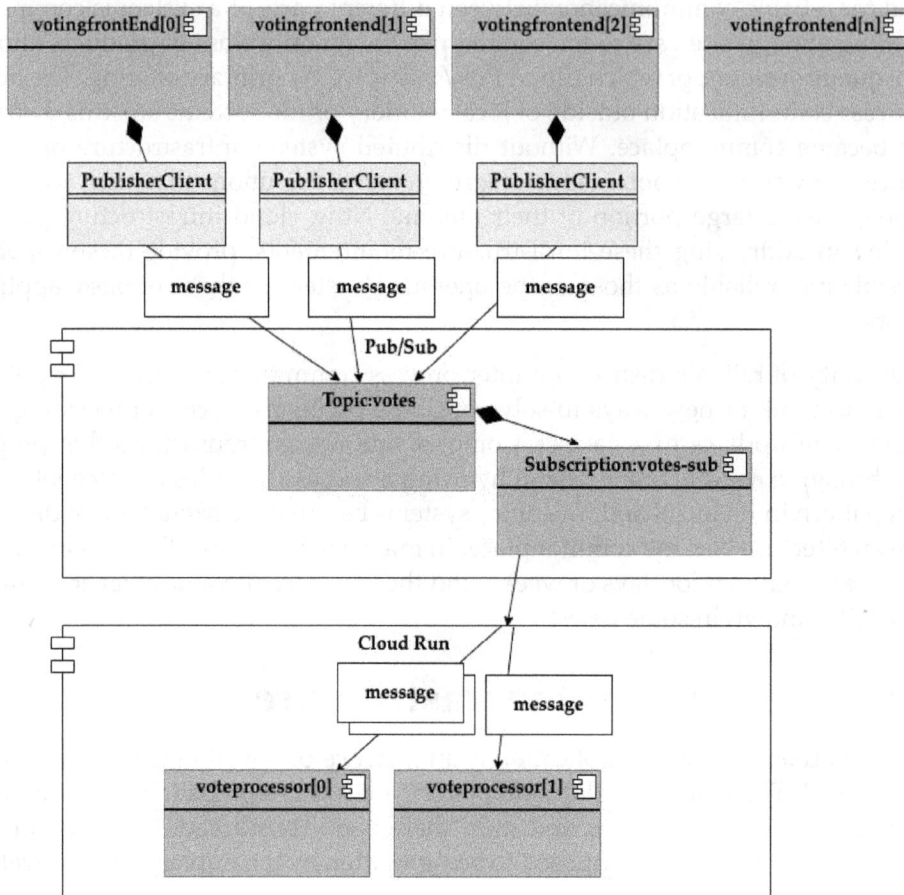

Figure 14.7: Worker pool design pattern using GCP

Implementing the worker pool design pattern would have been a much larger task without the GCP services that we have leveraged. The additional benefits of Google Cloud Monitoring, resource management such as auto-scaling, and features like automatic redelivery and durability guarantees make our voting application of a higher quality than our own development team could have produced without taking several orders of magnitude more time to do so.

Final thoughts on generic roles

The voting application that has been built and illustrated in this book is only a portion of a larger system. The other features of the application are important; we could not launch and run a voting application without them, but the focus of the book was narrowed with specific intent.

We will now outline and briefly describe a more complete view of the overall talent voting system. Then, a comparison of the voting application that was the focus of the book against the other features will highlight how the explored features were selected and what distinguished them for special attention as a case study for GCP development.

The complete voting system

The casting of votes is the moment or slice for which the system exists, but it is only a small portion of the entire system that must exist to enable it. Without features to configure and support the voting application, it would be impossible to manage the voting process. The relatively small portion of the entire system that is directly used in the voting process is in keeping with many systems in which the critical functions are outweighed by the support ecosystem.

One analogy, in a very different yet relatable example, is the human brain. The brain is the center of consciousness, of self; it is where the *I* resides and is the part of our body that we most identify with. The average adult human brain weighs 1.3 kilograms, out of an average total body weight of 70 kilograms. The brain, the center of a person's being, is only 1.8 percent of their body mass, with other systems and parts of the body outweighing it by a factor of 50. Likewise, the voting application may be 2,000 lines of code and configuration information, whereas the features that support the voting application might be 10,000 lines in several dozen modules.

The supporting cast for the human brain includes the skeleton, musculature, circulatory system, and lymphatic system, among many others. We will list and discuss the major analogous subsystems that must exist to support the voting application:

- **Act entry and editing**: The performers themselves are represented in the voting application only by their unique identifier, the act-id, and a short name in the current round. It is certain that these IDs and names are references to a master list of acts, which is used to identify a performer across the rounds in which they compete. The entry of that data, along with associated contact and qualification information, must be done through a data entry application.

- **User administration**: While user identification and authentication are handled by an **Identity and Access Management** (IAM) infrastructure product such as Firebase Authentication, there will be a need to update per-user information that the system generates and maintains. For example, user voting history might have to be reset as part of mitigating a system or user error.

- **Round definition and act assignment**: The voting application that was presented only included one hard-coded round definition with a list of predefined acts. In practice, the system will generate the acts for a new round based on the voting results of the previous rounds and should include means for a human operator to modify that generated round data.

- **Round voting window management**: When a round begins, the voting also commences. The acts' eligibility for voting is determined by rules encoded in the policy engine. The production system will include a way to set the eligibility of each act in the current round as the round progresses. At some point after a round concludes, the voting window is closed, and the acts are no longer eligible for voting. The complete system will provide all of these features.

- **Voting results post-processing**: Once the votes are all cast and the message queues are empty of votes in flight, there must be a way to then report the results and trigger any actions that were blocked by the round being open for voting. There should be a series of dashboards providing various views of the results, such as regional and time-based intermediate results. The results might be staged into a pending review status, which requires finalization by a person or committee. These features have to be implemented and must operate reliably before the first voting cycle can be completed.

- **Operations support dashboards and controls**: The system cannot be assumed to always be working as intended. Dashboards that reveal the current state of the system should be available to confirm proper operation or identify a problematic state. Some controls, such as the ability to temporarily quiesce the system, causing it to reject user requests in a controlled and informative way, should be provided.

Reading this list of support subsystems, it is probable that some of them will be at least as large and as complex as the voting application itself. Multiply that by the number of these subsystems, six, and it is evident that the main voting application will be only a small portion of the total system, albeit a critical one. Like the human brain, the voting system would not be able to perform or even to functionally exist without its ecosystem of supporting sibling subsystems.

Voting application in comparison

These six systems that were identified are all critical, and their quality and performance are needed for the entire system to function. There is one way in which the voting application is distinguished from its siblings, which is why it was chosen to be the case study of this book. The combination of scale and responsiveness that is required by the voting application is unmatched anywhere else in the system. The reason for this difference is in the demand driver, the source of traffic for this feature.

The voting application is subject to steep increases in demand, which were projected in *Chapter 8, Making a Voting System Available and Reliable*. These requests come from voters and viewers of our talent show, who number in the millions. As well as the size of the audience, their behavior is somewhat unpredictable. We cannot confidently say that the voting activity will be evenly spread across all 12 acts in a round; one act may trigger every viewer to cast a vote. It is this very unpredictability that is the reason for taking a vote. If we could predict which acts would generate voting activity, we could predict the winner with high confidence.

Let us contrast this with one of the other systems: Act entry and editing. This is a database update function that is executed by one company administrator or official at an expected time. There is no scaling consideration to speak of: A single user executes a series of transactions against a few rows of data at a time. Latency requirements are also not a concern: while the application is expected to perform well, if the official sees a busy cursor for a second or two after each update, it will not affect our business.

The scale of the two features: Voting and act entry are of very different orders of magnitude so let us examine another case which has a higher workload than the entry of act information, voting results post-processing. This is a set of analyses and database actions that are driven by a set of queries against the voting results and user voting activity. The input is the aggregated voting activity, so the size of the input set is based on the number of acts and the number of voters. This can be large as the number of voters participating in a round can be high, but the nature of the workload is different than that of the voting application. This can be envisioned as a pipeline, running a small number of complex and expensive queries, whereas the voting application is a large number of concurrent, relatively small transactions. The pipeline can be thought of as narrow and deep, whereas the voting application is relatively broad and shallow. We could, in theory, speed up the post-processing pipeline by increasing the computing power used to process it, whereas horizontal scaling is a more effective way to address voting application performance.

The measures we could take to reduce the runtime of our post-processing pipeline are well understood and not specific to a cloud infrastructure product: In effect get a faster computer. The automatic horizontal scaling of frontends and backend processors based on demand is a key advantage of a cloud infrastructure service.

Google Cloud Platform for general distributed applications

The two previous comparisons illustrate that while GCP, or any comprehensive cloud platform, provides advantages to an entire set of distributed application features, there will often be one or two requirements of the application system that make the use of cloud infrastructure necessary. In many cases, a well-thought-out use of a cloud platform enables otherwise infeasible application capabilities.

Aside from satisfying the killer requirements of the voting application, GCP adds value to the rest of the system. Automatic or generated monitoring, the deployment of versions by Cloud Build, and the inherent load balancing of frontends all reduce the toil and boilerplate artifacts that would be needed to develop, deploy, and operate a system using independent, classic service infrastructure. While GCP may be the only feasible means to satisfy some requirements, its adoption improves the entire application development and performance overall. There is a learning curve, and GCP is not as convenient or as concise as some specialized application frameworks and libraries, but as the scope of an application grows, the advantage of a comprehensive platform increases.

Conclusion

This chapter concludes the book with an examination of our voting application as a case study in distributed application systems development. The reader was shown how to view the application in its more generalized form, both as a business system and as a collection of technical features and their implementation.

The larger voting system that surrounds and includes the voting application was described, and the voting application was distinguished from the other subsystems by its dependence on specific GCP capabilities.

The chapter reveals that our application is an implementation of a general distributed systems design pattern. With these examples, the reader is well equipped to find opportunities to reuse the specific work, but more importantly, the methodologies used throughout this book to more quickly build reliable and successful software applications, which make good use of modern cloud infrastructure.

Join our Discord space

Join our Discord workspace for latest updates, offers, tech happenings around the world, new releases, and sessions with the authors:

https://discord.bpbonline.com

Index

www.ingramcontent.com/pod-product-compliance
Lightning Source LLC
Chambersburg PA
CBHW061746210326
41599CB00034B/6800